# JOURNEY TO THE INNER CIRCLE, AND BEYOND

## One man's search for his true self

*Written through and experienced by*

## BLAISE EAGLEHEART

*Brian to create*
*Continue to create*
*the world you choose*
*To live in from*
*moment to moment*
*Regards Blaise*
*April 14, 2009*

Agio ❧
PUBLISHING HOUSE

Agio
PUBLISHING HOUSE

151 Howe Street, Victoria BC Canada V8V 4K5

*For rights information and bulk orders, please
contact:* info@agiopublishing.com *or go to*
www.agiopublishing.com

*Journey To The Inner Circle, And Beyond*
ISBN 978-1-897435-32-8 (trade paperback)

For more information, we invite you to visit
*www.NaturalMovementCentre.com*

Printed on acid-free paper that includes no fibre from endangered
forests. Agio Publishing House is a socially responsible company,
measuring success on a triple-bottom-line basis.

10   9   8   7   6   5   4   3   2   1 a

## ACKNOWLEDGEMENTS and DEDICATION

*My unconditional love is extended to those persons who have afforded me an opportunity to look deeper within my creatively unfolding inner self. There have been many who have supported me along my inner journey, although not all were consciously aware that they were doing so. From my interactions with the many, I was presented with many new ways of looking at life here on Earth.*

*It was the child in each of them that supported and nurtured me during the most crucial points along my various inner journeys. It is to the creatively free-flowing child in each of us that these following pages are dedicated.*

# AUTHOR'S NOTE

*Written October, 1984*

I have written this journal to record an ongoing experience of how I have come to feel the worlds that exist within the world of man. Discovery of these ever-existing, ever-unfolding worlds has come about gradually, by consciously travelling inwardly – through many inner-dimensional aspects of reality – to find my truth. I have ventured within and beyond time sequences and space allotments as they are commonly known to be, and journeyed into the multi-dimensional framework of my mental, physical, emotional, and spiritual bodies, experiencing to the fullest the challenges and opportunities that I have knowingly created along my earthly journey.

By taking the gifts that these self-created lessons presented, I was able to form new ideas and create new unfolding experiences that eventually evolved into an enlightening inner journey of a special and unique kind. It is a journey filled with feeling and with awareness, that had its beginning in a very vulnerable stage of my life on the physical plane and moves through a wide array of experiences filled with both illusion and truth.

Many lessons were learned while interacting with and observing the birds, animals, plants and terrain in parks and wilderness areas. Many more lessons were learned by interacting with and observing the myriad aspects of my own body, mind, and spirit journeying to my innermost *centre*, and beyond.

This transformational journey to the inner depths of my physical, mental and spiritual dimensions of reality continues to infold/unfold, unfold/infold with a flexible and free-flowing creativity. It is a consistent place of being where all things exist as they truly are: without judgment and comparison; with unconditional acceptance and quality; with love and compassion, with being and living.

Be prepared to enter into a world of illusion, of feeling, of question, of sensitivity, of awareness, and of truth. Be open enough to seriously question the realities that exist and circulate within your current life concept and belief structure. You, too, might develop a burning desire to fully connect with your own creatively unfolding inner truths. Enter into and explore the depths of my experiences by creatively moving through your own personal experiences of your life journey. These freeing inner worlds are the one common thread all mankind has that will allow him to ascend to the higher aspects within the God Consciousness that he is.

Once you begin your inward journey to the *centre* of your own beingness, you might never want to return to the structured world you have securely anchored yourself in. This unfolding journey – within the following pages – may very well be the end and the beginning all in one, or else it could merely be a resting place for you to gather new thoughts and insights about the world you have knowingly or unknowingly created for yourself.

# AUTHOR'S NOTE

## Written October, 2008

I have always had an affinity to the mountains, ocean, and woods, finding great inner peace and connectedness when I was out in Nature – alone. Because I didn't feel comfortable talking to anyone about what was happening in my life, I went to where I was most at home, which was in Nature. I knew that the experiences in my life were mine and mine alone, as was my viewpoint regarding what my life was about. Bearing that in mind, I went on a singular journey looking for information about my own existence.

I invoked the inner teacher within me, the all knowing intelligence that was functionally activated at the moment of my conception. I traced my beginning as a human being backwards through time. I wanted to know where my beginning actually took place, knowing that if I knew this, and it was applicable to myself, it also had to be applicable to a child, and therefore it would have to apply to each and every person on the Earth.

The experiences I wrote about that became the journal were directed into book form by a few people I had met along my journey who encouraged me to do so. I had no desire to make this into a book. It was only documented as a reminder to myself of the experiences I created for myself in order to find some answers, and also to invoke the inner intelligence (teacher) to share the wisdom that could be breathed between the lines of the actual experiences I manifested.

As I wrote of my experiences, I realized that the words were coming out of me in a natural flow. I was reliving the experiences as they originally happened and receiving the wisdom between the lines, thereby imprinting both within my own brain matrix simultaneously, the end result being that I created my own consciousness from what my brain imprinted. The process had an electrical current and flow of its own design. I did not control the direction or the outcome. I only created the opportunity to have the experiences. I did this by asking purposeful questions. I knew that all the answers would come forth from my intelligence if I asked the right questions in the right manner.

The journal started on the outer edge – my earthly life and how I interacted in that life with other people. It slowly moved inward. In the beginning pages I wrote to myself key phrases that became my philosophy amongst all the turmoil that was occurring at that time on the outer edges of my earthly life. Certain people arrived in my life who gave me many tools that I openly accepted and used for my own purposes to help me unravel the complex network of concepts and beliefs that I had integrated into my life ever since I was born. I took their gifts, experienced them, and made them mine. One such gift came from a psychic who introduced me to 'Buddy' – whom I recreated and gave life, to act as a part of me that would share wisdom. That wisdom was not part of the complicated matrix that I was introduced to by my parents, religion, school, friends, etc. I used the same tool (Buddy) to recognize the ability to create a knowledgeable entity that existed outside the restrictions of time and space. I used characters in Nature with whom I interacted to extract information from my many different experiences.

The experiences written about are real. The journal was directed by an intelligence within me that had its own design, flow, reasoning, purpose and timing.

Since the journal was written in the way of the warrior searching for answers that were hidden behind the questions, it was not necessary to change very much of the writings, because it was not intended to be written for others. It was written for me looking for answers in my evolution as a person. Using natural cycles in Nature as a guide, I used recurring language structure in the written experiences to observe how consciousness is multidimensional in its own design. By contrast the standard method of writing a book for others in a linear fashion is illusionary because it is directed not created.

As it was written almost twenty years ago from a person's point of view who was taking layers of himself apart level by level from the outside to the inside, it was not fitting in 2008 to decide how the flow of the book should go. The intelligence that wrote the book does not need to be edited for, within the pages you will read, every facet of human experience has been touched upon. Some chapters contain experiences that are entertaining, insightful, exciting and some chapters contain information that will appear to be heavy, thought provoking, off the wall, or inspirational. Chapter 7, for instance, came through the process of automatic writing, and the text of that chapter was written strictly by the intelligence within me. I made the journey to the place where it occurred and consciously created the altered state to allow the words to be directed to the paper by asking questions. It is a very difficult chapter because it introduces a new viewpoint of 'mind' – unique to my own line of questioning.

The book was written to leave behind; not something to go forward with. As I peeled the layers away and asked more truth-seeking questions, I knew that in order to find the answers I would have to give up my life to the intelligence that first consummated my life journey at the moment of my conception. The evolution of the journey from the outer world in Chapter 1 to the experience of my death in Chapter 11, my ideas, my questions, my insights, and my knowledge was transcribed to paper in the event I did not survive the journey. In my consciousness I knew that to find the truth I would have to be willing to give up my existence, not intellectually, but emotionally, and through experience, not through words. I trusted that the intelligence within me would honor my desire for the truth of my own existence without destroying me in the process. I knew from observing Nature's interplay that the creative life energy creates and sustains all life. I also inherently knew that I became that life-giving energy at the moment the sperm and egg fused in the blue arc at the moment of my conception.

The process of editing this journal showed me that consciousness is multi-dimensional not linear, and opened me to seeing each person as a multidimensional expression of life.

*... In the beginning, there is quiet. From within the depths of the quiet comes movement. From movement comes thought, and the thought is the movement. The movement unfolds from within its central core. Thought is the movement of quiet, which creates the voice of all language. The language is the means by which the movement expresses itself. The language and the thought are one in the same. The thought and the movement are one in the same. The movement is one within itself and within the quiet. The quiet and the thought are one in the same ...*

# TABLE OF CONTENTS

# CHAPTER 1

# THE OUTER WORLD SHIFTS

I am sitting on the warm sand, looking out over the large body of water that lies before me, not really focusing on any one image either in my vision or in my thoughts. I am feeling as though my very existence – mentally, physically, and emotionally – has been shaken right down to my innermost core. I am desperately reaching out and grabbing for fragments to hold on to in order that I can establish and maintain a sense of security in what I am choosing to do at this particular time in my life.

It is with mechanical movements that I have been moving through this day, although not really much different than any other day during the past four months. Time and space, as I have known them to be, have come to a sudden standstill. I feel as though I am suspended between two fixed points in time. I have no concern for my future, for I have come to see that the future is only an illusionary concept within my thought processes. All I feel compelled to do is to search back through my past experiences, in the hope that I might be able to find some pertinent information that will help bring about a resolution to the life-altering crisis I have been experiencing for some time.

I have been sitting in the same spot on Mystic Beach and sitting in the same position for almost six hours. My muscles are quite stiff and sore, as I have not been accustomed to sitting this still for such a long period of time. My head is throbbing from recalling so many of those traumatic past experiences in my life. All the joints in my body ache. I am not any clearer now than I was when I first arrived this morning. I have turned my world upside down and inside out, and I have yet to come up with any answers. All I have been doing is analyzing, over and over again, each and every experience that has ever taken place within my past relationships. Like so many other times before, I am feeling frustrated and confused.

I stand up to do some easy stretching exercises to help bring my awareness back to my body and away from everything else. I need to get the circulation moving again, so I decide to go for a walk. Without thinking about it, or having any resistance toward what is happening, I begin to move. I am aware that I am being internally directed to and physically pulled toward the far end of the beach. It is as though my body has taken complete control over itself. My thoughts have no impact upon its movements. I try to stop it from moving any further, but it is futile. The pace is slow and steady, and there appears to be a determination from within to arrive at a specific destination. I am not at all concerned with that which is unfolding before me, for I have an inner sense of knowing that I am in no danger.

I walk for nearly three hundred yards before my body finally comes to a standstill. I am now positioned, not more than an arm's length away, in front of a massive rock wall that towers some eighty feet above the surface of the sand. I am feeling so small and so insignificant standing here before it. Rather shy and foolish, too, as I do not have any clothes on. It is totally out of character for me to feel this way, in that, for some eight years now, I have only frequented the beaches that have allowed me to be in the natural state.

The wall is shaped much like a semi-circle. Upon further examination, I realize that I have come to rest approximately at the centre point of its arc. It doesn't matter in which direction I choose to look, ninety degrees to either side of straight ahead, all I can see is rock. I am completely embraced by it, and I am feeling very humble. I feel as though I am being observed and that it knows exactly who I am, right down to my finest vibrations. I know that I cannot hide anything from it, and I also know that I have no intention of hiding from it either.

The sun is shining directly above and behind me, and I can feel the warmth of its rays penetrating the entire back half of my body. In contrast, there is a cool, light breeze dancing across the entire front half of my body, from my head to my toes. I am breaking out in goose bumps all over, but only on the front half. It is as though I have been split precisely in two, with each half experiencing something completely opposite to the other at the same time. It is an incredible experience. Everything that is happening is becoming more intensified. I have never felt this way before. I am not used to being not in control.

There are three- to four-foot waves continuously breaking on the sand behind me. The noise created by their movements starts to reverberate off the wall that engulfs me, and it begins to resonate through every inch of my being. It is becoming overpowering and irritating, and there is nothing I can do about it. I am totally powerless. I am aware that I am becoming a human tuning fork. I still do not feel that I am in any danger from what is taking place within and around me.

Without prior warning, deep-rooted feelings begin to churn inside me. I begin to yell at the rock face – screaming into its outer armour – about how I have come to see the world around me, "Everything I have ever done in my life has never worked out. All that I have ever believed in is bullshit. No one loves me. No one cares about me. What's the point in living here if nothing ever works out? My whole world is a mess, and I'm falling apart."

I end my verbal barrage by asking, "What do you think about all that? Well? You're so smart, tell me. Well, I'm waiting."

Minutes pass, there is only silence. Even the noise from the waves breaking on the shore behind me has ceased. I continue to stare into the vastness of the structure that lies before me, and I am in complete awe of its strength and its stature. Ten minutes elapse, still no answer.

Once again feelings begin to swell from deep within, and again I begin to scream into its outer armour. This time, however, it is on a slightly different note. As I begin to speak, I can once again hear the noise of the waves breaking behind me. "I am a very successful businessman, and I have made millions of dollars. I own six extremely expensive houses in different parts of the world. I can have anything in the world I want and desire. I am the world's most powerful person."

I end my dialogue by asking, "What do you think about that, eh – Well? Aren't you impressed with me? Say something. Damn it, say something."

Again, I stand waiting. Nothing is coming back. Just as before, there is only an eerie silence all around and inside me, a silence that is probing and penetrating into the deepest levels of my being.

I have been standing here for about ten minutes, reflecting upon all that has taken place, when, without it being initiated by conscious thought, my head begins to turn to the left. The rest of my body follows until I have completed a one hundred and eighty degree turn. I am now looking directly at a log that is partially buried in the sand some twenty feet in front of me. As I stand watching, the tide comes in and I witness the most amazing and yet very simple event take place. As the level of water rises, the log begins to slowly make its way out of the sand until, eventually, it is floating freely. I continue to observe the interchange of movement patterns between the log and the sand. What I see unfold next opens me up to a whole new way of looking at my life.

The waves are gradually pushing the log higher up on to the shore. Every fourth wave is much larger than the three that precede it, and it has lots of momentum behind it when it arrives. So much so that the wave tosses the log a little higher up on the beach. When the wave recedes, the log becomes stationary on

the sand once again. The sand doesn't seem overly concerned that the log is resting on it. Likewise, the log doesn't seem to be overly concerned that it is resting
on the sand. From what I can sense, they both have an equal and harmonious
relationship. There is no visible friction between them whatsoever, only total
and unconditional acceptance for each other; two separate entities moving and
interacting as one. I cannot get over the simplicity of it. It has been right here in
front of me for all of these years. I just haven't been open to seeing it.

Through this experience, I see the possibility that all of my inner turmoil
has been created entirely through the way in which I have come to perceive my
outer world. Nature has clearly shown me that everything in life is expressed in
simple ways, and that it is only me who chooses to make it all so complicated
and so divided.

While I am driving back home, I wonder if I can use Nature in some further
capacity to aid me in resolving all the conflicts I have created within my inner
and outer worlds. I am also questioning the feasibility of developing a relationship inside myself like the one I had observed between the log and the sand. I
ask myself, "What will it take to develop that kind of peace and harmony within
my worlds?"

## July 10, 1982

I have been sitting on the railing of my sundeck, contemplating how I can most
effectively bring about some major changes in my life. As I see it, I only have
two workable options. I can either move very slowly by involving others from
my outside world, or I can jump right into it and do it all at once from within
my inner world – a world I am just beginning to become aware of. They are both
very frightening to me, in that each will require me to take a risk. Which route
will bring me the quickest and the purest results? This will be the direction I
shall travel. I begin to look at it all more closely and more seriously.

If I choose to do it from the outside, I will have to involve others who will
not be able to either hear of my world or see any part of it clearly. Because of
this fact, they will only bring with them more confusion. I would have to keep
analyzing everything that is said, over and over again, in order to try and show
them how my world has been put together. I know that is impossible, for no one
else can see my world of personal experience – only me! My experience is my
experience. Others might think that they understand how my world is, but only
I truly know how it is.

I have been clearly shown this on many different occasions during my life journey. There has always been a struggle for power and for control, for inevitably someone has always wanted to be right. People never really wanted to listen to me to hear what I was saying. They only wanted to listen to me so they could tell me what I should or should not do. That only brought with it non-acceptance and frustration. This is definitely not the direction I want to proceed in. I begin to look at the viability of doing it the other way, trusting only myself.

As I sit here on the railing, gazing at the ground some fourteen feet below, I wonder if it is at all possible to jump up off this deck, leap over the railing and land safely and softly on the grass below, all of this while keeping my eyes closed. I know that sitting around thinking about it isn't going to bring me the answer. I will have to create the experience in order to find out.

Standing on the deck with my hands on the railing, I take a deep breath, and with my eyes fully open, I leap over the railing and drop gracefully and smoothly to the grass below, complete a forward role and stand up. I think to myself, "That was easy. There's nothing to it."

I return to the starting position. I repeat the same procedure once more. Only this time, as I clear the top of the railing, I close my eyes. As I make contact with the grass, I complete a forward role and stand up. I open my eyes. It is really easy. There is no real danger of me causing any injury to myself, as long as I let go of wanting to control the flow of the unfolding experience, and trust completely in my inner sense of knowing. I am excited! I rush back up to the starting position, eager to meet the challenge. I cannot wait to do it again from beginning to end with my eyes closed.

As I stand here anticipating how it will be, my thoughts begin to wander all over the place. I begin to seriously question myself as to the reality of actually doing it. The longer I wait, the more I think, and the more fearful I become. I fear that I might be creating an experience that will severely injure me. I am concerned that I might break an ankle or two, or twist one or both of my knees, or even more devastating to my being, land face first in the grass and break my neck. I begin to sweat heavily just thinking about all of these possibilities. I know that I cannot jump and make it safely as long as I have any one of these thoughts running through my mind.

I enter the house and occupy myself doing other things that will help bring me back to a calm and peaceful state inside. When I am feeling relaxed and at ease, with no thoughts generating fear, I return to the deck, walk up to the railing and, without any hesitation, close my eyes and leap into the air. The journey I am on through space seems to last a lifetime. But from within the darkness and sensitivity of my inner being, I emerge victorious.

Although my landing is a little on the rough side, I do manage to land without causing any injury, do a forward roll and stand up. As I open my eyes, I let go of all bodily control and collapse onto the grass. I feel a tremendous release of energy move through my entire body. I have clearly been shown that, without doubt, I can trust my inner path completely. All I will have to do is surrender my whole being, without any want or desire for control of the outcome, and the rest will take care of itself. I have found my path: It is within me!

✳

The house sold in September of 1982, and I moved into a one bedroom apartment in a quiet section of the city. I was now only five minutes away from the ocean. I spent as much time as I could sitting on the beach, sorting through all the emotional garbage I had accumulated in my life. I continued to work as little as possible, just enough to pay the bills and put food on the table.

In February 1983, I decided that it was time to get out of the construction business once and for all, so I sold my truck and all my tools. I figured that with the monies I had received from the sale, I could follow through with the development and sale of an exercise machine for which I had been securing Canadian and American patents. I also saw that I could easily survive for a year without having to worry about working at a steady job. Sorting out my life was still the priority and the focus. I wasn't at all concerned as to how long it all might take. I just knew that nothing else seemed important. I had to know the truth, the truth about who I am. I had a sense that somewhere behind all that anger and frustration there was a very warm, loving, sensitive being who had much goodness to offer the world.

✳

Things began to happen in March 1983 that promoted more of my spiritual growth. On a recommendation from a friend, I visited with a woman who claimed to be a psychic. She specialized in spiritual readings and spiritual healings. I had never heard of that kind of psychic before, but I was willing to create the experience to see if I could use any of what she might be able to tell me to bring more harmony into my life.

She had mentioned that there were a few belief patterns that I had adopted earlier in my childhood, and suggested that those patterns might be the major contributors behind the confusion I had been experiencing. A lot of the information she had presented with regard to my early years was very accurate. I could easily follow all of what she had said, and I could also see how it might very well have been an influence in my current situation.

The aspect of the reading that had intrigued me the most, though, was the fact that she went into what she referred to as a trance-like state in order to do it. She had mentioned that her guides were these 'entities' who were responsible for bringing forward all the information she presented during the reading. She had also been clear to say that she was only acting as a vehicle through which the unfolding process could take place. I had also heard her say that we all have our own guides who are with us all the time, and who are here to help us progress through the different stages within our development while we are on the physical plane.

During the reading, it had come up that I have three such guides assigned to me. Two of these entities would not manifest themselves through me until such time as I had attuned myself to the appropriate vibration for them to be of service; they were associated, in some way, with "healing of a high planetary nature." The one who is currently with me had said that I could call him 'Buddy' if I desired to communicate with him. He was apparently here at this time to aid me in bringing order into my life. It all sounded so exciting!

I had been totally fascinated by the whole experience. I had been introduced to a whole new world. A world that I had never even heard of before that day, yet one that I immediately felt very much at home in.

It was during May of 1983 that I received my next initiation into the world of psychics, and in the re-awakening of my own psychic abilities. There was a Psychic Fair being held in town. I had decided I would take it in to see what, if indeed anything, it had to offer me, and possibly even have one or two readings done.

When I arrive at the site, I am amazed at the number of so-called psychic people who are busy demonstrating their abilities through various mediums: tarot cards, palmistry, numerology, spiritual healings, astrology, etc. I am not at all sure how I should go about selecting the appropriate person to give me a reading. I am afraid that I will not pick the right one. I eventually decide to ask for my own inner guidance by attuning myself to my body and asking it to lead me to the person or persons who can most effectively shed some light as to where I am heading in my internal development. I am not at all interested in my outer world stuff. To me, at this particular time, my outer world is an illusion that has no substance to it.

I am directed to a person who uses tarot cards as a means of presenting personal information to her clients. She also does spiritual readings. She, too, uses the services of her guides in one way or another, but it is in a totally different manner than my first experience had been, two months earlier. This person does not have to go into a trance in order to access the information for the reading.

The main focus of the reading has to do with my emotions. She mentions that I have become entangled within my own emotional fabric and that unless I do something to resolve this situation, I will eventually be consumed by them. There has been a lot of good, useful information presented to me, and I know I will be able to use all of it. It will only require time and patience on my part.

She also makes reference to a guide who is presently influencing my movement on the physical plane. He is my initiator and my protector. She says that she can actually see him – only his facial features – suspended in the air off my right shoulder, just above my eye line. The reader next to her also confirms the existence of this entity in the same place. They both mention that he is a coastal native Indian, some sort of medicine man or shaman. I become excited! Yet at the same time, I am very skeptical of all that has been presented. I am not one for believing anything unless I can experience it for myself. And even then, I make a point of never trusting what I experience with my physical senses. I leave her booth with many questions running through my mind, mostly to do with the validity of what I have been seeing and hearing around me.

I am walking along the aisle, seeking out another reader, when I come upon a person whose specialty is aura readings. The aura is supposedly *the visible part of the electro-magnetic field that surrounds the human body.*

She gives me my predominant aura colors, along with a brief interpretation of what they mean, although nothing really specific. Before I leave her booth, I am told that she is going to be giving a workshop entitled *Awaken Your Sixth Sense* on the day following the closing of the Fair. After a brief discussion of the format, I decide to sign up. It feels right inside; nothing ventured, nothing gained!

On the appointed day, I walk into the room where the workshop is being conducted, feeling like I am entering into a whole new dimension of reality. Each person attending, has a distinctive look. Their energies are very much different than those I have been used to encountering in my normal day to day existence.

Upon entering, I am met by the psychic, and she once again gives me my aura colors. I am pleasantly surprised to hear that they are still the same as when I had my first reading a few days before. I somehow thought they would be different, and that if they were, I could then call her a fraud, demand my money back, and internally deny that anything I had experienced at the Fair was real.

After lunch, we came to the section of the workshop that was focused on a guided meditation entitled *Finding Your Own Wise Man*. We all sit on our chairs, settle into a relaxed, comfortable position, close our eyes and take a few moments to centre ourselves before the journey begins. When all are ready, the psychic proceeds to take us through the experience.

As she speaks, I can see vividly within my own mind's inner eye, all that is being described. She begins by creating an image of a rainbow, moving through each of the seven colour bands and giving a brief description of how each of them relates to a particular aspect of my physical being.

On completion of this introductory exercise, I have successfully altered myself into the alpha state of consciousness – where my creative process is fully engaged and functioning perfectly. I am slowly moving between the fluctuating thin veil of reality that separates this earthly dimension from all the other dimensions that simultaneously exist within it.

I find myself coming to rest standing in a large, open meadow in the middle of nowhere. My eyes are fixed on the plush green grass that surrounds me. Spotting this blanket of green are bright yellow and red flowers, each of them uniquely different in their expression, yet all the same in their radiant beauty. As I raise my eyes, I become aware of the quietness and stillness in the air. Not a breath of wind can I feel upon my body, and not a sound penetrates my outer ears. My inner ears pick up and vibrate throughout my entire physical embodiment the rhythmical beating of my heart and the ebb and flow of each breath as it moves through my lungs.

It is such a beautiful and peaceful environment I have created for myself. All the different colors, in every possible direction, are extremely rich and vibrant, and very healing to my soul. I am quickly becoming invigorated and alive with enthusiasm. As I look even higher, I can see majestic mountains that stretch out before me, snow-capped and barren faced, symbolizing tremendous power and stability. I can see the soothing powder blue sky that is gently and lovingly embracing all that lies below it. Not a single cloud can I see. There, standing all alone directly above me and all things on this Planet, acting as the vertex to the unfolding universe, is the Sun. It is continuously shining forth from its central core, radiating warmth in all directions and giving of itself entirely out of pure and unconditional love.

I slowly begin to turn my whole body in a circular movement, absorbing all the visual stimulation unfolding before me. It is all so pure and so perfect. As I complete a one hundred and eighty degree arc with my eyes, I become aware that I am standing on the threshold of a pathway that is lined with bright blue and white flowers. I have this deep-rooted inner urge to follow it. I am curious as to where it will take me.

It eventually guides me to a thicket of trees. Tall and stately they are, reaching high into the air, heading toward the ever-loving Sun. I am a mere speck in comparison. The pathway meanders through the maze that the trees create. I find myself moving ever so slowly inward into the maze, travelling deeper and deeper into the darkness created by the tight-knit canopy of the trees, eagerly looking back towards the light every fourth step or so, just to make sure I keep my bearings so I do not lose my way.

Then, as I look backward once again to glimpse at the light, it is gone. What was once light is now fully consumed by the darkness. I turn again and look ahead to where I am going. It is now bringing forth a small glimmer of light. Now all is completely reversed to that which I had observed only one step before. I stop for a moment and wonder if I could have possibly turned myself around, perhaps in all the excitement. I quiet my thoughts and wait. When I am absolutely sure that I am indeed heading in the appropriate direction, I continue on my way.

With each step that I take, the light becomes brighter in its essence and larger in its mass. I begin to move more quickly, becoming lighter in my movements as I travel along, keeping my focus always on the light. I do not concern myself with the many possible obstacles that might trip me up along my path, for I know, instinctively, that no harm will ever come to me as long as I keep my intention pure and my focus on the guiding light.

I soon find myself standing on the edge of a very large circular opening, surrounded by massive, radiating trees that are continuously giving forth the pure essence of life in each pulsation of their breath. The Sun is shining down from above, centrally suspended above the opening. Around the inside perimeter of this opening lies a body of water – a magical lake that is absolutely absent of all movement. It is a perfect natural mirror, reflecting back clearly all that enters into its plane of existence. The water is crystal clear, with intermixed textures of blue and green, depending on which angle the sunlight chooses to enter its surface. The shoreline is lined with glistening white sand and blue flowers, just like the ones that lined the outer pathway, only this time they are acting as a divisional boundary between the trees and the lake. I am in total awe of the whole spectacle that Mother Nature has provided for me to witness. I am consumed by it all. I am all of it, and all of it is inside me. It is such a beautiful gift to receive.

As I continue to let my eyes wander aimlessly, I catch a glimpse of what appears to be another human being on the opposite side of the lake, sitting in a squatting position with his head bowed between his knees, as if he is sleeping. I quickly proceed to make my way over to where he is stationed. I want to know who this person is. I also want to know how it is possible that he has arrived here before I did.

Upon closer examination, I can see that he is wearing next to nothing – a white loincloth hangs loosely from around his waist, and a simple piece of white cloth, much like a turban, encircles his head. Beside him lies a long pole – a staff used for walking, perhaps. I am too afraid to ask him, for I think I might be wrong.

I cautiously walk up to him and say, "Excuse me, sir."

There is a gentle stirring in his body posture, and he slowly lifts his head and turns it so that he is now facing me. He looks right at me, eye to eye, and then seemingly climbs right inside my whole being – at every level. I can actually feel him looking into every darkened space within me. His eyes are dark black in color, almost as if the pupils have been completely dilated, thereby blocking out the iris. They sparkle like diamonds in the sunlight. The white part of his eyes is pure and bright, like freshly fallen snow.

He is an extremely wise person. I can sense this by just looking into his eyes. They are like two open doorways into the universal knowing. And he radiates love in all that he is.

In a quiet and gentle voice, he asks, "Can I help you?"

I quickly and nervously respond, "Aaaah, no. I mean, yes, yes, you can."

I am still off centre and in another world of thought. I see something in his eyes. It is a sense of a place that I know exists somewhere, and one I am very much familiar with. I am also not absolutely sure as to where it is located, or if indeed it really does exist. It is all rather confusing. We continue to look deeper into each other's eyes.

I decide I need to know some answers, so I ask him, "Who are you?"

"I am what you see."

"What does that mean?"

There is a short pause within our verbal communication. I am not getting anywhere fast. I am not at all sure how I am supposed to ask the questions. The answer he has given does not make a whole lot of sense to me. As I stand here wondering what my next line of questioning should be, he begins to speak in a direct and intense manner, yet still remaining soft in his expression, "Are you looking for someone?"

"Well, I'm not sure. I think I am. And even if I am to find someone, I'm not at all sure that person would be the one I am looking for."

I realize that I am beginning to confuse myself with my self-doubt.

"How will you know, then?"

"I don't know."

"It is possible that I am the one that you are seeking?"

"Are you?"

"Am I?"

"Are you the one? Of course you are. You are the only one here, and I'm talking to you. So you must be the one. Forgive me, this is all so new."

He looks at me with his kind and gentle knowing eyes, and a soft smile covers his face. He slightly bows his head in acknowledgement of what has been said, and then continues to sit motionless, looking and moving deeper and deeper within the depths of my being. I can feel all sorts of things shifting and moving on many different levels.

"Are you the wise man that I am supposed to find?"

"Is that what you want me to be?"

"Yes. I would like it very much if you are the wise man. For if you are, I will not have to look any further."

"So be it, then. I am the wise man that you seek."

"If I ask you a question, will you answer it?"

"Know that if you ask me a question, I will answer it. But first, you must ask it."

"Is there something out there in my outer physical world that I can effectively use to help bring about more peace and harmony into my living expression?"

"Study the visible signs that Mother Nature provides for you, and you will soon discover all the necessary tools that will allow you to grow and evolve into all that you already are. You will not need the services of others to show you the way. All that is needed by you is the purest of intention to find the true meaning behind human existence. People that you encounter along your journey will merely reflect toward you your innermost thoughts. If you can clearly see them in that reality, then you will be able to perpetually expand your vision on all levels."

"Thank you for your insightful words. They are truly a gift. I will always treasure them."

Somewhere, in a distant dimension of my conscious awareness, I can hear the soft voice of the psychic mentioning that it is time to leave this place of inner calm and prepare for the journey back into her present reality within the room.

I also hear her say, "Your wise man may have a gift for you to bring back," and to "ask him about it before you leave."

As I take leave of the wise man, I say, "I must be going now. It sure has been a pleasure meeting with you. Is it possible that I can come back here and visit with you again?"

"It will always be as you desire. I shall always be here within the deepest depths of your being. All you will ever need to do is ask with the purest of intention. That will always open up the different doorways to our communication." With a soft smile on his face and a piercing look in his eyes, he continues, "Remember, my friend, that before any of this inner communication can take place, you must be willing and wanting of it to take place. The purer the intention, the purer the communication."

I nervously say, "Yes, intention, purity of intention. I will always remember. And thank you again."

I turn to walk away. A strong feeling of peace and tranquility surges throughout my entire being. I am ecstatic that I have found a new friend who is willing and eager to share with me all that he knows. All I will have to do, for that to happen, is be sincere and pure within my intention. If I am, I will be given all I will need, and at the appropriate time.

I take five rather large steps, pause for a moment, then swing my head around and glance back his way for one last look. He is still in a squatting position, head leaning slightly forward, completely motionless. I wonder if there is any connection between him and the guide who is apparently watching over me at this time. I have to find out for sure. I take one small step toward him, debating whether or not it is really important to ask him this question. I do not want to risk any embarrassment by being wrong.

Before I can say anything, he lifts his head, turns my way so that our eyes meet once again and proceeds to say,

"Yes, I am the one that you refer to as Buddy."

He had known everything I had been thinking. I now fully realize I will not be able to ever hide anything from him. There is another question I need to know the answers to, "But the other two people said that you were a coastal native Indian, some kind of medicine man or shaman?"

"I wear many different faces and assume many different interchangeable roles, depending entirely upon the dimension, or dimensions, of reality you wish to travel on."

"What do you mean by that? I am so confused. You continually speak in words I do not understand."

"I cannot explain any of this to you now, for you will not be able to fully comprehend that which is spoken. Know that it shall be shown to you as you continue to unfold from within your darkened inner void. Trust completely in your inner creative process, and be patient."

"Oh, do you have a gift for me to take back?" I cannot believe that these words have actually come out of my mouth. I am not at all sure what I should do next.

He motions for me to come closer. As I start to move toward him, I observe him pivot his upper torso around and reach down to the side of his body shielded from my vision. He brings up into full view a small object. It is a square container that has a matching removable lid. It is all dark blue in colour and neatly packaged by a fancy wide ribbon and a multi-looped bow, both of which are powder blue in color. With a full smile on his face and a twinkle in his eyes, he hands it to me. I bow my head to show my gratitude as I reach out and take it.

"May I open it?"

"It is as you wish."

I carefully untie the bow and the ribbon and slip them both into my pants pockets. I remove the lid. To my surprise, there is nothing in the box. It is completely empty. I have a funny feeling that I am being made to look like the fool. I am embarrassed by my own stupidity. How could I have fallen for such a low-down trick as this? I can feel my face becoming hotter, and cold chills race uncontrollably up and down my spine. With a sheepish look, and a quiet, cracking voice, I respond, "There, there is nothing in here. It's empty."

"On the contrary, my friend. A container such as this can only be of service when it is empty. Strive more in your world to be like this container. In order for you to be able to do that, you must first empty yourself of all that you have learned since your arrival here on this plane, so all that you do know can be brought forward and shown to you. If you continue to judge and compare all of your creative experiences with your earthly physical senses – taste, touch, hear, smell, and sight – you will continue to miss the gifts contained within each of those unfolding experiences."

As I stare into the darkness within the box, my eyes are becoming unfocused within the depths of this endless void. I am replaying over and over again the words he has spoken. Some of it I understand and can readily identify with, but most of it has gone right over my head. I get a sense that it is all so simple. Everything he has said has been spoken in very clear and simple terms. It is only me, in my own inner struggle with trying to be someone, who is making it more than it actually is. I once again bid him farewell and walk away.

As I stand at the edge of the water where the path begins, I pause to take one last look at all that lies before me. I inhale a deep breath, turn around and quickly make my way into the darkness. As I move through and beyond the halfway point in my journey, the darkness unfolds a pulsating beacon of light for me to follow, one that will ensure my safe arrival to the edge of the timbers.

In a fleeting moment, I am once again outside the thicket of trees, retracing my footsteps along the flower lined walkway, eventually coming to rest at my original point of entry. I bow my head, close my eyes and project a rainbow into my inner mind's eye, ascending slowly through each of the colored bands and their resonating vibrational frequencies.

As I complete my journey through the last band – which is also the first – the rainbow disappears. I have returned back into the confines of the meeting room, and I am listening to all the subtle noises the other people are making as they too begin to arrive back. I take a long breath and open my eyes. What a journey. Wowee! Unbelievable! I am bubbling over with enthusiasm. I can hardly wait until I am able to make the inner journey again. I feel like a child once more.

For the next few minutes, selected people share their personal experiences of what had taken place. I cannot find the appropriate words that will even begin to describe what I have seen or heard. So I do not even try. I just sit grinning from ear to ear, somehow knowing that my life is never going to be the same as it was before I came through that doorway at the beginning of the day.

We come to the last section of the program. It is entitled *Discovering Your Own Psychic Ability*. As a tool for discovery, we are going to be focusing on psychometry: 'interpreting the energies contained within an object that belongs to an individual.' The purpose is to give the person insights into events that might have already taken place in their life, that are presently taking place in their life, or that might be taking place in their life in the future.

I am paired with a woman whom I did not know prior to coming to this workshop. I am to give her a short (five minute) reading, and then she will give me one. She hands me her watch, which I loosely hold in my left hand. As soon as I have it in my possession, I start to receive clear images of events, as well as words to describe what these events are all about. I present to her as clearly as I can all that I have seen and heard. It is mainly focused on events that have already taken place, and also on one scenario that is presently taking place around her. To my utter amazement and joy, she confirms that all I have mentioned is true.

I am overjoyed to find out that I can actually do it, and with such accuracy, too. It is all so easy. It appears that all I have to do is get out of my own way

– stop the process of thought inside me of how it should be – and just let it happen. If it is pure, and done with the right intention, it will always happen.

I am now beginning to see the value of the gift the wise man has given me. Is this all there is to life: Getting out of my own way?!

I wonder if this is the answer I have been looking for: Stopping my thought processes from trying to control the structural alignment of all things, and allowing my creative inner talents to unfold accordingly.

CHAPTER 2

# THE NEW WORLD EMERGES

Within a matter of days following the wise man workshop with the psychic, I had fully opened the door leading to the mansion inside me that housed all of my psychic abilities. These were the ones that I had full use of in my early childhood and, for some unknown reason, the ones I had chosen to turn my back on in favor of a more sensually stimulating 'real' world. Although this door had been fully opened, I wasn't absolutely sure that I really wanted to cross the threshold and explore its dimensions.

In my quiet times, Buddy encouraged me to come forward and surrender all of my fears (of myself) unto this mansion so I could enter it unattached and discover the magic within its depths. I had decided, however, to take it one step at a time. I consciously began to attune myself to the unfolding of the inner process of creativity from within the depths of my inner world. At the same time, I was slowly pulling back from the confusion and abstractness of the outer world that surrounded me.

I truly began to see and feel that there was possibly another world within me that would allow me to transcend all the illusionary realities I had created and supported for so many years. I was able to connect more strongly with my friendly inner voice – Buddy. The more I sat quietly and attuned myself to my inner vibrations, the easier it became to communicate with him. He was the one saving gift that I had attracted into my life to help me make the transition from the one dimension of reality in my outer physical world, to other more subtle dimensions of reality within my inner creative world.

My outer world – the one that is entirely controlled and powered by my five earthly senses – continued to provide me with unlimited opportunities to experience all of my fears and frustrations. My inner world provided me with the clarity needed in order that I could continue to unravel the chaos that I had created while travelling along on my life journey. This inner world also helped steer me in the appropriate directions that enabled me to begin the restructuring of my thought processes, and the total re-examination of my experiential world.

As I began to realign myself, within the context of the inner and outer realities of my new awareness, I found that my diet also had to go through a major purification process of its own. This was vital so that I could continue to attune myself to the higher vibrational frequencies unfolding within my being on all the different dimensional levels. I began to eat sparingly during my day, once around noontime and once around seven in the evening. I was consuming mostly raw vegetables, raw fresh fruits, and a mixture of granola and raw nuts, water, and popcorn – lots of popcorn, as roughage. I continued to listen to my body, as to when and how much it wanted to eat.

The inner and outer textures and forms of my physical body began to change. The hard outer shell of muscle slowly began to melt away, being replaced by a more streamlined shape. It was as though there was a whole new body already under the one I had been moving through within my outer world. It was more fluid and graceful in its expressiveness, and more alive and free within its creative interpretation of what life is all about.

I continued to move very slowly and cautiously in all that I did, being extremely sensitive to my own vulnerability and wavering centredness. For a period of time I chose to keep a diary, of sorts, listing the various special processes that occurred while I was transiting through the numerous dismantling stages within my outer world. It became an effective tool that I used frequently, and it kept me heading in a life-supporting direction. I also used it as a form of expressional meditation, allowing me to soar like the eagle into the open sky, receiving insights about myself and the universe. At the same time, it allowed me to remain grounded to the Earth like the little mouse, taking care of the mundane things that were right in front of me.

And so my journey of introspection begins....

## July 25, 1983

I am choosing to use the word God in all of my communications as a reference to the creative process of unfolding energies that are ever-present and functional within my being. The spiritual path, or any other reference to spiritual realities that I make mention of, relates specifically to the presence of and inter-connectedness of the God energy within all aspects of living matter on Earth – human, animal, plant, and mineral.

I am but an instrument of the light that has been created through the loving eyes of God, and who has been chosen to fulfill certain needs for myself and the many others who have come here to experience the physical plane called

Earth. I am a mere void, an image of the darkness from which the light was created. The light brings forth God's power within me to create the necessary experiences to fulfill the lessons I have come here to learn, and to pass on the information I become aware of to other individuals who seek to create their own inner spiritual path – a path that continuously unfolds from within.

I am the ongoing creation of a living human being that has evolved from light by means of the spirit within me. I have been detained for a period of time since I arrived here on this plane, believing that my physical embodiment had a separate life of its own. This was primarily brought about by the supporting and maintaining of the ego structure within my being. This structure was created by my intellectual thought processes, and it has been the means by which I have sustained my existence.

I have only recently come to be aware that my physical body has been given the gift of life by the presence of my creative spirit. I have spent thirty-two long years on this physical plane living under the illusion that I was someone, and I have done everything possible along my journey to support that belief. I have created many good stories, within the framework of my evolutionary process, to justify all I have chosen to do. I have done very little in allowing myself the freedom to enjoy the experiences I have created in my life.

I have spent most of my time trying to get everyone else to fit into my world, without the slightest concern for fitting into theirs. I have fought to survive, at what, I am not at all sure, and never have been. Perhaps, just for the sake of fighting! I have been drained of my own life-force by reacting to what others were doing and saying. I have spent very little time, if indeed any, creating the things that I really wanted and needed in my life.

At almost thirty-two years of age, I am now beginning to seriously question all that I have ever done and come to believe in. I do feel that I am only now commencing the continual process of re-connection, on more of a conscious level, with the life-giving creative spirit that lies within the central core of my being. I have obtained an element of peace and harmony within my daily life that has given me true insight into the purpose of me being on this planet at this time. There have been countless numbers of people that I have already connected with and been nurtured by in my evolutionary growth, and there will be countless more to come in the years ahead.

> I am but a sun shining forth my own light, to spread warmth
> and love on to other suns, and to help those who have yet to

awaken to the gift of the sun that lies within their central core of beingness.

I am here to enjoy the experience of living with those who wish to live and to love within the creative process of life.

*July 26, 1983*

During the past week, I had come to believe that I was not in control of creating the things I wanted to experience in my life. I thought there was a greater force directing me, one that I had no power to interfere with. Well today, during my visit with Buddy, I became consciously aware that I am indeed in creative control of my own life. I always have been. I am totally responsible for all that I have chosen to create in my life thus far, and I will continue to be until the day I decide to leave this plane of reality.

I am now aware that I have been fighting the natural current in my life, so to speak, for I have always had the free-will to make the necessary decisions concerning the important issues that have surrounded me. All through my early years, up to and including when I turned thirty-two, I always did the things that I did so I could get recognition and acceptance from my peers. I continually used my outer world as a guide for centering myself, instead of aligning with and listening to my true inner self.

I am feeling much like a new flower just beginning to blossom, radiating its warmth and showing its beauty to the world surrounding it. The unfolding flower contributes in the only way it knows how in order to make the world a more peaceful and loving place to live in. I am excited to know that from here on in I am fulfilling what I have come to be creatively focused on: Helping myself and other beings find their own personal purpose for living on this plane, and to give back to my outer worldly structure all that I can. The best way, and the only way, for me to do that, is for me to be me.

I have taken a whole year off work in order that I might straighten out my life. I am becoming more aware of the deep-seated burning light within me that burns in the awareness of the God presence. The light that I speak of is the light of creation, and it is represented by the Sun in our solar system. The Sun shines forth light and warmth and gives life and purpose to all things. Each person, through his or her own individual divine light, gives life to all living things that he or she comes into contact with, regardless of the plane of reality they are on.

I have been shown a glimpse of the state of oneness that exists within me.

I have manifested inner peace, balance, contentment and harmony within my being. I have become aware of my true inner power: the power to create what I want and need in my life, according to my inner truth. I have also become aware of my feelings and my moods, and what causes them to manifest. Moods are possessions, whereas feelings are values.

Miracles begin when I take full responsibility for who and what I am. All that is needed by me is the desire to change, regardless of the time period necessary to complete the process.

I see that the process of change is far more valuable than the actual change. The value comes from the experiences I allow myself to go through in order to gain the freedom within my being and the eventual unlocking of the spirit fire that lies within my heart.

The key to living a full life is 'balance'.

## July 27, 1983

Today, I find myself on the verge of a new breakthrough. Financially, I am down to my last fifty dollars. Bills keep coming in and everyone is demanding their money. My outer world is generally looking really chaotic and very unstable. My physical, outward side is having a difficult time dealing with all that is taking place. It wants to panic and create havoc. It sees itself as being out of control and with limited power. My inner world is becoming more stable, bringing with it more peace and harmony.

For the past month and a half, I have been getting the same message from Buddy when I ask, "What do I do about all the pressures coming from my outside world?"

He has consistently answered, "Do nothing, and all will eventually resolve itself. You must trust only what you feel in your heart, and release what you think in your thoughts. Become quiet and still in all of your movements, and your path shall be illuminated."

I deeply feel that there is nothing for me to fear. I know that I am in the process of breaking away from the influences of old, habitual patterns of behavior that have been created and supported by my past programming and conditioning. I am freely opening myself to a whole new world. I am continuing to create a world of peace and balance within my being. I do feel that this peace and balance will eventually manifest itself within my outer physical world.

I am praying a lot these days, aligning myself with the Creative Principle – God energy – and asking, with the purest of intention, for guidance in all that I do. I know that I am being well looked after and that no harm shall ever come to me. I am now moving in my life under the purity of the all-encompassing truth. I know that truth, in its purity, is always supportive of life. I have attuned myself completely to my inner world for strength and support. I am finding that I am much more focused and centred when I am in that space.

I am now seeing that all the relationships I have ever had, both internal and external, have served their purpose. It is now time to proceed on a slightly different journey, in a much more supportive direction, that is strictly guided by a facet of true spiritual self – Buddy. Buddy is helping to bring me out of the darkness that surrounds my outer physical world and into the light of my inner world. I am realizing that I am in a transitional stage between these two worlds, and I am learning to be more patient and tolerant toward myself. Through observing this unfolding process, I am becoming more humble.

I feel that I have reached my inner spiritual resting place – a place that is very peaceful and harmonious. I am still feeling a strong connection to my outer physical world, and I desire to be secure within it so that I might give back to it all that I am able. I am no longer worried about surviving in my outer world, or even concerned about making ends meet, for I am now aware of my inner ability to create all that I need in order to live on this plane.

The best way for me to explain my philosophy toward life, is for me to live it. By living it, I will allow all those I meet to witness my creative form and expression of movement, and I will encourage them to take from me whatever they feel they can use. It is important for me to be all that I am in all that I do, and at all times. In so doing, I shall save the speaking of thousands of words.

> I shall continue to listen to my dreams. I shall also strive to listen more, and to become more aware of the obstacles I create in my life that stop me from achieving my dreams.

> Truth is like the wind: It cannot be seen, defined, or grasped. It can only be felt within the unfolding moment.

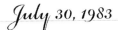
*July 30, 1983*

I have this strange but wonderful feeling inside me, almost like I am living in a fantasy world where nothing is real yet everything appears to be real. All things on the outer edge of my physical world appear to be very scrambled. As of today, I only have thirteen dollars left in my bank account, and I am not aware of any other monies scheduled to come in. One part of me wants to freak out and blow off some steam. Another part of me says, "What's the use, that won't help alleviate the problem. If anything, it'll make it worse."

When I communicate with Buddy, I continue to hear that I should do nothing. I am blindly trusting that Buddy knows the way through all of this, and I am choosing to follow his direction.

Most of the friends I had in my life (before I started making changes) have pretty much left. I no longer desire to keep ties with any of them, for I see that they are all living their lives entirely in the outer world of illusion – the one that is strictly governed by the five senses. When I had mentioned to them about my new inner world awareness, especially about my conversations with Buddy, they all laughed and poked fun by saying such things as, "Aren't you taking this whole thing a little bit too far, Blaise? I mean, talking to voices in your head. Come on, let's get real."

They were subtly inferring that I might be going off the 'deep end.' Or this one, "Be careful with what you say, and to whom you say it, or else those little men in the white coats will come and take you away and lock you up for good." I knew then that I could not share any of my new inner worlds with anyone.

My relationship with myself is one of grandeur. I am feeling lighter inside and more at peace with my surroundings. I am also feeling more at peace with who I am and with what has been happening to me. I am feeling deep within my being that the old awarenesses I have been moving with are slowly moving out, making way for newer and more powerful and sensitive awareness which I have slowly begun to integrate into my daily routine. The changes that have been taking place have been very subtle and very pure. Because of this I know that they will be around for a long time. I know that they are very real and that they support my life – all that I am and all that I am becoming.

I continue to move through old patterns of fear and anxiety, and with the continued support from my inner guidance, I am making tremendous breakthroughs. I am aware that the patterns of past programming and conditioning will probably come and go, and that all the worn out ones will eventually disappear as I implement newer, more supportive ones that will aid me in my evolution towards light.

I see that it is important for me to be with other people and to share living experiences for the sheer enjoyment. This will allow my inner wisdom to be presented to me through the experiencing and feeling, with not so much emphasis on thinking and philosophizing.

Life is only great when I am living from creating, not when I am sitting back wishing and thinking. I am praying that I find more time to play in my life, and also that I never have to work again in this lifetime. Play is whatever I choose to do in my life that is creative and free-flowing. Work, on the other hand, is what other beings try to get me to do that impedes my creativeness.

I know that inner peace can only be attained by returning to the darkness within the void. The void (symbolically) represents death. Out of the void comes a new life, a life that is spontaneous and purposeful, provided that I see the light of creation within the darkness of the inner void, and not the coldness of that darkness.

It has been a long and sometimes difficult transformation thus far, but one that I am happy I have created. It has been oftentimes questionable as to whether the inner voice I communicate with is real. As I write these words to paper, I am aware that the inner voice has always been available to me, and that in my past I have chosen not to acknowledge it. I am also aware that it is the only source of support I have, and ever will have.

As I sit here on the water's edge, I am creating that whatever lies below the surface of the water represents the contents of my unconscious mind. I am also creating that all the things existing above the water-line represent the manifestations I perceive from within my conscious mind. I see that the realities within my outer world are open to interpretation from how I choose to see my inner world. I cannot possibly see the things in my outer world unless I am aware of them in my inner world. Things only exist within my inner world as they truly are, in any dimension of reality, and they are subject to change in my outer world, depending on how I choose to perceive them at any given time.

'Loving' is valuing other beings for their creative uniqueness within the context of the ordinary world. 'Loving' another person is seeing that person wholly and appreciating them for who they are – their ordinariness, their failures, their magnificence – each and every unfolding moment. Being 'in love' with another person is an illusion, a possession, wanting only to see that person in the way that I want them to be in my world, without any sensitivity to who they really are in their own.

I may find the road and begin my journey in an innocent way, sure of my truths, only to get caught up in the illusions of those who might want to follow my truths. I, too, would then become a victim of their illusions made reality.

If I am to speak of goodness and of love through the way in which I live, and then allow myself to be accepted as someone greater than those who would wish to follow me, I would indeed be a fool.

*August 3, 1983*

As I write this to paper, I am feeling very strange inside. I am feeling as though I am falling into a thick blanket of warm air, immersed in total darkness and unsure of myself, but very clear as to where I am going to land. I am afraid, and I am excited. I am afraid of not knowing. I am excited, for it feels right. I have never experienced anything like this before. My whole world is dying around me, and at the same time, it is all being re-born again. I have consciously released all that I have from within my being. I have been sucked down into a darkened shaft so far that I am now beginning to travel in a different direction. I can actually feel the surging motion coming from deep within my physical body.

I have been on a trail of poverty for so long now, never quite having enough to do what I wanted. Now it feels as though my life has come alive with riches – inner riches. I have lost just about everything that has had any value in my outer world. Yet I have gained all sense of value within my inner journey. I have consciously witnessed the connection to the oneness of the One – I AM. I have only seen a brief glimpse, but it was just enough to let me know that I am heading in the right direction – the direction of my own inner truth.

Last evening, I was sitting at home looking at the conditions surrounding my life, once again feeling that my outer world was on the verge of total collapse. I had received four letters in the mail from the companies to whom I still owe money, all asking me to balance my accounts. My bank manager phoned and wanted to know when I was going to be able to pay off my outstanding loans. I started to fracture within my mental processes. I began to panic. My whole body began to shake, and I felt sick to my stomach. I wanted so much to disappear from the face of the Earth. I owe so much money, and I have no way of paying any of it off at this point in time. (I have been juggling my financial commitments around for the past six months, hoping that a business deal I have been working on for a while would be finalized. When it goes through, all of my money problems will be taken care of.)

I decided to go to bed early. I couldn't stand the fact that I thought I was out of control. I laid down and prayed that my life would be taken during the night. I didn't want to live any longer. I was getting swallowed up by my outer world, and I couldn't stand it. My whole body trembled for almost an hour before I finally fell asleep. I felt as though I couldn't go on this way anymore, for it was taking an incredible amount of my personal energy to maintain the game I was playing. I didn't know how to stop it. Death was an alternative, a last resort.

I died all right, only it was symbolically. My eyes opened early this morning, just after sunrise, and I was greeted with a horrible shock. I was still very much alive. I got up and started to walk around. My body began to shake uncontrollably once again. My stomach became tighter as each moment unfolded, and I felt as though I was going to vomit.

I decided to do a layout with the tarot cards to see what, if any, light could be shed upon my situation. What came up was very confusing, at first. The cards symbolically related strength and control within change. It didn't make any sense. I was feeling weak all over and totally out of control.

I then sat on the floor and went inside to have a visit with Buddy, to see if he could help in any way. I went through my usual meditation form in order to enter into the state of awareness where I could communicate with him. I then proceeded to ask if it would be possible to speak with him. He acknowledged in a supportive way that it was.

I asked, "What do I do now?"

There was no immediate response, as was usual in our communication. Instead, what came back was another question, "What do we do now?"

To which I heard myself answer out loud, "Make my outer world as peaceful as my inner world by straightening out what is going on in my outer world – stop everything!"

I thought that it was all just a game, with the inner voice, Buddy, being an entity that I had created (within the scope of my imagination) to allow me to escape into my fantasy world so I could hide away from the real world. I had to leave my apartment. I couldn't stand to be there any longer. It was too confining. I needed more space. I felt as though I had been tricked, that I had been made out to look like a fool. It was all a joke, and the joke was on me, only I wasn't laughing. I became angry and frustrated. I left and went down to the ocean for a few hours in order to calm down.

It was during that time that I became aware that I had somehow crossed over the inner creative threshold into a new dimension of reality. I was now able to connect with Buddy – my Higher Self – directly. What this means, I am not at all sure at this time. Perhaps this is part of becoming a whole being: my inner voice and outer voice are actually one in the same; that my thoughts are the same as Buddy's thoughts. Maybe I no longer need to ask, for I already know.

I felt completely empty inside. I had no emotions. My body began to release very subtly the stored up tension being held within its muscular tissues. My intellect saw clearly for the first real time, without any resistance, that my creative spirit is the sole creative aspect behind my beingness.

As I walked along the Ogden Point sea-wall I sang a song, one that was being spontaneously created as I moved along. It was a song of such strength and intensity that my whole body vibrated with excitement. At one point the clouds parted and the Sun shone through, laying a pathway of light before me on the water, beckoning me to follow it back into the source of all life. I knew then that I had made a major breakthrough in my spiritual journey.

As I continued to walk, I asked myself this question through my outer voice, "What is it I must do now, now that I have gotten to the point of nothingness within my beingness within my inner void?"

The response from my inner voice was lightning quick, "I have two choices: I can either give up totally and be forever more at the mercy of my outside world, or I can pick up the pieces of my outer fractured world, as well as take all the information I have recently received from within, and put it to practical use to create a loving and peaceful environment for myself."

I decided then and there that I had come as far as I could by peeling away the outer layers of my person. I had arrived at the innermost core of my being, and I had peeled it away as well. Behind it I found emptiness. From this emptiness comes the possibility to create any reality on this plane, the permutations of which are mind boggling.

It is now time to put everything back together and make it all work in my favor. By listening to and really hearing all that is spoken to me, I shall find the necessary information to overcome all the obstacles I have created in my life. I am the void from which the creative light does shine. The light is the creator of all life and the power by which all things are given life.

I am growing in all ways with the creative light of God energy moving through me. I am whatever I choose to be. I am no longer choosing to hold on to what I thought I was. I am now creating who I want to be in my outer world expression. I am creating this by releasing all thoughts of who I think I am.

I am now aware that all aspects of my outer world physical identity have to be released in order for me to find total spiritual peace and contentment. I must give up my total self, as I know it to be, in order that I might unfold my real Higher Self. Only by turning my energies inward, shall I be able to observe my true spiritual awakening. I must move through my spiritual identity in order to make each moment a creative experience.

> There are always gifts to be received when I am given obstacles to clear in my life. It is in the clearing of those obstacles that I am presented with the gifts. Life is exactly what I choose it to be.

> I am given the opportunity to dream. And in the same breath, I am also given the power to make my dreams become living realities.

> I can view the experiences in my past as obstacles to clear, or I can see them as opportunities to learn from. The choice is up to me, as always!

## August 8, 1983

Today began on a high note. When I awoke this morning, a message came through loud and clear, "Take each day in its entirety. Do not look any further ahead than the situation at hand." It continued to reverberate over and over again within the frontal part of my head. So I got up, went into a meditative exercise and shifted my awareness into an alternate state of consciousness, to see what else I could get in touch with.

Something came up from the other day when I met with an old friend at the corner store. During our conversation, he had pointed out that I was resisting the natural flow of my life. I had immediately become defensive in my communication with him and very protective of my physical space.

This morning I looked deeper into that situation. I became aware that the patterns from my past experiences, centred mostly around 'being a success,' are still very much a part of me. I clearly saw that to become successful, I would have to stand on my own two feet. Past programming and conditioning had set me up to support the belief that that was the way it was supposed to be. I was following in my father's footsteps, looking for his approval and acceptance in all that I did. I had told myself the story that if I became successful, it would stop my father and I from having any kind of life-supporting relationship, for I would then have something he had felt he had lost a few years back. So long as I was not successful, there would still be a chance that we could develop a close relationship. I had put the blame entirely on him. I hadn't been willing, until now, to take ownership of any of it. I now see that it is all my stuff. It doesn't have anything to do with him. It never has.

All the fears I have created during the last thirty-two years have not supported me in being successful. What would I have to complain about if I was? I have always lived my life in the future time frame, repeatedly putting deadlines in front of me, inciting non-supportive emotions to surface when these deadlines were never met. I would mentally create certain things I wanted in my life. Then, as the time approached to bring them into fruition, I would create further situations to ensure that I would never get them. Not so anymore! As of today, I am beginning an entirely new journey. I am now focusing on living each day as it arrives, and I am choosing to stay within the framework of that day in order that I might create an orderly outer physical world. I am excited about what I am choosing to create in my life. I am no longer afraid of succeeding in my undertakings.

I proceeded through my meditation seeing myself positioned on one side of a swinging arched doorway, restraining myself from entering into a new room on the other side and receiving the gifts it contained. By aligning myself with my Higher Self, I was able to ease my way beyond the doorway and close the door behind me. I was able to do this by moving very slowly with clear intention and pure focus. I am now aware, at all levels within my being, that this particular pattern of behavior is worn-out, and that it shall have no further impact upon my life. I shall only use it in the future as a reflection of how things were, to aid me in freeing myself from other functioning patterns that might still be attached to it.

I am creating each day as it arrives, and living each moment as it unfolds. I can only give love outside of myself when I choose to create it from within and extend it outwardly. I am living entirely from within the depths of my being, always keeping my focus on who I am and what I am to do here on this plane. I am focusing entirely on the present time frame, building a stronger reality between my inner spiritual self and my outer physical embodiment that is controlled by the five earthly senses. I am also allowing my Higher Self to guide me to my destiny. The work continues, but the load is becoming lighter.

An experience can only occur in the present time frame within the time sequence of now. I can only see the true experience as it unfolds, not before it happens or after it has already happened.

An experience has no judgment or comparison attached to it, for it has no memory.

## August 11, 1983

I am no longer afraid of getting into a relationship with either myself or another human being. I have now become aware of the particular pattern that has created that fear. It has been the rejection of my intuitive feminine side by my intellectual masculine side that is controlled and limited by the outer world five earthly senses. My linear, one dimensional masculine side always has to be right in whatever he involves himself in. He has maintained his power by always being in control of any given situation. He has never been open to consciously acknowledging my multi-dimensional feminine side.

I have been living totally in my outer physical, masculine-oriented world, always trying to perceive what was going to happen in my future by engaging my insightful feminine side in a dialogue. I would then go about setting things in motion in my outer physical world to ensure that I never achieved those objectives. I could never afford to let my feminine side be right. If she was, my masculine (ego) side feared he would have no further purpose on this plane. It has always been a fight for survival for my masculine side. The only thing is, he is the creator of the game and sole player. He can never win at the game, but continually insists he can.

My masculine side would always make sure that the relationships I became involved in, never worked out. Born a male, my feminine side was always attracting new relationships. The women I became involved with were all moving from within their masculine sides, thus creating a supportive polarity. When I had felt I was being rejected by these women, I would engage my powerful masculine side within the relationship and slowly drive them away. I was very insensitive to myself and other people when I operated strictly from my masculine side. I now see that this pattern has been created and supported by my past programming and conditioning, beginning first with my relationship with my mother.

As time progressed, my masculine side became more domineering, and decided he was going to be my protector (from what, I am not sure) thereby suppressing my feminine side. I have had to expend a lot more of my personal energy in order to keep my feminine side out of the picture and my masculine side in the controller's seat.

I am obtaining an element of balance within my being. I am now recognizing my feminine side as the creative force that is connected to the universal consciousness of man and God energy. I also see my masculine side as that part of me that connects me to and allows me to express myself on the physical earthly plane. I am now aware that both are important, and that their unification is very much needed and necessary in order that the lessons I have come here to work through are completed. I now see that both are ready and willing to move towards supporting each other in reaching this higher ideal.

There is only one true Higher Self that creates all that exists within my inner and outer worlds. The Higher Self exists *without* thought for its own personal identity. Thought for power and for control is always trying to prove that I am someone, that I am somehow important. It lives and thrives on creating illusions in my outer world, and then becomes totally consumed by what it creates. So doing, it creates more distractions in order to keep itself busy.

> Awareness of what is real is seldom ever achieved by mass numbers.

## August 15, 1983

I feel that I have made a gigantic leap forward in my evolutionary process. I am now living as much as possible in the present moment, and I am finding so much peace within this new awareness.

I rode my ten-speed racing bike out to Swartz Bay yesterday to visit with friends. I wanted to see if I could apply all that I had been learning on my inner journey to improve my outer world physical performance. The distance I rode was twenty-two miles. When I was heavily into training my body, mentally, physically and emotionally in the early and mid-seventies, I used to race out there in one hour and five minutes. It had been seven months since I had worked out seriously, and I was curious as to what would unfold within the experience.

I successfully completed the journey out there in just over fifty-five minutes. As I was pedalling, I was able to focus all of my attention onto the God energy that is always creatively moving within and throughout my embodiment.

I was able to use it to increase my physical power. By relinquishing all of my personal physical power, and surrendering all that I was in form, I was able to focus on letting the creative light shine through me. This provided me with an incredible surge of energy that continuously circulated throughout my physical body, enabling me to propel my bike faster and more efficiently through time and space.

It has become increasingly more apparent that my physical body really does not exist in the way that I thought it has. I now see that it was not my physical body that had performed all those feats of wonder during my training years. It was my creative spirit that had been responsible for the magic continually being created within and without my bodily form. I had been consciously connected to this creative force during my early training years, from 1972 to 76, but in a much different way. It had been strictly expressed on the outer physical plane. This time around it is much more subtle in its manifestation and encompasses all planes of reality inwardly and outwardly. I am only now beginning to get a sense of what it was that I had access to back then.

When my creative spirit is in control, and the God energy is able to move more freely through my physical embodiment, my performance level is acutely heightened. The vibrational frequency on the spiritual plane is much higher and far less taxing than the vibrational frequency on the earthly plane. The reasoning behind this discrepancy is primarily attributed to the high concentration of thought resistance being continually generated on the physical plane, compared to the constant, ever-unfolding flow of creative energies that are always accessible on the spiritual plane.

When I had consciously created my body as a golden yellow void surrounded by pure white light, I was able to change the consistency of my physical form. The yellow void represented the God energy, and it was the moving force behind my physical body. The white light surrounding the void was symbolic of the purity of my intention to find my truth within the movement experience. As my intention remained pure and unwavering, I was able to focus all of my attention onto the circular movements of energy within the swirling vortex of the void. I was then able to use those creative energies to move me faster through time and space with greater efficiency.

I have become aware of some interesting facts this day with regard to exercise and peace, balance and harmony within my being. I have reached back into the void of darkness to find out where the light of creation comes from. I have found that it comes from God, the eternal source of all light and all life. I am but a humble servant of the light, who has been manifested into form through the use of a physical body. I am able to use the creative light of God through my being in such a way that I am able to shed light and insight upon myself, and also upon others who might be seeking to find the balance between reality and illusion.

I am creating a world of peace, harmony and balance from within the depths of my being. I am moving through the doorway that has been representative of the way I have chosen to live in the past, and that door is closing behind me forever. I know that I might want to return to that room at some time in the future, in reflection only, but I no longer feel compelled to live there. In front of me another door is opening, one that will eventually lead me to the total realization of my true inner self. I am doing this with the help of the God energy within me, and I am seeking continual guidance and support as I journey along.

Learning comes from listening and acknowledging, not from thinking and speaking.

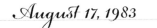

## August 17, 1983

I have just concluded another quiet, introspective time sequence, reflecting upon the observations I have been witnessing within the current flow in my life. I have become aware that my emotions are in need of closer inspection. I see that it is important to relinquish all of my attachments on this plane, to all people and all objects. I must not want anyone in my life. At the same time, I must allow myself the total freedom to share time and space with as many people as I can. To do this without attachment in the present time frame will ensure that my emotions do not have an opportunity to surface and disrupt the delicate balance within my being.

I am continuing to observe all people in an open, loving manner so that they might shine their own unique creative light upon me. I pray to be open enough within myself to receive the gifts they have to offer, and that I might be able to use these gifts in a reflective way to aid me in my spiritual growth. I seek only to find my truth – universal truth – and to live this truth through the awareness of the God energy within me.

I have transcended through the second inner doorway, the doorway that leads to complete freedom from all past experiences in this life. I have entered into my inner void, the place where nothing exists in form, and from where everything comes.

I am focusing on today, and no other day, for the only day that exists is within the unfolding day. Yesterday has slipped away into the total abstractness of my memory, and tomorrow will never arrive. Time is no longer of any significance to me, other than to remind me of my obligations and appointments in my outer world.

I had a wonderful journey out into the wide open country yesterday, driving, walking and talking with a friend. I had found I was able to stay in the present moment for almost all the outing, and receive so much more out of the experience by being there totally. Living in the present moment, I am much more peaceful as a person, more human in my feelings, and more aware of the subtle forces constantly interacting within the natural elements. Although I have this awareness within, I am remaining humble enough to know that I am only now beginning to open up to all the different creative energies available to me, and all mankind, when I come into the full awareness of and utilization of my Higher Self.

My Higher Self continues to provide me with an open doorway that connects the limited physical plane – limited by time and by space – and the unlimited spiritual plane – which is unlimited in that there are no time and no space restrictions, for it encompasses all time and all space.

The small portion of the physical brain we all employ – where the outer world thinking process originates from – keeps us grounded to the earthly plane. When we seek out and unveil our true Higher Self, we are given the opportunity to open ourselves to the other portions of the brain that allow all of our energized thoughts, in their purest form, to become our greatest creations. With these conscious creative thoughts, we will be able to create a more enlightened and serene world. We will be able to make contact with the natural elements in a very different way, one that will put us right in the *centre* of Nature. We will be able to attune ourselves to the harmonious flow of the natural elements, and we will be able to communicate as Nature communicates within Her limitless boundaries. There will be an opportunity for unlimited communication with all forms of natural entities (plant, animal, mineral), without ego – language, thinking – getting in the way.

All dimensional levels within the complex structure of the human brain will expand inwardly, bringing with it the availability for man to utilize the vastness of creative energies that make up this earthly plane, and that are the building blocks for all living expressions of life. We must do 'nothing' in order to attain this level of awareness. We must do nothing except let the layers of illusionary concepts of reality, and outdated belief systems, peel away far enough so that the physical manifestation of these realities might be uncovered and encouraged to surface, becoming fully operational and functional within each one of us.

> I know that I have the free-will to change, provided, of course, that I want to change. Sometimes it appears to be a lot of work to bring about change, and I think it would be much easier to stay the way that I am. In reality, though, it takes a lot of work to stay the way that I am, for change is continual.

## *August 20, 1983*

I had contemplated today about who I am, and came to the realization that I am no one, and that I do not exist. My personal reality, and the focus behind my living expression, is based entirely upon my concepts of reality and belief system. The 'I' and the 'me' of my person are illusions that have been created by the ego of society.

It now appears I spent my first seventeen years on this plane fighting to establish who I thought I was. I then moved through the next sixteen years struggling to maintain that identify. Today, I have come to the full conscious awareness that I have never really existed. It has only been my intellectual thinking – ego – that has been endeavoring to sustain its existence within the limited structure of the egotistical world it has been creating.

My Higher Self – Buddy – has been reminding me that there is nothing I can currently do about the imbalances within my outer world. He has said that they are illusions, and that if I choose to continue giving them my full attention, I will be supporting them in being real. I am continuing to put all of my trust into the movement of my inner process, and I am consciously releasing all desire to control my outer environment. I know that in the end all will work out as it should, for that is how I am creating it.

My intellectual thinking has been trying so desperately to show its power, and not having much success doing so, mainly because my intellect cannot create things in the world of spirit. It can only use what exists here already. My Higher Self, on the other hand, is able to create anything it so desires within the world of my intellect, including all those things that have yet to become a physical reality. I am now aware that I have not been allowing my Higher Self to create nurturing experiences within my living expression, for I have always given a false sense of power and control to my intellect.

Today, my intellectual knowing has consciously acknowledged that the situations 'he' has repeatedly set up in the past have not been totally supportive of me evolving into the true being that I am. (This has been the first big step that he has taken on his own initiative. It is showing me that he might just be sincere about really wanting to align himself with my Higher Self. It was definitely a major breakthrough.) He has also come to fully realize that the creative God energy is far too powerful for him to contend with on an ongoing basis. He cannot possibly match it or defeat it. With the creative God energy, I am to do nothing, and through the doing of nothing, everything will happen as it should. This is the exact opposite to the way in which my intellect moves within the framework of my outer world.

I have now become aware that the 'I' and the 'me' are nothing more than thought forms of energy that have been condensed in their vibrational frequency, in order that they can identify with and function within a physical form and shape through the manifestation of a human being. The 'I' and the 'me' are not part of that energy form. They are only concepts and beliefs of what that energy form represents. Energy is forever changing, interacting, and interchanging. It cannot be harnessed or contained within a static concept or belief system.

The purpose of living on the earthly plane is to live totally within the experience of the moment, as it unfolds, and to learn from that unfolding experience, moment to moment, through the duration of that experience. That is the movement of my spiritual free-flowing form, through and through. The 'I' and the 'me' hold on to the experience and have it exist in the past or the future time frame. My Higher Self is always aware that the unfolding experience, and the emotions attached to that experience, only exists within the present unfolding moment. My true inner feelings arise only at the time of the unfolding experience, and that is when they really need to be expressed and acknowledged, not in the past or the future time frame.

I have given up all desire to fight for preserving who I think I am, for I now know that I am no one. I have given up all desire to prove that I am someone. Now that I have done so, I only wish to move forward and align myself with my true creative self, and live the rest of my years on the earthly plane attuning myself to the purest spiritual essence that connects and bonds all things together.

When I ask myself who I am, in my new awareness, I see that I am freedom, open to all experiences, emotions and feelings at any given time. I am no one, in particular, yet I am everyone I can see, touch and feel. I am all there is. I am pure energy, in its natural form. I am as much a part of life as I am of death. Death is only life changing its form of expression. To live entirely from moment to moment is my new awareness.

The purpose behind my living expression is to be void of all accomplishments, and to be actively involved in the creation of many different experiences. Experiences that will help me become more of who I truly am, and that will help me, as well as others, to create a world that is motivated by love, peace and equality.

## August 22, 1983

The amount of noise in the front part of my head is deafening. I have become aware that my intellectual thought process is a continuous chatterbox, sometimes spewing out things of great interest. But in most instances, the dialogues are filled with meaningless, ego-oriented stuff that is concerned with either the past or the future. I am focusing all of my attention on to the here-and-now. With the continual help from my higher planes of awareness, and the God energy within, I will soon overcome all of my dilemmas and be able to live totally within the present moment unfolding.

I have become aware that the here-and-now is a frightening place to live in. I have also seen that it might be a difficult place to stay in all the time. It is much easier for me to create new experiences from old experiences, as I am able to intellectually recall (by the use of my memory) any one of them any time I choose, totally reliving them over and over again – which is also impossible, for, in reality, I am never the same from moment to moment. This keeps me from becoming bored with myself and the predicaments I have created in my life.

Past experiences keep me at a standstill within my relationship with my Higher Self, and also with others outside of my self, for I tend to continually draw conclusions from the experiences I have had, rather than allowing for the creation of new ones.

I speak about being happy in a relationship with another person, only I base my happiness on either what I get out of the relationship or on what the relationship is doing for me. In this type of situation, I really do not have a relationship. What I do have is a workable concept or belief of what the relationship is. If it was a true relationship, there would always be continuous growth and expansion on all levels.

The here-and-now is the only view from which to look at a supportive relationship. Loving the person with whom I am in a relationship gives the relationship an opportunity to grow on all levels. Loving is to be in total acceptance of someone, including myself, at any given moment; to become someone, anyone, in any given moment; and to act spontaneously according to that moment's desires, wishes and aspirations.

I am not so concerned with stilling my thoughts altogether. Rather, I choose to have my thoughts stimulate new growth and expansion within the present time frame. Growth and development cannot take place within me if I am continually living in the past or floating somewhere in the future. The future time frame always makes it seem like life will get better. I can always imagine new changes coming in my life, but if I fail to implement these changes in the present moment unfolding, there is very little chance they will ever come to fruition.

Personal power is only beneficial when I choose to use it creatively in the present moment unfolding. If I choose to continually put all of my attention, within my thought patterns, toward either my past or my future, I will be continually giving up all my personal power to my past or my future. Thus, I will have very little or no power at all within the present unfolding reality to manifest the things in my life I would prefer to have.

> The outer world I choose to live in is under my control and my direction. It is how I choose to see that outer world that determines how effective it will be for me.

> I am the way that I choose to live. I choose to live the way that I am.

## August 24, 1983

"Is it necessary to go through an experience in order to understand it? Is it possible to help another person through their traumatic experiences?" I was asked these two questions yesterday by a dear friend, and I have been looking at them seriously since then to see if indeed there is an answer to either one.

In my awareness, it is not necessary to go through a similar experience in order to assist another person who might be going through a traumatic experience. My experiences are my experiences. They are created by me so that I might learn the lessons I have come here to learn. What may be a gift of life to me might turn out to be the unwelcome death for someone else.

I might do another person more harm if I choose to give them the understanding they want, and in the way they want it – sympathy and concern. It is not possible for me to know the depth of another person's experience, or to know how they are feeling from their movement through that experience. They are in total control of creating their own experiences on this plane, and only they know what lessons they have come here to learn. If I am to be of service in the way that they want, then I will be supporting them in not learning their lessons.

If I am to become aware of my inner truth, and ask for support from my Higher Self, then I will be aware of how I can best be with that person, and how I can best give them the support they need so that they will be able to receive the gifts from their lessons. Hopefully, my actions will enable them to see their own predicament from a slightly different perspective, so that they might find their own answers and resolve their own situations. Just by being there, without telling them what they should or should not do, and unconditionally loving that person, I am allowing for growth and expansion on all levels for each of us.

I feel that the key for me is to return to the source from whence I came, and to seek the truth behind the ultimate purpose for living here on this physical plane. When the truth is known, all other categorizations of life forms cease to exist – life is! Truth cannot be talked about. It just "is" within the unfolding moment. Truth cannot be described, for it is a feeling for and a connection to the oneness that exists within all things. This feeling is too vast and too great to reduce into words. Truth can only be experienced within each person, separately and independently, and only an individual will be able to express his truth. It will be continuously expressed through the way in which he moves through his outer world.

I cannot give truth to anyone, for I have nothing to give. I cannot be given truth, for there is nothing to receive. I cannot learn truth, for there is nothing to learn. I must unlearn all that is not my truth, and in so doing, I shall find my truth. Truth cannot be learned, for it already exists within the reality of all things. Truth is the eternal gift of life that is available to any being who asks for it to be shown from within the depths of his own person.

The journey is only as long as I choose to make it. The miracle of change occurs when I begin.

> Understanding things is not necessary, for it signifies stability.
> Having awareness is necessary, for it signifies an ever-changing,
> unfolding of life. It is better for me to be flexible and fluid, than
> to be structured and brittle.

The least amount of resistance in my life will put me in the flow of my life.

## August 27, 1983

I had a quiet meditation this morning, during which I asked my Higher Self, "What is to become of me, and what do I do now?" I did not get an answer that directly related to that line of questioning, but what I did become aware of through the dialogue could only be described as being totally conscious. I looked at all of my desires and wishes and became aware that I have been constantly searching outside of myself in order to find those things that would fulfill my life. Even in the very existence of an unfolding day, I have always created things to do that would occupy my time. I have been seeking out books on numerology, astrology and the tarot, as well as psychic people, and relying on all of them to bring relief into my inner and outer worlds. It shall no longer be that way. As of today, all that stops!

The message I had received was so clear and so precise: "Do not give power, none whatsoever, to any object or person outside of myself." In my conscious awareness, no one really exists outside me. All people and all objects are perceived within me, within the limited functions of my five earthly senses.

Loving is a state of being where time does not exist.

## August 29, 1983

I am aware that everything in my outer world is an illusion. I see that it is only when I allow any form or shape – mentally, physically, emotionally – to manifest itself within my living expression that it becomes a reality. I might be able to see a lot of different structures within my outer worlds, and be able to look at them from many different angles at any given time, but it is only when I am able to take a particular perspective of any one of those angles, and use it within an unfolding experience, that it becomes a reality.

To look at something before I experience it will lead me to support the illusion that something is happening and that it has substance. To look at an experience after it has already happened, and try to evaluate it, is also creating an illusion, for the experience no longer exists. To recall any part of that experience, I would have to rely on the accuracy of my memory, which is very limited in its operation. My memory is entirely dependent on my five earthly senses for its accuracy, and my five earthly senses only exist on a one dimensional plane of reality in any given time sequence.

The emotions that were being created at the time of the unfolding experience would no longer be available. The emotions that are within me when I am in the process of recalling a past experience, are totally different from those emotions that were present as the original experience unfolded. As a result of this reality, I will only be able to roughly interpret what those emotions could have possibly been.

Each and every time I go through the procedure of recalling a particular past experience, I will water down the original experience and build up the effects the experience had upon me. If it has been a non-supportive kind of experience, I will probably create more pain, anger, frustration, etc., in order to punish myself.

There is no reality within an experience if I choose to worry about it before it happens, or if I try to bring it back after it has happened. The only reality that exists within my world is when I am in the process of creating an experience. The active aspect of any unfolding experience brings about the functional reality. The passive or non-involved aspect of the experience, thinking about the experience before it happens or after it has happened, brings about the reality of the illusion. Time and space are the two major contributors behind the creation of all illusions. By judging time sequences and space allotments, I continually create new illusions. By comparing and judging my experiences, I will inevitably create an infinite number of illusions, for no two experiences will ever be the same in either their physical expression or their mental, physical, and emotional transformation.

I am ever-changing in my form of expression. The reality of the experience is in the awareness I obtain from that experience. The total experience needs to be lived and digested at the exact same time. Insights only come from being involved. Involving myself is to create an experience – a reality. A reality is an expression of my thoughts and feelings in any given time movement through space.

I am the true creator of all that I choose to do here on this earthly plane. I was given the gift of a physical form when I first incarnated here. I must use this form to fully discover the realities of this illusionary world, and all the other worlds within this world. In this lifetime, I must move through the physical earthly plane learning to distinguish between illusion and reality. Realities reflect the goodness within the worlds I choose to live in and continually create from moment to moment. Illusions reflect the non-supportive influences within the outer expressional worlds that everyone else wishes I would live in.

To distinguish between reality and illusion is a simple task. That which occupies my personal space within any given time sequence, and involves any one or all five of my earthly senses, is a reality for me – and for me only! Others may be in the same time and space framework as I am, but their perception of the particular experience we all share is never going to be the same as mine. It will be theirs, and theirs alone. To me, their perception is the illusion and my perception is the reality. To them, my perception of the experience is the illusion and their perception is the reality. My reality is my reality. It is only a reality at the time of the unfolding experience: Not before and not after.

We are all given the same opportunities to create and fully experience many diverse experiences within the duration of our lifetime, but we seldom take full responsibility for creating them. I am now choosing to take full responsibility for all the experiences I choose to create in my lifetime.

> Be at peace with myself, and that peace will spread to all those beings who choose to become part of my interactive world. For however long, it does not matter, for they will soon begin to live their lives in peace, for like attracts like.

> By relinquishing all control, I am in full control.

✳

During the following four-month period (September through December, 1983), I continued to chip away at the hardened, outer crusty surface of my belief system, and the concepts of reality I have been identifying with within my living expression, so that I could look further into my perceptions of how I have thought my world to be. There were many occasions on which I had seriously thought about giving up on the inner voice that has been guiding me, and going back to being the way that I was before it all began. Whenever I would start feeling that way, I would always bring back (into my present moment reality) some illusionary conversations I had had with others.

I would recall dialogues that would make me stop and look, with all seriousness, at what I was choosing to do in my life with regard to my status in my outer world. People were always either directly or indirectly telling me: that I should get a job, a real job that would pay me some money (I had been giving free lectures at a college and teaching free martial art classes); that I should "get off my ass" and get back into the mainstream of the work force once again and "make something out of my life" (reminding me over and over again that I had the skills available to become very successful in my outer world, but I just wasn't using them); that what I was choosing to do in my life was all just a cop-out; that all I was doing was running away from my life, rather than moving with it.

There was one time along the way that I almost bought it all. I had been hanging on to a very thin thread of hope, and it slowly started to disintegrate. I was feeling overwhelmed by my outer world financial commitments, and I seriously thought about getting back into the work force so I could get out from underneath all of my debts. I was considering putting my inner journey off until such time as I would be hassle-free within my outside world. I began to think that maybe, just this once, all those people were right, and that what I was really choosing to do was take the easy way out. I decided that I would have to look at it all more closely. I knew that before I could go any further along on my journey, I would have to be absolutely clear about my intention, either way, or I would lose everything.

I altered my perception and observed it all from a new angle, one that I had not seen before. I saw that the people who I interacted with were clearly reacting to what I was choosing to do in my life. But why? Why should anyone care whether I make it in my outer world?

Upon closer examination, I saw that I only react to someone, or to something, when I am overcome with fear. When this occurs, I find that I am not in control of the situation. In this particular instance, the reality was that I was choosing to look at my life – the way I had structured it – so that I could find my own personal truth. The question that arose was: "Are they reacting to me, or are they reacting to the truth?" I knew that it wasn't me they were reacting to, for they hadn't reacted to me in all the years I had known them. It had to be that they were reacting to me looking for my truth. Why would they need to react to me wanting to find my truth? Perhaps they were feeling threatened by what I was choosing to do in my life.

For some reason they didn't want me to keep looking. If I continued to do so, then they, too, might have to look at the way in which they were choosing to live within their belief systems and concepts of reality. They didn't want me to keep looking, so they tried everything possible to discourage me from continuing. I then asked myself this question: "If looking for my truth is no big deal to anyone else, why are all these people reacting to me doing so?" The possible answer was that they were all afraid of searching within themselves for their own truth, and they were frustrated with me because I was seriously looking for mine. I also began to see that I was a constant reminder of what they were afraid of. I further recognized that it was entirely their problem, not mine. I knew that I was doing exactly what I was supposed to be doing, looking for my truth.

I know that what I am choosing to do is not going to be an easy task. There will be many self-created obstacles from my past to move through, as well as many opportunities to expand my internal awareness, before my journey will bring me to a balanced and harmonious state within my being. What has made (and continues to make) this journey a challenge is the fact that there are no outside teachings for me to look to for support and for guidance. I have no outside teacher who: will hold my hand and assure me that I am moving along my path in the appropriate manner; is available to fully explain all that I am experiencing and learning; will come to my assistance to console me when I become all caught up in thinking about and trying to fully understand all that I have been learning.

All I have available to me for support and for guidance are two distinct voices (Buddy and the wise man) that exist within the depths of my inner void, with whom I carry on different dialogues, and who keep saying they are here at this time to initiate me into the higher levels of awareness that are attainable within me and all mankind.

There were times when I would question myself regarding the direction I was heading. I would sit and begin to look at it from the perspective that: "If I am indeed going about my journey in the most appropriate way, why aren't there more people doing it this way? And why haven't I met anyone else who is choosing to do it all from within himself?" All the indications from my outside world showed me that I was going about finding my truth in the wrong way.

I then altered my perspective once again. This time I proceeded to look at it from where I had come from within my living expression, from what was already in my experience. I didn't have to look at it for very long before I could clearly see that where I was going in my life really couldn't be any worse than where I had been. It was easy to remember all the frustration and anger inside of me when I was heavily immersed within the confusion of my outer world. How much different I have been since I have been moving in the direction of my inner world.

There has always been a knowing feeling deep inside me that words cannot describe, that has always made me feel warm all over whenever I have put my full focus and attention toward travelling along on my inner pathway. On the other hand, when I recall some of the more traumatic experiences I have had within the texture of my outer world expression, I get cold chills racing throughout my body, and sometimes I even break out in a cold sweat.

The two inner voices that I have been conversing with lately are very quiet and non-judgemental in their expressions. They have always been soft and subtle in the manner by which they have chosen to communicate. It is in a very supportive, loving way. They are always acutely aware of how I am feeling from moment to moment, and they are extremely sensitive to what it is I need to know next. When I have needed to be shaken up a little, they were right there to make sure I got the message. This would only occur when I was getting pulled back into the old way of looking at my worlds. They would crate a very simple experience in my outer world that would wake me up and realign me with the objective of finding my truth.

The information I have been receiving from my inner voices has always been simple and pure in its presentation, its purpose, and its function. I have been observing the simplicity of all that they have shared with me, in all that is around me. At first, it was not at all like that. They gave me nothing in the way of support or direction until such time that I had opened myself up to being fully committed to finding the purest vibration of my truth. Even then, the information they gave only came sparingly, little bits here and there. I had to keep proving to them and to myself that I was sincere in my acknowledgment of wanting to find the purity of my truth.

I was continually being initiated into the multi-dimensional unfolding of my true inner self. As I moved through each of the outer layers of my earthly image, I was given a different angle of perception that I could use in order to help me get through the next layer. I had to move one layer at a time. It was like putting together a jigsaw puzzle, only I was taking my outer world image-puzzle apart.

At times, the information I was receiving had been so clear that I could see it and feel it on many different levels within my being, but I became frustrated because I wasn't able to use it all in the right way. I was informed that it would be a matter of time before I would be able to fully integrate, into my everyday living experiences, all that I was being shown by them, and all that I had been seeing on my own. In order for this procedure to take place, it would be necessary to continually realign myself – mentally, physically, emotionally – with my true inner self as I proceed to move along on my journey.

The changes that have been taking place within my being, on all levels, are very subtle in their manifestation. These changes will continue to unfold in the years ahead. Apparently, what I have been experiencing over the past year, and what I will continue to experience during the next two, are only the initial changes that are necessary for me to break through the outer layers of the hardened shell in which the real me is encased. Once I make it into the inner dimensional avenues of my beingness, everything will take on a whole new texture of expression. In a session with one of my inner voices, I was given some insight into what might possibly be ahead if I continue in the direction I have been moving. The following is a section of that discourse,

> ... Your physical body will go through a complete purification process – re-structuring, re-shaping and re-forming the structural and muscular alignments of the physical composites – in order to be able to handle the higher frequencies of energy surging through it. The dietary aspect of your human form will become altered somewhat, with the eating of simplified foods in the natural state. Your need to eat will be much less, as your newly tuned body will be able to fully utilize the higher vibrational energies that these simplified foods contain. The need for your body to rest – sleep – will not be necessary, as your body will be able to attune itself more readily to the higher vibrations of natural energies that make up all matter on the physical, earthly plane. Your brain will go through tremendous growth periods – where your senses will develop whole new characteristics within their expressions – as it continually opens itself, within itself, to the higher levels of awareness that exist on this physical dimension of reality and all the other dimensional planes of reality within this physical dimension. The means of higher communication – without the use of words – will be operational in such a way that pure communication with all life-forms on the planet Earth will be available to you, the degree of which is forever unfolding ....

When I asked for more information to help clarify all that had been presented, I was told,

> It is not yet timely for us to fully explain all that you have heard, for you have not been purified enough, at this point in time, to hear any of what has been said – hearing it at a level of knowing, which is beyond thought, itself. You will be opened up to

all of this, and much more, very slowly, so that you will be able to fully comprehend all that is presented at the time it is being presented. Your learning will arrive to you through many different forms, and it shall wear many different disguises. Be open to embracing all that comes to you each and every moment you are awake, for your food for growth is always within that which you attract....

The inner voices repeatedly encouraged me to put my trust into the process that is gradually unfolding within me. And that even though it all didn't make a whole lot of sense to me, the time would soon arrive when it would. It was also mentioned, more than once, that my innocence and trust would be my ultimate protection against outside influences, and they would allow me to move spontaneously in the appropriate direction, and at the most opportune time.

It sometimes appeared as though the inner teachers were dangling a carrot in front of my face, so to speak, putting it there to entice me, to make sure that I didn't become bored with what was taking place around me and lose interest in what I was doing. It has been an effective tool for them, for I have yet to waver from the path I have been on. Initially, there were times when I had thought about quitting, but I always ended up using those times as opportunities to reflect upon where I had come from in my living expression. I also used them to find the peace in where I was at that moment. If anything, those experiences had enabled me to become more focused and open to looking deeper within the darkened areas of my past so that I might utilize more of the creative energies I have been told exist within them.

Each and every day, I was evolving. Oftentimes I would change my awareness of what I had thought was real three or more times in a single day. I would see something within me in the morning as a truth, and by later that same afternoon, it was an illusion.

Those who were choosing to be around me were having a difficult time coping with all that has been happening. They have been busy trying to figure out and fully understand what I have been doing in my life, while I have been busy doing it. I could never adequately explain it to them, for it was always changing.

I have cautioned them all, on many occasions, to let go of the pictures of me they have been carrying around in their memory banks, as to who they think I am, so that they might be able to see the real me that is continually unfolding. Of course they were not able to hear my words, nor were they able to get a sense of the changes I was going through, for they were not going through any themselves. They were holding themselves rigidly within their solidified belief systems and the structured concepts of how they saw the world around them, while I was busy dissolving my belief system and all of my concepts of reality.

It was frustrating for them because they were not able to see any of the changes that had been happening to me. All of my changes have been very subtle so far, and only manifesting themselves on the inner levels.

I have never been able to effectively explain what has been taking place within me, for I have never been quite sure myself. I have been feeling my way through it, step by step, as I have moved along. When I would arrive at a place within my self where I would begin to have an idea of what was happening, I would see that it was pointless to try to explain where I was, for I would have already passed through that place and into the next level of awareness. What I had seen so clearly only moments before, was now no longer true.

The best thing to do was to keep to myself. I wouldn't be able to discuss any of what I was going through with anyone, for what I was choosing to do – finding my own truth by going deep within myself – goes against everything that is structured and functional within the world of man. It is more fashionable to look at one's life in a group setting, or in an environment where one has to pay large sums of money to learn about one's own self from someone else.

In India, I would be considered a very holy man, wanting to look into my life this way, but in my own country, I am viewed as a crazy man. Somehow, that doesn't make a whole lot of sense. But then again, what ever does in the outer, competitive world of man? I know that I have to do it all on my own. There is no other way possible that will allow me to free myself from my own self-imposed prejudices about myself and everything else in my worlds.

I had mentioned to those who chose to be around me, many times during our communications, that they should not hold on to any of the words I might use in my dialogues. I was clearly seeing that words were only words, and they were not totally representative of my truth. All the words I had attached myself to (along my life journey) had been very much responsible for me being the way that I was. I now knew that words weren't worth anything any more, and that I would have to release all of my beliefs about their meanings. The only way that would be possible to investigate, would be if I kept speaking words and listened to the words I spoke, at the same time, to see how I was choosing to use the words, when I was choosing to use the words, and the purpose behind using the words I chose. I also needed to become more aware of whether I was using too many words, or words that didn't have any specified meaning within the unfolding dialogue, or words that supported my death rather than my life. Negatively oriented words (such as *can't, it's hard, it's difficult*) support my death, for they limit me in what I can do. Positively oriented words (like *love, peace, harmony*) support my life, in that they are creative and unfolding within their expression.

I am becoming more aware there are many different levels of awareness within me, within the inner and outer dimensions of the physical earthly plane. I am not at all sure, at this point in time, how they are all connected, or if indeed they are, but I am sure I will find out as I continue to move along on my journey.

*

It wasn't until the middle of December, 1983 that I had finally surrendered my total being to the two dialoguing voices from within. I trusted them with my life. They had shown me on many occasions that they were sincere in their purpose and their intention. There was no longer any resistance coming from within me in regard to the certainty of the direction I was heading. I knew, within every level of my being, that I was heading in the appropriate direction in order for me to find my ultimate truth. I became a humble servant of the universe, ready and willing to do whatever I was instructed from within, and I was prepared to listen, with full attention, to all the information that would be presented. I knew the only way I could live was if I played on the edge of death: One aspect of the old me would have to continually die so that one aspect of the new me could unfold and live.

My fears have been very instrumental in attracting into my space all the non-supportive energies from my outside world. That was part of my outer initiation into the higher levels of experience on the physical plane. If I could move through all the illusions I had created within my inner and outer worlds, I would be given many opportunities to experience the dimensional avenues that exist within and beyond the earthly plane.

I had been informed that it would not be possible to find the purest expression of my inner truth so long as I was still holding on to, in any level of my awareness, anything in my outer world. It would be necessary to resolve the disharmony within my outer world affairs. It would not be feasible, or acceptable, to walk away from any of the situations I have created within my living expression. I would have to go right into the heart of all of them and find a harmonious solution for each one. Only by doing it this way could I hope to enter into the deepest depths of my inner void.

This would be the first of many tests that would determine whether I was worthy to go on to the higher initiations. I would have to succeed in bringing harmony into my outer world before I would be permitted to move on. I was given just one step at a time, and no more. I was not instructed as to how I should go about moving through each situation that would present itself. I had been told I was the creator of all that would eventually arrive, and that I was very much aware of the total composition of each of the situations arriving. I would have to attune myself to the structural fabric of each of them in order to make my way through them and neutralize them.

As I continued to move along step by step the pieces slowly began to fit together, providing me with a clue each time that would show me the next step I needed to take. It was indeed day by day, moment to moment. It was becoming absolutely clear that I was the sole creator of all that I had ever experienced in my life, and that I was the only one who would be able to undo all that I had done. I was on my own, as I always am.

I knew that I would have to face all the outer world financial strain being funneled my way. It was the tail end of all that I had created before I chose to make the major changes in my living expression. I sat down one day and wrote a letter to each of the businesses to which I still owed money, and made them fully aware of my financial position. I told each of them that I could not bring my account up to date. I agreed to send each a small token payment every month, to show my good intention and sincerity. I then made the necessary phone calls to the other sources I owed money, to let them know that I didn't have the funds available to clear up my debts, and that as soon as I did, I would forward the balance to them without hesitation. I mentioned that I was not negating my responsibilities. It was only that I had come into some difficult times and there was nothing I could do that would bring about a speedy resolution to my dilemma.

I had to finally let everything out about my outer world affairs. Up until that time, I had been keeping it all a secret mainly because I was afraid of what people might think and say. I thought they would say that I couldn't make it in my outside world. I feared that I would be viewed as a failure by my father and the rest of my family, including myself.

I had to stand up and acknowledge to my outside world what it was I was choosing to do, taking a good look at my life. I didn't tell the financial institutions that, though, for they would have freaked out completely. What I did choose to tell them truthfully was that I was starting up a new business that was centred on the development of functional exercise equipment. I let them know that I had recently been granted a Canadian patent on one of my machines, and that I was waiting for the USA patent to come through. I also mentioned that

I had investors from the USA who were waiting for the patent to be finalized before they committed their money; and that when the patent arrived, I would be able to generate the necessary funds to bring my accounts up to date. It would take a lot of patience on everyone's part, for the patent process takes a long time to complete.

Although this has been the current flow of the process, I am not at all guaranteed that this machine will be the ticket out of my dilemma. I remain forever trusting that I am being directed in a life-supporting direction, and that peace and harmony will continue to manifest in my living expression. I know that if I was meant to go under at the mercy of my outer world, it would have happened long before now.

In an overview: I see that everything that has happened, and that is currently happening, is supportive of my life. The exercise machine has been something I have used as a positive life-support, a tool that I could put all my focus on to when things got too hectic. I have continually used it as a means to remind myself of the creative gift of life that is forever unfolding through all that I am choosing to do. It has also helped me to stay focused on the present moment, and has aided me in staying out of the past. It has definitely been a creative gift in so many ways, regardless of how it all turns out.

## December 20, 1983

As I am driving along the road that is taking me back to the place of my physical birth, I cannot help but think that this journey is going to be very meaningful; that for some reason, there is a specific purpose in going there at this time in my life. I have a feeling it will serve as a catalyst for greater experiences that will eventually present themselves as I continue to move along on my life journey.

The energies inside my body are beginning to vibrate at a much higher frequency than what I am normally used to. I begin to tremble, however subtly, as I attune my whole being to the process unfolding within me. I have never experienced anything quite like what is moving through me at this time. I am also very much aware there is more actually taking place, on the many different dimensional levels within my being, than I am consciously able to acknowledge.

As the car rounds the corner, I see a flickering shadow of an awesome presence as it dances across the windshield and disappears into the cloudiness of the late afternoon skyline. At first, I think it is my eyes playing tricks on me, for how can there possibly be a shadow when there is no direct sunlight visible to cast one? I quickly flash on to a vision that had been presented to me by a facet of my Higher Self soon after I left Victoria.

In this vision, I had been shown that by attuning myself to the basic Laws of Nature, it would be possible to connect with and manifest on the physical plane the spiritual essence of any single facet of Nature (animal, vegetable, mineral, and the four elements: Earth, Air, Fire, Water). I would then be able to utilize these to aid me in resolving the mysteries of the universes within the universe that I perceive within and without my physical embodiment.

As I move through the next bend in the road, what I am greeted with sends pulsating electric shock waves throughout my entire being. It is an overpowering sight that leaves me gasping for breath. There in front of me, not more than fifty feet away, and hovering at about fifteen feet off the surface of the road, is a very large, powerful looking Bald Eagle. He is gracefully flying on a parallel course to the one I am on. I cannot get over it. He just seemed to appear out of nowhere.

Every so often, he looks my way. Whenever he does, I can feel cold chills moving up and down my spine. I have a feeling that he is a sign of some kind to let me know that I am being well looked after, and that there is no need for me to worry as long as I am in his territory. I continue to observe him over the next three miles, at which point he looks my way one last time, his eyes piercing right through me and setting my insides on fire. He proceeds to dip his left wing and then his right, as if to wave at me, then he quickly ascends to the open sky above and disappears behind a stand of trees on the hillside.

I drive for another five miles until I come to one of the parking lots on the shoreline of Long Beach. It is one of the most famous beaches on the West Coast of British Columbia. It is mile after mile of sandy beach, for as far as the eye can see, and when the tide goes out, one can walk out for a quarter of a mile or more.

I get out of the car and begin to walk toward the far end of the beach, pondering all that has taken place on my way up here, especially my magical encounter with Bald Eagle. I continue to walk very slowly and aimlessly, realizing that there is no need for me to be in a hurry, that there is no place for me to go, and there is nothing for me to do. All that I will need while I am here lies before me. I need only be open and receptive to what is being presented.

I am directed to a small clump of rocks on the edge of the water. I climb up, searching until I find the appropriate power-spot, and I sit down in a cross-legged position facing South. (I was once told that Nature provides many power-spots. These are places where there is a higher concentration of creative energies that can be utilized to aid a person in realigning himself to the higher vibrations of creative energies within himself and all of Nature.) I close my eyes and ask my Higher Self to present me with a sign so that I might know why I have come back here at this time.

I wait for a few moments, and then my inner voice begins to speak. I am told that while I am here I will meet a very wise old woman who will help re-structure and realign the creative energies within me. By doing this, I will be able to resonate more harmoniously with the higher vibrational frequencies that are locked away deep inside my beingness. It is this vibration that represents who I am, the part of me that I had turned my back on when I was seven years young. The wise old woman will also make clear to me the purpose of my existence. I am also told that I will meet a young boy who will be able to give me much insight into what I am doing here on the earthly plane, and also, what it is I am to do while I am on this plane.

After sitting and contemplating the words of my Higher Self for more than twenty minutes, I have a distinct feeling that I should get up and leave this area and not dwell any further on what has been said. I stand up and proceed to walk back across the sand, en route to the car. I have a sudden inner urge to stop and look out over the water. I decide to take this opportunity to ask my inner teacher for another sign, this time I ask if it will be possible to have a sign that I can identify with on the physical plane. No sooner do I finish asking, and the sign appears. The thick grey mass of cloud that engulfs the entire area ruptures in one specific spot, and the clouds begin to separate. From behind the deteriorating covering, the glistening sunlight streams through. It is not the full illuminating Sun (with its magnificent, pulsating energy field) that shines through, but rather, it is the pure outlined circular shape of the Sun. It magically lights up the water in front of me, extending toward me a walkway I can follow in order that I might return to the source of all life.

As I stand motionless, staring into the circular shape of the Sun, I can feel something beginning to stir from deep within my being. My body is beginning to feel warm all over. An innocent and peaceful smile takes form through my lips as I acknowledge that I have returned home once more. It is pure magic. I am alone within myself, experiencing the simplicity of life. I know that this is only the beginning of many such gifts I will receive as I move along my life journey. Within minutes, all has returned to its original setting; the thick grey bands of cloud once again fill the area. I take a few long, slow, deep breaths, feeling my connectedness to all that is around me.

For the next day and a half, I explore the townships of Ucluelet and Tofino

– the place of my birth – wondering what these two tiny settlements might have been like when my family lived here (I was nearly a year and a half young when my family moved to Victoria). I continue to drive around, allowing myself to be directed to wherever it feels necessary to be in order to experience totally the feelings that surface. I am becoming more aware of my affinity to the mountains and to the open sea.

As I drive along the highway heading out of Tofino, I come to the turn off point that will take me to Radar Hill. It is blocked off by a removable barricade. It is winter, and the road leading to the summit can be very treacherous under certain conditions. I know that I have to get to the beach area below the hill, and that this route is the only way of getting there. I carefully remove the barricade, slip the car through, and then replace the barricade in the same position. In so doing, I pretty much guarantee myself complete isolation down on the beach.

I park the car in the parking lot and begin to search for the semi-obscured trail that will eventually take me to my destination. I had been warned ahead of time that the trail down is fairly steep in places, and that because of the weather (it has been raining quite heavily for two weeks now) it will be extremely difficult to maneuver along the mud banks.

It is a long and tedious hike into where I want to go, but once I get there, the effort I have gone through is insignificant compared to what I receive in return – a desolate beach. It is a delicate mixture of smoothened sand and protruding rock formations. Driftwood is lying scattered all along the shoreline, intricately arranged by Mother Nature, forming many complicated geometric configurations. It is definitely a once-in-a-lifetime experience, a spectacular sight to behold. There is a fog bank that takes up residence some 300 yards from the shore, and the colour patterns within it blend perfectly with the overhead cloud design. The result leaves me feeling like I am standing in the middle of a place that can only exist within a fantasy world. I am now aware that I have come to the edge of the world as I have know it to be, and that I am the only one here to enjoy it.

I stroll up and down the beach area, looking at every inch of what is continually unfolding before me. I can feel subtle electricity running through my body. It is almost like a sexual excitement I am experiencing. I have this uncontrollable desire to remove all of my clothes, to be totally free of man's world (and all of man's earthly problems), and be one with all the elements that surround me.

I find a sheltered spot where I can leave my clothes so they will not get wet. It has been raining hard and steady since I arrived, more like sleeting rain. The wind is blowing off the water at about forty miles per hour, and the surrounding temperature is a chilly thirty-six degrees Fahrenheit.

I come out from behind the trees and begin to walk along the edge of the water. For a few moments in time, I am completely closed off from everything surrounding me. I am feeling as though I am actually here but not here, as well. I wonder if it is possible that I can be in two places at the same time. I am beginning to feel that I am being watched by more than one set of eyes, that someone or some thing is observing me from the nearby underbrush. I proceed to move inwardly and ask my Higher Self if he wishes to comment on the feeling that is surfacing within my conscious awareness. What comes back is very simple and direct. It is my own internal fears of being alone in this world that are being presented to me. There is no other being or animal form lurking in the underbrush. I am instructed to let go of my limiting thoughts so that I can enjoy the totality of the unfolding experience. I am also assured that I am being well protected, and that no harm will come to me.

Something is happening inside me. What, I am not at all sure. I suddenly break free from my entangling thought processes, and verbally shout into the open air my desire to be totally free within myself so that I can enjoy the simple magic that completely surrounds me in this ever-changing fantasy world. I jump on and over the logs that clutter the shoreline, and I dance uncontrollably on the hardened surface of the evenly toned textures of sand. I run in and out of the water, jumping over the waves as they head for the shore. I dance with the wind as it caresses and nurtures my naked body. I ask the wind if it wants to play, to which it acknowledges that it does. We continue to dance with each other, neither one of us leading, yet both of us are flowing in and out of the creative process. We are harmoniously moving as one within each of our movement patterns. We use the sand, the water, and the conglomeration of rock formations that pattern the surface of the sand, to express our creativeness and our ability to harmonize.

I cry out with joy at the freedom I am allowing myself to have for the first time in my life, and I can feel this ecstasy penetrating into every square inch of my physical embodiment. It is an exhilarating feeling that is flooding into my being. My heart begins to beat faster and harder, and my lungs demand more air as I race back and forth along the surface of the beach. I am taking every opportunity to be absolutely free and spontaneous in my expressions, with whatever presents itself within the reality of my physical senses.

After moving in a creative way for well over an hour and a half, I suddenly slip back into my normal awareness of thought projections and seriously begin to question the possible effect that these activities are having on my physical body. I am not sure why I have found it necessary to do this, for I am feeling comfortably warm all over. The only notice of the cold that I am aware of is on the tips of my fingers and tips of my toes. The area around my heart is on fire, radiating streams of warmth throughout the rest of my physical embodiment. I am quite surprised that I did not feel the cold while I was playing. My thought processes want to know why this is so. The more I look at it, and the more I think about it, the more I am beginning to feel the embracing cold air.

As I walk along the edge of the water, heading back to where I have left my clothes, I ask to be given a gift that I will be able to take back with me, one that will continue to support the new shift of awareness taking place within me. I stand quietly for a few moments, gazing out into the obscure depths of the fog bank. I slowly bow my head to acknowledge the elements of Nature, to show my appreciation for the opportunities of interacting with them. I then disappear into the trees to put my clothes on.

As I come out from behind the trees, my vision is captured by a sudden movement at the edge of the water, almost at the exact spot where I had bowed to the elements of Nature. As I turn and fix my attention onto the object, everything appears to stop moving. I proceed to walk over to where the object is lying, and what I observe before me makes my insides tingle. It is a piece of driftwood measuring close to six feet in length and having the exact thickness, texture, markings and body shape as a snake. My first thought is that it is a Boa Constrictor, one of the three snake forms that are part of the martial art discipline I am studying.

This particular snake form has its head raised and semi-twisted in a spiral configuration, almost as though it is just starting to climb up a really skinny sapling. The head section is raised some twelve inches off the surface of the sand, and it is looking directly at me as I pick it up out of the water. At the point where the body separates from the sand, there is a rectangular shaped white rock – two inches by three inches – firmly embedded into the structure. It is affixed to one side and does not interfere with the main body alignment. Rather, it supports the snake in raising its head by acting as a counterbalance.

This is truly a magical gift, one that I interpret as promoting softness and love of self. The snake, to me, symbolizes the potent power of transformation and change. It also represents the attunement to a higher vibration of energies I am capable of tapping into and fully utilizing within my living expression. These energies will enable me to transcend time and space as I know them to be.

I could have sworn that I saw the snake moving through the water when I first came out from behind the trees. It appeared to be moving through the water just like the Garter snakes used to when I played with them in the swamps when

I was a young boy. I had walked by that very spot where the snake was lying not more than five minutes before, and there was no sign of any driftwood near the shore or floating in the water. I am now thoroughly confused, mainly because the area where the snake had materialized is completely sheltered from the incoming waves. I cannot come up with any rational explanation as to how it had gotten here.

Upon my arrival into this area, I was greeted by a powerful looking Bald Eagle, and now I have been befriended by a magical Boa Constrictor. My internal thought processes have been actively engaged, and I am now beginning to question all that has been taking place. I am not at all sure what is real any more.

The following morning, as I am preparing to go back to Victoria, I receive an inner calling from an aspect of my Higher Self to go back to Long Beach one last time. I am to seek out a power-spot on the northern end of the beach, and once I have found it, I am to sit and wait for a message regarding the wise old lady and the young boy.

As I leave the car in the parking lot and head for the beach area, I am internally being directed toward a large section of boulders that lie partially submerged under the sand. This will be the place where I will sit and wait.

As I sit and attune myself to the unfolding inner process, I once again ask my inner teacher to give me a sign to show me that I am at the right place, at the right time. Almost immediately, the clouds part and the Sun shines through, just as it did on the day I had arrived from Victoria. It once again lights up the water in front of me and provides an extended walkway so I can return, once more, to the source of all life. I close my eyes and become quiet and still, waiting patiently to hear the words that will come from within my inner void. The message is short and to the point, "The wise old woman is all of Nature, all that the Almighty Creator has manifested here. The young boy represents the child inside you. The same child of knowing that arrived here on the day of your birth."

It is all so simple. So simple, in fact, that I begin to laugh out loud. I instinctively know there is much more that needs to be acknowledged in all that I have experienced since I left home to come to this place. At the same time, I have an internal knowing sense that all I have experienced is really nothing at all; that all of what has taken place is only the beginning phase to a higher initiation of some kind. It is now time to leave. Without further delay, I make my way back to the parking lot.

I sit in the car, looking out over the beach area spread out in all directions in front of me, sifting through the barrage of thoughts moving in and out of my mental picture screen. They are all coming and going so quickly that I cannot sort through them fast enough. The noise level within the frontal part of my head is becoming unbearable. I am not sure how to stop it. Instantaneously, everything becomes quiet. It is now so quiet that the silence is deafening. I wait patiently to see what will unfold next.

My own external voice begins to speak, "I have come back here to the place where I had first entered into this physical plane, and in so doing at this time, I hereby relinquish one aspect of my transitory living expression so that I may begin another."

There is a short interruption within my outer communication, as I am being presented with more information from my inner teacher. When the internal dialogue has concluded, my external voice continues,

> It is apparent that the life I have been living up until now has fulfilled its primary purpose. It is now appropriate that I begin a new life, with a new focus and moving in a new direction, one that will allow me to enjoy all the fruits that this physical plane has to offer. And to do all of this without fear. It is time to live my own life through my own desires and my own aspirations. By returning to the beginning once again, I have been able to re-connect with the child energy inside me. The little boy now wishes to be released into my outer world so that he might give freely, to all mankind, the love and goodness he has to offer. In returning to the purity of the child, I am now free within myself to explore all the different avenues of life, beginning with accepting that all things on the physical plane are here for me to experience without becoming attached to any of them. Other beings will be attracted to me because of my innocence, love, compassion, truthfulness, humour and spontaneity. I have a whole new lease on my life, with a whole new beginning. The old patterns are still very much around, and still need to be acknowledged, but no longer supported. I will only support that which will aid me in aligning with the purity of my truth.

I swing the car out on to the main road and head for home. I drive for about two miles before I start to get an inner feeling that I am being watched over from above. I roll down the window, stick my head out into the cool, damp air and look up into the sky above. Flying on a parallel course to the one I am on, is my friend, Bald Eagle. It is the same one I met upon arriving here. I continue to watch him as I drive. Every now and again, he looks my way, making sure that I am still following the road that will take me home safely. (The 'road' is the path I am moving on, and 'home' is my truth.) This is definitely not your average Bald Eagle. This bird is special. Whenever I observe him, words cannot be found to describe the feeling that is awakened inside of me.

He keeps moving from one side of the car to the other, crisscrossing the path I am on. He is playing with me. I have almost run off the road twice, as I am desperately trying not to lose sight of him. We continue this playful interaction over the next two miles, at which time, he once again dips his wings, as if to wave at me, and then quickly ascends. He disappears beyond the limited vision I have through the car windshield. I stop the car so I can get one last look at him, but when I get out and look, he is nowhere to be seen.

# CHAPTER 3

# THE UNFOLDING INNER DIMENSIONS

## *February, 1984*

I have just stepped out of the shower, and am in the process of drying off, when the phone rings. With water still dripping from my body, I enter the living room and answer it. It is my brother, "Hi, Blaise. Listen, something has happened – it's Dad – he's back in the hospital."

For a brief moment, I can feel a lump in my throat as I hold my breath. My heart skips a beat and then begins to beat faster and harder. I take a long, steady breath, swallow, and after a slight pause, ask, "How bad is it?"

There is a long silence on the other end. I can sense that he wants to answer but is having some difficulty managing the raw emotions surfacing within him. Whenever he goes to say anything, his voice cracks. After what seems like an eternity, he responds, "His heart has given out a few times, there isn't much hope." His voice begins to crack more as the emotional impact continues to surface. He says, "I don't know – can you come over?"

I ask, "Where are you, at the hospital?"

He responds rather nervously, "Yes, the Jubilee."

I quickly say, "Sure thing. I'll be right over."

Pictures begin to race across my mental picture screen. I do not know what else to say. I am at a loss for words. It is all so sudden. Dad had been in the hospital once before, just a few months ago, but all the indications from the doctors were that he was getting much better. After a short pause, I continue, "I'll be there in about fifteen minutes. Take care and – listen – everything will be okay, you'll see."

I hang up the phone and continue to stand motionless, looking aimlessly out through the sliding glass window. All time comes to a sudden standstill. There is no movement coming from either the internal space of the apartment or the visible world outside. My body suddenly becomes cold, and I can't find the necessary strength from within to move it.

I consciously alter my state of awareness to see if I can intuitively pick up on any information that will shed some light on Dad's condition. As I quiet my thoughts, I receive what I am looking for. It is clear to me that Dad isn't going to make it. The ordeal he is presently experiencing will be his last. Hearing this information snaps me back into the present unfolding reality and drops me, instantaneously, back into the moveable world.

I make a few phone calls to cancel the appointments I have scheduled for the day. I put on some clothes and leave for the hospital. I find myself walking, and then running, then back to walking. I can't decide whether I should be in a hurry or take my time. Thoughts about life and death dance across my thoughts. I am hoping that it is all just a part of a bad dream, and I want to know when I am going to wake up. I really do not want to accept the possibility that this is actually taking place.

Many times prior to this, I thought about him dying. Sometimes I even wished that he would die, especially whenever we would have a major disagreement or flare up. My self-created ego would get all bruised within the interaction, and I wanted to lash out at him for what I thought he had done to me. I had always wanted to see him as my archrival, instead of as my friend. I never really thought it would happen like this, though.

Thoughts of guilt flood my thoughts, "Could I possibly be responsible for what has happened?" This thought and more, most of which do not make any sense, continually dart in and out. When I finally stop all the noise, I am able to get a clearer perspective on what is actually taking place. I am able to see that Dad is totally responsible for his own actions, no different than I, and that there is no possible way I could have caused any of what is happening.

I enter the hospital and ask for directions as to where they are keeping him. As I get off the elevator, I take a left turn around a corner, and there in front of me, standing motionless in the middle of the hallway, with an absence of colour in her face, and body trembling, is my mother.

I walk up to where she is standing, gently place my arms around her and give her a hug. There is very little reaction within her to the gesture I have made. I can sense that she is trying to be the strong one. Like so many other times in her life, she isn't about to let anyone know just how scared she really is.

By this time, my brother and sister have joined us in the hallway. I give them each a hug and then we all go into the waiting room. Within minutes, I have received the whole story of what has happened. It somehow does not seem to be as bad as what I had first thought after speaking on the phone with my brother. Now comes the waiting.

This is only the beginning of what seems like a lifetime of waiting, waiting for something to happen. I know for certain that Dad isn't going to make it. What I do not know for sure is the amount of time we will all have in order to say the things we want to say before he leaves this plane of reality. The question that is most important for me to look at is, "Is it possible that a harmonious solution can be found to heal our relationship on all levels before he leaves?"

From deep within I know that a spiritual solution will be the only way of reinstating the purest vibration of unconditional love into our relationship. There are too many roadblocks that we have both put up against each other and the rest of the outer world to have it any other way. These self-imposed obstructions are keeping both of us from being truthful to ourselves and to each other. There has always been a lot of friction between the two of us, ever since I can remember. I can recall an incident that had happened when I was only six years old, and I am sure there were others that had occurred even earlier than that.

The incident that had taken place when I was six has been very instrumental in shaping the manner in which I have moved through my outer world over the last twenty-eight years. At that time, I was playing baseball in an organized league, and I made a great play within one of the fielding exercises. The coach had taken the time to personally compliment me in what I had done. I was extremely proud of myself for what I had accomplished. When I rushed up to my father to tell him my good news when I got home, he just sloughed it off as being no big deal. That really hurt me inside. I chose to take on that hurt and own it. I became very angry and frustrated with his attitude toward me. I saw him as being very insensitive.

From that day on, I programmed myself to move in my outer world in a certain way. I repeatedly told myself that I would be better at everything I did than he ever was or would be. I took it all on myself and became focused on fulfilling this obsession; becoming harder and more critical of myself and refusing to acknowledge any of that which I had to offer the outer world of man in my own unique way. I began to put all my attention toward the things outside me. The harder I worked the less acknowledgment I received from him. This infuriated me even more. I continued to be harder on myself and more bitter toward him. I blamed him for almost everything that did not happen in our relationship. It was through this one experience that I had created the 'tough man' image with the 'I'll show you' attitude that has been my trademark for too many years.

Here I am thirty-four years old, and I am only now finally getting around to realizing that I have been carrying all this extra baggage within me – baggage that has never even belonged to me in the first place, and that has never once supported my life. All of it illusions, and all of it created by other people. I owned it all and made it all very real in my world. When I was growing up, I spent the majority of my time reacting to what others were doing and saying, continuously going around in circles, never really finding the joy or the peace with being in one place within my thoughts. I was constantly running away from my own inner truth and attaching myself to everyone else's illusion of how the outer world was. As a result, I was dying inside.

The nurse enters the waiting room and mentions that we can go in and have a visit with Dad as often as we want, but only two of us can go in at any given time. She also encourages us to keep the visits short because he is really in need of all the rest he can get. They do not give much hope for him making it through the night.

I walk into the room, make my way up alongside his bed, reach out and gently take his hand in mine. He slowly opens his eyes. There are no words I want to say. I only want to let him know that I am aware of what is happening inside him. It is a bit ironic, and at the same time sad, to see a man who has spent the greater part of his life climbing some of the roughest terrain along the British Columbia Coast, falling trees and gaining a reputation as a hardnosed woodsman from Nova Scotia, now in his final hours, lying flat on his back with tubes running down his throat and nose, and a needle in his arm. They also have him plugged into a machine that keeps his heart beating. Without it he would not be able to live more than a few minutes.

After a moment of silence, I ask him a number of yes/no questions to see if I can help in any way to make him more comfortable. He has never allowed anyone to help him during all the years I can remember, and I can sense that it isn't easy for him to have people wanting to do things for him now. He is an extremely proud man who doesn't believe in showing his weaknesses to those around him. In his current situation, he really doesn't have too much to say about the way things are going, for he is totally helpless and cannot do anything for himself.

They have him plugged into two machines that continually monitor his vital signs. Each time he moves his body quickly or coughs, they start making weird noises. It is unnerving. Whenever the noise starts, I think this is going to be it; that he is on his last breath.

I have very little emotional reaction to what is happening. I do not want to cry. I cannot bring myself to wanting to cry. As I see it, there isn't anything for me to cry about. To cry would show that I am being selfish in my intention, that I am hurting on the inside and feeling pain. The truth is clear and obvious: He is the one who is in pain and the one who is suffering.

Each time during that day and the following three, whenever I went into his room, I began to reflect more upon my own life. I looked at the occasions where he and I had crossed paths, locked horns and dueled on all levels – mental, physical and emotional – in order to make our presence known to each other. I also reflected on how we both continually struggled to gain more power from each other by using whatever means we could.

He had determined his belief systems many years before I had arrived on the scene. He had structured it according to the manner that best worked for him, and he wasn't about to change any of it for anyone, especially me. I could never make any sense out of the things he came to believe in, or in how he was choosing to live his life, and I wasn't about to be swayed into believing any of it just so I could get close to him. It always seemed that the more we struggled with each other, the further apart we got and the more stubborn we became.

I had accumulated many beliefs as I journeyed along on my life's path, none of which I had ever felt particularly secure with. Nevertheless, I held on to them as tightly as I could, for I really didn't have anything else to replace them with that was any better.

It is now the fourth day. I enter his room and ask if he feels as though he is going to make it through this ordeal alive. His eyes become larger, almost as if he is startled by the question. Many times (in fun) he had talked and kidded about dying – that he was ready to go at any time – but I don't think he had envisioned it happening quite like this. He nods his head, signifying a yes answer, yet he and I both know that he isn't going to make it. He just wants to be strong in his own way, not wanting to show the outside world his fears or his vulnerability.

The next time I enter his room, I ask him outright if he is going to die. I have played the game with him long enough and I cannot go on pretending that he is going to get any better. I take his hand in mine and say, "Look, Dad, it's okay to be scared. We're all scared, too. Let's be honest with each other."

At this precise moment, I know the exact time and very day on which he will be leaving the earthly plane. I will now have plenty of time to help prepare the rest of the family for his departure. He then gives his response to the question I have asked. He shakes his head from side to side, indicating that he is not going to die. Looking into his eyes, however, I can sense that he knows he is on the last leg of his earthly journey.

His bed is next to the window. I turn away from him and gaze out the clear pane of glass, looking at what lies beyond. I want to know the answer to, "Why has it taken both of us so long to tell each other that we love and care about each other?" and "Why did we have to wait until now?" I turn back to look at him. Gently clasping his hand in mine, I quietly say, "Dad, I love you very much. I always have."

As I finish the sentence, our eyes pierce through each other's outer armour and we see, for the very first time, each other's true colors. We squeeze our hands together to solidify our bond. I lean over the railing and give him a kiss and a hug, both of which we have only allowed to take place on about three different occasions during the past ten years. As I stand up, I can sense that he is having a really difficult time holding back his tears. So I decide to leave to spare him any further embarrassment.

As I make my way down the hallway, I can feel tears beginning to swell to the surface of my eyes. As I sit in the waiting-room, I begin to cry. I ask myself over and over again, "Why has it taken so long? It all seems so stupid and so pointless. Why was it necessary for him to take himself to his death bed before he would allow himself the freedom to tell those who mean so much to him that he loves them?" I continue to cry for a good five minutes. For the first time in sixteen and a half years, tears are flowing freely.

The last time the tears had flowed so freely was on October 10, 1967. That was the day on which my older brother died. The circumstances surrounding that experience in my life had a very sobering effect upon me. So much so, that I had completely turned off my internal waterworks system.

✳

It is during the early hours of the tenth day that my father leaves this limited dimension of reality to move through the thin veil that separates it from all the other dimensions of reality. He once again returns to the oneness of all things, to move in the pure form of spirit.

I am standing beside his bed, holding his hand in mine, when he takes his last breath. I can see his physical body become denser and more firmly rooted to the structure that has been supporting it. I can also sense his spiritual essence preparing to transcend the limited boundaries of time and space.

I close my eyes for a moment in order to give them a rest, for I haven't had much opportunity to sleep during any of the days he has been in here, and it now appears to be catching up to me. As I stand here, something begins to happen within my being. My whole physical body starts to rotate in a clockwise direction. I am creating a spiral movement, of sorts. My feet are secured to the floor and my shoulders are leading the movement pattern in wide circle formations.

As my body is pre-occupied with doing this, I am becoming more oblivious to the world outside me and more acutely attuned to the internal process unfolding within the deeper levels of my being.

There is a certain calmness that prevails throughout me, the likes of which I have not experienced before. I feel myself consciously leaving the physical form I have been occupying, moving deeper within my inner void of darkness (to where my spiritual essence resides) until I am able to align myself with the same vibrational frequency as my father. Here we are face to face in a much different expression of reality, one that is so much higher in its vibrational resonance.

It is an environment of pure and all-encompassing light. There are infinite colour variations within this void, comprised of ever-changing textures and hues. There are no words being exchanged between us. The communication is the purest form I have ever witnessed. The closest expression on the earthly plane would be the process called telepathy. It is all concluded through the exchange of vibrational light energy: Each hue of a light variation carries within its vibrational essence a structural message that, when aligned with other hues of light variations, becomes the transformational building block for all physical matter on the physical earthly plane.

I am neither in my physical embodiment nor am I in the physical embodiment that belongs to my father. We have both had to transcend through the deepest layers of our multi-dimensional bodies in order that we could arrive within this void. It is a place that connects all expressions of human existence. One can only reach this place by going inward within oneself, for the inner true self is the only part of each of us that knows how to get to this place. Words cannot adequately describe all of what I am observing while I am here.

The message I receive is very clearly presented by one of my inner teachers, "There is no need to fear death, for death is only a transformational aspect of life that can be expressed through an unlimited number of multi-dimensional mediums."

We quickly move from the free-form levels of reality within the inner worlds to the peripheral edge of a much more defined outer physical world. We are now suspended directly above his bed, looking down upon the two motionless figures still occupying the tiny curtained off space. Dad is lying on the narrow bed, and I am standing right next to him, still in the exact same position I was in prior to closing my eyes.

I have been experiencing something I cannot fully explain. I am having a dual sense of a living expression. I am simultaneously aware of being in my physical body and not being in my physical body. The aspect of my being standing beside the bed, holding my father's hand, knows that there is another part of my being floating independently above the bed. The aspect of my being independently floating above the bed knows that the aspect of my being standing next to the bed is consciously aware of it.

Within the confines of the small cubicle, my father and I journey throughout lifetimes of human existence. I can see all things within the wholeness of how they were created and expressed ever since the beginning of time.

I know that what I am being shown is symbolic of the unlimited freedom I can experience while I am still on the physical earthly plane. All I will have to do, in order to attain this state of beingness, is go within myself and release all of my preconceived ideas as to what I think this plane is about. I have been shown the basic formula of how all life comes to be created on this plane, and I have seen that it is not how man has come to describe it in his writings. Man has adapted his perceptual knowledge so that it fits into his controllable structure, thereby totally trapping himself by it. The purity within the structure of all things can only be acknowledged when one is able to experience each one of them independently and separately, as well as wholly, at the same time.

This is my father's gift to me. The decision he is making at this time, to leave this plane, has a duel purpose to it. Firstly, it was important for him to create what he did along his life journey so that others could learn their lessons, and so that he too could learn the lessons he came here to experience. Secondly, this is to serve as a transitional pivot point in my living expression, mainly having to do with what I am to do here on this plane.

It has been explained by my inner teacher that I have successfully navigated my way through my own self-created obstacle course while, at the same time, maintaining my focus and intention upon the highest possible vibrational frequency – universal truth. I am seeking to resolve all aspects of disharmony within my inner and outer worlds through the full utilization of the purest vibration of love. I have been given the gift contained within this lesson. I have also been shown how I can further use this gift to help me transcend the limitations within my own world, so that I can move on to a much higher vibration within my living expression.

It all doesn't make a lot of sense to me at this time. I only know that there is much for me to look at. I see that it is not advantageous for me to continue looking at things within my outer world using the common everyday means of perceiving – the five outer world senses. Rather, it is important to attune myself to using the higher vibrational "seven senses" that allow for unrestricted expressions of creativity within my inner world.

Everything is black. There is an incredible sensation of movement pulsating throughout every inch of my physical form. It is as if I am being rocketed through a large, continuously expanding and unfolding void. Then, all goes blank.

I open my eyes and look at the clock hanging above the bed directly in front of me. I have only been gone for approximately one minute thirty seconds. I proceed to focus my vision toward the bed where my father is lying. As I do this, I can feel my state of awareness shifting through an unconscious process that is new. As my eyes begin to lose the clarity of the image of my father, I begin to see the spiritual essence of who he really is. I am watching it slowly ascend within his physical body and gradually disappear into the higher realms of vibrational existence.

I continue to stand here, not really too sure about any of what has just taken place, or what, if anything, I should do next. I only know one thing for certain, and that is I will not be able to tell anyone about what I have experienced within these few short moments.

A few minutes later, the nurse who has been looking after Dad enters the tiny space. She asks if she can do anything, and she also offers her condolences. She becomes very emotional, breaking into tears. I can feel from within her being that she cares for and loves the people she assists on this ward. I can see how it would be very difficult to be close to someone for a period of time, especially if they were dependent on you for everything like Dad was, without becoming attached to them in some way. I gently embrace her in a warm, loving, supportive way, and thank her for the kindness and love she had extended to my Dad while she watched over him.

God and I are the only ones who know that I do not need to be consoled. In fact, the truth of the matter is that I am ecstatic and overjoyed with all that I have been shown. I will have to be careful not to show to the outside world my exuberance, at least not until after the funeral.

I leave the hospital and go to break the news to the rest of my family. They all take it quite hard. There are many tears, and expressions of anger and frustration surface around all that has happened.

I proceed to assist Mom in whatever way I can, always being cautious within myself to be continuously sensitive to the way she is feeling. We make all the final arrangements concerning the legal matters surrounding Dad's death, and we confirm the details of the funeral service.

✳

While the service is being conducted at the church, I can feel the vibrational essence of my father present in the room. I can sense that he is watching over the proceedings and giving comfort and support to those who need it. I begin to consciously alter my state of awareness, much in the same manner that had taken place in the hospital, letting my eyes stray unfocused so that my vision becomes semi-blurred. I focus my attention to the area surrounding the casket, and there he is outlined in white light (those are the only words I can summon that will even come close to describing what he looks like, and they are by no means adequate), effortlessly suspended above the wooden structure. As he looks my way, I begin to smile, for I know that he is not suffering in his new environment. I can sense and feel all that he is; he is the purest form of love. He continues to stay around until after the ceremony concludes at the cemetery. When the people begin to disperse from the grounds, he departs.

After the service, everyone is invited to come back to our house for some food, beverage, and emotional support. I circulate throughout the house, watching and observing how each person is handling the reality that Dad is no longer going to be around. There are many who are feeling ill at ease, as they didn't have the opportunity to tell him while he was alive how much they really did appreciate who he was, and how much his friendship had meant.

A few people come up to me and comment that I am taking all of what has happened rather well, and that I am being the strong one for the rest of the family. They seem to be into making me out to be some kind of family hero. They obviously are not able to feel what is actually going on inside me. They think it is important to be strong, to hold in all their emotional feelings. I can see they didn't get the same message behind my father's death. He was the one who believed that all emotional feelings should be suppressed inside, and that is what killed him: the fact that he never gave himself the opportunity to clearly state how he was feeling. The times when he did express himself, he always attached a judgment or comparison to it.

Some of the people do not want to hear my response as to how I see the whole experience – that Dad and I had arrived at a harmonious and loving acceptance of each other in our relationship, and that I had taken every opportunity while he was in the hospital to be totally truthful toward myself and toward him, owning all of my own past critical judgments and expressing a desire to see him for the person he truly was.

I realize that it is all too far over their heads. I am also aware of the fact that I am very much different in the way I view the outside world of man, and in the way I acknowledge the inner worlds that exist within each of us, than all the other people who are gathered in the house. I receive yet another gift from my father's passing.

I have been keeping myself busy looking for the hidden gifts contained within all the experiences that have taken place during the last twelve days. I feel that if I am not able to receive one insight about my life from Dad's passing, then he would have died for no reason. At the beginning of my spiritual journey, I had become aware of the reality that there are gifts to be sought after and treasured within each and every experience created by me or someone else.

A person has to be prepared to look for these gifts if they truly want them. I am prepared to do that, and it seems that many others are not. It is not so much because they do not want these gifts, but rather, it is that they do not know that these gifts exist. I see that they all want to put their attention and focus on to me so that they will not have to deal with their own fears about dying. We have all been reminded this day that death is inevitable, and that some day it will knock on everyone's door.

The most precious gift I have received out of this whole experience is: "Life is far too short to hang on to limited beliefs and concepts of reality. When I die, all of those things that I thought were so important won't amount to a tiny drop of water." I have also become aware of the fact: "Life is far too short and too precious to be taken for granted."

I can see and feel, within my own sensitivities, that most of the people who have gathered together are very frustrated within the complicated textures of their own lives. They have become too trapped by their own inability to see past their own habitual thinking, to fully realize that there is a huge wonderful world that exists outside of oneself, one that offers unlimited freedom to whoever dares to venture out there.

✳

For weeks after the funeral service, I continued to extract valuable information from the experiences I had created within the scope of Dad's death. I intently observed people reacting to the truthful reality that he is gone, most of them hoping that if they could avoid talking about the way they were feeling, that somehow it would all just disappear. The fact that Dad is gone will eventually be accepted by all as time moves along, but the self-created restrictions within their own lives will remain. We are all accountable for those things that we create within our living expressions. It is through those creations that we determine how we are going to live, and eventually, how we are going to die.

## April 1984

By going more and more inwardly within my own being, I am able to begin resolving the uncertainty around who I am. I am also able to sense more clearly the continual unfolding of a whole new world within me. In order that I might reach this new world in totality, and maintain a stable position within it, I must give up completely the world that has been created and dominated by my outer five earthly senses.

I continue to open to the many different dimensional levels of reality that exist within my inner world. My sensitivities toward myself and to those around me have become more acute. My intuitive faculties have become more pronounced and functional within everyday situations, and the format I have been using to express them is gradually changing and evolving.

I am not totally satisfied with any one of the levels of reality I have begun to experience within my inner world. I cannot help but feel that there is a whole lot more behind all that I have been seeing and hearing around me. I feel that I have to keep letting go of newly acknowledged truths, seeing them only as illusions except within the moment of their unfolding. I cannot afford to hold on to any one of them. Yet at the same time, I must go into the very heart of each of them with the purest intention of finding the simple truth behind what they actually stand for. I have only now realized that what I am dabbling in is not to be taken lightly. If I falter along the way due to my carelessness, my life shall be taken. Whether this is to be symbolically or physically, I am not at all sure.

*

I have recently entered into a dimensional reality of ongoing experience that circulates with and expresses itself through the medium of spiritual entities – or spirit guides. I have so far been able to attune myself to their ever-changing vibrations. I am now able to flow freely within these different levels of reality to bring forward pertinent information concerning the structural alignment of the physical earthly plane, and also to present information of a personal significance, pertaining to certain questions I am asked by those who come to counsel with me.

These entities have the ability to take on many different forms and shapes, and I allow them to manifest themselves through me however they so desire. I am not at all concerned about protecting myself against possible harm from these various entities, as I know that I am moving within a higher vibrational frequency, and that I am being well looked after and protected in all that I choose to do.

I had been invited by a friend – who taught an upgrading skills class for people re-entering the work-force – to come and give a series of presentations on the subject of *Looking at your life, past programming and conditioning.* I had been her guest on a few other occasions prior to this engagement, and I had always found my experiences there to be rewarding, in the sense that I was given much symbolic information regarding myself and the way in which I was choosing to move through the other world of man. I got to see just how much different my world is in relation to the normally accepted world of the outer structure called Society.

There were always between ten and twenty-five people, of all social backgrounds, who would attend these lectures given through me. This particular morning had started off much like the ones before. My friend introduced me to the group, and then gave me the go-ahead to intuitively create the flow and the movement of how the day would unfold. I was never quite sure what direction the dialogue would take once I opened my mouth. I was never concerned about the content of what was being presented. Before I would begin a session like this, or anytime I was going to be in front of an audience of any size, I would attune myself to my Higher Self and ask that only the purest vibration of truth be presented, and I prayed that my intellect would stay out of it altogether.

I have been talking now for nearly an hour and a half, and things are beginning to unfold in a slightly different manner than what I have been used to experiencing. There is another distinct voice that keeps moving into and out of the audio range of my inner senses. It is asking for my permission to speak through me. I repeatedly decline its request. Previous to this day, I have only allowed the voices of other entities to be channeled through me when I was doing individual readings. I had never allowed it to happen in front of a group before, of any size. (I thought that all I really needed to do was leave the space available for these entities to come through while I was out in the public eye, and that would surely mark the end of my non-existent but working-on-establishing professional career.) I wasn't at all sure how it would be received by those who were attending. I rationalized that it was better to be safe than to be sorry. I couldn't afford to gamble.

I manage to stall the entity off until coffee time. We stop for a fifteen-minute break, and during this time I become aware that all is quiet within. I assume that the entity has gotten the message and has decided to return to the void from which he came. Well, I soon discover that this is not to be. I again stand up in front of the room and begin to speak. I am now aware that the entity has returned, this time more determined than before to express himself.

As I continue to speak, I am aware that I am not able to keep my focus or attention on my outer dialogue. I am totally consumed by the dialogue going on inside my head. A woman begins to ask me a question that has to do with something I had said just before we broke for coffee. At the exact same time as she is speaking, I am receiving, by way of the inner dialogue, a tremendous influx of information that specifically has to do with her early childhood. I am seeing visions of experiences that she had encountered, and I am hearing detailed descriptions of each of those experiences. I can see very clearly how the particular experiences she had back then are somewhat responsible for the dilemmas she is currently experiencing within her living expression.

The voice within begins to speak louder within the confines of my head. I am looking at the possibility of making a decision. I am not sure what I should do next. Almost instantaneously, I clearly see that I can no longer deny this experience from unfolding. I have to let go of my conscious thoughts of control and allow whatever is to be presented to come through uncensored. "Let go and trust in me, I mean you no harm, Let the truth be spoken" begins to echo through my inner channels.

Without any warning, there is a release of some kind within me. I instinctively know that it is the appropriate time to allow this experience to move. I ask the woman for her permission to allow this inner dialogue to be presented in front of everyone in the room. I mention that this dialogue might contain some important information that could possible shed some light on the current situations in her life. She says that I can speak freely. I proceed to ask all the people in the room for their permission to allow this experience to unfold. When all have agreed, I continue.

With astounding pin-point accuracy, her past is presented. The information channeled through relates to a few traumatic experiences that had happened when she was four years old. A few of the recalled events are not so favorable, in that they bring back memories that have been covered over with a heavy layer of emotional scar tissue. For the most part, the information helps her connect pieces of her past with experiences in her present world, and it affords her the opportunity to do with it whatever she wants.

After the channeling process stops, I ask if she has any further questions she wants to ask regarding any of what has been presented. She mentions that she does not. I am thinking that this will be the end of it, and that I can now go on with the rest of the presentation. But this is not to be the case. Hands start to go up all over the room. There are a number of people who want to know if I can give them some insight into possible experiences that had taken place within their childhood, which could be affecting them within their current living expression. Once again I give the inner voice permission to speak, and as before, the information is right on. My inner voice accurately presents six people with insights regarding their current situations.

I have been clearly shown that what I have experienced is a treasured gift, one that I can utilize effectively to aid those people who want to bring about resolutions to the dilemmas that might be consuming their personal energies.

I have become aware that I have entered into another dimension of reality within my being. I can clearly see that there is much I can make use of by being open to it. This is just another one of those ever-expanding awarenesses within the psychic realities, and I am becoming more focused on how I can use it positively within my daily experiences.

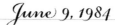

## June 9, 1984

I am continuing to go deeper within the depths of my being, looking to resolve all the conflicts that are associated with my past and circulating within the framework of my present unfolding experiences. I am no longer choosing to analyze any of my past experiences. I am now choosing to use them in a reflective manner to aid me in clearing up all of my illusions.

I have been receiving messages from within to attune myself to the higher vibrations within me so that I might move along in my evolutionary process. I have been doing psychic readings for people lately, and I am now aware that I have been neglecting to listen to the content of the readings. I now see the purpose behind doing readings for other people. The information that is channeled through is actually just for me, and no one else. The people who are attracted to me are gifts from the Life, presented to me to show me where my resistance patterns are, and to give me an opportunity to work through them so that I can move more into the light that lies within the *centre* of my being.

The higher vibrations are those that resonate with my Higher Self, the source of all-knowing. The lower vibrations are those that are associated with the intellectual, analytical thought process, the part of me that is trapped within the limitations of time and space within the fragmented framework of the physical plane.

As long as I continue to attune myself to the physical plane, I will spin within the constant confusion that man is continually creating in his outer world. It is a world that is dominated by power and greed. When I am feeling the essence of people, and living through my spiritual awarenesses, I never crave for the sensual distractions that are so predominant in the competitive world of man. Whenever I focus on the outer world of man, even momentarily, I get sucked back into old, non-supportive behavior patterns that are the result of past programming and conditioning. I then start to crave more personal power from everyone and everything around me.

I am now aware of the textural differences between the inner and outer world. I am now feeling that it is appropriate for me to return into the depths of my past experiences so that I can acknowledge and amend all the judgments and comparisons I have made on myself and everyone else during those earlier confusing years.

I am now seeing that I have used my past relationship with my father as the cornerstone for every other masculine relationship I have created within my outer world. Through the years, I have always had difficulty relating to my male friends – especially those who have exhibited power within the movement patterns of their daily living expression – mainly authority figures. Whenever I have found myself being confronted by this type of individual, I have automatically returned to the solidified structural foundation I had established within the relationship between my father and me. I would then become harder, tougher and colder within the texture of my outer world expressions. My energies were focused on one objective, to make sure that I would get my own way and come out on top in any situation.

I have always kept people on the most outer edge of my world, only showing them what I wanted them to see. I have been so busy creating illusions in my outer world that I have had no time within the quietness of my inner world. As a result of this movement pattern, I have become very insensitive to my own feelings. I have continually created people in my life who have supported me in becoming tougher and more demonstrative in my outer world expressions. It was all so perfect. I did it so well. I see that this has happened mainly due to the initial programming and conditioning stages I went through with my father. I am now seeing that I can change this particular programming pattern any time I choose, now that I fully recognize where it was first created. I am now in the process of altering that behavior pattern on all the different levels within my being. I am fully aware the old pattern may very well come back again and again, and that when it does, I shall move it in the same way as I have done today. Eventually, that pattern will lose its importance and its impact.

I have chosen to keep all the people who have entered into my life at a distance, mainly because that was the safest way for me to maintain control over every situation that was affecting my outer world – a world of illusion.

When either men or women approach me in a non-threatening way within a relationship context, there is no struggle for power or control. I freely and openly extend my loving energies toward them and give them whatever I can in support. At the exact moment there is any hint of them being a threat to my security, I automatically return to the old pattern I had set up with my father.

## September 23, 1984

I have been sharing some time and space with an herbalist friend of mine. I have been accompanying her on nature walks and helping her with the harvesting of some plants so that she can make the necessary tinctures for her business practice. She has also been showing me some of the many different edible plants and roots that exist in abundance within Nature, describing the various ways that these can be prepared and administered to hasten the healing process within the human body. I have also been learning, through other channels, about how the different animals attune themselves to various plant material and berries when they are out of sync with their own natural environment, instinctively knowing the medicinal properties behind each one.

Lately, when I have been going to the woods, I have been attuning myself to the wide variety of edible specimens that are around and available, always eating only enough to whet my appetite. I have been finding that I have much more personal energy, and that I do not tire as easily when I align myself with the natural food that Nature provides.

Today, my herbalist friend and I shared the day together, encompassing a wide range of experiences: walking along a beach out on the west coast of the Island, reminiscing about individual past experiences along our life journeys, sitting and walking in a wooded area out in the country, and looking further at the varieties of edible plant life common to Southern Vancouver Island.

To start the day off, we went to the local health fair. It was being held at a community centre in the heart of the city. It was being sponsored by the Alternative Health Practitioners. It is a group that I had once belonged to, but have not been active in for some time as I have been too busy looking at my life and healing my internal and external bodies – mentally, physically, and emotionally. I have not felt as though I wanted to or could afford to work on other people when my life is still in so many pieces.

I had been studying various bodywork disciplines over the past few years, none of which were quite what I was looking for. They didn't show me anything I didn't already know, so I ended up developing my own system based on a natural phenomenon demonstrated freely and continuously throughout Nature's expression. I call it *Spiral Alignment*. It works on the principle that all muscular tissue structures within the human body are connected and supported (by fascia) through a series of spiral formations that can either be wound up or wound down, depending on and according to how the mental patterning has constructed them and how tightly the emotional fabric is holding them together.

I thought that it was time to reconnect with the people I had once circulated with, within this field, before I chose to seriously scrutinize the mechanical structure of my life (it has been just over a year since I first entered into isolation). I had decided before reaching the premises that I would enter into the space with the full intention of acknowledging each of the practitioners as people, and that I would open myself up so that I could aptly receive the gifts they had to offer: "What could I learn about myself through the unfolding process?"

As I move in and out of the various lecture rooms listening to the different practitioners give dissertations about what they do, I imagine that each one of them is a reflection of me. As a result of this reality change, I get to observe myself actively participating in many different roles. What I become aware of is that each of these people firmly believes: that they are someone; that they actually do something important; that they are somehow important because of what they do; and that they think they have something to offer the public that can help eliminate their problems.

I continue to walk around and observe. I visit every booth and read much of the literature spread out on top of the tables. It all has to do with what each individual focuses on within their practice. The longer I look at it, the more confusing it all becomes. How is it possible that any of these people can offer anything that will make this world a more peaceful place to live in? I need to explore this question more closely because this is what I had thought I wanted to do as my profession.

I position my physical body directly in the centre of the large auditorium. Standing motionless, without any thoughts running through my mental thought process, I continue to observe all that is unfolding before me, waiting to see what will take place next. I keep shifting my sense of reality, slowly isolating myself from everyone else and gradually dissolving my bodily form until I have become totally separated from my surroundings. I can see everyone, yet no one can see me.

I observe, over and over again, people I know really well walk right past me – some as close as two feet – completely unaware of my presence. I am continually shifting my inner awarenesses in and out of the collective thought process in this room. What I see and hear contradicts each other. My eyes show me signs and literature that speak of what certain people do and how they go about doing it. What I hear on the inner channels of communication is totally opposite. I receive from each of the practitioners thoughts of doubt about who they are as individuals, about what they are doing within their living expression, and about how they are manifesting things in their outer worlds. I see people living their lives in fear, judging themselves and each other, trying desperately to solidify and justify their very existence. If they can help others make it through their difficult times, then they will be able to justify to themselves, and to everyone else, that what they are choosing to do has some value to it.

The organizational body that sponsored this fair is supposed to be a network of skilled professionals who want to share their ideas as to how we can all improve the quality of life on this planet, and also, how we can all effectively bring about life-supporting changes within our own daily living expressions. I continually see that they, in their wanting to help, end up suffering more, for they become totally dependent on others to give them a purpose of being.

I continue to move in and out of the ever-changing textures that flow from moment to moment. What appears to be very real on the outside is somewhat of an illusion on the inside. There is no one who is really what they say they are, and no one actually has anything that they can offer to anyone else. How can they, when they too need someone outside themselves to help them through their dilemmas?

I have been clearly shown that this environment does not hold the answer I am looking for. It is all too limiting, too confining, and too structured. I know deep within that I will not be able to find my truth in these surroundings. I can't see setting up a practice that offers something to someone and still be able to pursue the only thing that means anything to me. I know that if indeed I do set up a practice, I will become trapped within the belief that I have something to offer. It will also support me in wanting to be *right*, and that's the last thing I need in my life. That's how I got to be where I am today. It is also the very thing I want to get away from.

I have seen enough. It is time to leave this place and venture back out into the natural elements in order to charge my energies. All this looking is depleting my reserves. I gradually alter my state of beingness so that I am once again wholly visible within the physical dimensions, moving and breathing like everyone else around me. I go in search of my friend. It doesn't take too long before I find her. I wait for her to finish her dialogue with her friend, and suggest that I have had enough and am ready to leave whenever she is.

We leave the city and head out into the country, out to where my friend has a small cabin. We sit around for a few hours before heading to Matheson Lake for a bit of a hike on a trail that loops the lake. It will be a good way to finish off the day. I am excited about the walk, mainly because I have never been to this particular place, and I know that new places usually bring with them new experiences.

We arrive just before the Sun goes down. As we begin our journey, I sense some possible danger in what we are about to do. I check with my inner teacher and receive confirmation as to what I am feeling. Although I am alerted to the possibility of danger, I am also assured that no harm will come to either of us. It is meant to be more of a caution, warning me to pay strict attention to what is happening around me, to keep my thoughts focused on the here-and-now, and to observe everything as it unfolds.

As we continue along the trail, my friend mentions that there is a section on the far side, nearly three quarters the way around, that is made up entirely of cedar trees, and that if we get there after dark, we will have some difficulty making our way through them. I externally acknowledge what she is saying. I am not internally thinking very much about what she has said, for it is not in my previous experience to be out climbing around in the woods when there is no light. I mention that I am totally open to whatever will present itself.

The further we walk, the darker it becomes. I soon begin to question the feasibility of us being able to make it through that section of the trail in time. Then the inevitable happens. Everything goes pitch black. And I mean black! One moment we are walking in dim light, and the next we are immersed in total darkness. Nature has a way of changing rather quickly; sometimes to the extremes, like now.

We both stop cold in our tracks. We have lost the direction of the path. My friend mentions that there is a dry creek bed we should feel around for. If we are to find it, that would give her an indication as to where we are in relation to everything else, and it would also provide us with a direction to take. As she takes a step, I lose sight of her. I can hear her moving around, but I can't see any part of her. I call out and ask her to reach out her hand so I can link up with her. I then proceed to walk toward her voice until we connect. We are standing almost nose to nose, and I can't see her. It is the first time I have experienced such darkness.

We walk around for what seems like an hour, although I am sure it is no longer than a few minutes, looking for some kind of indication that will show us we are back on course. Nothing comes up. We continue to stand in the middle of nowhere, not knowing which way to go.

I decide to take the initiative and say, "I know the way out of here. Let's go this way."

I make a gesture with my hand, as if she can see me, and proceed to walk in an unknown direction. I want to show her that I know what I am doing, and that I can use my new internal awareness to get us out of this situation.

On the fifth step, I walk face first into the centre of a big cedar tree. Feeling a little flushed with embarrassment, I quietly say, "Oh, I guess this isn't the way. Let's go back."

I am sure grateful that it is as dark as it is, for at least I don't have to go looking for a hole to climb into. I am already in the best hiding spot there is. Nature has quickly knocked me off the pedestal I had placed myself on. I slowly retrace my footsteps and decide to head in what I think is the opposite direction. I am now beginning to lose my patience. After only taking a few steps, I once again walk face first into another cedar tree. My intellect starts to panic, and it verbally (internally) begins to spout off, "Some savior you turned out to be. At least she didn't run into any trees when she was leading."

My friend and I talk about staying in the woods all night. There doesn't seem to be a lot we can do except wait. I stand motionless, slowly retreating to within the depths of my inner world. I want to connect with one of my inner teachers to see if it is possible to get out of this predicament before the Sun comes up. I hear my inner voice begin to speak, "Let go of your desire to be free. Recognize that you are free. Surrender your entire being to all of Mother Nature, and let Her guide you out. Open your eyes and follow the light that you see. It will guide you and protect you."

I open my eyes and look straight ahead. The darkness becomes alive with small, shiny white balls of light. There are millions of them everywhere. I have never seen such a spectacle like this before on the physical plane. I blink my eyes three or four times, hoping that my vision will clear. I had been specifically instructed to follow the light, but which one? I continue to stand still, gazing out into the sparkling void of darkness. My body remains motionless. I am thoroughly stunned by all that is happening. I want to know what I am supposed to do next.

I verbalize to my friend, "Can you see those lights in front of us?"

"What lights?" she asks. "I don't see any lights."

Just then, a strange phenomenon unfolds before my very eyes. Four of the tiny light spheres combine their individual essences to bring into existence one much larger, twirling, circular light that throws off showers of magnificent colours in every conceivable direction. It is absolutely breathtaking. Within seconds, all the smaller white lights lose their brilliance and disappear into the depths of the darkened void – back to where they came from. The one light that remains becomes a glowing orb, and it slowly begins to move. It moves in a zigzag pattern, and then becomes still once more, effortlessly suspended in the engulfing darkness. It seems to be waiting for me to do something.

The voice from within begins to speak, "Follow the path that opens before you. Trust completely, and do not question."

I take off in the direction of the light. Still holding my friend's hand, we begin to make our way through the surrounding bushes. There is no path to speak of. We are making our own as we go along. We climb higher and higher until we eventually arrive at a place where the darkness brings forth some natural light. I can now faintly see the outlines of the surrounding treetops. The guiding light suddenly vanishes into the depths of the eternal void. We proceed to make our way to a small knoll and look for indications as to where the main trail might be.

As we stand here, my intellect once again becomes active and bubbling with enthusiasm. It will never miss an opportunity where it can be in total control of any situation, or where it can have authority of any kind to make itself look good. As the unfolding moment of truth arrives, it strikes another mighty blow. We are trying to figure out which direction will lead us back to the car. Should we go to the left, to the right, or straight-ahead? We converse back and forth for a few moments before I decide I am going to do something. I once again take full control of the situation, "I know the way out of here. The path is over this way. Come on, follow me."

I take one large step into the darkness, overjoyed at the possibility that I really know what I am doing. I think to myself, "This is great, a chance to redeem myself. I'll show her this time. I'll be mister wonderful."

I am feeling cocky, and I start to get caught up in my thinking. I am only looking for gratification. Within a darting moment, my illusion is totally shattered. I am about to be humbled once again by Mother Nature. There is no solid ground upon which I can plant my foot. Without time to regain my balance, I fall head first over the edge of a rock face. It is a good ten feet to firm ground. The time sequence in between falling and landing seems to go on for an entire lifetime. My body changes its form many times as I float through the air. I let go completely of wanting to control the unfolding experience, and not a moment too soon, either.

My left shoulder makes contact with the slanting ground at about the same time as my head lightly brushes by some rocks that are protruding from the bottom of the rock formation. At the other end, my right ankle – I am walking in bare feet, as I always do when I come to the woods – smashes against a small clump of rocks, opening up four narrow cuts.

Upon surveying this situation from an inverted hanging position, simultaneous to hitting the ground, I direct my attention toward my friend and verbalize a warning so that she will not meet the same fate as I, "Be careful of the first step – it's a rather long one."

I am beginning to see the humour behind all that has taken place within the darkness. I begin to laugh at my own foolishness. It is all such a wonderful gift. I direct my attention totally inward, and I acknowledge all that has taken place within my intellect. He, too, begins to verbalize his feelings, "Okay! Okay! I got it. I got the message. I won't try to control it anymore. I'll get out of my own way, you'll see."

I have once again been given the opportunity to experience the unfolding of creative forces from within me. They are experiences that are very magical in their application and extremely simple in their foundation. Nature definitely has a lot to offer me. I am only now beginning to get a broader perspective of what might be possible under the guidance of the natural elements.

# CHAPTER 4

# THE WARRIOR'S INITIATION

Early in autumn of 1984, deep in the woodland of Goldstream Park, I lean over the top of a fallen tree and scoop up a few handfuls of cool mountain water from the gently flowing creek. The water is alive with the life-giving energies from deep within Mother Earth. It is much like drinking the nourishing nectar from my mother's breast. I take a small piece of licorice root from the moss-covered bank alongside the trail, scrape off the excess dirt and outer layers and put it into my mouth. I bite down on it very lightly; just enough to break open the hardened outer casing. When I can taste the sweetness of its essence, I begin to gently suck on it. I know that I will not have to eat anything else for the entire day. Today is to be a very special day. It is my birthday, and the message I received this morning was that it was truly going to be a new 'birth' day.

I awoke this morning to a friendly and pleasant greeting from one of my inner teachers. Within the communication, I was given a few clues as to how the rest of my day would unfold: "Go out into the elements of Nature, as pure as you are able to find them, and attune your entire being to all that surrounds you. Become all of what you observe, and be prepared to venture forth along the path of the warrior. Know that you shall be challenged severely within yourself, even to the point of physical death."

A friend had picked me up early this morning and drove me to the entrance of Goldstream Park. On the way there, I was very quiet. I really didn't feel much like conversing with anyone in my outside world. I was focusing all of my attention within the depths of my being, continually attuning myself to the changes that were taking place. Many of these were on the highly sensitive, subtle levels of expression. They were constantly resonating outwardly and manifesting themselves on the outer edge of my physical body – rippling waves of energy moving from my toes to my head, then from my head to my toes. They produced a chilling sensation throughout my body as they moved.

From the park entrance, I proceeded to walk up to the main path that would

take me to the bottom of Little Niagara Falls on Niagara Creek. I took the man-
made trail to the top of the falls, along the way planning my next move. I decided to make my journey into the woods last for the whole day. My plan was to
follow the creek up as far as it goes, to trace it back to its origin. Symbolically,
it is very much the same thing I am in the process of doing in my life: following
the route of my inner pathway to its source in order to find my spiritual connection to myself and all living things on the earthly plane.

I remove my runners, tie the laces together and loop them through the back
strap of my squall jacket so that they hang from behind me, thereby not imped-
ing my ability to climb. When all is secure, I continue on my way. I come to a
place where I will have to do some climbing if I want to follow through with my
original plan. I stand and look at the steep rock face for a few minutes, knowing
I am going to have to make a decision fairly soon as to what I am going to do. I
know I have a choice. I can either climb straight up the unknown face or retrace
my footsteps back down the river to the top of the falls until I reconnect with the
main trail, circle up and around to the top side of where I am now, and then hike
back down to the creek once again. I decide that there is only one way to go, and
that is straight up. "This is to be my first challenge of the day."

I easily scale the first section of the rock face. It allows me the opportunity
to gain some sense of confidence in what I am choosing to do. This approach is
all so new, as I have never done any rock climbing prior to this day. I am confident that I can feel my way through it, as long as I don't hurry and only take
one step at a time. I know that I am entirely on my own out here, and that it is
really important to be totally present while I am here, especially knowing that
one inappropriate move could be extremely hazardous to my health. There were
a couple of places along the climb route that I had found to be very slippery.
When I was moving over these areas, I witnessed some resistance within my
body, mainly from the thought I kept having about falling and hurting myself. I
notice that when I am thinking about what is going to happen to me, rather than
staying in the moment, I become weaker in my body movements.

Halfway up the main face, there is a five-foot-wide ledge and an entrance
that leads to a very shallow cave. It appears that this cave has been dug into the
side of the rock wall. I crouch down and enter into its plane of existence, moving as far into its depths as I am permitted. I sit quietly with my back against
the end wall so that I am looking out toward the opening. Closing my eyes and
remaining still, I ask my inner teacher to clarify what the cave might have represented in the years gone by.

As I continue to sit, I receive some visual information within my mental picture screen that shows me that there is a connection between this cave and a sacred native Indian ceremony. I only receive short glimpses of what it entails, not really enough to get a clear picture. I ask that I be given the gift this space has to offer. I wait for a few minutes, but nothing further comes through. After sitting for close to fifteen minutes, and attuning myself to the ceremonial vibration, I receive an inner calling to continue on my journey. I acknowledge the space and the sacred energy it contains, and then I leave.

I begin to ascend the second and most difficult section of the rock face. This part is much trickier than the first, in that the handholds and footholds are a lot smaller, fewer and far between. The higher I climb, the less there is to hold on to. I am becoming scared, and my physical body starts to react to the thoughts of fear I am creating within my mental process. I feel trapped inside. I want to go on, but fear what will happen to me if I lose my balance and fall. It is a good forty feet straight down and nothing but rocks to meet me. If I turn back, I will have failed in my endeavor and my fears will have controlled me.

I am literally hanging on to this one section of rock by my fingernails and toenails. I can feel the tension beginning to accumulate in my fingers, quickly spreading to my wrists, forearms, and up into my shoulders. I begin to panic. I have visions of the rocks down below, and my face, meeting under very unhealthy conditions. I take a short deep breath, alter my reality and ask for directions from within. There are no words presented by my inner voice. I am definitely on my own. I got myself into this situation, and I am going to have to get myself out.

It is becoming very clear that this route is not the healthiest one for me to be taking. Although it appears to be the shortest way up, it also poses the most risks. I decide to go back down to the ledge once more and figure out from there what I will do next. But first, I have to get down!

I slowly lower myself until I come to a place where I can securely anchor my body, giving me enough freedom to remove my runners and squall jacket. I feel that they would be more of a hindrance if I have to make a jump for it. I tie the laces of my runners together and throw them down toward the entrance of the cave, hoping that they will end up somewhere on the ledge. No such luck. They hit the ledge, bounce once and proceed to fall back down to where I had originally started from, landing directly in the centre of a shallow pool of water. I throw my squall jacket toward the opening of the cave. It, too, takes one bounce on its way through and drops over the edge, landing in the water right beside the runners. I am beginning to get the message loud and clear: I am not supposed to be going up this way. The signs I have just been given are confirmation that I have to go back to the beginning and select a new angle of approach.

I slowly begin to make my way back down towards the ledge and cave. It is so close yet so far away. It is a good fifteen feet below the level of my vision. The tension within the musculature of my physical body increases with each movement. It is now becoming a race against time, and I fear that I am losing. I am still about six feet from my destination, desperately holding on, praying that I can keep it all together. Then the inescapable happens. I start to lose my grip. I panic! Thoughts of 'fear' and 'death' flash over and over again on my mental picture screen.

"Oh, God, what do I do now?" I wonder if I can possibly make it to the ledge. It is below and at a slight angle to the right. It would be a dangerous and tricky move. "If I let go and push off at the same time, I just might have a slim chance of making it." There is no way of avoiding it. I will have to give it my best shot. I go totally blank, absent of all thought and desire for control. I release and push off with all I have inside. I am falling freely, not at all certain where I am going to land.

I make contact with the ledge right near the edge, momentarily losing my balance. I am teetering with the doorway that separates life and death. I instinctively redistribute my weight, moving my centre of gravity down to just below my knees, and at the same time, I fling my arms aggressively toward the cave entrance. It is barely enough to put me on the supportive side of the line. I quickly regain control of my movements and leap toward the door of life.

I stand motionless, looking out into nowhere. My heart is pounding against my chest wall. My physical body is zinging with a highly energized current that has been created through all the excitement. "That was too close for comfort."

I am now becoming more aware of the seriousness behind the communication I had received from my inner teachers this morning, and that I am being tested by him. I am being made ready for the higher initiation. I know that if I make it through this day, and still be alive, I will be able to utilize the powerful new awarenesses that will be presented to me through my movements. In order for all of this to manifest itself, I will have to remain clear in my focus and pure in my intention so that I might see the gifts within all that will unfold. I must remain centred within myself and see everything outside me as an illusion that is presented to me to either support me in my journey or to distract me from completing my journey. It is up to me to be sensitive enough to see through the facade of what I think is out here, and to feel the texture of that which lies within this environment.

"I must go on!"

I now have to go back down and retrieve my runners and squall jacket. I cannot go back the same way I had used to come up, for the rocks are too slippery. I begin to look for other alternatives, and notice that there are two strands of plastic coated wire diagonally secured to two small saplings roughly twenty feet apart. There is also a much heavier piece of wire looped through and firmly attached to one sapling and hanging freely at one end. I figure that it will be long enough to get me about three quarters of the way down. From there I will be able to climb down the surface roots of a tree growing out of the side of the rock face near the bottom. I cautiously move across the two wires to see how securely they are fastened at the other end. Everything looks and feels right, so I return to my original starting place, take hold of the loose wire, and carefully lower myself to the ground.

I shake the water out of my runners, scrape the dirt off my squall jacket, and begin to assess the situation from different angles, looking for another plan of action. I see that I really only have two options available, the same as before: up the rock face or backtrack to where I first began. It is all very clear and simple.

Something inside tells me it is important that I take the route up the difficult face. I have to rise to meet the challenge. I will have to make the seemingly impossible task possible. In all the years I had spent training my physical body, I never once allowed an outside challenge to get the better of me, and I am not about to let it happen today. I inwardly know that this unfolding experience is the key component to all the other experiences that will present themselves during this day. Without completing this test, I will not be able to open the door to that part of me it represents, and the gifts that are behind that door will elude me forever.

I walk around and look at the face from every conceivable angle. I map out a possible route that I am sure will allow me to get to the top safely. It will require that I go back up to the ledge the same way I came down, then follow the other two wire cables to another section of the rock face and make my ascent from there. It all seems simple enough. I once again tie my squall jacket around my waist and loop the tied laces of my runners through so they hang behind me. Without further delay, I start on my way.

The first leg back to the ledge is easy. I then make my way over to where the two wire strands are connected to the two saplings. I proceed to traverse across the rock face, eventually coming to rest on a root structure belonging to the fir sapling. I decide to sit and plan my next course of movement. When the inner impulse arrives, I continue on my way. My journey is being complicated by the thick patches of moss that cover the rocks. It is very difficult to find dependable handholds and trustworthy footholds, ones that will bear all of my weight without giving way. Deliberately and methodically, I climb higher and higher.

My first challenge appears. The next connecting point of the climb is sideways. There is roughly a five-foot gap between two sections of rock, too far for me to straddle safely. Anchoring my feet, I remove small patches of moss and slowly lower myself to a horizontal position, suspending myself between two jutting surfaces of rock. As I lie across the opening, I swing my right foot over and above my head until it comes to rest on a narrow ledge. My toes securely grip the rock structure and I am held in place. I know that once my leg is stretched this far, there is no way I can go back to where I started. My drive for danger is becoming greater with each step, as is the challenge. I hastily make my transition and very gingerly guide my body across the moss-covered face with minimum support and maximum risk.

There is something about the element of danger that excites me. It is a real rush. The further I climb, the more obsessed I become with it. Knowing that I am dancing on the thin line that separates life and death creates an exhilarating feeling within my inner awareness.

I maneuver my way along until I come to a fork in the route that I am creating. I have to make another choice as to the path I will select to get me to the top. I survey my options and then choose the path to the left side, and proceed in that direction. I take four short steps and come to rest on a small outcrop of rocks. They are wedged into the side of a natural fold in the face of the rock that has been split and molded by Nature's hand. This provides me with a ledge to stand on. As I continue to stand here, I am aware that it is not at all solid. In fact, I can feel the rocks beginning to crumble beneath my feet. I know that my time here is limited, and that I will have to come up with another alternative, and fast.

Just above where I am standing on the outcrop, and over to the left a good four feet, there is another small ledge protruding from the main rock formation. I begin to make my way over to it, and none too soon either. As I stride and transfer my weight laterally, the outcrop comes loose and tumbles twenty feet down the slope and becomes lodged in another opening. I am now aware that I won't be able to return by this route, for the gap between the two sections is too wide. There is no going back now, even if I want to.

I begin to look for handholds and footholds that will allow me to go up to the next level. No matter where I look, I cannot see any visible means that will allow me to ascend any further. It is clear that I am stuck. I stand here on this shelf-like structure (which is no wider than the width of my two feet, and about as long), for what seems like a lifetime, looking for options. I remain calm and centred within myself. I am trusting that all will work out in a life-supporting way.

My intellect becomes active, looking for distractions in order to keep itself busy. As long as it does, it won't have to deal with the fact that it is the one who is responsible for getting me into this predicament – by wanting all the power for making the decisions. To defend itself, it creates an illusionary dialogue, "This is all just a dream, and soon I will wake up to that realization. When I do, everything will be fine."

The other story, and most popular by far, only because it chooses to repeat it four times in the span of about thirty minutes, is, "There is a man walking around up there, and in a few minutes, he is going to come to the side of the bluff. He is going to say, 'Could you possible use some help!' At which point, he will drop down one end of his climbing rope and proceed to pull me to safety. Once I get to the top, he and I can exchange wonderful stories about what has happened."

Of course, there is no man walking around on top, nor will there be, for I am out in the middle of nowhere, where there is only me and all of Nature.

As I gaze over my left shoulder to the ground below, the dialogue from within my head continues, "I wonder what would become of me if I fell. How badly would I get hurt? Maybe, just maybe, I wouldn't get hurt at all."

I seriously look at the possibility of making a jump to another horizontal platform I had passed on the way up. It is below me about eleven feet. I will have to make a standing long jump of a good seven feet in order to come anywhere close to making it. The dialogue from my intellect continues, "It would be a gamble, but better than staying where I am, because where I am is nowhere. I'm stuck, and I don't see any possibility of getting out of here. It's a fine mess you got us into this time. When will you ever learn?"

There is another part of me that begins to dialogue. It is another facet of my Higher Self, saying, "Stop it. I am not going back. I am going upwards and onwards. There is no sense looking back trying to undo that which has been done. What's done is done, and nothing can change that. There are no realistic solutions behind me. Taking that course of movement only supports my death. If I am to give in and fall to my past, I will surely injure myself quite severely. Am I so rooted to where I have come from that I am totally blind, or am I free within my own direction that I can move ahead unconcerned?"

My intellect doesn't want to hear any of this. It isn't interested in looking at the situation at hand and finding a workable solution. It wants to look back to and seriously dwell upon that which has already taken place. It also wants to look ahead and create an illusion as to what it wants to have happen. When it is challenged regarding this unproductive chatter, it becomes quiet.

I wonder if this experience can possibly be the beginning of the physical manifestation of all I have been hearing and seeing over the past few months within my inner channels of communication. Perhaps this is to be the first trial in my outer world dimension of reality. It only makes sense to have a blending of my outer world experience with the clear visionary aspects of my inner world teachings. This is the only way there can be a balance maintained within all of my movements, on all levels.

I can feel another transitory movement pattern of unknown description (within the dimensions of reality as I know them so far) stirring and evolving within my being. I sense that I have done this very journey once before, in another incarnation. I had been a member of a native Indian tribe that lived along the coastal region of British Columbia. Back then, I had been involved in a ceremonial initiation called *Awakening of the Warrior*. The ritual had four major stages. What I am now doing was one of them. The elders would take a young man who was being initiated into manhood to a place that was similar to the one I was now in, and he would have to get himself out. The only way a warrior could go was straight up. The only way that feat could be accomplished was if he completely let go of the image he had of himself as a boy, and surrendered his entire beingness to Mother Nature so that he could be totally transformed through the four elements: Earth, Air, Fire and Water.

There is an interchange taking place within my being on many different levels within the inner and outer dimension. I can see on the outer surface of my bodily form that I am transforming into and out of the warrior who was being initiated. I am even given glimpses of what he looked like. I can see and feel his shoulder length hair, and I am able to touch the headband that keeps it in place. The warrior is not wearing any clothes on the upper half of his body, except for a ceremonial bracelet on his left wrist. There were painted markings in various places on his face, arms and chest. These were connected to the other parts of the ceremonial ritual he had already completed. This was to be his last test within this particular initiation.

I keep shifting from the present reality into the reality of the warrior a long time ago. I am somehow able to move through different dimensions of time and space, simultaneously being in two places at the same time.

I begin to feel the texture and structure of my thought patterns changing, attuning to those of the warrior. I begin to hear the voice of the warrior speak through me: "Am I afraid to die?"

There is a short pause, and then the dialogue continues: "No, I am not afraid to die. A warrior fears not death. A warrior fears nothing. A true warrior would rather face the challenge of death and die, than give up and go back. For a warrior, there is only death. For in stalking death, he finds the true meaning behind life's expression within himself and within all living things."

It is becoming clear that I will have to let go of my thoughts and align with Nature so I can find a way out of this circumstance. I am caught in a doorway looking both ways, trying to decide what my next move should be. Below me is certain death if I make one mistake in my physical movements. Below me, some sixty feet straight down, there are jagged rocks and boulders. Directly above me, some sixty feet or more, is my freedom – a new living expression. I decide that I will become the warrior once more and seek out my death so that I might live. The supporting of life is first and foremost in my thoughts. I know there is nothing in my world worth dying for, especially not my fears.

The dialogue from my inner teacher continues, "Disregard all that you think you see, and realize that for every situation created through the natural elements, there is also a corresponding solution available in order that it can be moved through. There are no obstacles in the natural elements. There are only opportunities for creative expression."

I can feel my internal awareness altering and changing. Like the artist who chips away at the stone in order to unveil a masterpiece, I begin to peel away the thick, heavy layers of moss that cover the rocks in front of me, knowing that underneath it will be my way out. I eventually manage to uncover just three holding positions, one for each foot and one for my left hand. The only hold for my right hand won't allow me to move any higher. It will only hold me where I am.

I once again play back the communication I had received earlier, feeling almost certain that I am missing something. I know there has to be another piece to the puzzle that I am not aware of, one that is in plain view. I look up in the direction I am heading, and there above me, not more than four feet away, are two small bushes that appear to be growing out of an indention in the rock's surface. I know that they are the piece I need in order to complete my ascent. They have to be, for they are all that is left. The question I ask myself is, "How do I go about getting to them?" There is no way I can reach them with my hands. I remember that I still have my runners hanging behind me. I cautiously bring them forward and remove the laces. I tie one lace to each shoe and then tie the two laces together in the middle. They are tied in such a way that between each shoe there is a distance of about six and a half feet.

There isn't a whole lot of room on my small perch to allow me to make a good upward throw, so I have to improvise. While holding one of the runners in my left hand, I carefully fling the other shoe out to my right and up so that it will loop over the bushes. After five failed attempts, I finally connect. Slowly, I edge the bushes toward me. Their stems are flexible enough that I am eventually able to reach them (at the exact same time as the runners become unhooked and fall away). I gently pull on one of the stems. It starts to come away from the rock. I softly pull on the other one. It, too, begins to come away. I put both stems together and give a light pull, being extremely sensitive to the reality that I might only be afforded one opportunity to use them. If there appears to be the slightest chance that I might make it, I will take it. I might just be able to use them, provided that I don't pull on them too hard, using them more as a means of stabilizing the weight distribution within my body. I notice that directly below the spot where the two bushes are rooted, there appears to be a possible handhold or foothold. But first, I will have to get there.

I am standing on the small ledge with my right foot. My left hand is on a trustworthy handhold. My right hand is gently but securely holding on to the two bushes. My left foot is busy searching and testing for a stable enough rock from which I can push off. Without any further resistance, the moment of truth is about to unfold. Before I can consciously initiate a movement sequence, my body begins to lift off from its launching pad. As I begin to move, I take a deep breath. I am using my inward breath to make my physical body lighter, thereby not putting very much pull-pressure on the two bushes. I am focusing on: "Don't move unless I breathe," and "use my breath to move me." There is no hesitation within my movements, only freedom.

My intellect arrives back on the scene spewing out nonsense, as it usually does, desperately trying to regain control of the unfolding situation, "Who ordered this move? I haven't given my permission for this to be taking place. This is the wrong decision. Don't you know that it's too dangerous to take this course of action? You're going to be sorry, you'll see. Don't let it be said that I didn't try and warn you."

Fortunately, all this is totally ignored by the functioning aspect of my Higher Self. There are more important things that need my full attention.

It is too late. There is no way I can stop now, even if I want to. I am in full motion: "So far, so good."

I successfully make it to the spot where the two bushes are rooted. Everything checks out as I had felt it would. Handholds and footholds present themselves without me having to look for them. My body appears to instinctively know where all the necessary placements are. I don't need to use my outer eyes to find them. I start to get excited! All I can think about is getting back onto solid ground. I move quickly from one hold to another, making my way higher as I move.

Then, my vision of freedom comes to a sudden and abrupt halt. There are no more visible security holds anywhere. My good fortune seems to have run out. My body begins to shake uncontrollably. My legs start bouncing up and down and my arms begin to vibrate lightly. I am beginning to think that this is it; that I have definitely come to the end. Here I am, insecurely fastened to the face of this rock bluff nearly eighty feet above the ground, hanging on to two fist-sized sections of exposed rock that separate my life from my death. I have been moving on a grade that is twenty degrees shy of being vertical.

A thousand thoughts race through my thought processes all at once, causing a blow-out in my master thought circuit. I am filled with an unearthly calmness, one that begins altering my state of awareness. I am once again beginning an interchange with the warrior. I now exist totally within the physical embodiment of the warrior. I feel a sudden surge of strength and power flowing through my being. I am surer now, more than I ever have been, as to who I am and where I am going.

I externally verbalize to myself, "I am not afraid to die. I welcome death. If you want me, come and take me. I always welcome the gift of a new life."

Something is happening within the process of altering my awareness. The voice of the warrior begins to speak through me once more, "Allow me to be as I was back then, the pure living essence of my brother, Cougar. Let me move with the agility and the sure-footed swiftness of the cat."

There are distinctive physiological changes taking place within my physical embodiment. I am completely changing my form and shape. I am looking at my hands and witnessing them go through a total transformation. They are changing into paws, like those of a cat. Fur is replacing skin, claws are replacing fingernails. I look at my feet. The same process has affected them in the same way. I cannot believe what I am seeing with my own two eyes! It is all utterly unfathomable. I can feel my face slowly going through some brief metamorphosis. My eyes are changing in their texture and shape. My vision is becoming more acute. Looking out through my new eyes, I became aware that the whole front of my face has changed. I now have whiskers sticking out from both sides. I have somehow been changed into Cougar.

I am observing myself slowly sink my claws into the thick, moss-covered surface and into the contours of the exposed rock. My breathing pattern has also been changed. I am now breathing with short, pulsating breaths. My body is charged with a sudden surge of power, the likes of which I have never before experienced. I begin to push off with my hind legs at the same time as I am lunging forward with my front legs. I begin pulling with my front legs when they make contact with the surface so that I can snap my pelvis under in order that my hind legs can be edged forward. Through this action I am propelling myself in an upward, forward direction. So light are my movements, and so precise, that my newly formed body moves swiftly over the almost vertical surface.

Within seconds, I have successfully made my way to a level section of ground about ten feet from the top. I position myself next to a tree, securely bracing my body between it and the dirt bank. I gaze back down to the bottom some one hundred and sixty feet below, totally awestruck at all that has taken place. I wonder how I ever made it to where I am. The metamorphic process I had gone through earlier is now beginning to reverse itself. I am observing my total embodiment, internally and externally, hastily returning to my own natural vibrational frequency – back to man-form.

I continue to sit quietly for about fifteen minutes, attuning myself to all that surrounds me. I am giving thanks to my internal creative process for having been given the opportunity of experiencing the challenge of the warrior; and also for being guided into finding the true gift of what my life is all about.

I proceed to make my way to the top. I traverse along the upper stretch looking for an entry point that will offer me a chance to get back down to the flowing water. I navigate my way through the densely wooded area and then climb back down the grassy bank until I eventually reconnect with the river. I continue to make my way along its narrow, winding channel. I am back on course. I am now eager for whatever new challenges will present themselves. From each of them, I will certainly be provided with another opportunity of connecting with the deeper aspects of my true inner self.

When I had completed my climb up and over the rock face, I had a feeling that I was beginning a quest of a high order: A quest to seek out death; to move beyond the superficial reality of death; to discover that death is really non-existent; that transformation comes to me only by way of death; and that to die unto my own self is, in itself, a precious gift, for within that death a new life is created.

I know that I am embarking on an extremely potent and powerful pathway. I am being carefully directed to and initiated into the all-encompassing spiritual quest of a warrior. Through this experience I will find my ultimate association with, and my affinity to, all aspects of life on the earthly plane and all other planes within this plane.

While I had been sitting quietly on top of the rock face, I was presented with a very clear inner vision. I was shown many aspects of the native Indian way of life, not so much from today, but rather from many years ago. A very wise old elder – a medicine man extraordinaire – came to visit and to speak. He shared his many insights regarding the powerful magic Nature has to offer anyone who chooses to ask for it.

I had been initiated into the sacred teachings of his people. He had mentioned that as I progress along on my life journey, all of these teachings would be presented when I am most able to use them in the appropriate manner to aid me in finding the purest vibration of my truth. He had also mentioned that it would be important for me to keep attuning myself to the natural elements and aligning to the purest vibration of selfless expression. He went on to explain, "All creative power lies within the essence of the natural forms of life; the ability to totally surrender one's own identity so that a new life may be started and supported. There are no wants or desires in the simple expressions of life. There is only selfless giving of oneself."

He had cited that he had belonged to a tribe that held Cougar as a very sacred animal. Apparently, these people were able to transform their physical form so that they took on the complete physical characteristics of Cougar. Only those who had been inducted into the high order of the council, within the medicine man's entourage, could be initiated into the depths of the sacred teachings. They had believed that when they passed on from this world, and then came back again, they came through the living spirit within Cougar's form.

The warrior with whom I had interchanged was moving within the purity of the sacred teachings. He was a very special warrior to his people, for he had many extraordinary powers that were not available to any of the other members of his tribe. He was able to take on the physical identify of any form of life whenever it was necessary. He was known to his people as the *shape-changer*.

The elder had also introduced me to Raven. He had mentioned that Raven and I were brothers, and that as brothers, we would be able to communicate with each other. He had then showed me how to go about doing that before he returned to the void within.

As I sit motionless, I can hear Raven calling within my outer world. I open my eyes and look directly above me, and there he is circling effortlessly just above the treetops. As I sit here, I alter my state of awareness in the manner I had been shown. As I do, I can hear Raven speak these words, "Welcome, my brother. There is much that we can share. Know that while you are in my territory, you will be guided in all that you do and protected from all harm. Before you enter into the playground of Nature, attune yourself to me, and I will alert you to any possible dangers."

I reply, "Thank you, my brother. I have listened to your words, and I shall heed them. You know, I am having a hard time believing that this is actually happening."

Raven responds, "My brother, it is not a question of believing. It is purely an act of doing. Out in the purity of Nature, there are no impossibilities."

I sheepishly begin, "Forgive me—."

Raven quickly cuts me off, "There is no such thing as forgiveness within the purity of life. That is strictly a product of man's world. It is not necessary for you to speak while you are out here until such time as you own your total freedom."

On those parting words, he disappears through the spreading treetops.

I close my eyes once more and reconnect with the wise elder. He expands more on what Raven had said. When he is finished, he vanishes within the depths of my inner void.

When I give in to the separation between myself and Nature, I begin to see just how inter-dependent we all are on this earthly plane. I see how everything supports everything else, even when it does not wish to support it. The more we all try to move away from supporting something, the more we all move into supporting something else. It is purely a magical and mystical web we all weave together.

As I continue to make my way up the creek, I ask to be shown a sign that will prove that all of what I have been experiencing thus far on my trip is real and of some value in my spiritual growth. Within minutes of asking, my gift arrives. As I come around the bend in the river, I see Little Bird sitting on a massive boulder. He is singing his song of life. He has come to reassure me that all of what I have been exposed to is very real. He stays with me for a few hundred yards, bouncing freely from rock to rock, always managing to stay at least four feet ahead. At one point, I stand motionless, watching him hop about from place to place, sensing that he is not at all concerned about anything that is happening outside of what he is doing.

I wonder if it will be possible to attune myself to him so that I can verbally communicate in the same manner as I am able to do with Raven. I look at him, quieting my thoughts, and allow my outer eyes to lose their focus. I shift my awareness to another vibrational frequency, and to my surprise, I begin to hear his words as they are being channeled through within the depths of my being, "You are doing the right thing, my friend. Know that within the depths of your being. Let go of your concerns for the confirmation of all that you have been observing during your day. For it is all very much a reality, just as I am."

I ask, "Will I always see you when I come out here into the natural elements?"

There is a short pause and then he quietly says, "I will be moving in and out of your living expression as you become more open to what Nature has to offer you in your growth. Know that you are always protected and well cared for while you are out here. Continue to attune yourself to all that you see, and you will receive many gifts. Out here everything is supported within its ever-changing living expression."

As I stand in the creek, I squat down and scoop up a palm full of water to moisten my lips and mouth. When I look back to where I had last seen him, there is nothing more than the unreliable memory of what I thought I had experienced.

I push up the creek until I come to another rock face. The thought of another climb excites me. This time there is no hesitation coming from within. There are no questions or absurd statements coming from my intellect. I haven't heard from it since that outburst during the first climb. It is all so clear that I quietly affirm to myself: "The way of the warrior is to seek out death, to defy death, and then to live through and beyond the experience in a whole new way."

I proceed to scale another almost vertical trail next to the rock face. My being is free and light within its form, and there is no resistance coming from within my physical body toward any of the movements I am making. Like a cat, I move swiftly, wholly, and effortlessly up the trail. It is basically hard packed mud with protruding clusters of rock, and it offers me very few places to secure my footing and hand positions. I rely mostly on my initial forward momentum to keep the movement unfolding. I also align myself to all that is surrounding me. As with the first climb, I become one with whatever I am moving over. Being part of it, it will support me totally, for all of that which encompasses me is supportive of my life. As before, had I been afraid of dying, I would have been resisting the natural flow of what Nature has to offer me.

As I reach the top, I gaze back at the beautiful view that is stretched out below and in front of me. I begin to feel an all-embracing cooling sensation being generated throughout my body. I am feeling that it is indeed a great honor for me to be where I am, and that there is no special gift more important to acknowledge than life itself. I am continually being shown just how simple life really is, and how much there is in life for me to discover. This is especially true when I let go of all my preconceived concepts of reality and beliefs of what I think it should be. Life is definitely bountiful, but only if I choose to see it.

There is no aging process within the purity of Nature. Things and places are what they are. When they are no longer what they are, they become something else. Everything supports everything else without taking away from that which it is. A tree dies, and within that process falls to the earth, providing food and fertile ground for other trees and plants to grow on. I had noticed old wind-fallen trees supporting and nurturing much smaller trees, as well as moss, fungi, and a multitude of other species of plant and animal life forms.

The textures of colour that I am observing along the riverbank are being presented with just the right shade of sunlight, in contrast to the ever-changing darkened areas, to create the effect of a fantasy land. The hues of transparent light that are a once in a lifetime creative expression of Nature, are bountiful in their manifestations. The rays of direct sunlight are intermittently piercing through the irregularly slotted openings between the sprawling limbs of the tall trees, and spreading their streamlined tentacles over all the life forms that are anchored to the floor of the Earth. As the wind blows lightly, the illusionary aspect of the Sun proceeds to move smoothly and effortlessly across the open sky, creating spectacular, ever-changing and ever-unfolding patterns of light that continuously dance their way through the gently swaying trees. The seemingly transparent mist rising from the Earth's floor adds more magic to the already powerful display Mother Nature has provided. I am in complete awe of it all.

I continue to make my way up the creek to its origin at the top of the mountain, to the place that continually supports its creative expression – a lake. I have concluded my journey at the very centre of its existence. I have followed the meandering creek to the source of its life, and as I have travelled along, I have witnessed its forever changing yet always remaining the same simple truths. Before me, in the middle of nowhere, yet at the same time everywhere, lies the perfectly still and reflective water of its creative energies, reflecting outwardly only that which is brought within its plane of reality. It draws from an endless supply of nourishment from the creative Mother to allow for its own life, as well as to provide a flowing expression of life for the creek. I have continuously seen that Nature, in all ways, supports Herself in all that She chooses to create.

I know that this journey I have made today is very similar to the inner journey I have been on for some time now. The experiences that have unfolded so far are confirmations that the direction I am heading in is supportive of me finding my truth. I also know that I will soon arrive at the still and reflective waters that exist within the central core of my being. Once there, I will be able to draw from an endless supply of nourishment so that I might bring forth my total creative expression and present it to my outer world.

Now that I have arrived and have seen what I have seen, it is time to continue my journey down the creek, for there is still much to see and to do. The trail looks very different in some places. I frequently position myself where I can gaze both ways in order to get a more complete perspective of all that I am seeing unfold before me, and also all that I have already seen on my way up. I can't get over how everything has changed, and yet I really know that nothing has changed.

I realize that it is only my perception of how things should have been, as opposed to how things really are, that is changing, and my life is now beginning to take on a whole new meaning in that regard. I clearly see that all things are merely in a constant state of transition. It is the time sequence that holds them in their illusionary form. It is the letting go of the time sequence that allows for all things to make the transition together, thereby keeping everything in a constant state of equilibrium.

When time is fixed into a static mode of existence, all things age, but left to be free-flowing, all things remain in proximity to what 'is' – according to the natural laws that govern this physical plane. It is within this proximity that the natural magic occurs. Life supports life. Death supports death. Death supports life. Life supports death. All of these are just the transitory stages of expressive energies within the creative flow of the four elements – Earth, Air, Fire and Water.

I follow the same route on the downward trip that I had used coming up, with the exception of the first climb I completed. There is absolutely no way I was going to try that one again, especially knowing that the path I used in my ascent had been severed in two places.

The hard-packed mud trail I used on the way up offers very few handholds and foot supports, so is a little trickier on the downward climb. I have to make all the descending connections in the blind. I literally have to feel my way along. As I am more able to release myself from time sequences and space allotments, I find that I am able to implement one of Nature's Laws – surrender and become part of – and harmony is restored within my being. The descent is quick and exciting. When I reach the bottom, I once again become alive with enthusiasm to challenge death one more time. I know that there isn't anything I am not prepared to do in order to remain a warrior.

I make my way up to the top of the railway trestle and proceed to walk on one of the steel railroad tracks, closing my eyes just to make it more interesting. I start to wonder what it would be like to walk on the outer-most edge of the narrow steel plate that is part of the trestle's structural framework. (The outer structure consists of two one-inch thick pieces of steel that have a one and a half inch gap between their inner surfaces). It would definitely be a challenge worth pursuing. I know that there is only one way I am ever going to find out. Knowing that I am not afraid to die, I confidently move my body towards the outer-most edge of the structure.

I bring myself into position and cautiously place my right foot so that its centre-line, running through from heel to toe, lines up in relationship to the centre-line of the outermost one inch thick strip of steel. Once I am feeling secure within this placement, I quickly position my left foot ahead of my right and stabilize myself by concentrating all of my awareness within the *centre* of my being. I surrender myself unto myself and unto the steel strip. I become one with it. When this embracing alignment is complete, I begin to move.

On my left side, I have my attachment to living: the security the trestle structure offers me if I need it. Directly on my right, lies my obsession to experience death: if I lose my balance, I will free-fall hundreds of feet straight down towards the rocks below. My internal process is quiet. My intention and focus are laser-like in their expressional movements.

As I complete my fifth long step, I realize that there is no longer any point in doing what I am doing. I have clearly shown myself that I am indeed a warrior, and that I am not afraid to die in order that I might live. It is all too easy now. There is no more challenge to it. I take three more steps and then stop. I reposition my feet so they are resting at right angles to the two steel plates, giving me a full three and a half inches of support. As I stand, looking out over the various segments of my journey that are spread out before me, I have an overpowering impulse to jump into the abyss. I want to fly freely through the air like Raven so I can experience the total freedom of having no attachment or commitment to the gravitational forces of the Earth. I become curious as to what it would feel like to just let go and fall freely. I begin to feel myself swaying back and forth ever so slightly. The more I think about it, the 'higher' I get from the thought. As I am seriously contemplating this move further, I begin to hear the voice of my inner teacher speak these words, "A wise man is one who takes himself to the edge of a cliff, knowing that he is not afraid to die, for he fears not death. A fool, on the other hand, is a man who takes himself to the edge of a cliff and then jumps to prove that he is not afraid to die. It is far better for you, my friend, to remain a wise man."

## November 29, 1984

On November 25, 1984, exactly one day shy of five years from when I first started martial arts training, I walked away from my official involvement in it. I was choosing to take what I had become aware of within the mechanics of my own being, and also what I had witnessed within the movements of other people, and move on, out into the purity of all of Nature. I would take it all into the spiritual realms of reality.

I know that it was the most appropriate time for me to go and live within all that I had been observing; to become it, in totality, in all that I would choose to do each and every moment I am still alive and breathing. The warrior's path is to move within the darkened depths of himself so that he might bring about the most efficient and harmonious way of moving through the world around him. His own world, and no other.

I had started taking classes in November of 1979 after meeting my teacher at his house, where he was giving a hands-on demonstration on massage and using acupressure points to balance energy flows within the body. He had invited me to be part of a demonstration on the energy flows and how they are negatively affected by certain internal and external situations. Through that demonstration I was awakened to another new internal world (of energy flows) that had its beginning in China a long time ago. I wanted to know what he had become aware of through his many years of internal and external martial arts training. The day after our meeting, I arrived at his house, knocked on his door and asked if he would teach me. My journey into this new world began.

The system I had studied, Chien Lung, incorporates movement patterns – on a physical, mental, emotional and spiritual level – of three different animal families. There is the snake family (Python, Boa and Cobra), the cat family (Tiger, Black Panther and White Leopard) and the Dragon. The ultimate position that one can attain within this system is Dragon. All-encompassing in his nature, Dragon is able to create the complicated movement patterns of any single animal, or move within the multi-dimensional interplays of all six, consecutively, at any given time. He is the master of change and adaptability, for he has no distinct form.

Dragon was created when Tiger, representing the extreme of the outer, physical hardness of power, mated with Boa, representing the extreme on the inner levels, focusing on the subtleties of power within softness. Through their dance together and their eventual intercourse, Boa swallowed Tiger: the hardness engulfed by the softness. After the appropriate incubation period, Boa was turned inside out by the movements of Tiger, and thus Dragon was born into the world. He is the perfect blending of the hard and soft energies. These are the same harmonious energies that are locked away within the depths of each of us, if only we choose to look.

I have been studying two animal forms in the cat family, knowing that they have been inherently within me since I first arrived here on this plane of reality. They have been the main driving force behind all of my earthly expressions. The way in which I have chosen to move within my outer world has been through the heart of Tiger. The way in which I have come to see through the illusionary aspects of my outer world has been through the movements of Black Panther, in that I have always been very much aware of the underlying current of life that is enclosed within the darkness – the Unconscious Mind.

I have been Tiger in all that I have chosen to do in my outer world. The predominant characteristics of this animal are: head-strong, always one-pointed in his thought process; likes to dominate in his outer world; does everything on the outside edge of life's expression; is impervious to any kind of pain once he has become focused on his objective; always has his purest and most focused intention on the total destruction of his opposition – a single blow delivery to get the job done, for he likes to conserve his energy; has a strong physical body that he uses effectively; is aggressive in his nature; and he will always initiate the first move in whatever he does.

I have been Black Panther in the way that I have moved within the darkened areas of my living expression, searching for the unknown (in the sense of not being consciously aware of) patterns of behavior that have been responsible for the way in which I have shaped my life. Black Panther is always stirring below the surface of things, looking intently, actively observing everything that enters into his world. He always waits for the most appropriate time before he makes any conscious movement within the directional aspects of his life. He is not aggressive like Tiger. He is more aware of the subtleties within the mental energies that exist around and throughout him.

As I had progressed through the outer layers of my being, I began to get a wider appreciation for the ever-expanding depth of the Chien Lung system. I also began to see the extent of what it actually had to offer me, and also to others who wanted to become more consciously aware of the inner mechanics of their emotional fabric and mental structuring, through the observation of their daily thought processes and how they affect their movement in the outside world.

It was within the broadened philosophy of the system that I had been encouraged to participate in as many alternative health related workshops and seminars as I could, so that I could open up my awareness within the structural composition of my bodily form. I had believed that if I was to do something within the course of my movements, either within a class atmosphere or outside on the street, that caused an injury to another living being, I had to have the sensitivity and knowing available to be able to restore balance into that part of the body I had impaired.

I am truly aware that no one person really wants to hurt or injure another living being, just the same as he, himself, would not want to be hurt or injured. It is only the complicated structures of the inner frustration and anger (that have been created and supported throughout the many years of programming and conditioning) that a person actually wants to vent from inside himself. I was studying this particular discipline in order to become more aware of how I could live my life to the fullest expression possible, not so I could find out how I could lose it.

I had learned a very simple technique within the first eight months of training that showed me how, with just the right amount of pressure in a particular spot in the throat area, I could easily take the life of another human being. Just knowing that offered me the opportunity of never having to try it out to see if it would actually work. I didn't feel that I wanted to test it out on someone, and I surely wasn't into having someone test it out on me. From that day onward, I have not been so interested in fighting, although I did my fair share of it through sparring in the dojo. I chose to spar so that I could observe the ways in which I would move against certain types of people. I used it as a means of becoming more sensitive to the people who were around me, especially the ones who were unconsciously supporting me in making changes in my life.

As I progressed into teaching, I had instructed my classes within a holistic environment, always encouraging those who came to become more aware of their movements and more in tune with their feelings. In order to do that effectively, I integrated emotional trials and creative mental exercises that incorporated many of the multi-dimensional aspects of one's self. I used continual, ever-flowing, body-opening, supportive movement patterns. I also fostered the spiritual awareness of one's own inner teacher in all that unfolded within a class format.

I do not believe that total freedom within any form of movement, whether it is mental, physical or emotional, can ever come through the utilization of structure. I had become aware a long time ago that any kind of structure is the element that is totally responsible for all the different resistance patterns locked up inside each of us.

Within my teaching, I acted totally from a place of spontaneity and sensitivity, usually intuitively attuning myself to each of the people who came to class so that facets of themselves – the ones they feared the most – could be presented to them within a workable, free-flowing and functionally effective manner. Initiating their fears in this way, each student would have the opportunity to acknowledge them and move through them with love and support from those around them. The ongoing opportunities to bring about new changes within their awareness would always present themselves. What the people chose to do with them was entirely up to them. Everyone was supported in moving at their own pace, whatever made them feel most comfortable.

I never believed that anyone was ever coming to my classes because they wanted to hurt anyone. I knew that they were just frustrated in their own inability to express themselves freely within their outside world. All they really wanted in their lives was to feel good about themselves as a person. They also wanted to have a safe and supportive environment in which they could release some of their pent up hostilities so that they could find the opening to change some of the things they didn't like about themselves.

I had often sparred with people who had a tremendous amount of non-supportive feelings bottled up inside that they needed to release. I would encourage them to take it out on me, only I wouldn't hold on to any of it. I figured that it would be far better if it were me, who had a choice, rather than their child or other loved ones who might not be as sensitive to what was actually going on within the deeper levels of their being.

I was getting people excited about looking at their bodily form, as well as the body forms of the others who were in the class, in a much different way than they were used to. They could use their body as a tool, to be used in such a way that they could learn more about themselves. I found it important to continually emphasize that they could become as creative as they wanted within their movements. All they would have to do is let go of the thought processes that were keeping them from being free and creative within their mental, emotional and physical expressions.

I recognized my own gradual transformation while I was instructing. I saw that I was becoming quicker in my seeing, more sensitive in my feeling of the subtle energies that surrounded everyone, faster in my application of physical movements, and stronger in my bodily form, from just observing those who would come to my classes. Whenever I saw something reflected in their bodies that was holding them in a certain way, or keeping them restricted in some way, I chose to see it as a direct reflection of what was happening within my body. By moving through each perceptual experience in this way, I was able to further align myself with what I had seen and fully integrate it into my body and my daily physical experiences.

I haven't had serious, repetitive work-outs on the physical plane for nearly two years now, although I have done the odd bit of sparring with various people over time. I have never allowed myself to get out of shape within the creative awareness of my thought processes, so my body always knows how to respond to any given situation, according to what it has already done previously or to what it is open to creating within that unfolding moment. There is an old saying that I choose to identify with my everyday movements. It is simply stated: "My body knows!"

I never really wanted to teach a martial art *per se*. I realized early in my initial training that it just wasn't me. The expression of it within my outer movements wasn't at all supportive of me staying involved as an active participant. My body resisted a lot of the forced stretching movement, in the sense of their aggressive application. Afterwards, I would always suffer for a few days with soreness in the muscle structures that I had been forcing to open. Each time I would go into it deeper, for I wanted to know more about how my body worked and what made it do what it did. I always used myself as a guinea pig. To me, theories didn't mean anything. I never believe anything unless I can experience it first hand. Even then, I never get hung up believing that is the only way it can be. I know that everyone's body is different, and that no two bodies will ever perform in the same way through a determined set of movement patterns.

I would never allow anyone in my classes to do anything I had not already experienced and acknowledged within my own body. Within all of my excise formats, I was always looking for the most effective and efficient way in which to initiate a movement sequence so that I received maximum effectiveness with minimum resistance.

From December 1983 through May 1984, I had been involved with a stage theatre production of dance and martial art movement. Within the context of the martial art piece, we re-created the two major worlds that exist within each of us – the hardness of Tiger and softness of Boa – and showed how, through the merging of those two opposite aspects, the world of Dragon was created. This is the same level of awareness that we all aspire to attain within our life of time. I had landed the lead role as Tiger, an appropriate character for me to be creating and moving with, for I was always wanting to be at centre stage capturing the full attention of whoever would acknowledge me.

What I had found happening through the course of those various productions, was that my desire to play the role of Tiger was slowly diminishing. I had found that it was taking an incredible amount of my personal energy to fulfill my duties as Tiger, and that I wasn't getting anything back in the way of supportive energies from the audiences. If anything, I felt as though I was being sucked dry by them. What I had seen was that I was projecting to the people in the audience their own inner fears about the sometimes rampaging Tiger that gets loose within their beings and stirs up so much inner turmoil. I sensed they didn't want to acknowledge this reality to me or to themselves. In some instances, there were hundreds of people attending the showing, and I had felt, at most times, that it was me against all of them.

Our last official engagement of this production consisted of three showings that were scheduled during a week of festivities on the downtown waterfront. It was within the course of those three performances that I began to seriously react mentally, physically and emotionally to all that was taking place around me. I started to become ill-at-ease from my active participation in the shows. My Tiger heart was slowly losing its flair for aggression and its thirst for power and control. He now only wanted to run away and cuddle up to himself, away from the crowds, away from the noise and the hype, and away from all the sensual stimulation he had been focusing on.

It was during the last show that all hell broke loose, and the concrete, hard-crusted dam that was inside me holding everything in check for so many years, finally gave way. Mentally, I had reached the end of the line. I was ready to pack it in long before we were scheduled to go on. I had lost the purity of my intention within my thought process. I felt as though I was coming apart. The images that I had held of myself as being someone and being important were starting to disintegrate, and my emotional reactions toward these thoughts were begging to let the full impact of their presence be felt and heard. I knew that I had to somehow keep it all together until after the show. That was always one of my chief patterns: I had to be the strong one and keep it all together. I couldn't afford to let everyone else know that I was just like them.

As the total production came to a close, it was very clear, like it had never been before, that my days of playing either the role or the reality of Tiger were finished. I would not do it ever again. That aspect of my Tiger's nature – the outer aggressive nature – was completed. It had served its purpose in my living expression.

It was also apparent that I could now move on and put my focus and attention toward the exact opposite of the Tiger form I had brought to life; to move within the circle of Boa. Within my movements with Boa, I would be able to reconnect with my own inner sense of self-love, and I would be able to move with it on many different levels within my being. I would become softer in my outer world expressions. I would also be able to bring about a blending of the hard and soft energies within my being, and use these energies more creatively to bring into existence within me a world that is based on love of self and love of all mankind.

I took off my costume and threw it into the garbage can. That was it! I was definitely ready to move on in another direction, as there was no resistance coming from within in regard to the decision I had made.

I remembered the snake (piece of driftwood) I had found on the beach below Radar Hill near Tofino (during the latter part of December 1983). I went home and took a rasp to the outer layers of flaky wood until I brought the main body to a polished state. It was exactly the way I had envisioned it when I first saw it on the beach. I couldn't believe it at first, but then I realized that it couldn't be any other way. It was my outer world confirmation that it was indeed time to move in that direction.

Internally, I continued to move within the aggressive manners that had consumed me for so many years, looking for the gifts of softness contained within the structure of each. The more I was able to observe what I was in the process of doing as it unfolded, the easier it was to see the subtleness that Boa represented, and how much more power the softness has to it.

In my teaching, I conveyed to those who came to class that there was no such thing as a martial art; that all there ever is, is movement. Martial art is only one expression of a movement form, and it is only a concept of thought and not a pure reality in life. Nothing exists here on this physical plane of reality unless there is movement.

I presented the following to my students: "There is no need to focus all your attention onto learning a particular martial art discipline. When you do, you become trapped and limited within the structure of that system. You would then take on and begin to believe that how you were being taught was really the only way it could be. Then you would soon discover, especially when you looked more closely at other martial art disciplines, that how you thought it was is not actually the way that it is. If you stopped and tried to figure it all out, it would just make you more confused, for then you would have to start defending the reality of the system you are studying. Every system within the martial art category is functional and purposeful within its expressional existence. If that is so, then which one is right? They all are. So why get hung up on believing that one is any better than another? If you do, you will become trapped, and it will be your thoughts that trap you, not the system. The system – any system – is always pure within its creative expression. It is your thoughts that distort the purity of truth it contains.

"It would be far more beneficial for you to learn about and become more aware of the mechanics of movement within your own body. Look at everything you do seriously, with the right intention and right focus, and you will be able to do whatever you choose totally unobstructed by the judgments and comparisons that inevitably come from someone who says: 'I know.'

"Do a punch once at a slow speed and follow it right from the moment you begin the movement pattern until it finally hits its target. While you are doing that, it would be most important that you put your full attention onto what you are doing, while you are doing it. That way you will be able to feel how the movement comes about. You will also be able to see the progressional steps that are so necessary in order that you hit the target where you want. You will be able to feel all the different muscles that are used and are affected within the mechanical range of that movement. You will be able to feel through your whole body what happens when you hit the target with that punch. There is no need to do a particular movement pattern hundreds of times while you are asleep, when you can do it just once while you are fully awake.

"If you know the mechanical rhythm of your own body, you will be able to move in harmony within all the other expressions of rhythm within the world of man, and also those that exist outside the world of man in the higher states of awareness. The more time you spend doing an exercise, the more unfocused you become, for an element of your mind will create thoughts that will make sure that you have to work harder in order to get what you want. As a result, the Mind of thought will have control of you, instead of you having control over the Mind of thought."

In my class teaching, I was focused on opening people up to their inner creativeness, to the playful child that lies within them, but all they wanted to do was shut their creative, free-flowing child down. They were more interested in learning how to defend themselves against an attacker, for they wanted to be able to handle themselves in any situation. They couldn't hear and see the plain and simple truth: If they weren't in the action, in the front row participating, there wouldn't need to be any action. They wouldn't need to fight. It was almost like they didn't want to hear that they didn't have to fight any more, or to know that there was a way available that supported them in living and expressing their lives in a creative, loving way – one that would ensure that they would receive all that they needed on their life journey.

All movement within any of my class formats was done from a free-flowing form of expression. Nothing was ever completed from a static place. (Nothing in Nature is ever done from a static place. Out in the natural elements, all there is, is movement.) Emphasis was put on having the body open up naturally, by having the body move within itself, not against itself. Forcing the muscles to stretch creates pain, whereas moving the body within itself – by doing certain types of movement patterns that fully utilize opposing muscle groups, aligning with each other and moving harmoniously – creates a release. The movement creates an opening up of the natural kind. The results stay around for a lot longer by doing it this way, for the opening is completed through a natural expression of movement. Forced action always needs support. You need to work at keeping whatever you have forced open to stay that way. If you do it that way, your body will always be in control of you, instead of you being in control of your body. If you have to work to keep it, it really isn't worth having in the first place.

For a long time, I had been avoiding doing my own creatively expressive thing in my outside world. I was busy teaching body awareness through movement in a martial art atmosphere, and it wasn't working out. I was going into someone else's creative space and trying to adapt it to my way of living. I was compromising my abilities by shaping myself to its format. Either way I was not succeeding at being me. I was taking the easy way out, and the universe had served me notice a few times along my journey that my time in this environment was limited. When the timing was appropriate, I moved.

One evening while I was giving a class, I asked everyone this question, "What is the point of you being here, doing what you are doing?" I then proceeded to go around the room and ask each person if they would share their response. There were many and all of them different. It then came time to give my reply, and this is what I said, "The point of me being here is so that one day I will no longer have to be here."

That was my cue. I had gotten the message on all levels within me. I knew then that it was time to be moving on in my life journey. I could no longer continue teaching in that environment, knowing what I did. At the end of the class, I mentioned that I would no longer be instructing Chien Lung classes or any other type of class. I sincerely thanked the people who had supported me in growing and in learning about myself and all of us. I recognized that all of us in that room, each moving from within our own life experiences, were a representation of what the rest of the world was like. I then expressed to them very simply, "Life presents to each of us many creative opportunities if we are open to receiving them as such. This unfolding experience is an opportunity that is being presented to me to become more of who I truly am."

I bowed humbly to them one last time, and then I left.

✴

From my experiences within those walls, I received the gift of my life. I was able to explore the playfulness of the child within me, and I was also opened up to my own creativeness. I also became much freer in my outer world movements and forms of expression. I was being guided within my teachings by a source far greater than words can ever begin to describe.

I was but a humble student of the universe, who was choosing to move out into the freedom of all expressive forms, out to where the great learned masters live, out into the free-form expression of all of Nature. Within those realities, and within the realities of the death-seeking warrior, I moved on.

## *Christmas Day, 1984*

I arrive at the lake around ten in the morning. It is a glorious day. I am choosing to celebrate this day the only way I know how – by venturing out into Nature. It is so quiet and peaceful as I stand here on the rocky bank, taking into my visual awareness all that lies before me. The lake is mirror-still, reflecting back perfection to all those who ask to be shown their beauty. It is a picture of absolute stillness, to a degree I had never before witnessed. It is as though all forms of life's expression have come to a standstill, suspended in a frozen time sequence. I am the only visual sign of life that is flowing within the breath of life.

I acknowledge within myself that I have come to this place to ask for further initiations into the higher vibrational essence of life's expression. It has been two and a half months since I was given my first initiation into using the natural wisdom that abounds within me whenever I am out in Nature. I recognize that there is little in the world of man that can compare to the purity of the teaching available through studying how Nature continually aligns Herself within all facets of Her existence....

I had returned to the outside world after my first initiation enthusiastic and inspired to move through my life by reflecting back on what I had become opened to. What I had found disappointed me. It made me wake up and fully realize that I couldn't depend on any thing or any one to support me in moving in the way I was choosing.

The world of man is such a complicated one, for it is so divided. He has set up so many divisions within his own structure that he is unable to see the simplicity in anything. He continues to expand sideways on the evolutionary scale, becoming totally consumed by his desires for his earthly senses, using them to hopefully guide himself towards fulfilling his destiny. The only thing is, he is not sure what his destiny is.

I found that I wasn't able to trust anyone who associated with or indulged in the sensual world of man. Whenever I went to share with them my experiences, they always reacted to what I was presenting. I was talking about Nature and how it has the ability to show each of us, within everything we perceive around us, the simplicities of life, but all they could relate to, or chose to relate to, was the world of power and greed. They were forever talking about going to sign up for *this* course or *that* course. In our communications, they were always mentioning that they had bought *this* book, and that the guy who wrote it said life was *this* way or *that* way; or that *this* is the way so and so says it should be. They were making all these people outside themselves the authorities on how they should or should not live their lives. They were always ready to give up their whole beingness to someone they knew nothing about. It was much like watching blind men running around telling everyone they can see, yet they continuously trip over every obstacle presented along their journey.

I could see it was difficult for some people to just sit and listen to the content of what I was saying. They would always feel compelled to bring into our conversations judgments and comparisons about how they thought the world was, or how it should be. They were never into hearing that the outer world of man is only a reflection of how man's inner world is; that they are one in the same. They always wanted to debate the information I was choosing to present. As I saw it, what I was choosing to speak about was only my truth, and no one else's. What they were telling me, by their communications, was that I couldn't have my own truth, that I had to be open to seeing it their way – that somehow my truth was not valid. Because they weren't focused on finding their own truth through their own living expression, they possibly didn't want me to be in mine.

I have become frustrated within myself for being so naïve to think that what I have been learning out in Nature would be worth sharing with other people. I have been desperately trying to sort through all the garbage I have accumulated along my life journey, so that I could share with and be nurtured by my fellow man. What I continually see is that there is no possible way to find clarity within myself by conversing with my fellow man about what I see as being real in my world.

As much as man strives to have complete freedom of movement within his world, he continuously sets it up so he never achieves it. He is forever giving his own personal power to things of the sensual kind, and also to people outside himself, and he rarely ever acknowledges who he is within himself.

If a man speaks of and relates to only the things he has personally experienced in his life, and does so confidently, he could either be frowned upon or held in the highest regard. It would all depend upon the circumstances he creates in his life. He could be labeled (as in the example of an actively aggressive, competitive athlete who is stating how he has come to be exceptionally good at what he is doing) as being conceited, arrogant, snobbish, etc., if he poses any kind of a threat to the self-acceptance of the people he is relating to at the time.

On the other hand, this same man might be called confident, independent, successful and dynamic in his approach to life if he expresses himself in the same way within a business-oriented environment. An example of this situation would be: If all the members of a selling corporation are attending a motivational seminar, then everyone there wants to hear the latest hype about how they can boost their sales volume. If one man can get up and speak assertively about how he has become so good at what he is doing, and about how much money he has made and how he has made it, then he becomes a role model for everyone else to focus on. He is utilized to show each person there that they, too, can be as successful as he is if they only apply themselves in the 'right' manner.

In one instance, society openly accepts the man's behavior because it has to do with power and money, and the focus is on the man surrendering and conforming to that which is acceptable to his peers. In the other example, the man is not so readily accepted by society because his focus is on the accumulation of personal power, and it has to do entirely with how he sees himself as a person. There is no support from the outside world in this example, only from the inner world. This inner world is lived through knowing, whereas the outer world is lived through conformity to a certain accepted belief structure.

It somehow doesn't make a whole lot of sense. Everything that man chooses to create in his world, based on his thinking process, is created in pairs of equally opposing forces. When he creates the supportive, he also creates the non-supportive to (externally) do battle with and (internally) struggle with. This encourages him to work for the supportive creation which he already has inside himself – only he doesn't know that. It sure is a crazy world out there. It is far better for me, and healthier too, to be alone where I am so that I might receive, without being divided in order to do so, the subtle gifts of life as they are presented to me in the purest and simplest ways.

*

I am sitting quietly in the middle of a small open space on the top of a knoll, surrounded by scrubby trees and sprawling bushes, looking up into the cloud covered sky. I am perched on a small boulder that Nature has purposely positioned in the centre of this circular opening. I alter my state of awareness so as to encompass all of my surroundings, attuning myself to all the different vibrations that are present within their natural forms. I still my thoughts and proceed to align myself with Raven as I have done many times before. I am asking for a sign that will show me how I should be moving in my inner and outer worlds.

I wait for a few moments, and then I receive an inner impulse to open my outer world eyes. As I gaze out into the direction of the North Wind, I can see the growing image of Raven flying toward me.

As he approaches, he speaks these words: "Greetings, my brother. I hear that you have come here today looking to connect still further with the powerful forces within all of Nature. I acknowledge your inner desire to live your life to its fullest creative expression. Come, let us be here together and share with each other the simple gifts of life."

As he lands, I am able to witness a brief demonstration of the power and strength he has within his being. As he stands on a small tree stump directly in front of me, not more than six feet away, he begins fluttering his wings. As a result of this movement, he creates gusty currents of air that begin to strike the front of my body in wavy motions. The force behind them is almost enough to cause me to fall off the small boulder on which I am standing.

His wings are long and pointed at each end. They have to be at least four feet from tip to tip. His main body frame stands a good twenty-four inches in its overall height, from where his feet rest on the stump to the top of his head. His black colored coating of smooth feathers glistens in the early morning mist. His bill is fairly large and looks heavily constructed. The only part of him not of a smooth texture is the area around his nostrils. It is covered with feathers that stand up and stick out. It is a reminder that there are always imperfections within the perfections of Nature's expression, and that is what makes all of Nature so perfect.

His eyes are keen and sharp, as is his ability to sense all the movement taking place around him. His full attention is on everything simultaneously, missing nothing, for he has become all things. I even feel his presence stirring within my being, looking and probing into the structural facets of all that I am. The steely look from his glaring eyes pierces right through the thin veil of fabric that covers my physical body. I am slowly being stripped apart and dissected from the outside, coming inwardly layer by layer.

There is an accelerated altering of total consciousness unfolding within me, and I can feel my vibrational resonance shifting as well. It has a definite familiarity to it, although I am not able to pin it down to anything specific. Suddenly, there is a hastened interchange occurring. My total essence shifts from being in my own body into totally occupying his physical form. I then proceed to jump back into my physical form, then back into his. It is much like electricity jumping between two pieces of wire. In another instant, I am back to my normal state of vibrational frequency, sitting opposite my Brother, beginning to wonder what this is all about.

I ask, "What is the process that keeps occurring within me?"

Motionless and with total presence, Raven responds, "You are slowly being attuned to all the different vibrations that exist within the limitless boundaries of Mother Nature. You are also being aligned, by your own inner guidance, to all the different dimensional levels of reality that exist within you. You are in the process of integrating into your living expression those energies that will allow you to move in any world as a free man, free unto yourself, so that you may share your oneness with all those you come into contact with. The path you are on is the pathway that leads to the full realization of your true inner self.

"You must become aware of the fact that the process you are currently undergoing will require a period of time in order to bring about the necessary integrated changes on all the different levels within your being. It would be appropriate for you, at this time, to become more patient within yourself as to how quickly you want things to happen, and to allow ample room for the complete alteration to unfold in the way that it will. It is also important that you continue to focus your intention onto extracting from your past, and also from your present experiences, all the vital information that will enable you to free yourself from your own self-imposed limitations. Realize, my brother, all that you have done in your past has been of great benefit to you and the many others you have interacted with while you have been moving along on your life journey. The experiences that you have created have helped many a person move into their own light, and they have also offered others many opportunities to become more aware of the darkened areas within their own living expressions.

"You have been asking for and are now receiving the purest form of teaching available to man on this physical plane. As you progressively attune yourself to your interconnectedness to all living expressions of life, you will automatically infold to within the deeper aspects of your true inner self. This will allow you to bring to the surface more of your wholeness. It will also open you up to being able to see the wholeness of the universe within all things.

"There are no degrees of separation within the world you are choosing to create. The path you are on encompasses all expressions of life within the purity and simplicity of how they have been created. Strive to become more consciously aware of all the multi-dimensional aspects of your being, so that you may flow harmoniously with all your fellow human beings.

"It is advisable for you to move within the darkened areas of your past experiences with the laser-like focus and intention of the warrior, so that you might bring more clarity to your own present day as it unfolds before you. It will be impossible for you to reach your purest level of realization about yourself as long as there is still disharmony surrounding any of the experiences you have created in your past. If you continue to align yourself with the powerful light of truth, you will be guided and directed in the ways that are necessary for you to fulfill your destiny here.

"You have now decided to come out into this environment and seek the purest teachings from all the great masters. Remember, in all ways, that what you will learn out here will always keep you imprisoned if you always need to come out here in order to feel your connectedness to all that exists. Gradually, you will have to take all of what you become aware of out here back into the city and utilize it fully each and every moment through your daily living experiences.

"Do not believe any of what you think you see or hear out here, for if you do, you will become trapped by your beliefs of what you are thinking. It is important for you to know, my brother, that all that takes place out here in the purity of all of Nature has a purpose in its creation and its expression, and that it will aid you in your inner growth, as well as carry you on to your ultimate truth. Be forewarned that out here, nothing is ever what it seems, it is always what it is.

"Be very cautious about who you choose to relate your experiences to in your outer world. There are many who are now feeling you are a threat to their very existence. They would just as soon get rid of you completely, in any way they can, rather than confront you or be confronted by you. They may try to take your essence from you at any time, so move within the dimensions of your worlds with total awareness. As you become stronger within your being, and begin to project yourself into your outer world, there will be many who will try to gain control over your movements. All your training out here will prepare you, should these situations arise, so that you will be able to move through it all with the purity and clarity of the fearless warrior.

"Before you lies the journey you have been asking for. There are very few around, at this time, who are seeking to find a pure connection to the structure of their own roots by employing entirely the sacred teachings of Mother Nature. There are many who are involved in enlightening others as to how Nature has all these magical cures and remedies that will help them eliminate their self-created illnesses. These people have become so trapped by their own fragile emotional fabric that they are unable to align themselves, at the deeper levels within their beings, to all of Nature to receive the gifts they need in order to restore balance within their living expression. You have already seen an example of what I have spoken of: that day at the health fair. Oh, yes. You see, I know all of your thoughts. I know all the experiences you have ever had on this plane, as well as all the ones that have yet to come. So, let us go on.

"This is a journey you must make on your own. There are no other beings who can come to your assistance at this time. You must go deeper within yourself and attune yourself to finding your own purified truth, and allow this truth to be your guide, not your crutch. Trust no one that lives in the outside world. Look within for all of your food, and stay out of the unstable energies of the city as much as you can while you are still transiting through your initial transformational stages.

"Surrender your entire being unto the guidance of the all-encompassing creative force, and you will be looked after. There are no outside world situations available to you at this time, or ever will be available, that will aid you or guide you in finding your truth. You must decipher all the necessary information from the experiences that are within you. You must give up all wanting and all desiring, and ask for the guidance of the highest order from within to provide for you all that you will require in order to complete your journey.

"There is much for you to learn while you are out here, yet there is nothing you will learn out here that you do not already know. When you come out into the elements of Nature, be sure to check in with us. We will stay close to you at all times, so long as you need our assistance, guiding you and protecting you according to living life's expression to the fullest. Remember always that you are a student when you come out here. All that you need will be given to you when you are most ready to receive it. All that will be given shall be pure and simple, for that is the truth behind how life is.

"Trust us not, my brother, for we are as much your archrivals as we are your protective guardians. We support you and encourage you to succeed on your journey, but know that we will do everything possible to make sure you never succeed. That way you will never become dependent on us for your stability. It is like that throughout all of Nature: there is constant duality of meaning and of purpose. That is why the inner pathway is the purest one to follow, for it embraces all realities within the wholeness of truth.

"You have asked for the purest and the highest vibrations that are possible for you to attain while you are still on this plane, and this is the journey you are now undertaking. There is much that is hidden on this plane of reality, as there is within the planes of existence that exist within the inner dimensional pathways. You will be required to go deeper within your being in order to uncover the complete picture. The more you travel inwardly, the more sophisticated everything becomes, yet the clearer and more simple the answers are. Only you can determine where you will want to stop, for the internal journey is endless.

"Take one step at a time, and do not overlook anything that is presented to you. For it will be the simple things, the ones you think are the least important, that will trip you up and possibly even cause your death. Be cautious, and be careful – not so much of the things that exist outside of yourself, but rather, of your own thoughts about what you think you are doing or think you have attained. Your thoughts have the ability to bind you and to destroy you, and they also have the ability to set you absolutely free.

"Remember, too, that all of that which you have done for the greater part of your life has been in complete control of the way in which you have moved in your worlds. There is an equally powerful force inside you that does not want you to succeed in your endeavors. We will speak more about that at another time. Know that you cannot even trust yourself while you travel along your way, for your self – thought form – was that aspect of you that created all the imbalances within your inner and outer worlds.

"Look at all the signs that are readily available in Nature for the purity of the wisdom and the knowing. Do not think about any of that which takes place while you are out here, or after you have left here. Live your experiences totally while you are here. In doing so, you will be able to see and receive the gifts that the experiences will offer. There is nothing for you to take away from here. There is only much for you to leave behind. Allow all the information you receive to naturally sift through and filter into the deeper levels of your being.

"Attune yourself completely to finding your own truth, and open yourself to your own great love for all things within the vastness of the universe. The path of the warrior is one that must be walked alone. Only by doing that will you be able to be with all living expressions of life unconditionally. There will be many who will come to be around you as you make your way through your outer world, but you will not need them in order to make your world complete. Provided, of course, you make it through the training and the trials within your initial transformation.

"Each time you come to our living area, know that there is much for you to observe and to assimilate. I will be in contact with you when it is appropriate.

"Otherwise, keep your focus on your inner truth. We will take every opportunity to trick you, so trust us not. Yet at the same time, my brother, trust us in all ways. Rely on your inner feelings to guide you as to when we are your friends. You will only know what we truly represent when you are able to connect with your inner sense of knowing on the higher vibrational frequencies. When you are able to move from this higher place all the time, there will be no question as to who is your friend and who is not.

"All that you need is around you at all times, if you are only open to seeing it. Do not look too hard or for too long, or else it will pass you by. The secret of finding the simplicity in all that you experience is to release your thoughts. Behind those thoughts you will experience your knowing.

"It is time for me to go, my brother, as it is now time for you to involve yourself in today's lesson. I bid you farewell. And remember, you are totally on your own."

With these parting words he opens up his wings, gives one brisk flap and at the same time makes a short hop into the air. He is now airborne, quickly ascending to above the treetops. Then he disappears. I close my eyes and attune myself to the current vibration moving within me. I question how I am ever going to remember all he has said. But then I know that it really doesn't matter if I do. It will be far better if I live it all in my daily unfolding world, rather than trying to recall it all by using my memory. I sit for a few minutes longer, waiting for an impulse to come from within as to where I am to go from here. A clear picture of an exposed mountaintop flashes before my inner eyes. I know that this unfolding day will bring with it another sacred ceremony – one that will be quite a bit different from the last one, but will be the same in that it will be another initiation of the warrior.

I make my way along the trail, observing all that I can see in my outer vision. I am also listening to all the different sounds being made by the trees as they gently sway back and forth in the early morning breeze, and by the birds that call this area their home. At various spots along my way, I stop and attune myself to the reality of what it would be like to be a tree, wondering what I might have witnessed over the many years I have been rooted here, and what conversations I might have overheard from the people who walked on the trail beside me.

As I begin to ascend the first rocky section, I receive an inner communication to remove myself from the main trail – the one that is always travelled on by everyone else – and head straight up the mountain by creating my own trail. I am to move through my journey in any way I see fit, keeping my focus and intention on observing all the things I will encounter along the way. I will need to open up to the vision of my inner eyes, as well as using my outer eyes, so that I am not just focusing on finding my way. It will be important to let go of wanting to go anywhere in particular, and openly allow my inner guidance to take me to the places I need to be in order to receive the gifts that are there. I am to open my vision so that I will be able to see everything, to become totally aware of all the things that surround me without having to look at them. I am aware that if I only keep my eyes directly on the path, then I will only see the path and nothing else.

I spot a deer trail and decide I will use it to take me part way to my destination. I decide to attune myself to the essence of the Deer in order to learn something about my own behavior patterns from the natural wisdom that is shown within the way the Deer chooses to move in his environment. What I am discovering is that the deer trail criss-crosses back and forth across the hillside on a steady, manageable incline, allowing the Deer to slowly climb higher and higher. I am also aware the Deer always picks a route that will support him in arriving at wherever he is going, and by moving in this way, he is able to keep his own personal energy reserves full. The Deer never expends any more energy than he really needs to at any given time. I sense the Deer instinctively knows there is no place for him to go in his lifetime, for he continually ventures forth within the total openness of what Nature offers.

I, on the other hand, always take the route that will get me to where I want to go in the quickest possible time, and I usually end up being depleted in my energy reserves once I get there. I never really get to see very much of anything along my way because I am always so caught up in how I am going to get there, forever plotting my movements so that I have every detail figured out long before I do it. I am also into punishing myself along my journey by creating obstacles to slow me down, rather than being able to see that the process of what I am doing is a precious gift that I am giving myself.

About a quarter of the way along the first section of sloping ground, I am paid an unexpected but very welcomed visit by Little Bird. When I first see him, he is busy hopping from bush to bush, chirping away, vibrantly singing his song to the world outside him and celebrating his gift of life. I stand motionless for a few minutes, observing his every movement and attuning myself to him. I then proceed to speak, "Hello, my friend. It is truly a priv—."

Before I can finish my thought, he interjects, "There is no need to flatter me, my friend. I decided I would drop by and see how you are doing. I was observing you and your Brother (Raven) speaking earlier, and there is very little I could add to what has already been spoken."

With an inviting smile, I quickly say, "I would welcome your words, my friend."

In a quiet and direct manner, he voices his thoughts: "Perhaps I could share a few insights with you. It would always be important for you to allow yourself to be absolutely free while you are out here. There are no restrictions within the purity of Nature, only the ones that you choose to bring with you when you come. The way that you have moved in your outer world has been by programming and conditioning, and those things won't work out here. You will miss all of what is here for you to see. Become more spontaneous within the manner of your expressions. Take your life seriously enough that you find the moments to be open and free within yourself to sing your own song to the world and bring joy and happiness to those around you and to yourself."

I look down to adjust my foot placement on the sloping side hill, and when I raise my eyes back to where he was, he is nowhere to be seen. I have heard all of his words. They are so simple in their expression and so powerful in their meaning. I am now beginning to see how I am trapped within my expectations of finding something out here that will allow me to move differently within my worlds. I am now realizing it is all of that stuff I am still attached to that is holding me back from being open to what I already know.

I soon come to another part of my journey that will require me to release my thoughts and move with the grace and freedom from deep within me. I come upon a rock face that is covered with wet moss and a thin coating of freshly fallen snow. It will be very slippery and extremely dangerous. It will be important that I remain totally in the present moment unfolding. I will also be required to make my way up this particular face while wearing my heavy work boots. I welcome the challenge to go after death one more time, for I know that if I am to succeed in this trial there will be many gifts to receive.

I begin to climb, unaware of any impending dangers, totally free within myself to play and explore. I am moving without any concerns or worries about what I am doing. I am involved in the total creative process, watching it unfold before me. I then make the mistake of looking back towards the ground below, to the place where I had just come from. I start to react to what I am seeing, and I lose the clarity of focus and purity of intention within the inner movements I am creating. I look up to the place where I want to reach, wondering whether I am ever going to be able to make it. It is so close, yet I know that I will not be able to get there unless I first take control of my internal movements and deal effectively with what is happening right here.

I again look back at the ground directly below me. It is thirty feet straight down. Lying on the surface of the ground are a few rather large boulders and a shattered old windfall that has been recently blown over. If I am to fall, I could pick up some really nasty injuries. I think to myself, "I am forever putting myself into these kinds of situations, and for what? I never get anything out of doing this."

I once again look up to where I want to go, and then back to where I would end up if I am to fall. I become aware that I am once again reacting to my past – where I have come from, and also to my future – where I am supposedly going. The future is a non-existent place that is out of reach – a place I want to get to none-the-less. The past presents to me my fears, the things that will stop me from getting to my destination. Had I not come this particular way, I would not have created these fears. I can see that I am using the place I have just come from to dictate how I am choosing to move in the present unfolding moment. I can also see that I will be fine as long as I have my full attention on the thing I am in the process of doing. It is only when I choose to look back to my illusionary past, or ahead to my illusionary future, that I get pulled off my centre. That is usually when I start reacting to everything and everyone around me, totally negating all I have done that has been supportive of my life.

I close my eyes for a few long seconds. Taking slow deep breaths and centring myself within my beingness, I ask for some indication as to what I should do next. I begin to hear the welcomed voice of my inner teacher coming from within the depths of my darkened void, "Nature will not present to you any situation without also giving you the means to move through that situation in a harmonious way. Let go of your thoughts and surrender yourself to your fears. Do not fight with your fears, for to struggle with them will give them power. While you are in the openness of all of Nature, attune yourself to the wholeness of that which surrounds you. Open your entire being to the vibration of the cat, and you will know what to do."

I allow the altering affect of these words to continue moving through me, and I soon become aware of how the cat would move. My arms begin to move in a very different manner, as my hands are now being controlled by my powerful shoulder muscles. I adjust my position on the rock face so that I adopt a semi-crouched body posture. My breathing is also being altered. Each breath becomes shorter and my exhalations are more forceful, setting up a distinctive pulsating rhythm that promotes powerful movements. I can feel my whole body getting ready to explode as the energy inside begins to boil to the surface. I can sense how all the separate parts of my physical body are being synchronized to what is taking place within me.

I can feel a wave of energy beginning to surge through my body. It is centrally located in and around my navel, and it starts to move in two directions at the same time – one toward my head, the other toward my feet. As the two waves arrive at their respective ends at the exact same time, there is a recoiling effect upon my body. As the waves begin to return to the place of their origin, a tremendous surge of explosive power is unleashed. I bolt inside. I can feel everything bursting forth at the same time. In an instant, I am on the move.

I practically fly up the rock face. It all happens so quickly that I have no memory of what it is like. I am too involved in the creation of it. When I arrive at the top, I keep myself in the altered state I have been attuned to, as I want to move more in the way of the cat, to experience what it is like to have that kind of power and agility all the time. I continue to run all over the place, running through the bushes, up and over logs and scampering up sections of rock, always finding the appropriate way to move in order that my overall journey is not delayed.

My vision is focusing on the path that I create as I move, yet I can also sense everything else around me at the same time. My breathing pattern is the pulsating driving force behind what is occurring in my movements. Everything originates from my breath. The energies within my body keep replenishing themselves, and I am aware that I am not using very much of my personal energy while I am moving through these open spaces. It is as though I am able to draw on an endless supply of energy from all living things around me to fully utilize in my creative play. I am moving totally from within myself. I have a sense that every part of my physical body is involved in the creation of these movement patterns. I am also aware that all of my individual body parts are doing their equal share of service to ensure that I am getting maximum efficiency within each of my movement patterns.

I am being directed to a large secluded spot on top of a cliff. As I arrive near the opening, I immediately begin to alter my state of beingness back to my normal human-like vibration. The opening is oblong in shape, with one part of it bordering on the edge of the rocks and the rest surrounded by small, scrubby evergreen trees. Near the centre of the open space is a very large sprawling bush. It is hard to tell what the surrounding ground is like, as there is at least six inches of snow covering it and everything else.

I find a spot that I can harmonize with within my being and clear away some of the snow. I sit and wait for further instructions from my inner teacher. I use this time as an opportunity to reflect back on all that has taken place since I first arrived this morning. Time has a way of not existing as I sit recalling my communication with Raven and Little Bird, my insights from the way the Deer moves, as well as my experience of living in the awareness of the Cat. I am totally involved in the magic and the teachings that Nature has to offer me. At one point in my reflective state, I ask: "Why me? What makes me so special that I get to witness all of this firsthand?"

A very simple reply comes back from within the depths of my knowing self: "It is yours because you have asked for it."

I open my eyes. I have the distinct feeling that I have been off on another journey somewhere within the vastness of my thought processes – to a place where there is no thought. My body is feeling warm and very relaxed. I close my eyes once more, observing within my being all that is beginning to unfold.

I am instructed to remove my clothes, which are representatives of man's world, and to leave them on top of the bush so they won't get wet. The temperature is around 33°F – just above the freezing point. It is cloudy and there is no wind to speak of. I do not question having to remove my clothes, as I know that I am being protected and guided and that no harm will come to my physical body. I know that I am not partaking in this journey to create more pain in my life. Rather, I want to remove pain altogether.

I open myself to being receptive to all that is around me, making sure I do not separate myself from any of it. I know that if I do, I will get cold, and that through the coldness I will inflict pain and possibly do irreparable damage to my body. As long as I become attuned to the snow and the coldness in the air, I will not be affected by them; I will become them.

I proceed to move freely through the wooded areas, running and playing, expressing myself fully within the purity of the environment I am surrounding myself in. It is obvious that I am the only one who has ventured into this place. The snow is undisturbed, and it is clean, soft and pure. I am unconfined within the openness of life's expression. I am free to be creative in any way I choose to express it, without fear of being judged for how I am moving or for what I am choosing to create.

I continue to move higher and higher until I eventually arrive at the summit.

The scenery is breathtaking. Everything, for as far as my eyes can see, is pure white, and I have a clear 360° panoramic view. The wind is blowing, dancing all around and caressing me all over, tantalizing my body, encouraging me to be playful. I move gracefully along the uneven, snow-covered surface, being careful not to overextend my reach so that I lose my balance. The wind and I dance as we move, and we continue to play. I am without form in my expression and without thought in my movement. Moving and creating, becoming and dissolving with each unfolding moment, never concerned about space or about time. I am free to be whatever I choose for as long as I choose.

A shift begins to take place within the format of my creative expression. A visual image of the warrior shape-changer flashes across the picture screen of my inner eyes. I sense that this is to be the beginning of another of my initiatory sessions. Then the wise old medicine man comes into view within my inner dimensions, and I begin recalling bits and pieces of the information he has already related concerning the Indian way of looking. In a few seconds it is all over, and quiet reigns once more within the darkened depths of my being.

I stand facing each of the four directions in turn, bowing to each in acknowledgement of their ability to teach me what I need to know. I stretch my arms out above my head, extending my entire being toward the heavens above in a sacrificial way, offering myself to all of Nature and asking humbly to be accepted as a student of life's expression. I wish only to find my truth, and if it means that I must die in order to do so, so be it. I give myself entirely to the finding of my truth so that I might become self-less within my living expressions upon this Earth. I close my eyes and call forth through my outer voice: "Take me, Oh great Mother. Although I am only a humble and insignificant being, I wish only to serve my people. Take me and nurture me so that I might be of pure self-less service to all mankind."

Instantly, the clouds open up and the warm and radiant Sun shines through in all of its brilliance, showering me with life-supporting acknowledgment. The Sun appears out of the South, which, according to the Indian way of looking, is the direction of innocence and trust. I know that I have now been officially accepted as a student, and I will always remain humble in my knowing that there is a much greater meaning to life than who I think I am. The wind comes in a sudden gust and celebrates with me my joy and my love. I begin to hear the calling from Raven coming from the distance behind me.

As I do an about turn, I can sense the vibrational essence of two of my Raven Brothers. One is coming from the East, the other from the West. The West represents introspection, and the message he has is clear, "Move within the darkness of your own shadow, and you will find the reality of the purest light. The warrior moves into the darkness knowing that the light shall always prevail."

The East represents illumination, and his message is also clear: "The gift of wisdom will come to you when you are most able to blend – to the most balanced consistency – the teachings of your inner world and the lessons of your outer world so that they are one in the same in all that they represent. In so doing they will be reflecting a mirror image in all that they do so there is always harmony, no matter what situation you find yourself involved in. It will only be through the innocence and trust of the child within your beingness that you will succeed in finding all that you are seeking. The Sun is the *centre* of all life. It is symbolic of the pure child that you were when you first entered into this plane of existence. At that point in time, you were totally free from all prejudice – beliefs based on judgments and comparisons – about yourself and all other forms of life on this plane. In order for you to attain your purest expression of truth, you must return to the state of knowing you knew when you first arrived as a child."

I sit down cross-legged in the snow, letting everything that has taken place find its own resting place within the depths of my being. I alter my breathing pattern so I can continue to keep my body temperature at a consistent, supportive level. I had been instructed how to accomplish this by my inner voice of knowing. I close my eyes, breathing deeper into my *centre* of the universe, flowing further and further into the darkness of my creative void. I begin to move freely within the dimensions of reality within my inner world.

I find myself on top of a grass-covered plateau similar to the one where I had left my clothes, only this one is situated on top of a very high mountain. I am sitting on top of my world, looking out over all that lies below me and stretched out above me. The Sun is shining directly overhead. I am sitting much like I am on this snow-covered mountain. I have a sense that I am not alone in this place. I soon find myself observing a moving shadow that has been cast on the ground in front of me. I glance up into the Sun, and before I am partially blinded by the intensity of its light, I catch a quick glimpse of a very large bird. I close my eyes and wait for the burning sensation to clear away, knowing that when it does, I will be able to see again.

When I open them, I am staring directing into the eyes of the most beautiful woman I have ever seen. I sense that I know her well, but from where, I am not sure. She is sitting in the same manner as I am, cross-legged and without any clothes on. Her skin is golden in color. Her eyes are a deep and endless blue, and they are beckoning me to come closer. I extend my hand and touch her soft, smooth skin, gently stroking every inch of her face. I am aware of her outer fragility, yet I also sense the awesome power and strength within her internal beingness.

Our energies are continuously connecting on all levels. Feelings of love radiate from within each of us to each other, and the passionate feeling for expressing that love becomes overpowering. The sexual stimulation on the outside framework of our beings is nothing compared to the highest vibrational resonance that is manifesting itself within each of us. My body begins to flow with an electrical stimulation from a power source I have not witnessed before.

I move myself so that I am guiding her to the soft textured ground with no words spoken, our eyes never leaving each other's hold. Positioning her so that she is lying on her back, I tenderly lay myself down on top of her warm inviting body, smoothly easing her legs open so that my erect penis may enter into her welcoming vagina. We embrace solidly and our bodies become cemented together by a raging fire of pure high frequency love racing between each of us. Our beings are moving as one, continually opening to the deeper inner sensitivities that are present and unfolding. There is an ever-replenishing supply of energy stirring within each of us, and the pulsating force behind this energy is gradually building, waiting patiently for the most appropriate time to release itself.

The moment of creation is now at hand. As the moment arrives, my being is ripped from my physical embodiment and catapulted into her. Simultaneously, her being is being catapulted into mine. We have changed our expression, but our form remains the same. The seed of life from my body is propelled deep inside her body, bringing with it the creation of a new life.

We lie motionless, still looking into each other's eyes, seeing only the purest reflections of each other. Our bodies begin to recede in their individual ownership, and the common line we both share – where our bodies touch – begins to draw the outermost edges of our physical forms ever so slowly toward it. We are both becoming one within the union of the two of us. I surrender all of me, as does she. We each surrender unto the completeness of who each of us is. We are one in the same, forever divided but still remaining whole.

I now find myself alone in my bodily form and structure, yet we are still very much connected through our common spirit. I have no wanting for the outside physical manifestation of what I have just witnessed, for I know that I am whole within my being.

My breathing pattern begins to change once more, slowly bringing me back so that I am now fully aware of my outer surrounding environment, once again on the snow-covered mountain. I am not feeling any one sensation moving through my physical body. I am feeling at peace with myself. I am full of warmth. I continue to sit, asking for the significance of the vision I have just experienced. In a flashing moment, it is all so clear. I am truly excited! This marks the first time I have consciously been able to see it without asking for help from my inner teachers.

My own inner voice begins to dialogue, "The purpose of the journey I am taking in my life (at this time) is to solidify the communion of, and to bring about the inner marriage of, the two separate aspects of my being so that I might create a new life. It is a life that is based on truth and honesty within the expressional forms of love.

"Today I have planted a seed of life within myself, and it will only be a matter of time before it becomes a creative reality in my outer world. We had our eyes fixed on each other because we were mirror reflections of each other, neither one being any more or any less that the other. We were one in the same as illustrated by the fact we were connected by the front halves of our bodies. We attuned ourselves to that our hearts were beating as one. We did not need to speak, for true communication is without words. It comes through accepting and acknowledging each other in the wholeness of who each person is. It also comes with the acknowledgement that each is complete within themselves, neither one needing the other, yet each one ready to surrender to the other in order to fully realize the purest communion. Each half is equal to the other, and each half is very much necessary in order that a new life can be created. The gift is in the seeing that there can be no life created unless the female and male sides – representing who I am – unconditionally surrender unto each other without judgment and without comparison."

As I open my outer eyes and begin to make my way to a standing position, I hear the distant calling from Raven coming out of the North. Rising above the trees and heading straight for me are two of my Brothers. They are flying side by side, showing the equality of each to the other, neither behind nor ahead. As they complete their overhead pass, I see them merging their bodies into one, signifying the wholeness that arises out of the separateness. This is a confirmation of what I have already acknowledged within myself. I now know that I am opening up to the deeper levels of communication within me.

Raven circles around twice before deciding to land. Hopefully, he will share more of his insights. As he takes up his position on the small rock I have cleared of snow, we attune ourselves to each other for a few seconds, and then my dialogue begins, "Tell me, my Brother, why was it that when I first saw you flying toward me out of the North I saw two of you, but when you completed your overhead pass you formed into just one of you?"

Raven partially opens and closes his wings as he repositions himself, and says, "That is simple, my brother. When you first saw me flying above the trees, you had just come out of an altered state of awareness. You were looking out of each of your eyes independent from the other. Hence, you saw two separate images of the same object – me. As I flew over you, your eyes returned to their normal alignment within the visual structure through which you perceive."

I ask, "So there was only one of you all the time?"

As Raven looks right at and into me, he thoughtfully delivers his message, "Yes, you now see that you cannot trust any of what you think you see with your outer eyes, for you will never know for sure whether you are in an altered state or normal state of awareness. Most times people walk around in altered states of awareness, but they are not consciously aware that they are. Everyone continuously moves in and out of different states of awareness, and they are unaware of this. As a result, they become victimized by the particular altered state they are held in, especially if the state is not supportive of their creative expression. What you are learning inside you is how to enter into these multi-dimensional altered states consciously so that you can utilize them to aid you in finding your own internal truth. There is an infinite number of these altered states. Choosing the appropriate ones will get you to where you want to go. If you get caught up on any one of them, you will become trapped within the ever-unfolding universal void.

"You have now begun to experience the magic in the simplicity of life's expression by utilizing your inner eyes and attuning yourself to your sixth and seventh senses. Look at all things in the duality in which they exist, and know that life can only be created by bringing together these two separate aspects. Also realize that which is created from the two belongs to neither of them. It is a creative aspect of life that must be encouraged to express its own life according to its own inner creative light.

"Seek to bring the things from the outer edge of themselves in toward their *centre*. Once at the *centre*, all things give way unto a greater sense of purpose within the creative expression of life. If you work from the *centre* out-wards before you have cleared an appropriate pathway, there will be a tendency for you to become trapped by the snares that you have already set on your outer edge. Work from the outside and move toward the *centre*.

"When you have been able to fully recognize the existence of both of those edges, then you will be able to find a harmonious solution for maintaining a balanced relationship within yourself. From there, it would be important for you to be able to see that the two outer edges are connected by a very thin line, and that it will be through your ability to walk this thin line that you determine how free you will be in your living expression.

"It is the same line that separated you and your partner in your vision. Each of you were surrendering from the outer edge of your being in toward the centre thin line. This thin line was neither part of you nor was it part of your partner, yet it connected the two of you together. Looked for, it cannot be seen. All you will be able to see is the outer edges of your physical body. You cannot feel this line, for it cannot be felt. All you will be able to feel is the outer edges of your physical body. If you try to taste it, you will not be able to succeed, for all you will be able to taste is the outer edges of your physical body. If you try to smell this line, it will elude you, for all you will be able to smell is the outer edges of your physical body.

"It is only with your thoughts that you will think you know what I am talking about. Realize, my brother, that these thoughts you will undoubtedly have cannot possibly grasp where this line is. This line is continually shifting within the moment of its ever-unfolding creation. These thoughts of yours will always be focused on either the past or the future. There can be no thought within that unfolding moment.

"When you and your partner were exchanging your physical embodiments, there was no thought. Nor was there an awareness of the thin line that connected you. When you were both in the process of becoming the line, it, too, was in the process of unfolding. You must be able to see this reality very clearly, or it will cause much division within your being.

"If you can see, within your own inner clarity, activating and utilizing your sixth and seventh internal senses, then you will be able to see that the centre line is always in the process of surrendering and becoming, and that the outer edges are also doing the same. You must be able to see that it is not possible to have becoming unless you first have surrendering. Likewise, you cannot possibly have surrendering unless you first have becoming.

"Take us Raven, for example. The egg we bring into existence by our union cannot become a living expression until such time as it goes through a consecutive cellular division within itself. The outer casing of the shell serves as its protection from the outside elements, and it also provides, within its walls, a space for it to be nurtured in. When it is time for the new life form to come forth into the outer world, the shell casing must surrender itself unto itself so there can be a release of a new life. In each stage of the young one's life cycle, he must keep surrendering unto himself so that he can physically mature.

"Well, my brother, it is now time for both of us to be going. I trust that you have received enough food for today. It shall last you quite a while. Remember that all this information you already know. Allow time for it all to saturate your whole beingness. Until we meet again."

With a short hop and an easy flap he ascends to the open sky, heading off in a southerly direction. This is his last gift of the day. I see by his movements that I must continue to trust the process unfolding within me, and that I must be more patient and wait for the changes to manifest themselves in their own time.

I proceed to acknowledge all of Nature one last time, and then I head back down to put my clothes on. My body is still very warm, and I am still very much connected to all that is around me. I have become aware that when I surrender my entire being unto the natural elements, and become them within my aware-ness, I am no longer affected by them.

As I make my way along the lower trail by the lake, I meet up with another adventuresome person who has come out here to celebrate part of the new day. We exchange pleasant greetings and wish each other a good day.

As I am leaving the main trail and entering into the parking lot area, I stand and outwardly acknowledge to myself, "My Brother is right. Everything out here within my experience is very real when it is happening, but afterwards it's hard to believe that it actually even happened. Maybe it is all just a dream, and some day soon, I am going to wake up."

CHAPTER 5

# TRIAL BY FIRE

I went out into my day, seeking to discover the purpose behind all that I am doing in order to bring more peace and harmony into my living expression. As of late, I have been riding on a volatile roller coaster in my emotions. It appears that I am continuously being affected by all the garbage I have accumulated while travelling on my life journey. Just when I think I am making progress, wham! I get an emotional smack in the face to remind me that I really haven't gone anywhere. I know that it is all part of the process of moving into my own light, and that it will all work out in the end. I am now beginning to see that I just don't want a little change in my living expression, I want a complete overhaul, and I want all the necessary changing and restructuring to take place all at once.

I have been sitting on this hilltop for a few hours now, absorbing warmth from the life-giving Sun, looking back over all that I have been doing recently so that I might eliminate more of the resistance that is present in my life. I have been noticing that when I am out in the woods, or any other environment that allows for the natural expression of Nature, I am more open to receiving the gifts within the experiences I have while I am there, and I am more able to utilize my intuitive processes in order to extract the pertinent information I need at the time. I have had no difficulty dissolving the patterns of fear that present themselves when I am in a natural environment, but whenever I have been under the covering of the city, and moving through the darkened areas in my life, I have become trapped by my thoughts.

I have seen that when these thoughts have been circulating within my mental processes, I have become extremely dependent on the books and other tools I have accumulated along my journey. I have seen that these tools were becoming – or that they already were – a crutch. I now see that I have been more trusting of these tools than I have been of my own inner guidance. I have been running to these various tools whenever I have felt unsteady in my mental and emotional movements within my outer world. Whenever I have consulted the books on numerology, the i ching, the tarot, or interpreted different layouts with the tarot cards, the dakini oracle, or the viking runes, I have automatically changed the way I had been feeling to suit the outcome of the reading. In most cases, I would feel better, although there were a few occasions (where the readings had to do with time and patience regarding the many changes I had been going through) when I ended up feeling more depressed afterwards.

I have seen that I have been depending on these tools to change either the way I had been feeling or the way I wanted to feel within my thought processes. The tools have been controlling the way I have been choosing to move, instead of me controlling the manner in which I use the tools – to use them only in a supportive way to show me that I have indeed been heading in the right direction in my life. It really doesn't matter what I see or what progress I make when I am out in the woods, or any other place, if I am still going to be trapped within my own dependence on things from my outer world to determine how I find my truth.

I now see that I can no longer be out in Nature looking at all that is being presented, totally moving within my awarenesses from within, if I am continually going back into the city atmosphere and reacting to all the outside stimuli I attract. The city and Nature do not blend together. They are on opposite ends of the forever shifting scale of life. There is no connecting line that I am able to focus my attention on so that I might use both my outer and inner worlds effectively in my life.

I have found that what I have been doing in the city is creating thought patterns that would slowly encourage me to use these various tools. When I have been clear in the woods, and moving in my own light, I have never once even thought about them. I have never found any need to, as I could always clearly see all that was taking place around and within me. I know there has to be a way of correcting the imbalances between these two incompatible environments.

I am now seeing that if I can be clear in the woods, there is no reason for me not to be clear in the city or any other place that exists either inside me or outside. "How do I go about making this transition?" This is the main question I have been asking myself lately. I also feel that it is the key component behind my being able to utilize all facets of life's expression in order to grow into my own light of truth. I see that my main focus must be on my whole being, so as to become totally aware of all the different lines of movement within the levels of my outer world expression. If I am not able to do that consciously at all times, then there is no way I can live in the purest light of my own truth.

The solution seems to be quite simple. It is clear that I must act only on the internal feelings I am getting: I must rid myself of all outer world tools! This way I will only be able to rely on my inner feelings to help guide me through the outer world illusions I have created thus far in my life. As long as I continue to use outside stimuli to help me solve the predicaments I get myself into, I will continue to support the definite divisions that exist within my being.

"What will I use to centre myself on if I don't have these tools?" I see that it is possible I do not need to worry about centring myself. If I am to just observe all that takes place within my thought processes – not *do* anything about them – then it is likely that changes will take place on their own. I know from my past experiences that when non-supportive thoughts have come up, and I have reacted to them, they have returned more often and in greater strength each time. However, if the thoughts have come up and I have not done anything about them, mainly because they were not that detrimental in my life, then they would not come back as often. Even when they did come back, they were much weaker in their overall effectiveness.

I see that it is more important for me, at this time, to find more moments where I can be quiet and alone in my thoughts in order that I might find out what lies at the base of their structure.

## February 12, 1985

I have been walking along one of the back trails in Thetis Lake Park. It sure feels good to be out of the strain of city life, out to where the energies are more supportive and conductive of change. Things in my life have been continuing to swing between the highs and lows. Looking back into the darkness within my life's expression creates a lot of tension in my being. I am not at all sure why I react to the things I do. I do know that it is no longer necessary to analyze any of that which surfaces relating to past experiences. I know that none of it is real. It may have been real back when it was happening, and only when it was in the process of unfolding, but seconds later it was all just an illusion that was only real in my memory.

Sometimes the path I have been travelling gets to be a lonely one. Every person is a potential friend who wishes to support me, and at the same time, they are a potential enemy who wishes only to knock me off my *centre* and stop me from reaching my inner truth. I know that it really doesn't have anything to do with them, in the essence of who they are. Rather, they are only the reflections of those experiences that I have liked about my past, that have provided me with pleasure. They also represent the reflections of those experiences in my past that have brought me much pain. These people are the gifts that have been presented to me by my Higher Self so that I might clear up and rid myself of the many illusions I have been holding on to. It is only me, my lower earthly self, who is having difficulty moving through the illusionary aspects of what I have come to believe these people represent.

Sometimes it is difficult living in the shadows of the city life. There are so many things to watch out for in the normal movements within my unfolding day. I see the clarity and purity of the information I am presented with whenever I come out into the natural elements. I am also aware of how peaceful I feel inside whenever I am out in this environment. I have absolutely no worries in my life when I am moving totally from within the connection I have with all of Nature. There are no memories of those past experiences that still might have their emotional and mental tentacles securely wrapped around me.

I am aware that I have been totally responsible for creating all the non-supportive circumstances in my life. When I look back and reflect on them, I can never see why I would ever have created them in the first place. My own aspiration is to be absolutely free within myself so that I might live my life as creatively and lovingly as possible.

I am also aware of the reality that the information I am presented with when I come out here is of no value to me unless I can take it within me, and fully integrate it within all the different aspects of my being, and utilize it twenty-four hours a day, every day. I must be able to move in my outside world without being affected by any of that which is unfolding around me. I recognize that I am slowly taking all that I have been learning about myself and functioning with it in my outer world. I am doing this in such a way that I am now beginning to unlearn all those things I have been holding on to for all these years – things that have been very non-supportive in my life, and things that have never even belonged to me.

I sometimes become frustrated with the process of time and space on the plane of reality called Earth. I clearly see the significance of all that I have been learning about myself. I also see how I have wanted to implement all the changes within my physical world as soon as I have seen them within my inner awareness. I know that it is not possible for things to happen like that in my outer world, for everything on the physical earthly plane arrives here through an element of a time sequence that is connected to an allotment of proportional space, within which it can be manifested into a particular multidimensional form.

It is only possible to bring about the clear manifestation of all forms of life's expression, instantaneously, through the unfolding creative realities that come from within my inner worlds.

I see that the process of change I must go through is much like that of a new seed that has been freshly planted in the ground. We are much the same in that we are both in need of three primary ingredients in order that a new life may be encouraged to begin and then sustained once it is unfolding. This three-component support system that all forms of life's expression require is: fertile ground, sunshine and lots of love.

The fertile ground is representative of the void I have created within the deeper levels of my being in order to provide a nurturing place where the process of transformational life may unfold and express itself. The more I enter into the darkness of this void to remove the non-life-supporting weeds that have been growing and thriving there (the judgments and comparisons I have made regarding my past experiences), the easier it will be to create a new living expression. The ground that has been supporting and nurturing me along my life journey has been overgrown with weeds for a very long time. I am in the process of removing them so that I might express myself totally and freely within all of my movements in my outer world.

I know that I have become more anxious whenever I have seen new weeds surfacing within my living expression. I am also now aware that it is no longer necessary to go digging into the darkness of my inner void in order to find those weeds that are still obstructing me and preventing me from growing into all that I am. Knowing that the weeds already exist within my thought processes, I now only need to patiently wait for their arrival on the surface. When they eventually present themselves within an unfolding moment, I will be able to easily pick them out so that I no longer need to concern myself about them having an effect on me.

If I am to put all my focus and intention on arriving at the final product of who I am, then I will surely become more frustrated with regard to the amount of weeds I will see surfacing all the time. I won't be able to move either efficiently or effectively within my worlds, for I will always fear that the weeds will keep coming back. I fear that if they do come back, then people will see them and freely comment on them, and their comments will be unfavorable to all that I have been doing. If people are able to see my weeds, then they won't take the opportunity to acknowledge, either to me or to themselves, the inner and outer growth that has taken place.

If I am concerned, out of fear, that these weeds will always be around to affect me in my outer world expression, then I will end up attracting the necessary people into my life who will continually remind me of my fears. On the other hand, if I choose to focus all of my attention on to the weeds by observing them when they surface, and picking them only when they are unfolding, then I will always see the beauty of who I am at that moment, and also the beauty of who I am in the process of becoming. Each and every time I pick a weed, I am reminded of why I am choosing to pick that particular weed. It is because I wish to move into and become, within all of my expressions, the higher vibrational awarenesses that I had utilized freely and openly when I first arrived on this earthly plane.

If I am always focusing my attention on the weeds within my inner garden, then I will not be affected by the comments that others may feel free to make about them, for I will be well aware of them. As long as I already know about them, (where they have come from and how I can get rid of them), I will not have to do anything except be quiet and still within my movement. I will also know that any person who is so readily available to comment on the number of weeds I have growing in my garden, really isn't concerned about removing all the non-life-supporting weeds growing within their own internal garden (thought processes). If they were, they wouldn't have any time within their creative living expression to comment on the condition of my garden. It is a full time job being attentive to what is growing in one's own inner garden. If others are freely passing judgments in regard to the state of my garden and the number of weeds I have growing, then I know they are not really interested in finding their own inner truth. The truth of who each of us is, individually, is always shown within the final product that arises from the seed that was planted many years ago in the womb of our mother.

I am including the second component of the support system (sunshine) to ensure my growth, in that I am aligning my entire being with all of Nature's expressions. I am asking Her to nurture me in my endeavors to find my truth. I see the Sun in the open sky above as the same Sun that exists within my heart, and is the true source of all life inside and outside my being. The nourishment I am open to receiving while I am in the midst of Nature is the food that nurtures me in my inner growth. I know that there is an unlimited supply of nutriments in all that exists out here, and that all I have to do is ask and I shall be provided with all that I need.

In Nature I have yet to be turned away in my asking for support to find my inner truth, whereas in the city I have been rejected many times. I have been rejected in the sense that those persons who I have been attracted to were not at all interested in supporting me finding my own truth. Rather, they had wanted me to follow either their truth or the truth of the person they had been following. I knew that was not what I wanted to do in my life, so I continued to search.

I went about asking certain people in the city if I could study with them, not because they had something to offer me in being my teacher, but because I saw them as being equal to me. I saw that they would be able to effectively reflect back to me all that I might need in order to learn more about myself. In the same way, I had felt that I would be able to reflect back to them those traits that they possibly needed to look at regarding their own inner movements. They became angry with me. They wanted to be my teacher, and they wanted me to be their student. I knew that was not even possible in my reality, for it would automatically set up a measure of inequality between the two of us.

That kind of a relationship would only serve to create disharmony on all levels within me, for I would be allowing myself to be judged by the person who would call himself my teacher. This situation would also open me up to comparing myself, in all ways, to the one I would choose to hold as my teacher. I see that I could easily get caught up in the judgments and comparisons, so much so, that I wouldn't be able to clearly see who I truly am.

The persons that I have aligned with have shown me that to search outside my own being will always bring into my life journey much confusion as to who I am, primarily from the judgments and comparisons I would be likely to make.

I have recently lost the support of many people who have called me their friend, all because of my burning desire to find my own truth. I discovered that they would only be my friends if I supported them in staying the way they were. I mentioned that it would not be possible for me to support them in the illusions they were choosing to live under and still be able to find my truth. I have seen too many instances where people's sense of entertainment was to make fun of the hardships of another human being, or to tell stories about another being that were not true (based on third party information and not their own personal experience), or that they mentally, physically, and emotionally abused their own inner child or the creative child within someone else.

I know that there is a more supportive way to express myself in my outer world. I will not be satisfied until such time that I arrive within the totality of who I am so that I may consciously experience it. I know that under all the illusions I still have lurking within the darkness of my inner void, I am already in that state of totality, and that one day soon I will be able to bring about a harmonious solution to the many experiences I have judged and compared in my lifetime.

For some time now I have been receiving clear messages from my inner teachers to release myself from all of my inner and outer world relationships, including my internal relationships with the many different aspects of my being. If I am willing to do this unconditionally, then I will be able to commence new relationships with all those people who are presently circulating in my life on a whole different level of expression – one that is supported by truth and by love.

I mentioned to those who I interacted with daily, both children and adults, that I wanted to be able to sit down with them and listen to what they have to say. I reinforced to the children many times that they are the ones who really have it all together, and that they are the real teachers; that the adults – the ones who think they have all the answers – are the ones who distort the child's inborn purity of expression by filling their heads with all the belief patterns and concepts of reality that the adults had programmed and conditioned into them during the course of their life's journey.

I had to openly tell them that in the world I was choosing to live in, there was no distinction between life forms: that I couldn't love a person any more or any less than I would love a bird or a dog. In the world of spirit, all things are without labels. We are all the same in essence and in being. It is only man who is continually labeling everyone and everything, setting up further divisions within himself. Look at what it has all gotten him – thousands of years of unrest within himself and an endless number of futile wars within the outer world he moves in, people fighting and dying for belief structures and concepts of reality that are based on illusions. None of it makes any sense!

The third component of the support system needed to bring life into an expressional reality is love. I am loving myself in the purest way I know how – by doing what I feel I need to. I am continually supporting my internal growth by venturing into the shadowed areas of my life so that I might find more to live for; more of me, that is. I am centring myself within myself. I am focusing all of my attention toward my own living expression, and no one else's.

The outside world has sometimes chosen to see me as being selfish in my undertakings. I can see how it is possible that they might view my actions that way. I have heard people comment that it is wrong for me to care only about myself, that I need to think more about other people in my life and how they feel about what I am choosing to do. My reply to them has always been the same: "In order for me to become totally selfless in my outer world expression, and be of the highest quality of service to mankind, it is important that I put all of my focus and full attention on to discovering who I am not. That way, I will become more of who I truly am."

If I continue to go inside and connect with the true essence of who I am, then I will not be affected by what others are saying or doing. I would, therefore, be able to be of more service, for I wouldn't have any need to keep a group of people around me. In other words, I wouldn't find it necessary to justify my existence here on this plane. If I don't need anything from any person on this planet, then I can love everyone equally and unconditionally!

Once I say that I need someone, then I am putting straining conditions within the relationship. Sooner or later there will be imbalances created within that relationship. When I say that I will only love the person I am in relationship with, I am in fact imposing conditions within that relationship. This kind of situation will only bring about division within that relationship, and it will eventually lead to disharmony within my thought processes of what the relationship is all about. It is not the relationship that creates the imbalances. But rather, it is the thought of what the relationship is. This applies to all relationships. Whether they are inside or outside me makes no difference.

All thought has the potential for being very destructive if it is not seen for what it is. It can never be real, for it is entirely based on events that have either already taken place or that will eventually take place – maybe! All thought is concerned with creating and living illusions. I have never had any thoughts when I have been creating experiences that have supported me in becoming more of who I am. Thought can be a very powerful tool when I choose to use it to support my life. I use it in that way when I allow myself to create the thoughts that connect me with all other living aspects of life, and bring into fruition those experiences that encourage me to move more flowingly through my life. I have discovered that, within all of my thought patterns, I have inevitably wanted to be right – right about things that don't even exist.

## February 17, 1985

I find myself looking back over the events that have been taking place in my life during the past few months. I am becoming aware of some rather enlightening insights, pertaining mostly to how I see myself within my outer world.

I am continually amazed at how I have gone nowhere in my life, yet I intellectually think that I have travelled a long way, and that there is still a greater distance to go in order that I might arrive at my ultimate truth. I only think this way when I am moving within the boundaries of time and space.

Today, while I was out hiking with friends, I heard myself explain when they asked what an ego was:

> "To be totally concerned with the outer world developments is an ego state of being. The ego is only a creation that has been brought to a functional reality through thought. All thought creates the entire structure of the outer world of man. If one is focusing on the inner world of awareness, then one is involved in the spiritual unfolding of life."

It is rather funny to me how simple that was in its speaking, yet so profound in its meaning. I have known all of that intellectually for a long time now, but today I really got the full impact of it. It registered on many different levels within my being. I was definitely ready to hear it this time around.

Later in the afternoon, all the thought processes that normally take place within my Earthly Mind, came to a grinding halt when I dropped by a friend's house on my way home. She came out to the car, put her arm through the open window and around my far shoulder and pointedly said, "We have to look at our egos more, my friend."

I started to react inside. I became frozen in time. My body wouldn't and couldn't move. Cold chills moved like waves throughout my being, both internally and externally. My crystal-walled world had just been shattered, and all around where the walls used to be, streams of white light, representing truth, flooded in. Another illusion had been singled out and brought to the forefront of my living expression. Suddenly, I was being inundated with memories of experiences that had taken place only days before, all concerning the movements of my ego.

"It is all just a scam," is what I thought hours afterwards as I was sitting in my living room, wondering how things actually were in my outer world. How was it possible that I had missed so much? At the same time as I was questioning all that had been happening around me, I was also feeling very much at peace with all that had transpired. I had finally arrived at a place in time and space where I was able to call myself on creating, thriving on, and living an illusion.

I had recently created the illusion, from within my thought process, that I had to go somewhere outside myself in order to attain more personal power. I had come to believe that my personal power was being depleted whenever I needed it the most. Or so I thought. I was putting out to my outer world a message that I had some magical quality within me, and that with it I could heal people of their dis-eases, and that I was a psychic – whatever that is – and that I could perform numerous tricks within the psychic realities.

I was living off my own hype as to who I thought I was. I was having it fed and supported in more ways than one by my friend who supported me in my role. I had thrived on it right from the beginning, and it had been slowly eating away at me just like a cancerous growth on the move. I had started to judge and compare things, people, events, and even closer to home, myself. My ego wanted to know how much value I could have, how much of a price could I put on what was doing. Such a cleverly contrived play it all was. So much so that I had become immersed in it, and I could not see how I had allowed it to drown me in its essence for such a long period of time.

I have always gone out of my way to be recognized and accepted by everyone around me. No one, as I had created it to be in my world, had ever stopped me long enough so that I could see what I was doing to myself. That all changed rather quickly yesterday afternoon when I kept hearing the voice of my Higher Self repeat over and over again, "Listen, do you hear that" all the while another friend of mine was speaking of his experiences of living and studying in an ashram, in India. There was a lot of information within his dialogue with me that in one way or another validated all that I was choosing to do in my life.

I am now aware that I had slanted the entire discourse between the two of us in only one way – mine. I had very little regard for acknowledging him in his desire to find his own truth by whatever means he so chooses. I had a disturbing feeling circulating within me at the time of my conversation with him, one that I was choosing to look outside myself for its cause. There was one aspect of my being that was very much aware it all had to do with me, in the sense of my attitude. My friend was the gift that I had chosen to overlook in favor of something that was more sensually pleasing to my outer world expression, which was the thought of who I thought I was.

I had started to slow down all of my thought processes. I had attuned myself to the vibration of truth, and I knew that it would only be a matter of time before the non-life-supporting pattern would surface. I would just have to wait patiently for it to arrive, and when it did, I would only have to move with it in order to eliminate it from my living expression.

That afternoon when my friend came out to the car and mentioned the word ego, I had realized that this word was the key to the pattern I had been waiting so patiently for. At that precise moment, everything fell into place. I heard the power-hungry voice of my lower self screaming within the confines of my Earthly Mind, "I've been had again!"

Everything within my physical body went cold and I felt sick to my stomach. I had clearly seen that there was no point in me doing anything strictly for value. It is more important for me to do it for the experience only. The experience is all there ever really is. The value is only a judgment, and it can never be real.

*

Holding on tightly to my life will surely bring me my death. There is no need for me to have a fancy title or recognition of any kind for the way in which I am choosing to move in my outer world expression. It would only be of importance to every person who is outside me. If that is truly so, then they would only see the title that I would go by and not the light of the continually unfolding, creative being that I am. Living is a continual process. This is something I have mentioned many times before in my interactions with other beings, and have only today received the wholeness of its message.

*

Humbleness is knowing that all knowledge is useless. It is not important for me to know anything. Rather, it is more important for me to feel as much as I can within the unfolding moment of creating an experience. I have been holding on to all my knowledge and trying to make a living from it in my outer world. At the exact same time, I have been very much aware that the knowledge I thought I had was in fact an illusion, for I wasn't ever able to use it within my outer world and make it work for me.

*

There are no teachers in the outer world of man who have it all together. It is all just one big illusion. "The flaws of a man made perfect are the perfections of those flaws!" There are no absolutes here on Earth. When there are absolutes within my worlds, it will be time for me to leave this plane of existence. In my past, I have felt that it was necessary to go somewhere else in order to learn something more about myself from some other person, someone who supposedly has it all together. I am now clearly seeing that is all just an illusion, an illusion that had been created within my thought process to keep me from looking within my own being for the answers to my many questions.

I am now seeing that the story of my life is revealed within the still emotional waters on the earthly plane. The reflections presented to me must come from the still emotional waters within me, through my perceptions of what the reflections stand for. All forms of living expression are my teachers. As a student of life, I will continue to look into my own reflective, emotional waters in order to find the appropriate passageway that will lead me to the *centre* of the life force within me. My asking for guidance in all that I choose to do will assure me a safe and truthful journey. As long as I continue to ask with the purest of intention, I shall continue to receive all that I will need along my way, and at the most appropriate time.

In the past I felt that I had to go out into my outer world and converse with people around me about the relationship that exists between my inner and outer worlds. I now see, on many levels within my being, that it is not really necessary, for I am now aware that everyone outside me is only a reflection of who I am. I have known this intellectually for a long time, but I did not open myself up to the full impact of what those words actually stand for until today.

There is no one outside me to tell my words to. There is only me. There is no one outside me who will ever hear my words. There is only me. There is no one outside me who will freely act on my words. There is only me. I am all there is. Within me, there is every thing. Outside me, there is no thing. It is all so simple when I stand back far enough to take a good close look at it. So simple, in fact, that it is sometimes difficult to believe it could actually be that way. I am now seeing that, in my past, I have spent much of my waking time making things extremely complicated for myself.

✳

Talking is for thinkers, whereas acting is for those who wish to fully experience life.

I am creating and acting upon that which I am hearing from my creative inner voice.

There is no place to go that I have not already travelled to.

✳

I have come to the awareness that I have been defending my position of being on this plane of existence. Up until today, that is. I am now choosing to create my being here as an ever-unfolding process from within – a total living experience each and every moment that I am alive. There is nothing for me to do here. There is nowhere for me to go while I am here. I will always remain in the same position within my evolutionary process, in an endless dimension of reality where time and space do not exist.

Lately I have been struggling with living harmoniously within two worlds – the worlds of the ordinary state and altered state of awareness. I have not, in the past, been totally clear as to the distinctions between the two. I find that I am more comfortable when I am in an altered state of awareness. I only travel into the ordinary state of awareness when it is absolutely necessary.

Prior to today, there has been a tremendous power struggle going on within me between two opposing aspects of my self. One aspect of my self wanted the freedom to move away from the linear world of man. The other aspect of my self wanted to strengthen the ties of conformity and impose further restrictions within the linear world of man. Both were occurring at the same time. This is only one of the constant diametrically opposing dualities that surround me at all times, and that will continue to surround me until such time as I remove myself totally from living within the fixed structure of man's world.

Today I am choosing to free myself completely so that I may effectively move within any state of awareness I might require, in order to experience the many different levels of reality that I know exist on this earthly plane and beyond.

I am choosing to surrender to my outer world thoughts unless I am specifically asked by another person to render my awareness within another dimension of reality. I now see that it is not at all necessary for me to develop my sensitivities outside my person. The time has arrived for me to clearly put forth my purest intentions within the intricate textures of my own being: to open myself up to the self-unfolding experiences that are so necessary for the continual realization of my Higher Self.

I seek to find my truth, to be immersed within my truth, and to live according to the universal truths: truths that were here yesterday, that are here today, and that will be here tomorrow; truths that are forever changing, but in all ways remain the same.

✳

Obtaining a position of notoriety in the outer world of man holds me firmly to time and space. Certainly this is not necessary on this plane? "Do I really need to live within the limitations of the time and space element while I am here on this plane?" Perhaps it is necessary for a time, at least until it is no longer necessary to focus on time and space. Stillness and absolute peace will come to me when this moment is creatively manifested within my being.

✳

Discipline, of any kind, restricts the freedom of creative expression.

*

The conclusion I have arrived at from the internal dialogue I have had today, is that there is nowhere for me to go, for there is no place for me to arrive at. The place for me to travel to is within my own inner dimensions of reality. The price I have to pay in order to get there is the cheapest anywhere around. The weather for going there is always clear. I do not have to book my reservations ahead of time. I can pick my own departure times and arrival dates as I see fit, for there are never any rush crowds. The journey to the *centre* of my own creative universe is the only true reality that exists.

*

Everything that is presented to me in my outer world is a valuable gift that, when used properly, will aid me in my evolutionary process. Everything that is presented to me in my outer world is an illusion that has been put there to trap me, to confuse me, and even to destroy me. This can only happen if I choose to allow it to happen by failing to see the intricacies of how those illusions have been set up and constructed.

*

To get past the many different illusions that this plane has to offer takes lifetimes within a single lifetime. The cosmic puzzle is so utterly complex in its structure, yet when one looks into it seriously with the right focus and right intention, it all becomes so simple within its everyday expressions.

*

I no longer find it of any value to create the turmoil in my life between the total reality as I perceive it to be, and the illusions that other beings have wanted me to see. The other beings have been created by me to trap me here and keep me spinning between what I have thought and what I have felt. I now see that feeling brings with it a creative process, and that thinking brings with it reactions to those thoughts that it brings.

*

I am choosing to centre my entire being from within. From that centring will arise truth, peace, and unconditional love of myself.

*

The starting point and the finishing point are one in the same.

*

Life is limitless in its expressions. Death always has limiting factors surrounding it.

*

All movement within my earthly journey is a necessary part of my growing closer to the Creative Father (GOD) vibration within. I accept all that is within me as the truth. I also accept that all of what is presented to me outside myself is here to help me find my truth.

As it is with all other beings, all that I am choosing to do in my life is of benefit to me as a person and also to those who choose to interact with me. Whether they are aware of it or not, or whether they agree with me or not, we all need to receive the life-giving gifts from each other without laying judgments as to how each of us has come to see our individual truth. Whatever experience is created, whether positive or negative influenced, it all has a very worthwhile purpose in its creative expression, but little or no significance in the overall plan for clarity and use of right action within all forms of movement.

*

As the voice begins to vibrate through me, I can hear these words coming from deep within my inner void, "This is the *centre* of your being, your inner moving soul, the key to all that lies within the universe, complete. As you move through your daily living expressions, your attunement to this vibration continues to become a reality – a reality that is beyond all physical description. A place where time and space do not exist. A place where all things are One and are connected through the One. A place where life begins and life ends, and all the stages in between.

"As you continue to attune yourself, your ability to stay within this inner universe will become more functional, bringing forth for you the many gifts you have been pursuing: the gift of life in all ways. Know that this is your destiny. Attune your entire being to truth, and all shall be provided for you. Let truth be your guidance, and allow your inner truths to be your guide."

*

It is now time for me to move into the light that shines from within me; to follow all of that which is; to surrender to all that is, without want or expecting to gain control over that which does not exist.

## February 5, 1985

I have been passionately involved in Body-Mind development for the past eighteen years. During those years, I have been exploring and testing the capabilities of my mind on many different levels. I have also been testing the limits of my physical performance, severely sometimes, almost to the point of causing permanent damage to my body.

I have always pushed myself to the edge of life and death in all of my living expressions. There is something about walking the thin line between the two extremes that excites me.

I have been travelling on the path of the outer warrior, purposely stalking the many images death portrays on the outer edges of my world. I have created for myself, on numerous occasions along my journey, various death-defying trials in order to prove to myself that I was indeed a warrior, and that I was worthy enough to meet the challenges that would eventually lead me to knocking on the inner door – the one that would guide me to the deepest, darkest part of my being, to the ultimate *centre* of the universe within me, universal truth.

I was in incredible physical condition when I went through my initial testing stages in the early seventies. There wasn't much I couldn't do as far as events or experiences that would require body strength, endurance, and mental focus for long periods of time. I was training like a possessed fanatic, living and dying many times over in order to take myself to the outer edge of my capabilities, and beyond. I had to know what the limit of my ability was, and I wasn't going to settle for anything less. I trained by myself, for myself, and away from the crowds.

I trained with intensity and a meaningful purpose in all that I did. I did not allow my thoughts to keep me from looking deeper within the realities I had created at the outer edges of my physical expression. I focused all of my attention onto my physical body, being very sensitive to what I put into it and always giving it my utmost consideration in all that I did. If an activity didn't support me in finding my truth, I didn't do it!

There were many along my journey who tried to discourage me from continuing. I saw that they were part of my testing, to see if I could be easily led away from my path. I was well aware that I couldn't trust anyone from my outside world. There were those who supported me in what I was choosing to do, and they had built me up in their own eyes and in the eyes of others. There were also those who put me down, mainly because they couldn't see any value in what I was choosing to do.

I wasn't doing what I was doing to prove anything to anyone outside myself. I was doing it all for me. I didn't go to my outside world and broadcast to everyone what I was doing in my training. However, there were some people who had seen me while I was training, and they automatically judged what I was doing. I was branded as being weird and eccentric by my fellow sporting associates, mainly because I always trained using unorthodox procedures and never used the accepted forms of resistance training equipment. I always used the natural states of movement within my body to train with. I would move my body within itself, thereby using all the different opposing muscle groups. Training this way enabled me to become faster in my body movements, stronger in the way I moved, more balanced in my application of movement patterns, more flexible within my movements, and allowed me to eliminate all unnecessary stress and strain on my body parts.

I had been training every day, doing some form of intense exercise that always demanded my full focus and present attention, for nearly two and a half years. Then one day, while I was finishing up the last section of one of my grueling training sessions on the mountainside, I was awakened inside to the clearest of truths – the one that I had been looking for, and waiting for, for a long time. It didn't come to me in the way I had pictured it coming, for it had nothing to do with my physical capabilities, yet it had everything to do with my physical capabilities.

My body became vibrant with an incredible, pulsating energy force, one that I had been moving under for some time – only now I was aware that this energy force was increasing proportionally as I continued to increase the stress loads within the physical components of my body. The more I wanted my body to do, the more I demanded my body do, the greater the flow of energy was created from within me to ensure that I could do it all. There was a seemingly endless supply of natural energy being generated from within the depths of my whole being – physical, mental, and emotional. (My recovery time following these intense training sessions never exceeded five minutes. That was the maximum I ever needed in order to prepare myself for the next taxing experience.) This tremendously powerful buildup of pulsating energy (within all the cellular components of my being) was getting ready to explode. I was aware that I was putting too much energy through my physical form, quite a bit more than I actually needed at the time. I had to do something, and I had to do it quickly, to somehow vent all the excess energy from my body before it did some irreparable damage to my inside structures. I stood there stretching my arms up and out to the sides in order to expand my chest, totally letting go of my physical form by releasing an intense, high frequency scream from deep within my internal depths, releasing everything of excess from inside. I screamed these words to the mountain as well as to myself, "I've done it again. I've made it. I'll always make it. You'll never break me. Never!"

A cooling sensation began to fill my entire body. I closed my eyes and began to feel what was taking place within me. It was something I had never experienced before, and words cannot fully describe it. There was a peaceful calm that began to move through every inch of my being. I could feel the subtle changes taking place, almost as if they were being magnified by the process that was unfolding. Then, the light of awakening was turned on. Out of the peaceful environment from within came a soft, quiet voice speaking the words of the purest truth, the truth I had been looking for: "Blaise, you could continue training like this, the way you have been, for twenty-four hours a day, seven days a week, fifty-two weeks a year, for the rest of your living days on this planet, and you would never come to the end of your physical capabilities. Look closely and seriously at what you have done in the past. You will clearly see that you have always found a way to move through each and every trial you have ever created."

The message stopped me in between breaths. I clearly saw what it all meant. I was now free, free from doing any more of my outer world training. I began to verbalize to the night sky my observations from within, "All that I have ever done, is mine. It will always be mine. I don't have to do any of it any more. There is no longer anything I need to do in my outside world. I've made it! God, I've made it! This is all there is. There is no more."

I started to laugh, remembering the one thought I always carried with me, "that there had to be an end-point to what I was doing, and that one day I was going to find it." I have now discovered that there is no end-point, now or ever. The laugh was to celebrate my freedom. It was now all becoming so clear. I was finally getting the whole picture. I laughed harder and louder.

I walked back down the mountain, looking at all that had taken place, laughing and chuckling to myself, feeling totally at peace with all that I had witnessed. I knew that it was now time to move on in my evolutionary process, and to create new experiences with all the information I had become aware of. That night I quit training with such intensity in my outside world. I had seen that it was no longer necessary to do any of that kind of training – or any training, for that matter. I could always call upon the inexhaustible energy force within my being to aid me in moving through any experience I might create within my living expression. It was all so simple. I could now do anything I wanted in my outside world. Nothing would ever be too difficult. There would be no further need for these "trial by fire" training sessions, at least not in the way that I had been used to.

I was invited to attend a special 'fire-walking' ceremony on February 2, 1985. The twelve invited guests arrived by 7 p.m. We proceeded to sit in the comforts of a small but very cozy living-room, making small talk with each other, waiting for the instructor to begin the session. As the seminar got under-way, each of us had to stand up and share why we had come. There were a few people who had said they were skeptical, within their own reality, about the feasibility of actually walking on hot coals. A few wondered if it was indeed possible for anyone to walk on the hot coals without being burnt. Others were there strictly as a professional courtesy, to take pictures and write an article for the local newspaper based on their observations.

It then came time for me to stand. As I was about to introduce myself, an anxious feeling began to stir in my gut. I cleared my throat and then these words began to flow from my mouth, "My name is Blaise. I have come here this even-ing to complete my ceremonial trial by fire. I wish to be consumed by the fire, to become part of it and to be transformed by it so that I might never have to trial in my outer world again. I am choosing to do this so that I may be accepted, totally from within myself, to begin a much higher vibrational spiritual journey inward – to the *centre* of my being – to discover who I am. I am here to share this experience and opportunity with all of you."

As I sit down, it is clear to me that I am going to be initiated into a very dis-tinctive transformational experience. I know that all I want to have happen will indeed take place.

The rest of the format unfolds. The instructor presents a dialogue that covers such things as *fear*: that it actually represents False Evidence Appearing Real; how to confront your fears; how to move through your fears; and what is the basis for having fear.

At eight o'clock, we all go outside and prepare the wood, and then light the fire. Everyone is standing in a circle around it, no one speaking, everyone just holding hands and internally dealing with whatever is coming up in their own thought processes.

We then go back inside, where the seminar continues to unfold. After another hour has passed, we are ready to once again venture outside. We all remove our shoes and depart for the back garden. There is to be no talking until after the ceremony of walking on coals is concluded. We all stand around the fire and join our hands so that we have a complete circle formation. We all begin to chant these words, "Release your mind, see what you'll find, bring it on home to your people," while the instructor continues to prepare the coals, making sure they are well spread out.

He is making a pathway to walk on the coals. It measures about four feet wide by twelve feet long. Red-hot coals cover this walkway, coals that are close to 1200°F. The heat coming from them is so intense that I cannot stand anywhere near them without feeling the effects on my bare arms.

I position myself directly in front of the entrance to the pathway. I want to be there so that I can walk on my own initiative – not following someone else – as soon as the instructor demonstrates walking through. He will be the first, primarily to show that it can in fact be done, and that he won't get burnt while doing it. I am standing behind him, desperately wanting him to move on so I can go through. I have an overwhelming feeling to push him onward, on to the coals, so I can get on with it. I am not being at all patient with everything that is unfolding. I know what I want, and when I want it.

After what seems like hours of waiting, although I am sure it is only a few moments, the instructor raises his arms and takes off across the coals. I am ready to go as well, but I hesitate, not really knowing whether he is finished with all of his preliminary concerns. After waiting for a good ten seconds longer, and observing that he is not coming back to the front of the line, I slowly and surely begin to walk.

I feel like I am being pulled through a 'doorway' of some kind. It feels as though I am securely attached at my navel to a flexible cord coming from the other side of this doorway. My head is perfectly balanced on my shoulders, and my eyes are looking directly ahead at all times. When I begin to look down at the coals as I am walking, I feel my head being repositioned so that I am looking forward, almost as if I am being set up by some outside source as to how the ceremony is to be conducted. My body glides effortlessly across the glowing coals. I can't even feel my body's weight on them. They seem to crumble beneath my feet as I walk. It is just like walking on popcorn.

There is no sensation of any kind, hot or cold, registering around the soles of my feet. I know that I am in another form of the altered states of awareness, one that I am not at all familiar with. There is no one around me when I walk. All the other people seem to disappear. I don't see any sign of them until I turn around and start to head back to where I was originally positioned in the circle.

As I slowly walked the four long strides from one end to the other, I was not able to hear any of the chanting that has been continuously going on throughout the ceremony. When I had walked through the doorway, it was like walking into another dimension of reality that exists somewhere else simultaneous to the dimension of reality that exists outside the perimeters of the pathway.

I return to the beginning and proceed to cross the coals once more. Again I experience the same pulling-force directing me through the doorway and over the coals. There is a lightness quality within my body, and I have no awareness of the surrounding elements. I lose sense of everyone else being here. I am here, wherever here is, alone. When I walk on to the coals, the vibrational resonance of the surrounding air is very much different from what is evident outside that plane of reality. I am totally absent of all sensual stimulation while I am in the process of walking. When I come out on the other side of the doorway at the end of the path, all sensual stimulation within my being is once again activated.

As I am finishing my second walk, I feel as though I want to play in the bed of glowing coals with my hands. I walk up to the edge of the path, kneel down on one knee and proceed to put my right palm down on top of the coals. I feel nothing. It is like putting my hand down on a large piece of shredded wheat. The coals start to crumble as the downward pressure from my hand becomes greater.

All of a sudden, without any warning, my intellectual thought process becomes activated and starts questioning all that is taking place, scornfully warning me that "I'm going to get burnt if I continue to play" and to "watch out." Immediately, I become fearful that it just might be right this time. In my reactionary state of being, I am totally negating the two walks I have just completed. The fear that I have created in my thoughts has me right where it wants me. I quickly yank my hand back, bringing with it one small section of a red-hot coal that is securely lodged within the knuckle fold of my index finger. My fear has burned me internally and externally. A little blister forms, a visible reminder of the destructive power in fire if it is misused.

I stand back in a relaxed position. I am feeling all that has just taken place. I alter my state of awareness so that I bring myself to the place within where I am alone and free within the context of no time and no space. I proceed to walk through again mainly to eliminate my fear. I come back to the starting place once more, look at the palms of my hands and acknowledge them. I walk up to the entrance to the pathway, thoughtfully kneel down and press my palms down hard on top of the glowing coals. I leave them there for four seconds, then remove them for a second or two, then put them back down for another three second count. It is the same feeling I had the first time, only this time I am in complete control of how it is going to turn out. I stand up and proceed to walk through the glowing corridor one more time, looking at the unfolding experience from a completely different perspective. I am now seeing that I am all alone, and that I am no longer separate from the fire. I am creating the reality that I am the fire, and I know that fire cannot consume itself. It is an incredible feeling that I am experiencing, a definite void between time and space where nothing exists yet everything exists.

This is the end and the beginning all in the same stroke. I am feeling as though I have completed all that I need to, and I have done it cleanly. No more trials by fire, for I am now the fire. I am now able to change, at will, the elements within and around me. I accept my transformation into the reality of spirit, and I ask for the guidance of my transformational spirit to protect and nurture me in all that I will do. I bow reverently to the coals with palms coming together so my index fingers lie across my lips. The process of change and transformation is now complete. Or is it?

When I had prepared myself for this walk at the beginning of the evening, I had acknowledged the magical quality within fire and its creative abilities to bring about the reality of permanent change and transformation within me. I had also welcomed its cleansing properties and its ability to purify me. I had offered myself, in my totality, to be sacrificed to the fire so that I could make the necessary transformational step from my outer world into my inner world – the world of total spiritual awareness. It is the purest form of spiritual initiation I could ever receive. If it is necessary to physically die within the process, so be it. I want it all, and nothing else will ever do. I am an extremist in all that I do.

All the other people have finished their walks through the glowing pathway and are making their way back into the house. As I am about to follow, I hear an unfamiliar voice from within begin to speak, "It is now time for your initiation to be completed. In order that it may come to pass, you must walk to the centre of the pathway and allow the ceremony to unfold as it is destined. This is how it is to be if you desire to attain all of that which you have spoken of."

A wave of panic races through my entire being: "How do I know that I can really trust this voice? How do I know that he is not the voice that will lead me to my physical death?"

I stand here wallowing in my thoughts, slowly realizing that I am reacting to all that has been spoken. This means that the words cannot have come from my own limited thought process, for he would never have created that kind of experience in the first place. Besides, somewhere within all of his complexities, he knows that if I die, he is going to die, too. I know that I can't afford to take any chances. The stakes are getting much too high to take any of this lightly. One irrational move on my part will surely bring an end to my earthly living expression. I am a warrior searching for my ultimate truth, and I know that truth will protect me in all that I choose to do. I close my eyes, quiet my thoughts and attune myself to the highest vibration I know exists within me. With laser-like clarity and precision, I begin an internal dialogue: "Show me the truth behind the words that have been spoken. I demand it now."

I wait, nothing is coming back. This is the purity of truth I am looking for. It is shown to me in the form of silence. It is the purest form of truth there is. I wait for a few minutes within the void of silence, feeling all that is taking place. I am wondering what my next move should be. Just as I am finishing with this thought, an aspect of my Higher Self begins to speak within the quietness of my inner void, "I am a warrior. I am on my path looking to find my ultimate truth within this universe. I am choosing to stalk death so that I might uncover more of my own light. I choose to listen to the voice of my initiator and to follow his directions. If it means that I must give up my earthly life in the process, so be it. I am not afraid. I am no fool, either. My truth is my sword and my protector. I will do as you have asked. I am now choosing to put my death into your hands so that I might live unconditionally."

I slowly move until I am aligned with the entrance in the doorway, preparing myself for whatever is to unfold; preparing myself by surrendering all that I am not so that I might become all that I am. I quiet my thoughts and focus all of my attention on to my breath, deliberately drawing it in and letting it out again slowly, patiently waiting for an inner impulse other than thought to move me.

"Take me and transform me, for I am now ready." The impulse arrives as my inner voice becomes quiet. I begin to move, unhurriedly making my way to the centre of the pathway. All is peaceful within my being, for I know that this is what I have been waiting for. I am on the verge of entering into the world of spirit, and doing it in the flesh. I am now standing motionless in the centre of this potentially destructive walkway, witnessing the tranquility and peaceful-ness of just being here without any attachments to life. The air is absolutely still. There is no noise of any kind. It is much like being in a soundproof room. The coals are beginning to bring forth dancing flames. They are quickly rising higher and higher.

I am slowly being consumed by these flames. I can feel nothing. There are no indications of sensual stimulation coming from within or without my body. I am now becoming the flames. There is no separation between us. I am slowly being attuned to the transformational properties of the flames and the coals. This is to be my entry point into the creative essence of all that I am. I am aware that I am gradually being reduced to the same height as the coals that lie on the ground below me. I am slowly being devoured and changed by the tantalizing flames that have completely engulfed me, until all that remains of my physical embodiment is a small mound of ash that is now covering the coals.

"The transformational reality into the world of spirit – could this be it? Is this all there is?" At this moment, I begin to feel myself slipping from the surface of the Earth and falling through the compacted layers that make up its mass. As I make my way downward, I can feel the different divisions of cooling within the Earth's structure. Then I experience the coldness, the other extreme. It is becoming unbearable. I eventually descend into a large, cold, damp cavern that is pitch-black inside.

As I attune myself to where I could possibly be, the cavern begins to fill with light, letting just enough through so I can see about twenty feet ahead at all times. There are odd shaped fixtures suspended from the ceiling, long pointed structures that hang point down toward the floor. There are also long pointed structures that point up toward the ceiling. As I explore the boundaries of this seemingly endless space, I become aware that it has many different compartments and chambers. Some have low ceilings, while others have low, narrow archways. I spot nine rather friendly looking bats while I am scouting around, and they offer no resistance to my being in their domicile.

I make my way through the openness of the largest chamber. I can hear water dripping as I reach the far end, and I begin to feel coolness from a gentle breeze as it lightly brushes my face. These are the physical indications that are showing me that I am getting closer to where I am supposed to be. I spot a very narrow, low-ceiling tunnel. There will be just enough room to squeeze through, and no more. The tunnel appears to be filled with water, about a foot deep, and looks to be much colder and darker than the section I am standing in. All indications from within assure me that this is the appropriate way to be heading.

I am completely within myself in my thoughts and in my being. I literally have to feel my way through this darkened tunnel. I arrive at the far end, seemingly with no other place to go. It is definitely the end of the line. As I turn around and begin to head back, I notice there is another narrow, restrictive tunnel that branches off towards the left. There appears to be a dim light shining faintly at the other end. I am feeling very uneasy about seeing this new tunnel, and also the light that had awakened me to it. When I had originally moved through the tunnel, I had felt every inch of its walls and didn't feel that particular opening. Nor did I see any visible sign of a light. I decide to explore if further.

I continue along on my journey, keeping my eyes fixed on the light at all times. My curiosity is beginning to build, wondering what could possibly be at the other end. Suddenly, this confining passageway opens up into a large, expansive cavern of unbelievable beauty. The opening is completely saturated with gold and white light, of an intensity and purity I have yet to witness anywhere in any of my journeys. Within the darkness of the outer void, there springs forth this incredible paradise. As I look across to the extreme other end of this inner void, I see the most magnificent Black Panther I have ever seen or could ever have imagined. His outer coat of jet black fur glistens and shines as he leisurely paces about. As I make my way into this heavenly place, I feel my internal vibration changing. I am now being affected by the higher vibrational frequencies radiating throughout the entire space. As soon as I take my first step through the vertical plane that divides the tunnel and this room, Black Panther quickly alters his body position so that he has me in full view. He is motionless as he continues to watch me enter deeper into his territory. His emerald eyes sparkle like pulsating prisms as the light strikes them from many different angles.

Scattered all about this cavern are thousands of transparent diamonds that are circular in their form. They are totally suspended by their own means, and they are not moving. There is no visible indication of where the light is coming from that illuminates this space. The diamonds radiate soft colored textures of light everywhere.

Black Panther begins to slowly inch his way toward me, keeping his eyes fixed on my bodily form as he moves. I am not at all frightened by his presence. I am feeling quite at home and at peace with being in his company. As he approaches, he begins to speak, "I am the guardian of your true inner self. I am the master of the world which lies beyond the world you now know. In the deepest depths of your internal darkness, I prevail, bringing forth the truth when you so desire it. In order for you to arrive at your purest form of living truth, you must first surrender unto me all that you think you know."

As he finishes his dialogue, I notice there are three brilliantly glowing lights that appear to materialize out of nowhere, instantaneously, adjacent to where he is positioned. These particular formations of light are surrounded by a translucent aura, a dazzling white light. When these lights begin to move toward me, the intensity of their glow increases. It feels as though they are self-generating and amassing an enormous quantity of high frequency energy. The diamonds that are dispersed throughout the cavern simultaneously proceed to revolve, and the pulsating light configurations that shower forth are breathtakingly beautiful. Having all these sensations manifesting and vibrating at the same time on variable, high frequencies is too much for me to take in and resonate with all at one time.

The three lights come to a standstill at a place that is equidistant between Black Panther and me. We solidify the outer reference points of an equilateral triangle. The energy form within the structural composition of these three lights extends a wide beam of highly energized white light toward Black Panther, totally encasing him. The aura that is created protrudes away from his body in every direction a good fourteen inches. There are striking contrasts between his jet-black body, the enclosing white light, and his piercing emerald eyes. It is truly a spectacular sight to behold. I stand in awe of it all.

The three forces of white light turn and direct their highly energized laser-like beam at me, penetrating my own outer energy field and making a solid connection just below my navel. From this entry point, it is deflected in every direction in and around my physical body. Eventually, I too am encased in an aura of white light, no different than Black Panther. Then the beams of light connecting us all instantly disappear. But even though they do, I can still feel the strong connection I have to the three lights and Black Panther. It is an invisible energy bond that holds us perfectly aligned to each other. There are no time or space issues in this dimension of reality. All of my sensitivities are slowly being attuned to a tremendously high state of awareness, a state that is quite a bit different than any of the other altered states I have experienced previously.

From out of the stillness and quiet comes a clearly defined and articulate voice, "I am Father of all that is. From journeying within your own inner darkness, you have come to find the purity of your own inner light from the source of all light. You have journeyed into the central core of all living things, and you have now become directly connected to all those living expressions of life. In order for you to utilize your new gifts to help others, you must first return to and heal within you all those aspects of your being that are out of alignment within the outer world you are currently centred in on the earthly plane.

"Take back to your surface world all the awarenesses you have experienced within this void, and know that the day will soon arrive where all that you will do will benefit all mankind. Your friend, Black Panther, will always be with you in all that you do. He is the knowing part of your being that holds the light firmly. He will be ever-present to help guide you in the most appropriate manner so that the day will soon arrive when you will shine in the glory and love of Father. When you return to your outer world, you will be joined there shortly by your conscious manifestation of Black Panther within your being. Continue to find your truth from within, and always allow your free-flowing creative spirit to bring forth its own life-supporting realities from the internal world that is enclosed within the darkness."

At this exact moment, the three glowing spheres of light alter their state of physical existence and manifest before me a living humanized form. The figure is male. He is clothed in a long, flowing white robe. The long staff he is holding with his right hand is made from purified gold. He has long white hair and a long white beard. The light that envelops his face is so intense that I cannot make out any of his finer features. He slowly begins to fade away into the brilliance of the room that surrounds him until eventually he is nowhere to be seen. I have a strong feeling coming from within assuring me that he really hasn't gone anywhere, that he is somehow throughout the whole room, in everything that is here. As I glance down, I am aware that Black Panther is now positioned to the left side of my body. He is letting me know, in his own way, that he will be travelling right beside me in all that I choose to do.

I also have an inner feeling that it is now time to return to my surface world. My journey into the depths of inner darkness has only just begun as there is still much for me to do before I will be able to live in this inner sanctuary all the time. I know that I can return here whenever I need to be centred within myself, or whenever I need to seek counsel from the creator of the light. I slowly move away from my enlightened side and begin to make my way toward the tunnel opening. I am now standing directly in the centre of the archway that separates the two totally different worlds, and I have one last look and feel of all that I have just experienced. Then, I turn and enter the tunnel and head back to where I have come from.

I proceed to move out into the large, cold, wet cavern once more. I acknowledge to myself how very much different this place is in compared to the marvellous environment I have just encountered. I cautiously make my way to the opening that will take me back to the surface.

I am now aware that the opening is directly above me. I stretch out my arms above my head, take a deep breath and then exhale, releasing myself from all processes of thought. My formless form begins to ascend through the hole in the Earth. I can feel the temperature within the layers of the Earth changing as I progress upward. I finally reach the surface and centre myself within the mound of ash that represents the remains of my physical embodiment. As I begin to move towards the heavens, my physical body begins to materialize into a new form of expression. I have returned as I had left – whole. Now I have a much different awareness of who I am and a higher vibrational frequency to move from.

I have found the inner doorway that leads to the *centre* of my being. It is the connecting passageway that brings together all the different levels of reality that simultaneously exist within each single expression of reality. It is all-encompassing. The doorway will always be open for me to step through. It is hidden and protected by the most powerful force I will ever encounter – my fear! It will only remain hidden from me if I get caught up in and react to my fears. Going into the heart of my fears, and moving through them with the purity of focus and clarity of intention of the fearless warrior, will ensure that I am able to move freely within this open doorway whenever I so choose.

I consciously step back through the doorway and enter into the ordinary human expression of reality. As my body regains its full structure, the flames that had engulfed me hastily commence to recede. Within seconds, I am once again standing in the centre of the bed of red-hot coals. I proceed to look all around. It is all so new, and yet it is all so much the same. I proceed to leave the bed of coals through the doorway and make my way over to where the hose is so I can wash the dirt off my feet. As I do, I hear the back door to the house open and a voice calls out, "Blaise, is that you?"

"Yes, it is."

"We have been looking all over for you. We thought you had left."

In a manner of speaking, he was right.

"No, ah, I've been right here."

"Are you coming in? There is still more we need to do in here."

"I'll be right there."

I continue to attend to my feet. I turn off the hose and quickly make my way toward the back door. I glance back one last time at the glowing coals, and then enter into another expression of reality.

✳

I was awakened early this morning by an internal dialogue that was originating from a facet of my Higher Self. He was subtly mentioning that it was time for me to be up and moving. He had mentioned that there were many gifts that would be available to me within the unfolding moments of my day, and that it was not important for me to be lying in bed when I could be out creating life-supporting experiences in my outer world. He had reminded me that a warrior is always on the move stalking death, and that he never waits for it to come to him. I quickly slipped on some warm clothes and headed out into the darkness of the early morning.

I have no idea what I am possibly going to find of value in the darkness, but I have already become aware of the fact that it is no good trying to figure these things out with my thoughts, for they are seldom ever right. My body is moving very slowly and loosely as I make my way through the suburban side streets. I have a feeling that the course I am being directed on will take me somewhere in the vicinity of a nearby golf course. As I proceed to align myself with my inner directional guide, I become more still and absent of all thought. I am passively observing and absorbing all of what surrounds me. I am continuing to wait patiently for the inner communication to arrive so that I might know why I am heading in this direction.

The Sun is gradually ascending from behind the trees that line the outer perimeter of the golf course, and as it continues to rise, I am treated to an early morning performance by Mother Nature. The delicate rays of sunlight dance their way through the openings between the trees and glisten on the dew covered bushes that line each side of the pathway. I then happen upon a man-made path that divides the wide open, sprawling golf course from an adjacent subdivision of densely spaced houses.

This path is very symbolic to me, in that it represents the very thin line I am choosing to walk within myself, the line that separates my inner and outer world. As I make my way through this section of my journey, I become aware that I will be able to walk this fine line within me as well. I will only need to be patient and wait for the process to unfold in the most supportive manner.

As I pass hastily along the man-made path, thoughts begin to stir inside my head, adding quite a different texture to the unfolding process. I am thinking about many different possible realities, all of which are not that important, mainly having to do with man's world – the world of power and greed. I cannot stop the sporadic dialogue going on inside my head. One moment is so quiet and peaceful, and the next is so uncontrollably noisy. I am creating an environment within me that is breeding anxiety, and my body starts to react to the non-supportive thoughts I have been creating. The further I walk, the tighter my stomach becomes. The area around my heart is becoming heavier, making my breathing a little more difficult. None of this is making any sense, for there is absolutely no structure to it. I have never experienced anything like this before.

As I round the far corner of a large storage building on the golf course, I can hear the familiar squawking voices of two Crows. They are sitting in one of the overhanging branches of an oak tree, directly above where I have to travel through. As I continue to move closer to where they are, I become aware that the noise level within my internal dialogue is growing louder and more deafening. I am also aware that the noise coming from the two Crows is becoming louder and more irritating to listen to. I don't particularly want to go anywhere near those birds. All I really want to do is find a nice quiet place where I can hang out for a while so I can re-establish an environment of peace and calm within my living expression. As much as I think about escaping, I know that I will have to confront all of what is unfolding before and within me.

I can't help but think of the two other occasions in the past when I had created a definite division between Crow and myself. Consequently, I had been attacked. I have just now become aware that since those two experiences, I have always reacted to whatever Crow has done with non-life-supporting judgments and criticisms. I have been holding on to illusionary beliefs about what Crow represents to me.

My first encounter with Crow was when I was moving through a workout session in my backyard. That was in 1980. I was dressed in a black outfit and doing a lot of sudden, erratic movements, jumping high into the air as well as rolling on the ground. As I was going through my unstructured routine, Crow came on the scene and perched on the outside edge of the gutter of my next door neighbour's rooftop. He didn't have anything to say at first. Rather, he just sat and observed all of my movements. I figured that he was trying to decide who or what I was.

I did a series of jumping sequences that obviously had not made a favorable impression on him. He started to squawk, and then he proceeded to dive bomb me three times. On one of his bombing runs, I could feel his right wingtip brush my left ear. I panicked! I started to react to all of his movements. He now had me right where he wanted me. He was in complete control, and I could tell that he was thoroughly enjoying every moment of it.

I had been completely blown off my centre, and there was no way that I was going to get back on. I was too caught up in my reactive thoughts to be able to deal with it all effectively.

We continued to spar with each other. It was all so futile though, for he had already won the match. I had known all along that he had won. I was only seeking to save face. I eventually gave up and went into the house. As I left the battlefield, I shouted angry words his way and shook my fist at him, telling him to "bugger off!" I just had to get the last word in. I couldn't stand the fact that I had been blown off my centre by a noisy Crow. My intellect couldn't handle not having the control or the power.

Not to be outdone, Crow positioned himself on top of the roof this time and started to squawk more frequently and louder. I took it that he was laughing at me, making fun of my inability to keep myself centred and focused on what I was doing. He was soon joined by two more Crows, and after he related to them all that had taken place, they too began to squawk. I could still hear them nearly two hours later laughing and carrying on about chasing away this so-called fearless warrior who was apparently taking martial arts so he could protect himself.

The second run-in I had with Crow was a few months ago – January 1985 – when I was out on an early morning run in a wooded area at the University.

I had only covered about twenty-five yards when I spotted three Crows sitting on the telephone wires, directly overhead of where I had to travel.

As I approached them, they started to squawk back and forth amongst themselves. Memories of my first experience with Crow flooded into my thought process. I could feel myself beginning to react inside. I knew that they knew I was reacting. I also knew that something was going to happen because of it, and I was right.

As I moved along under them, I could sense that one of them was planning a surprise for me. Just as I was finishing that thought, I heard a deafening squawk in my right ear. At the same time, I felt something graze the top of my head on the right side. It was that pesky Crow. He had swooped stealthily down upon me, hoping to catch me off guard and knock me off my centre. Well, he succeeded. I was so startled that I missed my stride and leapt over to the right side of the road, narrowly missing a large hole.

He returned to the wire, now directly in front of me. He was waiting for the next opportunity to try it again. Meanwhile, the three of them continually talked it up, giving each other support and encouragement. Again I passed under him. I was getting a strong feeling that he was getting ready to make another move, only this time there was a reverse twist to it. I had become attuned to his body rhythm and connected to his vibrational patterns. Just as he left the wire, I swung around and surprised him. This time it was his turn to react, and he called off his assault, quickly pulling back on his speed and climbing into the air, circling me and squawking louder.

He was slowly succeeding in pulling me off my centre. I was reacting to everything. I was very much aware that I was not in control of the situation, and so was he. Feeling my frustration building, I finally became so outraged that I yelled all sorts of nasty obscenities at him.

As I hastily continued on my way, I could still hear the three of them hooting it up back on the wire, obviously entertaining themselves at my expense. I dared not look back, for I had already lost the battle, and there was nothing I could do to change that.

As I make my way through the towering oak trees of the golf course, recalling my two previous encounters, I sense that I recognize one of the two Crows confronting me this time around. He is the one who visited me that day at the University, the one who had so much pleasure watching me squirm and react to his antics. As I begin to recall the deeper feelings I had on that day, I start to react. He begins dive-bombing me over and over again, first from the front, then from behind.

The other Crow lands on a low branch, content to watch and cheer on his friend. Both Crows are continually squawking back and forth to each other. They won't shut up! I can feel myself beginning to lose it all, just like the other two episodes. I can feel my body starting to respond negatively to the high level of anxiety I am creating within me. The palms of my hands are beginning to sweat. My heart beats faster. I know that I have to somehow pull myself together or this Crow will get the upper hand once again.

I eventually break free from the covering of the trees and enter into the wide-open space. Crow chooses to stay within the protection of the trees, still making all sorts of noisy chatter, presumably celebrating his second victory. I cannot deny it to him, for he is winning. My only saving grace is the fact that I have come out into a space where there is no overhead support for him to rely on.

When I am far enough out of his sight, and out of range of their noise, I decide to sit for a few moments to reflect back on all that has taken place. I proceed to ask my teacher from within, "Is it possible to attune myself to the spiritual essence of Crow so that I might receive the gift he has come here to offer?"

I wait only a few seconds before I receive an answer: "Crow represents your movements in the world of man. He shows to you your inner fears about your-self and how you see yourself and how you see the world outside you. In his actions, he reflects those movements that most typify man's world and keep him separated from himself. You react to that which you think is real, and thus, that which you create does control you. To confront Crow is to confront a darkened aspect of yourself. In confronting the illusion of what you think Crow repre-sents, you will discover the plain and simple truth."

I know the texture of what is presented. I cannot put it into words, but I know what the inner feeling is. I am now aware of what has to be done. I proceed to take a shortcut through the bushes, back across the open field to the place where I had last seen Crow. I consciously alter my state of awareness and proceed to align myself with the vibrational frequency he is constantly attuned to, letting him know that I want to meet with him, alone. I tune into the resonating ener-gies from his thought processes and allow them to act as a homing signal.

As I continue to move along on my journey, I can hear him in the distance, and know that he is waiting for me to arrive. As I get closer, I see that he has positioned himself in a small tree at the edge of the pathway, at the same place where the path acts as a divisional boundary between the subdivision and the golf course. The tree that he is sitting in is situated on the other side of the centre-line, in the section that represents man's world. I begin to move toward him much in the same manner as when we encountered each other about thirty minutes ago. I don't want to give myself away. I pull in all of my external energies, projecting nothing his way that might warn him about the change of tactics I am going to use. I know that he will still be moving from the same pro-grammed state as when we first confronted each other. I also know that he won't be open to feeling the subtle changes that are evident within me.

I had put out to Crow that I wanted our meeting to be one on one, and he is accommodating me. I am right on line with his thought patterns. I can now hear him chuckling to himself, and he begins to talk to himself, "Here comes this guy again. Boy, is he ever a sucker for punishment. I'll let him have it one more time. It'll be a treat to watch him react to my movements and then run away. I'll wait for him to get a little closer before I let him have it. Then I'll start squawk-ing really loudly. That always works to get him going. Once I have him off his centre, I'll go in and finish him off with a few good dive runs. I haven't had so much fun in a long time."

I now know that I have him right where I want him. He cannot possibly win. He is too trapped within his own thought process. He is walking right into his own death. He is basing everything he is going to do on what his memory will provide for him. I am well aware of the game he is playing, and how it works. All I need to do now is to wait patiently for the appropriate point of insertion, and then I will have him.

As I draw even closer to him, he begins his irritating squawking, but I do not alter my line of approach. I am heading on a collision course with him. I have only one plan of action, to seek out and destroy. He now begins to realize that I am not reacting to his tactics, and I once again begin to hear his internal dialogue, "What's going on here? Why isn't he reacting to what I am doing? He did before. What do I do now? My plan of action isn't working. Why not? I don't understand it. It worked before. What do I do now?"

He is beginning to repeat himself. He is losing his ability to control every-thing within himself. He is reacting now, not to what I am doing, but rather to what I am not doing.

I do not change my line of action. I am going into this confrontation with no line of action other than to be quiet in my thoughts and pure in my intention to observe all that unfolds. As I continue to move toward him, he is becoming more frantic within his internal movements. His reactionary thoughts are taking him around in circles. He is now in total destruct mode. I continue to reflect back to him all that he is – nothing. I am giving him no power, no thought. Without my total support, he is nothing. He has now given me all of his personal power, and I didn't have to do anything in order to get it except let him give it to me.

He decides to fly off and seek refuge in another tree about twenty feet away. He is in the process of trying to regain his stability, to see if he can somehow regain control. He is desperately searching for a way to shift everything back in his favor, but he is so limited by his conditional thoughts that he isn't able to see the way the experience is actually unfolding before him. I look directly into him as I continue to walk toward him. I don't dare take my eyes off him, not even to blink. He is just about at his end. There is nothing he can do now, and he knows it.

I am waiting patiently for the right moment to unleash a highly intensified energy blast his way. He is almost worn out from reacting to what has been happening around him. He has just about used up all of his own personal energies.

"Just a few seconds more. Wait, don't rush it. Steady, steady – now!" I proceed to direct all of my intense focus and pure, high quality intention right at his heart. In a flash, I release a tremendous surge of electrical energy precisely at the target point. He cannot escape. ZAP! A direct hit – feathers go flying in every direction. He spreads his wings as if he is going to take off, and then, without so much as a peep, he disappears. I have sent him into another dimension of reality. He did not die. Rather, he has been transformed into another vibrational frequency, where he will wait patiently until his next journey begins.

I am totally amazed at all that has taken place. I know that there is more to this experience than what I have witnessed with my (five) physical earthly senses. I know that it is not possible for me to eliminate another living expression of life and still be able to find my truth. How is it possible that I could have taken the living essence of Crow? I have to find out what happened to him. I sit down on the grass, close my eyes, still my thought process and ask an aspect of my Higher Self to clarify what happened.

Immediately, my inner voice responds, "Your brother, Crow, is not dead, for he has never lived. The journey you have been on this day has only been a projection of your innermost thoughts. They have been creatively manifested for you to witness first hand all of that which is within you and holds you securely in bondage. The elements of Nature support you in growing and in living. They will not support you in dying or in causing the unnecessary death of another living expression of life so that you may live. You cannot believe any of what you see with the use of your outer eyes, nor can you believe any of what you perceive with your other four outer senses. Look at all of that which has taken place outside you as an internal process of clearing, and then utilize your 'sixth' and 'seventh' senses in order to receive the gifts."

I am not at all sure what to make of it. It all seemed so real when it was happening. I know that I saw Crow disappear, and I know that I saw his feathers go flying in every direction. I know that I will have to find out what happened so that I can be absolutely sure within myself.

I travel over to the spot where I saw him disappear and look around for the scattered feathers. There are none to be found! The magic of Mother Nature is just far too powerful for me to totally grasp, but I know that I am not to question any of it.

I must listen to my inner teachers only and not trust anything that comes to me from my outer world; not even from myself. As I have been cautioned many times before by Raven, I am not to trust my inner teachers completely, either. I must take what I am told and feel the essence of my truth from it, and not ever follow it blindly.

I look into all that has been presented, searching for the gifts that lie hidden behind the illusions. I see that Crow represents my fears. I also see that when I create experiences in my outer world, I create them out of fear and not out of the pure joy of what their gifts may bring to me. I also see that I have always prejudged my experiences before they have arrived, instead of acknowledging them within their unfolding process.

I am now aware that each time I react to one of my fears, I feed it some of my personal energy and support it in growing in strength within me. As the internal (dialogue) pattern continues to be nurtured and to grow, I become weaker within my outer world self-expression. As a result, I will react more against it until eventually I will lose my internal centredness. I am now clearly aware of the amount of thought-power my fears actually have. As long as I continue to support my fears, they will end up controlling me, and they will determine what I will do and not do within my living expression. I have observed that when I react to my fears, they become stronger in their substance and louder in their presentation, thereby overriding all the other awarenesses I might have that are more positive and life-supporting on many different levels.

I am now seeing that the only way for me to rid myself of and completely dissolve away my fears, is to go right into the heart of them. I must align myself with the essence of what each of my fears truly represents within me, and then reflect back to it exactly what it projects – which usually turns out to be nothing. At the appropriate moment, I must pull back all thoughts into the quiet depths within my inner void and watch – put nothing out and react to nothing coming in. When my thought of fear begins to react to its own uncertainty, I will insert with the simple truth – observation through quiet – and it will automatically dissolve itself back into the darkened void from where it was first created.

"I see very clearly that all of my fears are created by me, and that all of my fears can only be dissolved by me!"

# CHAPTER 6

# STABILIZING THE INNER RELATIONSHIP

## June 3, 1985

A friend picks me up in his car at around noon, and we head out of town toward East Sooke Park. We are going to spend the afternoon as we have done many times in the past five months, usually hiking and enjoying Nature and sharing insights about the common world of man, and also about how each of us has been growing into our own light within the movements of our own inner spiritual journeys.

Our time together is always so richly rewarding. There is so much internal food to share and to come away with from our communications, for they are invariably centred within the higher vibrational frequencies. Their focal point is mostly in and around the different altered states of awareness that are possible to create within our daily experiences. We are brothers in the sense that we share the same life pathway – although we have different living expressions – each heading toward a spiritual connection of the highest quality within ourselves.

On the way to the countryside, I express to my friend that I have been experimenting further with consciously altering my states of awareness into the higher realms of expression, and that I have been acknowledging more often the unconscious process behind those altered states. I also mention that I am not at all satisfied with the purity of the information I have been obtaining in regard to the many diverse relationships that co-exist and interact within my being.

This morning, while I was having an internal dialogue with an aspect of my Higher Self, I had been informed that it would be possible to attune myself to the two predominant facets of my Earthly Mind that are the foundational building blocks from which all other aspects of my being are created. These two facets are primarily responsible for nurturing the creative process of thought within my physical form. They are also responsible for the destructive nature of thought within my physical expression. Therein lies the danger. It was said that the particular altered state I would need to create within me could possibly have non-life-supporting side effects unless I was totally assisted by the outside world during the course of my venture. I would only be able to experience it fully if I was aided by someone who was willing to support me in finding out more about myself – someone who would be able to unconditionally accept me, regardless of what I might choose to do.

I had been informed that if I proceeded into this altered state with the right focus and the purest of intention, I wouldn't need to concern myself with the outcome. I would be free enough within all of my movements to live the experience totally as it was unfolding. The altered state that I would be aligning myself with would require me to walk a very thin line between sanity and insanity. I would have to cross over that invisible line many times in order to receive the pertinent information I was looking for.

I have already been warned by my inner teachers that, in the world of man, there are many institutions filled with individuals who have crossed over that line and entered into an illusionary, but very real to them, world of ever-changing abstract thought of what reality is all about. These sane individuals have failed within their endeavors to return to the supportive side of the line where constructive thought plays a meaningful part in their self-creativeness. They will remain stationed there, forever unconsciously formless, until such time as they can access a way back by using either their own internal awarenesses or the assistance of another person from their outside world. (This person would have to have the ability to consciously transcend the limits of his own structural fabric, so that he could purposely move within his own disillusioning living expression and guide that person back through the alternating, bridging doorway, back into a supportive alignment within the normalized vibration that is consistent with the world of man.)

It has also been presented that, for some time now, my inner teachers have been attuning me to the many different vibrational frequencies that are accessible within the altered states. They have been doing this so I would not have to concern myself with consciously entering into them on my own initiative. I have not been at the appropriate level of awareness, within all of my expressions, to be able to successfully enter into these altered states without causing further imbalances within my being on the many different levels – mentally, physically and emotionally.

My inner teachers have been protecting me by slowly introducing me to these multi-dimensional altered states, so I would be able to use them more functionally and creatively within my daily movements. It has been set, from the beginning, that once I have been attuned to a particular altered state, I have also been given the key component in the structural alignment of the necessary vibrations within myself, to recreate, at any time, that particular altered state, or any other altered state that might have the same common vibrational frequency within its composition. Once I have become aware of that structural alignment, I am able to return to that particular state of awareness whenever I choose. The manner through which I have been continuously introduced to, and supported within, the higher levels of awareness has been very convenient for me, in that I haven't had to do anything except be absolutely pure within my intention to find my inner truth.

The transitional stage that I desire to move within and explore today will require that I move within the deeper levels of my being and set up a conscious division between the two main formless aspects of my Earthly Mind structure. It has already been clearly put forth that once I enter into this altered state, I might not be able to return to my current form of living expression. Or that if I do return, I might not be able to function adequately within the realities of my own worlds as I know them to be. It has also been mentioned that I should move into this experience with the purity and openness of the fearless warrior, and pursue my everlasting creative living expression by stalking death.

As we take the turn off that will take us to the parking lot where the hiking trail begins, I ask my friend if he is willing to assist me in my undertaking, and only support me if I ask for his help. I tell him that his greatest gift to me will be if he can remain totally free of all thought in regard to what I am choosing to do. I mention that I am not at all sure within myself as to what is going to take place. I also mention that I will be all right as long as everything remains clear and free-flowing between the two of us. He agrees that he will be open to doing whatever I ask of him, and that he will support me on my journey in any way he can.

As the car moves along the narrow road, we talked about a course of action. He will follow me along whatever physical path I choose to take as the day unfolds. He will stay close at all times, always keeping me in his vision but remaining far enough away to give me plenty of room to expand the experience however I see fit. He also says that he will make sure I am not interfered with by any other person who might happen along the path. He assures me that I will be given every opportunity to look deeper within myself so that I might take another small step closer toward the *centre* of my being.

With all the outside necessities taken care of, I slowly begin attuning myself in the manner that I had been given during this morning's discourse with an aspect of my Higher Self. I had been given only the first step of how to induce this new altered state to ensure that I do not willfully take control of the unfolding experience. It will be enough to take me to my inner threshold, and then my inner teacher will direct the flow of movement from there. I will be required to surrender my entire being unto my higher vibrational self, and then move within the thin veils of reality that hold its composition together so that I might be able to reconnect with it on the other side on a whole different level of movement.

I close my eyes. I proceed to take a few long breaths, all the while disintegrating the outer form of my physical being, moving deeper within my inner darkened void, totally removing myself from all want and desire for control of the unfolding experience. I begin to propel myself deeper and deeper within the astral realms of reality until I finally arrive on the threshold of my creative process – an open doorway to move through. I am now teetering on the edge of two distinctively opposing vibrational frequencies that exist on either side of this forever-shifting portal. I release myself from being directed to either one of them, and I begin to freefall through the invisible boundary line that separates the two. All is quiet and serene. I am now moving within the expressional avenues of pure creative thought.

There is a sudden jolt as I am reinstated back into the confines of my structural body. My physical form begins to shake and vibrate uncontrollably as I am quickly trying to readjust to the sudden in-surge of high voltage energy I have brought back within me to this lower level of existence. I open my eyes. Everything around me is now very much different. I am feeling as though I am still positioned within the *centre* point of that threshold, only this time I can consciously feel it within the limitless confines of my skull. I have the distinct feeling that I am divided precisely in half, and that each half is very much in control of my perceptual images of thought, pertaining directly to those things that surround me. At the exact same time, I am clearly aware that I am also removed from as well as part of these two divided aspects of myself. I am somehow able to remain totally whole within the separateness of who I am.

A dialogue now begins to unfold within my internal thought process. There appears to be an active voice present within each of the two separate divisions. One has clearly identified himself as being my Higher Self. He is the aspect of my being that is the free-flowing creative process – that part of me that knows everything. He has all the universal information within his grasp. He is also the one who allows me to move between all the other dimensions of reality within my earthly expression. The other voice has identified itself as being my lower self. He is the aspect of my being that is only functional within the limitations of my five earthly senses. He is totally limited, within his movements, to earthly experiences. Thus, he is limited by time and space.

The chatter taking place within me is now beginning to increase in its tempo and sharpness. There is a definite power struggle going on for control over my entire living expression on the physical earthly plane. The dialogue is having an overall effect on the stability of my internal vibration. I am beginning to get very irritated with the amount of noise going on. I find that I am not able to bring an end to it.

I have just been reminded by my inner teacher that I cannot interfere with the two interacting voices in any way. This journey has been set up so that I am only an observer. I am being given a once in a lifetime opportunity to witness what normally takes place within my thinking process: a dialogue that continuously unfolds within, but one that I do not ever hear because I am usually so caught up in all the sensual stimulation within my outer world.

The confrontation is building to a point where my lower self isn't able to handle what my Higher Self is presenting to it. In his frustration, my lower self wants to literally peel back the top section of my cranium so he can escape. He knows that he is being shown the truth, and that he will have to be accountable for all of his irrational behavior patterns. He doesn't want to take responsibility for what he has done within his past movements. My lower self is refusing to give up ownership of my living expression, and the only defense he is able to use is his repetition of the words, "Stop it! Stop it!"

"Why?" asks my Higher Self.

"I'm very concerned. This isn't at all healthy for me. I don't like what you are trying to do to me. Let me out of here!"

"Deal with it, then. You know you cannot run away. There is nowhere for you to run. You are the one who has brought all this upon yourself. Now deal with it. You cannot hide from it, for this is the reality of all that you stand for. You are all that you are trying so desperately to get away from."

Fearful and panic-stricken, my lower self begins to run to wherever he can in order to escape, however temporarily. He doesn't know where to go, and he doesn't really care. He just wants to run so he can remove himself from the non-supportive environment he has created. He is deathly afraid that he does not have sufficient power within himself to direct the flow of the proceedings that are unfolding. And he is right!

As my friend's car comes to a gradual stop in the parking lot, a wave of fear begins to run rampant throughout my entire being. I am afraid that I won't be able to balance myself sufficiently, because of my internal divisions, to be able to move on my own initiative. I am also fearful that I will surely stumble and fall if I attempt to move on my way, and that the people who are in the parking lot might react unfavorably to all that is taking place within and all around me.

"Oh, God! What will everyone think?" replies my lower self.

"Is that all you can ever think of, your self-importance?" says my Higher Self.

I eventually become focused enough within my being to remove myself from the car.

I position myself next to some of the small trees that line the perimeter of the lot. I look out into the deep space in front of my vision, not really focusing on any one object in particular. I am totally involved with just listening to the eye-opening dialogue being generated from within my thought processes. I cannot believe how loud it is or how intense it is becoming. My lower self is extremely upset. He is continuously throwing out all sorts of non-supportive thoughts, thoughts that don't even support him in being around. (Before this encounter took place, I had no conscious idea that this degree of dialogue even went on inside me.)

The noise from this confrontational discourse is temporarily interrupted by the welcome arrival of my inner teacher. I proceed to ask him, "What is the purpose behind this manner of dialogue?"

He responds, "It is about power and control within your earthly movements."

I ask, "Where did all that aggressive nature and perversity come from?"

He goes on to say, "It has always been within you. You had not been attuned to it before now, for you had been asleep within your conscious movements on the earthly plane. The voice of the one who is full of anger is that part of you who had controlled your outer world expressions for the many years prior to that moment when you had awakened within yourself. He is strictly concerned with sensual stimulation from that which he perceives around him. His main focus is on having power-domination within all facets of your living expression."

With these few words having been spoken, he recedes once again into the deeper inner void of quiet, only to be replaced by the chattering voices of the other two.

My friend gets out of the car and moves slowly across my vision. He is wearing a pair of black warm-up pants and a bright red sweater partially exposed under a black squall jacket. Attached to his jacket is a foldaway hood that is loosely draped over his head. I have created a symbolic picture (within my mental process) of what my friend represents within my conscious reality. He is the physical manifestation of one part of the dialogue going on within me. I see him as playing the role of my self-importance, a facet of my lower self, in that he is totally covered in black and his face is almost entirely hidden from view. I also see him this way because of our prearranged agreement, in that he is going to be following me along the path to make sure everything is kept under control and running smoothly. I see that the hidden red sweater is representative of my inner spiritual guidance, the higher aspect of my being that unconditionally supports me in making this journey into the far and darkened corners of my inner domain.

I am now beginning to feel the effects of the high levels of anxiety that have been building within my body since I first began to hear this frantic dialogue. I am beginning to experience some weakness in my legs. I know that I either have to start moving so I can begin to dissipate this resistance buildup, or else sit down and become totally consumed by it. I know that I have to be on the move. I ask my friend, "Shall we go? I need to get moving."

He replies, "I'm right behind you."

My lower self begins to freak out at that suggestion. He begins screaming within the confines of my inner audio frequency, and then proceeds to create a new dialogue within himself: "Oh, No! Now, how am I ever going to handle this one? What did you go and do that for? Are you crazy or something? How am I ever going to make my way past those people without falling flat on my face? I'm never going to make it, and it will be all your fault. Oh, I know. I will look down at my pants and make like I am fixing them, so even if I do happen to falter a little, they won't suspect anything."

I am now beginning to feel very unstable within all of my movements. My mental, physical, and emotional equilibriums have been shifted slightly as a result of my initiation into this alterative process. I am feeling as though I have been divided into three separate identities, each of which is a presently functional living expression of who I am in part, but not wholly, within my Earthly Mind structure. It is difficult to put the living expression of this altered state into words. It is as though I am constantly in transition between being one way in my expression and another, never absolutely sure where I belong. I am not altogether sure whether I am going to be able to speak or to move, for there does not appear to be any homeostatic stability within my being. Perhaps there will be when I become fully adjusted to this new state of being. Or maybe there never will be! I am not at all sure. I am beginning to wonder if I should indeed be concerned about any of this.

Once again, from within the depths of my darkened inner void, my inner teacher begins to speak, "Trust completely in the unfolding process. Show no resistance within your movement and you will move through it all unharmed. React to any part of it and you will become lost forever within the unfolding illusionary realities that are continually being created within your thoughts. All of what is unfolding before you and within you is but an illusion, yet it is so frightfully real as well."

I finish adjusting my pants and begin to walk, heading toward the entrance to the trailhead some twenty feet away. I manage to maneuver myself so that I arrive at the entrance without losing my composure. I figure that if I can make it this far, then everything else will be simple. I am sure that I can handle anything that comes my way. This reasoning is coming from my lower self. He is scheming again, within his own predictable structure and form of expression, how he can get complete control over the unfolding experience, and how he can best maintain it once he has it.

My journey is now evolving on its own momentum. I head up the trail and my friend follows behind, keeping his distance so as to support me but not hinder my movements. My lower self is continuously nattering about losing control, having control, and protecting the image of who he thinks he is, an image that really doesn't exist, except within his own destructive thought patterns. Nevertheless, he is forever trying to get my Higher Self to support his reality concerning that image. Whenever my Higher Self confronts my lower self on any issue he is presenting, my lower self is always quick to react to what is said and he tries to run away so he won't have to answer to the truth.

Every once in a while, I hesitate on my journey and look back along the trail, and there is the outer world image of my self-importance hanging out on the trail, making sure everything is okay. He wants to keep strict control over how everything is developing. Whatever I see, and whenever I stop along the way, my internal self-importance always wants to create an illusion of what he thinks is taking place, so he can control it, to make sure that the story he makes up supports and protects the illusionary image he has of himself.

I come to a section along the route where I can hear the intensity of inner conversation building in reference to "stopping everything right now." It is mainly my lower self who initiates the subject matter. I can hear him saying, "I can stop all of this any time I want."

I am well aware that my two legs are still moving in the same direction and at the same speed. There is no visible sign that he can indeed stop any of it, even if he truly wants to. By saying that he can stop all of it, he is in effect stating that he is in control of the texture of the evolving experience. My lower self clearly states without any hesitation, "I'm in complete control of what's happening, and I feel no need at this time to stop. When and if I decide that it is necessary to stop this whole process, then that will be the most appropriate time to do so, and not before."

I begin to hear voices coming from outside me, somewhere up along the trail. They appear to be heading in my direction. My lower self begins to panic inside, screaming, "My image, my image! What will happen if these people know me? I might have to talk to these people. I don't want to talk to anyone. I just want to get out of here. What would I say to them? What are they going to do when they get here? I have to get off this trail and hide myself until after they've gone. That's it! That's what I'll do."

"No!" says my Higher Self. "You must stop your erratic behavior and confront this issue. You cannot run."

A few seconds pass by. I am still on the trail. My body is not moving. My Higher Self has momentarily taken over control of the proceedings. Along the trail comes a man who is carrying his young daughter on his shoulders. They appear to be supportively connected and flowing harmoniously. As he says, "Hello," the noise in my head vanishes, leaving me in a state of welcome quiet. I acknowledge his friendly gesture as he disappears behind me. I dare not look once he has passed. I breathe an internal sigh of relief, and as I do, the chattering utterances of my lower self return, all excited that he has handled the situation, and that it all worked out just as he thought it would.

I continue on my way walking very slowly, for I can now hear two more voices approaching from in front of me. I am beginning to react in much the same fashion as I had with the man and the little girl. My Higher Self again takes over control so that my lower self has to deal with it. Just as before, my lower self decides to disappear from the line of action. As the people approach, I am feeling much calmer inside knowing that my lower self has gone. I now know that this encounter will be no problem, for there is no fragmentation within my being. A woman appears from around the side of a tree, dragging behind her a very uncooperative young boy. Presumably they belong with the other two. The woman is displaying great patience with the way the boy is behaving. She wants to keep it all together, just like me. The two of us are very closely linked on this issue. As they come closer, I smile and extend my silent, supporting acknowledgement of what she is doing, and I verbalize a friendly "hello" as she passes and slowly disappears up the trail.

As I continue on my way, I am becoming aware that I have been holding my body rather rigidly in my movements. My Higher Self also picks up on it and begins to speak, "What would it take to let go of your physical form and stagger and stumble a little?"

Defensively, my lower self blurts out, "No way. And lose control?"

My Higher Self pauses and then gently says, "Try it. It will be good for you. You will still be in control. Go ahead. You can always return to the way you are now."

So after a few seconds deliberation, I feel the unyielding framework of my body begin to loosen. I am becoming soft and flowing, then back to hard and rigid, back to soft and flowing, then back to hard and rigid. My lower self sees that he is maintaining control, regardless of what he chooses to do. At this precise moment, I pivot around and see, standing on the trail with his back to me, the image of my outer world self-importance. I want to yell at him, "Look, self-importance, leave me alone. I would be a hell of a lot better off without you and your illusionary image." Then I remember that I am only an observer during this experience.

The inner discourse continues. My Higher Self asks, "When is it all going to stop? When are you going to take the veil down that you are hiding behind?"

My lower self, always wanting to maintain control, begins to respond, "I can stop this any time I want. I can stop it all right now if I choose."

"What is stopping you from doing that right now?"

"Nothing is stopping me."

"Well then, do it."

"I don't have to do what you tell me. I'm in control here!"

"Are you?" asks Higher Self.

"Yeah, I am."

"Well then, stop. I demand that you stop now."

I look all around me. I see that I have situated myself in the centre of a large standing growth of leafless Alder trees, comfortably supported by an odd shaped tree that aligns almost perfectly with the contours of my physical form. I am looking around to see if there is any symbolic reality that this place might represent in regard to the unfolding conversations within my thought processes.

I am aware that I am enclosed within a prison-like structure made up by the surrounding trees. The trees signify an expression of death to me. They are bare, exposed to all the outside elements. A picture is beginning to take form. The truth is slowly coming to the forefront of my awareness. It is now very clear that I am still in prison within the restrictive realities of my lower self, and that I will have to come to terms with that fact before I will be able to proceed any further along on my journey.

I begin to look at the trees more closely. What else can they show me? I can see that they are like bars that line a prison cell, and that they are restricting me in my living expression, forcing me to live within their confines. I have limited freedom. They are so closely spaced that there is no room for me to move freely within my creative movements. I feel as though I cannot stay here much longer, for the reality of my new discovery is beginning to affect me. I am feeling very nauseous. My head is now starting to throb. I feel that I am getting closer to the nerve impulse that controls the behavior patterns of my lower self.

The ensuing dialogue of my Higher Self continues, "Are you ready to get off your power trips now?"

"I can hold off for as long as I have to," replies lower self. "It's no big deal to me, you know what I mean? I'll still have control when this confrontation is over and done with."

"Yes, perhaps you will, but what about the next encounter, and the one after that. Will you always be able to avoid answering to the truth of what is really going on?"

My lower self commences to panic, for he knows all too well that he cannot stand up to or defeat the vibration of truth. It is too pure for him. He is totally aware that he has limits within his movements on this plane. He is just hoping that on one else will find out about his limitations. He is slowly beginning to crumble within his functioning abilities. He replies sharply, "Yeah, sure, I can handle anything. Anything you care to throw at me, I can handle, and for as long as you want to throw it at me. Come on, what are you waiting for?"

My lower self is now trying to entice my Higher Self into playing his game. My lower self continuously creates illusions within his inner world through his interactions with outer world stimulation. The more stimulation he can generate, the more power he can accumulate. Likewise, the less stimulation he receives from the world outside himself, the less power he is able to produce.

My Higher Self responds, "When are you going to stop all this nonsense? I know what your game is, and I am not going to get involved."

My lower self quickly reacts, "Okay! Okay! I'll stop it! I'll stop it!"

He is becoming more angry and frustrated within his verbal expression, for he knows that he cannot possibly win at the game he is playing. He again begins to speak, "Are you satisfied now?"

"Is this truth that you speak?"

"Sure, don't you believe me? I can assure you that I'm telling the truth."

"The purity of truth shall always prevail. We shall soon see if indeed you have spoken the truth."

I begin to hear more voices coming toward me on the trail. Once again my lower self begins to lose his sense of structural balance within his expression, and he panics! While my lower self is reacting to what is happening, I glance over my left shoulder and see the image of my outer world self-importance standing on the path above me, lurking in the background.

In a panic, my lower self says, "I need to get off this path, and I've got to do it now before it's too late. Let's see, where can I go? Where can I hide? Oh, no – there is nowhere to go. There are only these Alders, everywhere I look, all around me." He is generating fear within himself. The very thing he thrives on from his outside world is the very thing he is creating to destroy himself with.

In a rather stern voice, my Higher Self delivers, "So, you stopped it, did you? Now we both see the quality of truth that you speak. You know that you cannot possibly hide from the purity of truth, for it knows no boundaries."

Not liking what is being said, my lower self quickly responds, "Let me out of here. You can't stop me. I'm in control around here."

My body won't move. No matter what my lower self says, my body remains stationary. My Higher Self has taken over. He is now in full control, and quietly states, "It is now time for you to look more closely at the situation you have created within your irrational movements. You have been running from this, and everything else you have ever created, for far too long."

"I don't want to listen to anything you have to say. I'm getting out of here."

"There is nowhere for you to go. It is all right here, right now. This is all there is. We could work this through together, you know. Are you prepared to give it a try?"

My lower self hesitates for a moment, knowing that he has to move fast, for the external voices on the outer trail are getting nearer. Within his own frustration, he says, "Okay, okay, I agree."

My body moves slightly, just enough so I can change my postural alignment. My lower self now begins to fidget in his thought processes and his body movements. My Higher Self is containing him within the unfolding of the situation. I quickly turn around and pick two leaves from a sword fern conveniently growing next to the tree I am leaning against. I turn around and greet the people as they file past me on the narrow walkway.

My lower self quietly says, "Whew, I made it."

I look back just in time to see the people gradually disappearing over the top of the rise. They are making their way beyond my outer world self-importance, who is continuing to stand on the trail, patiently waiting for me to make my move.

I look down at the two leaves I have in my hands. I acknowledge that one symbolizes death, while the other symbolizes life. I turn around in a complete circle, and I fully recognize the prison walls that surround me.

My Higher Self asks my lower self, "Are you willing to work together and look honestly at all that arises?"

My Higher Self has firmly decided that there is not going to be any movement taking place within my physical body until such time there is a mutual commitment to finding and living the truth. My lower self checks out all of his possible alternatives and acknowledges that there is no escape for him. He sees that he is powerless. He now has no other choice. He reluctantly surrenders and agrees to move toward full cooperation with my Higher Self. With that agreement, I continue on my way.

My Higher Self knows that all things on this plane are more illusion than they are real. He accepts them in the light of their present moment of creation, and within the roles they play in manifesting the unfolding experience. He light-heartedly laughs and then addresses my lower self, "Why are you holding on so tightly to all those things you have done in your living expression, and to all those things you hope to do? They are all just illusions that you put value on. And for what reason? The joke is on you, my friend, for life is an illusion."

The voice of my transient inner teacher once again ascends through the darkness, this time with a brief explanation of what has just taken place, "There is a definite place on this plane for your lower self. He is very functional and necessary on the physical plane, for he is responsible for the creation of, and subsequent utilization of, those forms that already exist within the earthly plane. The Higher Self is directly connected to the universal knowing, and knows the purity of all of that which is within the earthly plane. Both of these aspects are important and vitally necessary in order that you might move towards your full creative realization. They must harmonize and work together or else all that you do will be futile. As long as they are struggling with each other, you shall remain divided on all levels within your being. When they are moving harmoniously in all ways, as one within their movements, then you will become and maintain your own individual wholeness."

As my inner teacher's voice withdraws, the voice of my Higher Self begins a dialogue directed at me, "All that you have done in this lifetime has been centred around your relationship with your self-importance. You have continuously blamed others for your own misfortunes within those circumstances you have gotten yourself into, and also within the experiences you have created for yourself. You have never once taken full responsibility for any of what you have done. All that you have ever focused your attention on and toward has been with power and greed as your motivator."

My lower self does not want to hear any of what is being presented to him. Like the elusive and evasive snake, he begins to slither away. My Higher Self seizes and maintains control of their interaction by presenting him with the plain and simple truth. My lower self struggles unsuccessfully to break free of the hold that has been securely wrapped around him. He is quickly using up all his personal energy defending himself. My Higher Self is doing nothing. He is patiently waiting for my lower self to tire himself out. Suddenly, my lower self awakens to the full realization that he is consuming himself, and that he has lost in all of his power-hungry endeavors. He must now answer to the truth, for he has no more energy with which to fight.

At this point in the action, my friend approaches and asks how I am. I quickly respond, "I'm fine. Everything is okay."

He mentions that he is going to go ahead on the trail, and that he will wait for me at the next junction. He passes by and carries on.

I continue to climb up a steady incline for a short time, feeling that there is something of significance to see at the top. As I break over the crest, I see my friend up ahead symbolically moving as my outer world spiritual guide. He is now wearing his bright red sweater out in full view, like a beacon. Knowing that he is ahead of me watching out for and protecting me assures me that my lifetime pathway is already marked out, and that it is clearly and brightly illuminated so that I might easily find my way to the full realization of my own internal purity of truth.

I am now beginning to get a full sense of what this whole experience is about. It is a journey into the *centre* of my self. It is a place where I am able to witness firsthand, in a removed and observational way, the finer intricacies of the mental processes that continuously unfold within my being. It is also about truth, the truth about how I have chosen to live up until now, and also about my truthfulness and honesty toward myself, within myself.

Within all the seriousness of what I have been seeing and observing, I am also aware that it is rather humorous at the same time. I begin to laugh. I now feel that I am starting to get the true purpose behind the teachings that I have been receiving out here. As I am engaged in amusing myself, reflecting back on the circumstances that have passed by, my inner teacher simply states, "Only the true fool is able to see the inside humour that lies within the illusions of life. It is by that humour alone that he is able to use his magic to bring about the creation of new life within all of his experiences."

My life is beginning to look a whole lot less complicated within its ever-changing expressions. As I make my way along the trail beside my friend, still internally chuckling to myself about all that I have seen, I externally verbalize my insight in a humorous tone, "Life is a joke, of sorts, and the laugh is on me!"

As I move ahead of him, I return to my internal observations. I am now choosing to look at my friend differently as well. I no longer see him as either my outer world self-importance or my spiritual guide. I see that he and I are actually one in the same, two facets of my self, no different than the two internal voices that have been dialoguing. I now feel that I am on the path to becoming whole within myself, bringing the two major divisions of my life's expression together under the guidance and leadership of truth.

My lower self is still trying to get out of the agreement he made earlier. He is starting to create new stimulation from old stuff, hoping that my Higher Self will engage him in his meaningless conversation. My Higher Self is wise to his antics and does not choose to involve himself in his useless, non-life supporting dialogues.

As I continue to hike along the trail, I eventually arrive at a crossroad where I have to choose one of four possible routes. I feel a compelling urge to take the trail up to the top of Mt. Maguire. Being clear in my choice, I begin my ascent. More things come up about honesty, finding the humour in all things, spontaneity of my movement, and the relinquishing of my self-importance. Many memories from days gone by re-enter my thought processes. I am now able to shed a new and supportive light on them, as to what they truly represented. There is an overall feeling of peace and harmony within my being. I am able to feel many subtle changes occurring on many different levels.

The climbing is becoming more of a challenge as the ground becomes steeper. My body knows exactly where it wants to go. There is no hesitation within my physical movements. I am aware of, at a much deeper level within me, what lies ahead along this trail. I will just have to be patient and wait for it all to arrive.

I begin to verbalize within my internal channels more of the enlightening insights I am seeing in regard to my life: "I see that there is no place for me to go outside myself to find the necessary information I need to fully realize all that I am. It is time for me to accept, unconditionally, all of those multi-dimensional aspects of reality that exist within me as creative gifts of who I truly am. There is nothing at the end of the path, for there is no path. I am the path as it unfolds within me. My life journey is always created in the here-and-now. It's all so simple, so very simple. The truth, all truth, is inside! What could possibly be at the end of this path I am on, heading up the mountain, if I am seeing all this so clearly now? Is this all there is?"

My journey continues. As I am slowly climbing higher, more things come and go until I begin receiving instructions from my inner teacher to take the next turnoff to the right. I am becoming anxious in my movements. I begin to externally verbalize more of my inner thoughts, "Could this possibly be the moment I have been waiting so long for – the moment of my truth? Could this possibly be the place where I am going to find out everything?"

I proceed to climb up and position myself so that I am sitting cross-legged under a sprawling branch of a scrubby evergreen tree. This tree is magically growing out of the top of a massive rock. I close my eyes and begin travelling inwardly, removing myself totally from my outside world, for I am seeking to find the true purpose behind being directed to this particular spot. Seconds pass before an inner teacher's voice presents itself. Within the purity and sincerity of all that it represents, I hear: "Self, meet self."

I am startled by what I hear, and yet I am not at all surprised. My internal dialogue continues, "Is it really that simple? Is the inevitable ending/beginning all right here? I am sitting here at the centre of the universe. I am all alone. My Self and my self, both Higher and lower. I am on top of the universe. I am in the middle of the universe. I am the ever-unfolding universe. It is all just one big joke, and the laugh is on me. It is all so profound, yet so humorous as well."

I begin to laugh out loud. I am feeling extremely light within my bodily form. I am aware of more subtle changes occurring within the deeper levels of my being.

As I am sitting here entertaining myself, I catch a glimpse of my friend as he leisurely strolls by. He sits nearby, and as he does, I begin to internally verbalize more of my insights, giggling inside as I do, "All that I have ever thought of as being important really isn't anything at all."

My enthusiasm is now bubbling over. I am beginning to laugh more openly, and my friend begins to join me, not at all sure what he is chuckling about. I proceed to engage my friend in a dialogue, "It's all so simple. *Why* is my next question."

With a slightly serious tone, my friend replies, "Be cautious of the question that begins with why, for it is much like the never-ending circle, in that it will surely trap you and keep you spinning forever, looking for the illusionary answer."

After a short pause, I respond, "Ah, I get it. It's to find the peace in the moment of creation. That's the only real momentary flash of truth that ever exists, only as it is creatively unfolding."

I begin to ponder over his statement about finding the answer to the question *Why?* My thought processes are now becoming more active. They are enthusiastically rising to meet the challenge. Suddenly, I am inundated with all sorts of solutions, none of which appear to be of the significant vibration to present to me the simple truth.

We both continue enjoying short outbursts of laughter, each of us, in our own unique way, celebrating the simplicities of life's expression. Time appears not to exist as I continue acknowledging the many insights that drift through my thought process.

After spending some time on top of the mountain, enjoying the panoramic views and insightful conversation with my friend, it is now time to be heading down the mountain, back into the vacillating connection I have in man's world. As my friend slowly disappears down the trail, I mention that I will be following in a few minutes. I decide to wait a little longer before heading back.

I commence my descent, feeling at peace with all that I have seen within the depths of my being. A totally different perspective of my inner and outer world is presenting itself as I continue to move along. I am replaying the tapes of this entire experience, wondering whether this experience has closed off an old way of living for me, or opened a whole new way of expressing my creative energies.

Will I ever have to return to that old way of expressing myself in my outer world? I see that I don't have to live there any more, that I do indeed have a choice of how I choose to live. I am now choosing to fully attune myself to this new altered state. I shall now make this the base structure from which I will move and continue to express myself in my outer world. As I proceed along on my life journey, I am continually opening myself up to more and more of who I truly am. I am feeling more conscious of all that is around me and more alive within my acknowledgement of the simplicities of life.

Life is presenting to me a whole new ray of sunshine, showering me with constant love and support. I am now seeing that it is time for me to take all that I have been seeing and hearing and integrate it wholly within every facet of my living expression. Otherwise, all that I have been exposed to will be meaningless.

I am clearly seeing *what* is of importance to me in my life, as well as *who* is important. I know, definitely, that my self-importance is no longer important. Being truthful and honest to myself within the present unfolding moment is of the highest priority. Is it truly possible for me to be absolutely free from the prisons I have ever created within my thought processes? Can this indeed be attainable? I see that it is a very real possibility, but only if I choose it to be that way. I can create anything I want within my patterns of thought to aid me in finding my truth. It is so simple when I look seriously at it all with the right intention and the proper focus.

I am standing, lightly leaning against the post that lies in the centre of the crossroad – where I originally made the choice to climb Mt. Maguire – contemplating the symbolic significance of where I am. I am beginning to hear a familiar chirping voice. As I swing my head around, I come eye-to-eye with Little Bird, and he cheerfully commences to speak: "Today I sing my song for you, my friend, for I have heard on the higher levels of communication that you have learned the true meaning behind the experiences you have created for yourself this day. As a result, you are now much freer within yourself to move closer to your purest inner vibrations. Take your new awarenesses back into your daily unfolding worlds, and allow them to aid you in transcending those life-threatening limitations you have imposed upon yourself. I would wish to caution you though, with all that you have attuned yourself to, it will be utterly useless to you unless you go back down into the dark depths of your being and resolve all the judgments you have ever brought against yourself and against others. As you continue to do this, you shall open yourself inwardly to the limitless possibilities within the higher vibrations. You have only just begun a new journey, my friend. Remember, the purest expression of truth can only be served in silence. I shall continue to observe you whenever you are moving within the life-supporting elements of Nature. You are being well looked after and cared for in all that comes your way and in all that you choose to do. Do not ever trust any of that which you have seen, or any of that which you will continue to see. For if you do, it will surely imprison you within your thought processes."

As he is finishing his words, my internal vibration begins to resonate at a much higher frequency. I am fully aware that my inner sensitivities are now coming to the surface of my physical expression, generating outwardly more warmth and love from my radiating heart and filling my whole being with a sensation of lightness. A new and powerful reality is unfolding from within. I am feeling a clearly defined merging of energies within my total consciousness. I am removing another layer of who I am not. I have an inner desire to respond to his communication.

Without further hesitation, I begin, "I would like to thank you for the support you have given me whenever I have had the honor of your presence while I have moved within the free-flowing creative expression of Mother Nature. Your words of wisdom have always been inspirational and of benefit in allowing me to align myself with the purest expression of my inner truth. I have only now become aware that I will no longer need your services or your support, for I have been fully awakened to the reality that you are a source of guidance that exists entirely outside me. Within that conscious realization, you have now become a trap for me. As long as I continue to align myself with you, I will not be able to move freely within the deeper levels of my being. I am now seeing, as I have never see before, that everything outside me is an illusion that is there to stop me from completing my inner journey to the level I desire to attain. I am now seeing that I must retreat to within the darkened depths of my inner void – to pull back from all the expressions of life outside me – in order to find the purity of my own inner truth. As I am now free of you, you in turn are now free of me. Good-bye, my friend."

Little Bird has this reply, "You have truly gained the purity of the wisdom from this day. I celebrate your joy and your thirst for life. Now that you are free from needing me, we shall be able to visit in future without a feeling of inequality. You are truly a warrior in every sense of what he stands for in his essence. Keep your focus like that of a laser and your intention as pure as the diamond. Good-bye, my friend."

As he disappears into the distance, I feel a sudden surge of pulsating energy moving in waves throughout my body. I am aware that my internal structure is realigning itself to a higher frequency. I am beginning to feel the presence of another familiar natural ally – Raven. I begin to welcome him as he approaches, "Greetings, my Brother. Your presence is always welcomed. It is good to see you."

As Raven lands on a low lying branch and folds his wings, he turns toward me and begins to speak, "Greetings to you, my brother. I have come to welcome you one step closer to attaining the fulfillment of the ultimate truth that lies within you. As you progressively move nearer to the central core of your physical expression, all of that which surrounds you will intensify, testing you continuously, and sometimes severely, to see if you can indeed maintain all of your movements by utilizing the creative light within you. Continue to search within the darkened areas of your being. There, you will discover all that you are by uncovering all that you are not. Realize that the price you must pay for your purest expression of truth becomes higher as you journey toward its full realization. Be cautious of those in your outside world who say they wish to help, for they will ultimately have a motive behind their eagerness to be of service. Be especially cautious of those higher vibrations you encounter within your inner dimensions of travel, for they too will try to stop you so that they might use your vital essence to make themselves more powerful. Trust no one, not even yourself. Trust always that which you feel from deep within your inner void, and never trust that which you think. Attune yourself to the purest vibration of truth whenever the need arises for you to do battle – on any level."

I ask, "What do you mean when you speak of going into battle?"

Raven replies, "It is not necessary to go into that at any greater depth than what has been given. Be totally present within all of your undertakings, and you will know what to do when the time comes."

I refocus my thoughts and direct a response to Raven, "Thank you, my Brother, for your clarity of insight and for your constant support whenever I have been moving in your territory. It has helped me tremendously while I have been moving along on my inner journey. I strongly feel that I am no longer in need of the guidance that you have to offer. I am now clearly aware that everything I need must come from within me. I am ready and centred within myself to accept whatever will present itself directly to me. I am a warrior seeking my ultimate truth. If it means that I must die in order to attain the purity of truth that I wish to align myself with, so be it. I openly welcome death in all that I choose to do."

"I will heed your words of caution, though," I continue. "Yet I know all too well, from our interaction on days gone by, that I cannot trust you, for you are the ultimate trickster. I will continue to consciously vacillate between the divisional boundaries that separate all dimensions of reality, so no one will ever be able to pinpoint the precise vibration I am moving from at any one time. I am aware that I have consciously created you within a dimension of reality within myself to serve a meaningful purpose within my alignment to my true inner self. That purpose has now been fulfilled. I am now free within myself from all wanting or needing of your services. You are now an illusion within my living expression. You are a fragment of reality, but you are not real."

Raven stands motionless as I finish my insights, and then he proceeds to say, "My brother, you have indeed gained much wisdom from all that we have shared. Now that we have attained a level of equality within our relationship, whenever we meet from now on there never need be any words spoken. May you continue to move in the purest light of your own truth. Until we meet again."

With his final word spoken, he releases himself from the branch and disappears through the trees and into the overhead sky. As I watch him disappear,

I acknowledge to myself that I have now arrived at the place where I clearly see that: "I am a fearless warrior in all that I do!"

## June 1, 1985

The type of relationship I am now in the process of creating within my being is one that supports me in becoming all that I am, and also one that affords me the opportunities to express my deepest, inner creative self in all that I choose to do. By moving into the heart of my fears to find where they have come from, and what they are based on, I am slowly eliminating the stranglehold they have had on me. I am consciously observing more of how the sophisticated mechanisms within my outer world thought processes function from day to day. I am finding greater peace and harmony within from not speaking very much to anyone. I am not finding it necessary to speak just for the sake of speaking. Rather, quiet and solitude seem like the appropriate action for now.

My whole inner and outer worlds, as I have known them to be, are beginning to fall away, and I am finding that there are new and very different worlds showing me their realities. I am feeling that I want to be more isolated from my outer world in order that I might become clearer about what is real on this earthly plane. I am choosing to further reduce, and eventually eliminate altogether, the resistance patterns I have created within my inner and outer worlds, by simply observing all of that which creates friction within me.

I have been thoughtful of what I believe love to be. I am aware that I cannot find words to adequately describe what it means to me. I cannot see it in any one person in particular. Rather, I am acknowledging it more and more in all expressions of life on this plane – animal, vegetable and mineral. I am looking into the feasibility of observing all facets of my life's expression without thought, thereby doing away with all judgments and comparisons and allowing the purity of the experience to present itself within its own unfolding.

An inner relationship is the only kind of relationship that can ever be totally truthful. I am now focusing on creating that kind of a relationship in my life all the time. I see that 'attentiveness' is the key to having it all happen. I am continuing to observe my inner and my outer worlds, and I am marveling at the growth that is taking place. It appears that the more I observe, the less my worries seem, and the quicker they disappear from my present space, thereby allowing me many more opportunities to see what is actually going on, at any precise moment, within a living experience.

I am experiencing a general emptiness in feeling as to the purpose of being here on this plane, restricted by the creation of my limiting illusions and confined in all that I do by time and by space. When I stop and take a serious look at it all, there doesn't appear to be much of a purpose behind living in or depending on the world of man. I do see that there is a meaning of a much higher dimension that is hidden behind all that this earthly plane seems to stand for. I am afforded many opportunities to realign and reconnect with the God energy that is the initiator of my creative expression, and to manifest that quality of light within all of my earthly movements.

I am aware that I have been trapped and confined here on this plane by being completely dependent upon my five earthly (physical) senses. However, I now see that I am changing that rather drastically within my conscious movements in my outer world. I no longer see any value in using my five earthly senses solely as a means of determining how I live within my worlds. I do see that my five physical senses are important here on this plane, for they are the only indicators that will allow me to experience fully all the expressions of life that are distinguished here. It is rather my 'sixth' and 'seventh' inner senses that I am now choosing to focus all of my internal energies on, allowing them to act as the guiding light that will eventually direct me into the central core of my being.

My sixth sense – which includes the utilization of my five senses but on the inner channels – is activated when I am able to 'see' beyond the ordinary range of my five earthly senses and their limiting qualities, to a place where these same five senses are not bound and restricted by time or by space. Within the reflection of each of those vibrations – each sense – lies limitless potential for me to use so that I might witness the simplest forms of movement within the most complicated patterns of life's expression. I now 'see' that if I shift my focus from the desires and wants that have been impregnated into the fabric of my earthbound senses, then I will be free enough from them to use them, without attachment, however it may be appropriate.

My seventh sense is directly associated with the universal 'knowing': The functional awareness of all living expressions that exist within all the dimensions of reality on this plane, and all the other planes of existence within and beyond it. My ability to 'see' all things in the purity of what they truly represent is continually available whenever I choose to free myself from holding on to those desires and wants that are interwoven into my physical senses. The 'knowing' manifests itself into my creative expression when I relinquish all of my thoughts pertaining to and affiliated with my five senses. In order for me to be able to 'see' and 'know' successively and consciously within my living expression, I must continually release myself, within my awarenesses, from those thought patterns that create any of what I experience outside my being as being real.

Whenever I judge or compare any of the realities I experience contained within the framework of my earthly senses, I get caught thinking about and analyzing all that I have experienced. By stopping my thought processes in all that I do, I am able to 'see' more of what is around me. I am also able to 'know' more about what is not within my sensory awareness. I am aware that my thought patterns have been continuously perpetuated by the limited qualities of my earthly senses, and that the depth, or lack of it, of what really lies behind the facade of my physical senses, has been perpetuated by the limiting qualities of my thought patterns. I am absolutely clear, within my awareness, that it is not possible for a creative expression to fully manifest through me as long as my thought patterns are activated and functioning.

I am now choosing to move beyond the restricting elements of my five earthly senses in order to experience the purest expression of 'seeing' and 'knowing' that is attainable within my being. I am forever releasing old habits – those worn-out thought patterns – that will no longer be of benefit within the newly discovered creative world that is ever-unfolding within me. I do not feel that it is of any great importance to replace them with other patterns, for they have never really existed. I have only perceived them as existing.

It all seems so simple once it all becomes so clear!

When one wakes up from a deep sleep and finds oneself in a strange new place, everything looks so much fresher and more alive. As each moment arrives, I am waking up more to the realities of who I am by shedding my old habitual patterns of behavior.

I am aware that the power of life and death lies within the structural reality of what I 'see', and that my ability to use that power source to create life or death within my living expression, based on my thoughts, is only available within the guidance from my 'knowing'. Others might think that they see and know what is happening within my worlds, but only I will ever 'see' and 'know' what is truly going on in my worlds by the full utilization of the ever-changing realities that comprise my inner truth.

I am aware that time and space only exist within the parameters of the earthly plane, and they are strictly held together and supported by my five earthly senses. I am aware that I control all time and all space in how I choose to activate my thought patterns. When my thoughts are focused beyond the limited dimensions of time and space, or my five earthly senses, there is nothing for me to control. There are only things to 'see' and 'know'. When I am effectively 'seeing' and utilizing my 'knowing', then I will be controlling all time and all space. If I focus my attention on time and space under the direction of my five earthly senses, then I will be prevented from 'seeing' and from 'knowing'.

Words – when I choose to verbalize them in my communication with others – affect the purity of my inner thoughts and the clarity of my intentions behind using them. It always appears that the clarity I have within my thought processes becomes somewhat distorted whenever I vocalize the extent of my outer or inner world experiences, especially if they involve any number of my physical senses. It is because of my desire to be supported by others in my reality (of what I want to believe happened inside of my experience) that brings about the distortion and causes my frustration. I am aware that whatever I choose to put forth in words is only a small fraction of what lies within the particular thought pattern relating to my experience.

I see that the choice of using a dialogue that totally supports the expansion of my five physical senses is a way and a means of being completely restricted to the earthly plane. To effectively live in peace and harmony, I must be free from my habitual compulsion to immerse my entire being into the controlling hands of my five sensory mechanisms. What I do see as being appropriate is to use my five earthly senses as a means of moving through my outer physical plane, creatively enjoying all the fruits it has to offer without being controlled by any of them. That way, I would only need to activate the necessary sense(s) as the experience is being created within the unfolding moment, and not bask in reflective thoughts or their translations after the experience has been terminated.

I am acknowledging more that my past is just that – my past. It doesn't have any relevance to how I am choosing to live in the present moment unfolding, unless I choose to align myself with my past experiences and bring all of those non-life supporting thought patterns forward into my flowering experience, to use them to learn from so that I do not bring disharmony into my total living expression. It is now time for me to allow all of those past experiences to be just that: experiences that have already happened, or that I have proposed, within my thought processes – by the utilization of my memory and supported through my evolving outer world experiences – have already taken place.

How do I truly know that my past is actually my past? The only sure proof I have of my supposed past is through the activation of my memory. How do I know that I can trust my memory?

✳

To be silent on the outside allows me to observe and to 'see'.

To be quiet on the inside allows me to observe and to 'see' all that there is in my world.

To be patient along my journey allows me to observe and to 'see' all that lies before me.

To 'know' all of what I have seen along my journey is real means that I cannot put words to it. To put words to the truth instantly changes it to an illusion.

Life is like that: continually unfolding before me, yet simultaneously terminating before me. To try and conceptualize that process stops the very process from taking place.

## July 9, 1985

I have been house-sitting for my friends since June 29 while they have been away on a holiday. I have acknowledged that I have been guided to come here by my inner teacher in order that I might move through another introspective phase. The purpose of being here is to look at and to resolve either the reality or the illusion within me concerning me being 'alone'.

I am reflecting back now, looking at how I had made the transition into this space so difficult on myself, creating all sorts of distracting situations that kept me from being alone with myself. There were people to see, places to go, things to do. All these and more were created by me to keep myself occupied – no different than I had been doing for almost thirty-five years. July 3rd and 4th were the first two days I had ever allowed myself to be entirely alone, cuddled up on the futon couch, sometimes in quiet, other times with soft, peaceful music playing in the background, lying perfectly still, aimlessly looking into the greater depths of the square room. After the initial shock of realizing what I had in fact created for myself, I gave myself permission to be there totally. I wanted to be consciously sensitive to the thought patterns that would inevitably present themselves, and then move from those thought patterns however it seemed appropriate.

I slowly began to strip away the outer layers of my ever-changing outer world as best I could, dissolving and fragmenting it into many clearly defined sections as I went. I sat on the couch and watched my inner and outer worlds, as I had constructed them to be within my thought processes, begin to fall away. The realities that I had been holding on to as truths for so long began to show me their other faces. Those truths turned into illusions just as quickly as I was able to observe them moving through my inner audio receptors. As I lie there, I had begun to seriously question, once again, all that I had been doing. I wanted to find the truth, the ultimate truth behind who I really am.

Was it to be found in discussing my thoughts with someone outside myself? Would they actually be able to hear any of what I was saying? On several occasions during the course of my life journey, I have presented some of my deepest thoughts to various friends who have held themselves at a supposedly high level of consciousness. I have always come away from our dialogues feeling that they had no idea how it actually was in my world. They were always too busy protecting their own illusions about who they were or what they were supposed to know.

I am now aware that what I was in fact doing then, and previous to those times, was trying to get other people to support me in not being alone with myself – my thoughts. If I could engage others into listening to my thoughts, and into sharing their thoughts with me, then I would not have to be alone with my thoughts. Had I taken every opportunity earlier to be alone with my thoughts, then I might have discovered, as I am in the process of doing now, that the majority of them were not supporting my life – only my death. A high percentage of my thoughts have been extremely judgmental of myself and of others, and very few of them have been totally creative within their unfolding expression.

After two days of quiet solitude, I had felt as though I needed to get out into the open air, away from the confines of the four walls that had been holding me in place, for a little fun and recreation with some friends. I went on a picnic-hike experience with a friend whom I have been sharing a fair amount of my personal time with. I had enjoyed and treasured the time I had been with her, as I always have. At the same time, I couldn't help but think about this underlying feeling I had: that I was really avoiding doing what I knew I had to do. That same evening, I went to another friend's house for dinner. While I was there, I had come to the full realization that I actually didn't want to be there. At some level of my being, I was being directed towards a small and quiet room where I was house-sitting. There I could be alone and have the freedom to look at my life without any distractions. Instead of resisting, I was rather looking forward to it as a welcomed relief from my chaotic outside world.

The fragmentation process continued. As I stripped away the outer layers of my being, I couldn't hold on to any one thing or to any one person, not even aspects regarding my own personal image – the ones that I had created many years ago and had kept alive for so long. I began to observe the mechanics of my outer world with utmost seriousness and laser-like intensity and focus. I had to find the origins of my truths as they truly existed. I had asked my Higher Self to help guide me through the complicated maze of illusions that are multi-dimensionally interlaced within the delicate fabric of my being, and to present to me all the different aspects of my being so that I might clearly see who I am.

What came up was 'relationship' – mainly the relationship I have with a close friend. I began to look deeper within the structure of this relationship to find out what it was based on. I quickly became aware that what was once a reality was now very much just another illusion. The beliefs that I had supported before, in the relationship being meaningful and purposeful, would no longer hold true. The agreement that the two of us had made to support each other in finding our individual truth, no longer had any substance. It became a crutch, with which each of us could play the game of avoidance from various angles, making it so that we wouldn't have to be accountable to ourselves for finding our own realities of truth.

I continued to peel back the outer shell of our relationship and discovered that if we truly had a relationship – one that was based entirely on truth – we wouldn't have to make an agreement with each other. If I am genuinely looking for my truth from within my being, then I will have to consciously be aware of all that is taking place around me all the time. To make agreements of any description, in order to search for my truth, means that my truth does not exist, especially if I have to go and search for it outside myself. The purest expression of my truth is forever continuously unfolding within me. The functional reality is that I am not always open to seeing it as my truth, particularly if the unfolding experience is non-supportive of my life.

Supporting each other in any way – hugging, supportive conversations, etc. – gives us a physically-oriented structure we can hold on to and rely on. It is a distraction that serves to keep each of us from looking deeper within the intricate complexities that formulate our beings.

When we begin to open the many different doorways inside ourselves – the ones that allow us to see the creative potential we have – we also simultaneously open up the opposing doorways (within our thought processes) that create fear and all the other non-life-supporting feelings that come from it. As a result, we stop ourselves from being more expressive of who we truly are. In reality, though, it is not our own true self that we fear. Rather, it is only the thought of who we think we are that we fear.

*

I sat this morning within the quiet of my inner temple and conversed with an aspect of my Higher Self on the following questions:

"Is it possible for anyone to hurt my feelings? For anyone not to hurt my feelings? That I have no feelings? That all I have in my world are my thoughts?"

My Higher Self then proceeded to respond in this way, "One must look at all these questions with intense seriousness. In so doing, the simplest expressions of reality may be observed. Let us look at them together, one at a time. Shall we begin?"

"Is it possible for anyone outside myself to hurt my feelings?"

"No. It is only through my perceptions, both before and after creating an experience within the limited range of my five earthly senses, that I am encouraged to pass illusionary judgments on myself. It is from these judgments that I decide how I will feel. I am solely responsible."

"Is it possible for anyone not to hurt my feelings?"

"No. Once again, it is only through my own perceptions of the experiences I choose to create in my outer world, within the limited range of my five earthly senses, that I will create a functional reality of the way I want to feel. I would do this by means of thought."

"Is it possible that I have no feelings?"

"Yes. It is very much a reality that my feelings do not actually exist."

"How is that so?"

"It is quite simple. A feeling arises from a thought pattern. It is through the mechanics of that particular thought pattern that one selects the appropriate feeling. One that is positive or negative – supportive or non-supportive of my life – in its expression. Let us look more closely at the example, 'hurt my feelings.' Looking at it with focused seriousness and right intention, what are feelings?"

"They are perceptions."

"Yes, but where do these perceptions come from?" asked my Higher Self.

"They come from somewhere within my formless mind."

"Yes, that is so. By what means do they come from my formless Mind into my conscious awareness?"

"They arrive and are immediately expressed through my thought patterns."

"Yes, that is so. Then are they not just my thoughts? Now, let us look at the word, hurt. What is hurt?"

"It is a feeling that I create from a past experience."

"Yes, but what exactly is it?"

"It is a word that I use to describe a certain way I am choosing to feel."

"Where does this hurt come from?"

"It, too, comes from somewhere within my formless mind."

"Yes, but where in my formless mind?"

"From my thoughts?" I answered.

"Yes. And now looking at it all more seriously: What is the difference between hurt and feelings?"

"There isn't any. They are both just thoughts."

"Yes, that is so. Then what is the true meaning behind the phrase, 'hurt my feelings'?"

"I don't really know anymore. If they are both just a product of my thought processes, then it is my thoughts that are responsible for creating my feelings, and not my feelings that are responsible for creating my thoughts. Does that mean that any negative, non-life-supporting feeling I manifest before or after one of my experiences, comes about because I choose to create it that way in my thought process? I actually choose, by utilizing my thought processes, whether I want to be angry or be happy with someone I have shared an experience with?"

"Yes. It is as you have spoken. An experience is just that, an experience."

"Is it possible to have a thought about an experience while the experience is still in the process of unfolding?"

"No. It is not possible. If I am creating an experience, then I must be there totally within the present moment as it is unfolding before me. If I choose to create illusionary thoughts, regarding the unfolding experience, while I am still moving within the unfolding process, then the experience is no longer in the process of unfolding. The thought process would then be unfolding, clearly bringing into the texture of the experience a judgment of how the experience was being perceived – one that would be either supportive or non-supportive of myself as a creative being."

## July 19, 1985

I have been hiking in the Olympic National Park, outside of Port Angeles, in Washington State, USA. A friend invited me to join him for a couple days of hiking and exploration.

I am moving lighter and faster as I continue along a path that has its beginning in the rain forest and slowly climbs toward the majestic mountains. My head pivots from side to side. My eyes are observing all that comes into view. I want to make sure I don't miss anything. I want to be totally aware of all that surrounds me. After continuing this particular pattern of movement over the course of two miles, I am slowly becoming aware that there is another way of seeing, one that I have not yet observed consciously, but one that I have experienced on several occasions while I have been in an altered state.

For some time now, I have been going out into Nature, and also the world of man, observing and studying the surrounding interconnected relationships in order that I might become more aware of my own patterns of movement. I have thought that this would be an effective method for helping me break free of old patterns of programming and conditioning. I have used the reasoning that my outer world is a reflection of my inner world, and that by putting my full attention on my movements within my outer world, I would be able to alter my inner world. I would also be altering my outer world (by consequence) in the process. I have had positive results whenever I have used this method, but now I am beginning to see a whole new light being shed onto this old way of moving.

I see that if I continue using this approach, I will indeed become more fragmented within my being, and not in a supportive way. When I look deeper into it, I see that using my outer world as a means of ascertaining the state and the condition of my inner world is an illusion. If I choose to separate these two distinct worlds, then I will cause a split or division in the realities I have observed. To look at things outside of my being means they are separate from me. How is it possible that I could ever hope to learn more about me if I have divided myself before I even begin?

Which one of my worlds is real – my outer world or my inner world? How is it possible for me to look at my outer world without judging what I have done, or analyzing any of what I have seen? In order to evaluate the mechanics of my outer world, and be able to see it in relation to my inner world, I would have to make a judgment of some description that would be based on the thought patterns I would be experiencing at that time. These, in turn, are affected by the experience I would be in the midst of.

My thoughts regarding my outer world experiences come from within me, and they have nothing to do with my outer world. If I now take this process one step further: How is it possible for me to alter the condition of my inner world, which is not governed by thought, by utilizing an analytical attitude that involves making judgments concerning experiences in my outer world which have never really existed in the first place? Viewing this reality from a slightly different angle: I now see that I have been judging my movements in my outer world – which is, in reality, my inner world – in hopes of changing the state of my inner world – which is, in reality, my outer world.

The question that races across my mental picture screen, the one that forces me to stop this whole process, is: How is it possible to analyze myself from within myself? For in this very line of questioning, separation is expressed and solidified in its form.

"There isn't anything out there. It is all in here, and 'here' doesn't exist," says a knowing voice from within the depths of my inner void.

Could this be true? How absurd! How silly. How simple. I stop and proceed to look at it all from a totally different perspective. But in so doing, I am aware that I am once again analyzing my inner world process – which is, in reality, directly associated with my outer world. I see that as long as I continue to follow this line of reasoning in order to discover my true inner self, I will be limited to using my five earthly senses. I will also become a victim of my own illusions – limited by my own limitations – by only being able to use the vision of my outer eyes, in hopes of seeing the realities that are contained within my inner world.

The process of using my outer world expressions to change my inner world movements is an illusion. This illusion has been created and supported by the restrictive limitations within the different factions surrounding my perceptions of thought, in relation to the experiences I create within the diversity of dimensional realities that exist on the earthly plane.

The inner voices I oftentimes communicate with – the ones whose interacting dialogues I attentively listen to within the inner channels of my formless mind – do not originate from within the vibrational frequencies that comprise the earthly plane. How do I know this to be truth? It is quite simple. Whenever I am totally involved in the creation of an unfolding experience while using any one or more of my five earthly senses, these voices are nowhere to be heard. To be sensitive to and in full use of my five earthly senses keeps me from breaking free of my own thought processes, to live and experience the various dimensions of reality that exist outside the earthly plane – but that are very much contained within the rhythms of light patterns that formulate the structure of this plane.

The purest and only possible way for me to become self-realized, or self-actualized, is by continuing to look directly at the underlying composite structures of the path I am on with total commitment and absolute seriousness. I am not speaking of the path that I continually walk within my daily movements on the physical plane, but rather the path that lies as a mirrored reflection to that physical path. I would refer to this path as the ethereal path. This particular path cannot be experienced within the limited scope of my five earthly senses, for it is positioned at a much higher vibration within its expression. It is not possible to approach this path by using any physical components of matter. This is the path from which all expressions of physical matter are created and sustained in time and space.

How is it possible that I might travel this particular path during my lifetime? The only way that I can get anywhere near this path is if I continually give up and surrender all of my thoughts, especially those thoughts that are directly related to the 'solid' consistency of all physical matter. I must relinquish all of my judgments and comparisons that were based on my five earthly senses. In other words, I must totally dissolve all aspects of reality within my conscious awareness so that I will be able to flow more harmoniously with the creative expression in each and every succeeding moment, from its creation right through to its termination.

> The inner rhythms of light – those that make up the structural foundation of my physical embodiment – fabricate the vibrations of pulsating energies that resonate outwardly from the depths of my inner being. These energies saturate the environment that I continually create to immerse myself in, and eventually they become unconsciously acknowledged by other beings or life forms as high frequency vibrations of light. They are openly received by their internal audio receptors, which translate the numerous variations of vibratory signals into transmittable audible sound waves within their own internal processes. Thereby bringing about the ever-unfolding creation of inner communications of thought that are confined and expressed within the limitless inner void, and externally verbalized outer communications of thought that are reactionary within their manifested expressions.
>
> These composites of various light patterns form the solidified existence of all expressions of physical matter on this plane. If I continually open myself to this full realization, then subsequent movement, in all ways, will allow me to connect (from within only) with all the possible variations of light patterns that exist within and beyond the earthly plane. What I will be able to readily access whenever I so choose, is: the total past experiences

that have ever existed on the earthly plane; the total present conditions of all expressions of life that are taking place within the continually unfolding moment; and the total future – all that will ever take place within all expressions of life within a future time sequence. All of this representing my movement within the superior vibrational frequencies that are unrestricted from the awarenesses of man, should he dare open the door that leads to these dimensions of reality.

If I am an observer within my own inner formless matrix, then I will be able to move unrestricted between the unperceivable veils that separate the higher frequency, inner vibrations where all light originates, and the lower frequency, outer vibrations where all light creatively expresses itself. My own formless matrix is the same as the universal matrix, where all the structural composites of light are created and manifested. These are the same arrangements that are responsible for manifesting into a functional physical reality all expressive forms of life – the infinite variations of light vibrations that make up all matter.

The high frequency vibrations of light energies do not formulate the operational structure of a single thought pattern or multiple patterns *per se*. Rather, all patterns of thought originate from within the structural alignment of the high frequency, inner vibrations of light. Thought patterns distort and alter the purity of the light vibrations that give them substance for their expression, by continuously being subjected to the interweaving and amalgamation of extremely complicated but highly simplified patterns of light vibrations. Eventually what occurs, within one's own thought processes, is the inability to distinguish between the simplified forms and complicated forms of thought patterns, as they forever dissolve in their structural arrangements and shift in their internal and external expressions. These thought patterns oftentimes, within the discourses that take place through verbal communication – either internally or externally – manifest themselves as indiscernible conglomerations of expressive impurities that are at the same time purities for how they have come to be created. Hence, what is clearly presented within any form of communication, whether internal or external, is an on-going unfolding of interchanging realities between clear, precise thought projections and scattered, incoherent thought projections.

A practical and functional example of how one can look at the various possibilities within the clarity and purity of thought projections can be found in a simple recipe: take one multi-speed kitchen blender, a quarter-section of a small peeled orange, a quarter-section of a small apple, a quarter-section of a banana, a quarter-section of a medium peach, half cup of plain yogurt, and half cup of unpasteurized whole milk. Each of these ingredients is pure within its purposeful living expression.

I am choosing to use each of the above ingredients to symbolically represent a facet of an experience that I have already had in my life, and the purity of how I had experienced it as it unfolded. The blender represents the internal mental processes of thought that are responsible for creating and verbalizing all of my communications, both internally to myself and externally to others.

I place the milk into the blender and add the yogurt. Both are pure within themselves even though they have been added to the same container. I proceed to turn on the blender to the highest possible speed, thereby thoroughly mixing the two ingredients together. Now they have become impure within their own functional expression, but at the same time, they have become pure in what they have come together to create. I now add the section of the apple into the newly formed mixture. Both the apple and the mixture are still pure within what they stand for. I proceed to turn the blender on to the lowest speed, chopping the apple up and mixing it in with the other ingredients. The main mixture is now impure within what it was, but at the same time, it is pure in what it has now become. As I continue to add each of the other ingredients in the same manner, and selecting different blending speeds, the same process of purity becoming impurity becoming purity occurs.

Each time I add another ingredient to the mixture, it would be the same as adding another facet of expression to my unfolding experience. Each time I blend the ingredients, I would also be blending together my thought patterns, as to how I saw my experience going or not going, by making judgments and comparisons about what I thought was happening.

Each time I blend the ingredients, it would be much like recalling the facets of my past experience and blending them all together to get a new texture of what the experience was all about. With the last ingredient added, the mixture has been continuously changing in its expression but always remaining the same within its presentation. This would be comparable to my thoughts about an experience that I have already had, in that the more times I recall the experience as each facet was added, the more it changes within its expression and remains the same in its presentation.

I now turn on the blender to the lowest speed possible, and allow it to do what it will for five seconds. At that time I turn it off, wait for five seconds, then turn it back on for five seconds, only this time I select the next highest speed.

I will continue to repeat this procedure until all the available speeds have been selected and moved through.

At each stage, the mixture is slightly altered within its composition and changed in its outward expression, but its presentation always remains the same. If I look at each of the blending stages as being symbolic of me recalling and reliving my initial experience over and over again within my thought processes, then I will clearly be able to see how many times I would have subtly altered the inner composition and changed the external expression of my original experience. My verbal presentation of the ever-unfolding and ever-changing original experience will always remain the same.

Can it all be so simple? It all sounds so clear and so simple within the reasoning process my inner voices – thoughts – have been engaged in. This is the very aspect I am looking at the feasibility of terminating within my current living expression, absolving myself from judging and comparing the extent of my experiences. How do I know that it is in fact so simple? Is there a way of testing the practicality of this information through my physical movements while I am still moving along this path?

From within the depths of my inner void, a soft and gentle voice begins to speak, "Of course there is. Let go of all thought in regard to controlling what you think you are doing, and allow yourself to freely experience all of what has been spoken."

As I proceed to take a step forward along the path that I have been following for the past two hours in the Olympic National Park, I continue to ponder over all that has been presented within my inner awareness. From deep within, there is an appealing invitation to bring into a full physical reality all that has been given. My excitement is growing. I can feel my physical body becoming more alive with a vibrant energy-force, intrinsically knowing the significance of all that is about to unfold, and seeing it as a glorious opportunity to immerse itself in creative play.

As I take a few more steps forward and downward, I can feel a propelling force being generated from within my central core that is insistent on taking over full control of the unfolding experience. The speed at which I am moving is gradually increasing. This self-generating force is discriminatively selecting the appropriate increments for the necessary speeds I will need to encounter along my way, in order to be able to fully realize the information given previously.

I am a good ten miles out and heading back toward the place where I had first entered into this learning adventure. I am travelling on a makeshift pathway that meanders through various overlapping expressions of forest life within a natural park-like setting. The texture of the ground I am moving over is extremely inconsistent in its physical characteristics. Some of it is smooth and well packed, then the ground abruptly changes to jutting boulders and protruding root structures, then loose gravel, loose dirt, flowing water that intersects its route at various spots, scattered small branches, and man-made elongated trenches. The portion of the trail that I am travelling over has been created on a 25-degree incline, and it extends over a distance of approximately four miles.

I begin to feel light and airy throughout my entire physical form. As I continue to move along at a quicker pace, I can hear a voice from within my inner void, "It is possible for me to fully realize all of that which has been presented from within my internal dimensions. In order for that to occur, I must let go of my physical embodiment, and all of my physical senses, so that I can be absolutely free from all concern for a few moments within my earthly time."

I know that I can trust this inner voice, for this voice is, in reality, a deeper aspect of my true inner self. Everything on this journey is but a mere reflection of who I am. It is a continuous unfolding of my own deeper, inner patterns of light that are forever connecting to and interacting with other forms and expressions of light energy.

The pace is now at a fast jogging speed, and it is steadily increasing as I move along on the ever-changing obstacle course. I am scurrying down the path shoe-less, sometimes feeling as though I am totally out of control, yet at the same time, I know full well that my inner self is in total control. I resign myself from having any active part in determining what is going to happen, and completely surrender my conscious thoughts to the quietness of my inner void. I have become an observer.

I am looking down immediately in front of where I am moving, thoughtfully observing with my outer physical eyes the most appropriate places to put my feet to ensure that I don't trip and fall. As the rhythms of light vibrations within my body attune to and harmonize with the surrounding vibrations of light energies that make up the texture of the path, my inner eyes take over full control. I am now aware that whatever my eyes fixate on, my feet automatically connect with, and with pinpoint accuracy. I am amazed at what I am observing. It is as though my feet have eyes. Or that my eyes, and my feet, and everything in between, are moving as one. All of my inner senses are synchronized to the outer vibrations of all that surrounds me. There is absolutely no separation between me and what I am connecting to on the path. I now fully realize that there is no possible way for me to become injured by this experience, for I am the experience that is presently unfolding. I am becoming whatever I see. What a feeling!

There is nothing to remember, for I have no thoughts. There is only the purity of the unfolding moment.

I am aware that I am not labouring for my breath. In fact, a few times I have found myself consciously focusing on my breath just to make sure I am indeed still breathing. My physical body is relaxed and totally fluid within its movement patterns. I am constantly shifting between my inner reality of creative light energies and my outer, functional reality of those light energies. They are continuously expressing themselves through the continuity of my physical movements as the experience is unfolding and terminating within its creative progression.

I want to push this experience to its furthest possible limit to see how many angles I can perceive it from. I am now aware that there is only one: This earthly plane is made up entirely of resonating vibrations of light energy. For me to be in tune with the natural flow of universal light energy at all times, it will be necessary to attune myself to all the various light vibrations that surround me at any given time. This will only be possible as long as I continuously surrender all of my physical senses, as well as my physical form, and offer myself totally as an instrument through which the creative life-giving universal energy can flow freely. In doing this, all that I will ever need for my inner and outer journey shall be provided for me at the most appropriate times.

It is all now appearing to paint a clearer picture within my Earthly Mind. The reality of all that I have been experiencing can be summed up in one simple sentence: The more I continue to surrender unconditionally to myself and to all of that which I perceive to be around me, the more I shall become who I truly am within my total living expression.

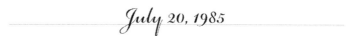

## July 20, 1985

It is the next day. I eventually come to the turn-off point posted along the path. This is the one that will take me to the top of Hurricane Ridge in the Olympic National Park. I decide that I am going to wait for a few moments before I make any further movements. As I am waiting for an inner impulse to arrive, I check the bottoms of my feet and remove a few shards of shaly rock from between some of my toes. I am feeling that I do not want to proceed up to the ridge. I close my eyes and attune myself inwardly to connect with an aspect of my Higher Self. I am looking for clarity as to why I have come here this day, where I am to go from here, and what I am to do while I am here.

I hear a voice from deep within my inner void saying that I am not to go to the ridge. Instead, I am to proceed in the opposite direction. I am to take the path that leads up into the mountain peaks. There appears to be no well-used trails to follow. There is only rock face after rock face for me to climb. I now know that this is going to be another initiation of some kind – one that will require me to again face my fears and, of course, look for death in all that I do. I acknowledge the guidance from my voice within the void, and I eagerly begin a new journey into the depths of my being.

Ever since I started on this path thirty minutes ago, some rather large horse flies (the meat-eating kind that like to take chunks of human flesh whenever they can) have been circling my torso and buzzing near my ears. It is now appearing that the higher I climb, the more of them materialize within my personal space, hoping to dine.

I am choosing to use this experience as an exercise to see if I can possibly keep the flies at a safe distance from my body at all times. I am consciously choosing to create them within my inner reality, and in so doing, I am creating the reality that they are not real. I see that they are only the physical manifestation of my powerful inner fears, and that they are continuously being created through my thought patterns. I travel inwardly, surrendering my outer physical form of flesh unto my inner creative form of light. In the process, I bring forth from within the creative void of my inner world, a wall of energy that extends fourteen inches away from my body. I am manifesting within my thought processes an invisible wall that will keep the flies out of my personal space.

My creative process has been functioning very effectively as long as my attention and focus remains on the present unfolding moment. I am finding that as soon as I alter my thought patterns in any way, the effectiveness of my invisible wall of energy disappears. The flies then enter through my weakened energy shield, land on a section of my body, take a quick bite and take off again, long before I have an opportunity to do anything. As long as I continue to keep my full attention on my wall of energy, I can keep them at bay.

I am looking at taking this experience another step. I am now choosing to create the reality, within my creative thought process, that I am in control of all time and all space in my world. This being the case, I should now be able to make these flies disappear instantaneously from my surrounding space. I close my eyes and attune myself entirely to the vibrational frequency of this inner reality. I open my eyes and discover, to my utter amazement, that the flies have all left. I am once again walking on my path alone.

As I continue to move, my thought patterns begin to waver from their steadfast awareness of the present unfolding experience. They begin to focus on bits and pieces of abstract thought, mostly in regard to other experiences that have happened in my past that are not at all supportive of my creative living expression. While this process is occurring, I am aware that the horse flies are quickly returning, and there appears to be more of them. Now that my protective energy shield is not working effectively, a few of them at a time hastily land, take a fair chunk out of my exposed flesh and then head out again, resuming their position on the outer edge of my weakened energy wall. Their buddies gather for a chance to enter and help themselves.

I continue to focus my full attention and creative energies within my inner world, to see if it will be at all possible to maintain this centring process so that I will not be affected by these pesky flies. I am finding that I can control them as long as I keep my energy focused within me, and as long as I don't react to what I think I am seeing taking place around me.

When my thoughts are clear and focused on the unfolding moment, I am supporting myself in finding out more about who I truly am, and I am also being nurtured by the experience I am creating. When my thoughts become scattered, and I begin to think about the meaningless, non-life-supporting experiences I have had in my life, I get easily pulled back into my old habitual patterns of movement. As a result of this, my thoughts turn against me, and I begin to spin uncontrollably within the illusions I have created. Whenever this process occurs, I become the victim of my own internal mental misalignment and my own emotional thinking patterns.

These flies are only an extension of all that I am. I have been choosing to react to what they have been doing. I have been expending a great deal of my personal energy in order to keep them away from my physical body. Even though I could easily have created and maintained the energy shield around me, they have been in total control, for they have had me reacting to their presence.

I am now aware that these flies are very much a part of the natural elements of this area, and that I am the intruder who has entered into their personal space. I also see that I have been trying to force my expressive movements within their territory, instead of harmonizing with them and becoming one with all that surrounds me. I am the one who is out of alignment. I must realign myself within myself. I need to realign my thought patterns and focus them entirely on the natural vibrations of light that resonate from me at all times. This is the light that interconnects all forms of matter on the physical plane.

My attunement to my surrounding environment is such an easy and simple procedure. So much so that I am surprised I do not use it more consciously within all of my movements. I am also sensitive to the fact that this is a relatively new tool that I have incorporated into my creative thought patterns, and that it will require a certain time sequence before I am able to fully attune myself all the time. It seems so simple once I see it!

All things that exist on this plane are never really what they seem. They are always what they are at the time I create them. I am sensing that there are multifarious levels of consciousness that are identifiable within a single level of consciousness, that allow me to discover the different awarenesses of who I might be.

In order for me to become more aware of the missing pieces of my life puzzle, I must continue to travel further into the darkened void within my thought processes. I must continue to look with laser-like intensity for the purest expression of truth that might be brought forth in the light of my creative energies. As long as I keep my awareness focused within the present unfolding experience, I will always be able to move effectively through all of my outer world expressions with the least amount of interference from outside stimuli. It is important for me to act accordingly, utilizing my own inner truths, and not to react to the many illusions that the lower dimensions of my mental thought might create in order to keep me from shedding new light within the darkened areas of my being. It now appears that the layers of sophistication within my mental thought patterns (that have been programmed and conditioned into me over the course of my life journey) are definitely losing their stranglehold on me. By focusing on the double-edged sword of truth within my universe, I will always be able to safely venture deeper into my darkened areas and bring forward, into the openness and flow of my living expression, more of who I naturally am.

By allowing this process to take place, I am able to walk along this trail knowing that I am in total control of everything that is entering into the scope of my unfolding experience. The flies continue to buzz around me constantly, but not one of them has managed to get past my fourteen-inch energy barrier. I am now maintaining a balanced and harmonious relationship with my surrounding environment.

At a point along the trail, I stop all of my outer movements in order that I can get a different perspective of what I am doing. I am feeling somewhat restless with the conscious realization that I have been travelling on the same common path everyone else would use when they come out here. I know that I am not like anyone else. I know that I am unique in my living expression, and that the path I am standing on does not resonate harmoniously with my inner vibration. It is too easy and too conventional. I am aware that whenever I have travelled on someone else's path, I have fallen asleep within my own conscious awareness, and I have also created more divisions within my internal perceptions of my inner and outer worlds.

As I gaze upwards I am feeling very humble, standing before the towering mountain peaks that are enclosing me. I know that the only way for me to go, from this point on, is straight up. This is to be my destiny for the day: to face all of my fears in regard to finding the true purpose behind living and dying within my thought processes. I close my eyes, putting my full attention on to my breath and focusing all of my energies within my *centre* core. I attune myself to an aspect of my Higher Self, asking to be given an internal sign that will steer me in the most appropriate direction so that I might learn my lesson(s) for the day. I am beginning to feel a tugging sensation coming from around my navel. This is the impulse I am waiting for. I open my outer eyes and begin on my way. I am allowing my internal awarenesses to guide me to wherever it is necessary.

I alter my internal awareness and attune myself to the movement patterns of a cat. While adopting a four-legged movement pattern, I thoughtlessly scurry over the shaly surface of the rocks. The climbing is easy, with handholds and foot-holds continuously presenting themselves to the harmonizing vibration of my inner awareness. I am spontaneously and creatively making my way higher.

Getting to the first peak has acted more as a warm-up. It has presented plenty of opportunities to familiarize myself with the do's and the don'ts of rock climb-ing. It has also given me ample time to attune myself to the surrounding terrain. As I stand on a shelf-like structure that is about a hundred feet away from the peaked point of this section of rock, I receive a very strong pulling sensation from the peak. It is much like a magnetic pull. A tremendous amount of energy is being generated by this structure. I am being asked from within to move within its alignment and receive the gift it has to offer.

Without any further deliberation, my body is assuming full control and is on the move. I proceed to move slowly and cautiously on a long and narrow ledge, en route to the outermost edge of the precipice. When I am only halfway there, I decide to stop and take in the spectacular view. I am now seeing that this choice has consequences. I can feel my body beginning to react to what I am in the process of doing. My heart is beating faster and harder. My legs are becoming weaker and are beginning to vibrate. My saliva is quickly drying up, leaving a dusty taste inside my mouth. Cold chills are racing up and down my spine, sending stimulating electrical shockwaves to the outer edges of my physical embodiment.

I hold on to two firm handholds and close my eyes. I am hoping to once again centre myself within my own internal process. After about fifteen seconds, my body has re-established its own equilibrium, thereby allowing me to continue. The voice of my inner teacher has assured me that everything will be okay; that I should trust completely in the unfolding process; and that I should let go of my thoughts as to what I think I see. Without any further hesitation, I proceed.

As I take my last step and firmly and securely perch myself on top of a small boulder about twenty-four inches square, I fully realize that I am now standing on the apex of this massively wondrous structure. As I look to my left, I am aware that the formation of rock I am standing on immediately falls away to a depth of well over a thousand feet before it comes into contact with another sloping incline. On my right, there is a similar drop off, only this one drops away well over fifteen hundred feet. I am in complete awe of all that is before me. I am up more than four thousand feet above sea level, getting a bird's eye view of one of Nature's most powerful settings – the mountains. As I continue to gaze aimlessly, I can't help but reflect upon how Nature always has a way of laying Her natural beauty out so that words can never be found to adequately describe what it is.

My body soon returns to its own natural vibrational rhythm. I am now feeling an inner urge to move on. I look behind me and see that there are still a few more rock faces for me to ascend. They are openly beckoning me to come and interact with them, to receive the precious gifts they have to offer. I am beginning to feel both anxious and excited at the same time. I am feeling anxious, for it all looks really dangerous from where I am standing. I am also excited to think that I am eventually going to reach the uppermost point of a peak that is well over 5,400 feet above sea level.

I once again begin to hear the nurturing voice from within, "Everything will be all right. Give up all of your fear, and you will find the peace you are looking for. You are well aware of all that you are doing. Trust your knowing. Let go of your wanting for control, and all shall be given to you."

I begin to have an outward verbal conversation with myself, "Am I willing to die? Of course not. I didn't come all this way to die. I came here to find a greater purpose to my living on this Earth. I am now ready to let go and live, live on the edge of my creative self-expression."

The vibrating energies within my inner awarenesses are growing stronger. My physical body is becoming lighter. My vibrational essence is slowly attuning itself to the vibrational frequency of Cougar. Using all of my body parts as one, and utilizing the pulsating driving force from my newly acquired breathing pattern, I quickly begin my assault. With each step taken, my physical body becomes lighter and more agile. I am not afraid, for there is nothing to be afraid of. There are only things to marvel at and to become part of.

A dialogue is beginning to surface from within the depths of my internal void. One voice represents an aspect of my self that is very competitive in his expression. The second voice represents an aspect of my self that is the direct opposite, the mirror image of the competitive one. The dialogue is now coming within the functional range of my internal audio receptors, and the discourse begins to unfold,

"It is me against the mountain," says the competitive aspect.

"No. It is not me against the mountain. It is me against myself, or else it is me in harmony with everything else," is the reply from the non-competitive aspect.

"I have to conquer this mountain."

"No. The mountain cannot be conquered, for it is part of everything else. It is even part of me."

"I have to make it to the top of this mountain, because if I don't, I will be a loser."

"No. It is not possible for me to be a loser, for I have already made it to the top. If I had not, I would never have begun this journey."

"I will have to push myself right to the edge in order to make it to the top."

"No. I have to let go and become part of everything else that surrounds me. When I have allowed myself the freedom to do this, then my way will be made easy."

"I know exactly what I need to do," says the competitor. "I need to let go of all thought. I also need to be with this experience totally as it unfolds before me. I must surrender and relinquish all thought, for thinking creates patterns of movement that focus on accumulating all sorts of power so that the thoughts can have total control over my living expression within a particular time sequence."

I recognize that there is a much greater force moving within the depths of my being that knows how to connect with all that I see in my vision. This force is part of all that I see before me all the time. It is only my self-created image of who I think I am within my thought patterns that chooses to play the game of life and death, making choices and creating friction so there will always be confrontation within the divisional aspects of my being.

I continue to climb until I finally arrive at the highest ridge of the highest peak. I gingerly make my way along the apex of the ridge, being very cautious and selective with every one of my movements. I am aware that one miscalculated placement of one of my feet could very well mean my physical death. This ridge measures no more than eighteen inches wide and goes sixty to eighty feet to the summit, over loose chips of shaly rock. I test the stability of the platform that marks the pinnacle of my adventurous ascension. This elevated platform that I am standing on measures approximately fourteen inches square.

I am receiving an enlightening revelation about this particular experience: The air at the top of this mountain peak is no different than the air I breathe at the bottom of this mountain. Once again I am clearly being shown that there is nowhere for me to go in order to learn more about me. There is no amount of tests that will ever provide me with what I need to know. I am really starting to get that it all really does just exist inside me. Never outside! I am aware that the outside has constantly been showing me that it is all inside. I have been continuously fighting to prove to myself that it does in fact exist on the outside. As I continue to stand here, I proclaim to my inner self that I have finally arrived at a place in my evolution where I am able to give myself the necessary freedom to move internally to lose the images and perceptions of myself that I have been carrying around for thirty-five years.

All of a sudden, things are beginning to happen within my internal alignment. Awe and excitement about the outside surrounding environment and view are slowly disappearing, and what appears to be replacing them is an inner environment of peace, calm, and quiet. I am seeing within my internal awareness that I am all of that which I see before me, and that everything I am seeing, I am only seeing within me. It is as much a part of me as I am a part of all of it. I am not viewing it as anything out of the ordinary, for if I do, I know that it won't be real. It is clear to me right now that the things that are real have no emotions attached to them, and the things that are illusionary have many emotions attached to them desperately trying to make them real.

I am now looking at this place where I am perched, not as the summit of the mountain but as the bottom, and that the bottom of the mountain is now the top. I am sensing and feeling this in the reality that I am choosing to create within my creative thought process. I will now have to go up the mountain, which is in reality down the mountain, in order to get back to the car. I see no real difference between the top and the bottom, except when I choose to judge them or compare them with each other or with other mountain formations. The view that I have within my inner thought processes is the same at the bottom as it is at the top.

Everything is the same at the top as it is at the bottom. It is all one in the same, connected in purpose, and yet every part of it is unique in its presentation. It is only me who is forever choosing to be separate from all that is around me. It is only me who wants all that I have been observing to be something greater than what it actually is. There cannot be a mountain unless there is something else to compare it to that is not a mountain. There cannot be the something else that I would compare it to unless there is a structure that has been identified as a mountain to compare it with. It is all the same, yet it is all not the same. It is only me who chooses to make it all so different within my perceptions. It is only me who chooses to separate each aspect of life from the wholeness of what it is. I am now seeing that I have done this in my past out of fear that I might just see how easy it really is, this thing called life. My life-giving gifts all come from within me. There is nothing that exists outside me. There are many different expressions of life here on this plane. I am now seeing that it is entirely up to me to find the ultimate balance within myself as to what each expression symbolizes in the texture of my inner journey.

It is only me, within my perceptions, who is making this whole outer world experience something special, giving it more power and existence than my own inner creative expression. I have been telling myself over and over again that I will have to work hard in order to become clear about those things in my past that have been stopping me from finding my truth. This is the story that has inspired me to keep looking to my outside world for the clarity of how to get inside.

A voice from within the depths of my inner darkness begins to speak, "Where is your uniqueness, your beauty, your strength, and your gift of self-expression in the world that you continuously surround yourself with? Where do all of these aspects of reality fit within your living expression?"

I stand motionless, listening to all that is being said, looking intently within my inner void to find the answers. I become frozen in my thought patterns. The possibility of me being so powerful and so unique in all that I choose to see and do has never before dawned on me in such a loving, supportive light.

The narrow point I am standing on is just over 5,400 feet above sea level. Directly in front of me, no more than six inches in front on my toes, is a sheer drop off of 1,000 feet or more. Directly behind me, not more than eight inches away, is another drop off. Only this is more of a gradual one – an 85% grade. It drops away a good 1,500 feet before it connects to an intersecting horizontal section of ground. I feel as though I have arrived at the top of my outer world. I am an unattached observer to all that lies before me, for as far as I can see.

I am clearly seeing that there is no real separation between me and what I see with my physical eyes outside me. I am aware that the beauty, the strength, and the power I have been observing outside me is, in reality, only a reflection of all that is within me. I have never wanted to acknowledge this reality before to the extent I do now. I have known all of this previously, but only on an intellectual level. Today, I am using more of my sixth and seventh internal senses. I am aware that what I feeling inside me stretches far beyond the limited realities of my five earthly senses. My physical body is beginning to tingle. The subtle energies within me are changing once again. I am free within my living expression if I choose to be. I am free to be whatever I want to be! The reality of being free is very real to me, more so now than at any other time. I am ready to make the quantum jump between my outer and inner world. I desire to move freely within the limitless layers of the thin veil that separates them; the invisible line that is forever shifting in its presentation. This summit that I am standing on is the symbolic physical manifestation of the thin line that divides my two worlds.

It would be all too easy to let go of my physical form and jump from where I am. I am not afraid to die. I am ready to die, to give up all that I am in this moment, for there is nothing worth hanging on to anymore. All that I have been seeing within this journey is making everything else I ever thought important appear to be pretty insignificant. I close my eyes and take a few deep inner breaths. I surrender my total being to Mother Earth and allow the pull of Her desire to have all of me, to take me however She sees fit.

I am now falling quickly towards the rocky surface below. I feel the coolness of the all-embracing air as it continuously passes through me. I am dissolving within my form as I am falling. I am abstractly becoming all of that which I have been seeing through my physical eyes.

My Earthly Mind begins to panic, for it does not want to give up its existence on this plane. It is desperately trying to find a way of moving so it can strike a bargain to ensure its survival. Out of the depths of my inner void, I can hear the ascending voice of another aspect of my Higher Self. This time it is much softer in its expression and more loving in its resonance. His message is clearly and precisely being stated, "Let go of your physical body. Let go of all that you think you are, and all that you think you are not, so that you may enter into the depths of your darkened inner void. You will then become the endless void where everything is separated in its expression yet always remains the same in its origin."

Instantly, the thoughts that have been active within the structural fabric of my petty Earthly Mind vanish. What I am now feeling in their place is a sensation that engulfs my being with a soft billowy consistency. I open my internal eyes for perhaps the first time consciously. What I now see unfold within me is an experience that comes with no words suitable to describe it. When I begin to search for a possible word that might come close, the unfolding scene begins to fade away and change in its expression. When I let go of my desire to construct thought around it, it comes back again.

I am beginning to wonder what is actually happening. I am not sure whether I am only dreaming about what is happening, or whether it is actually happening. I am continuously being carried from one level of awareness to another, and then to another, much like an elevator that is ascending an unlimited number of floors.

As I approach each level, the unfolding scenery begins to change in its composition but always remains the same in its presentation. The intricate patterns of light energies that are intersecting to form these various scenes of living expressions are constantly altering in their formation. Whenever I look at them, and begin to think about what they might possibly represent, they begin to dissolve. If I look at them without focusing on any one aspect of what is there, I clearly see that all of it has life within its most simple structures.

The rocks are expanding and contracting within the higher frequencies of their vibrational energies. Eddies of air are ruffling the pure energy rays of the Sun as they are continuously filtering down through the various levels of the different forms of matter. These rays of sunlight are striking my body from every conceivable angle. The ribbons of high intensity light are penetrating my entire being, filling me completely with the finer resonations of high frequency vibrations. These vibrations will enable me to harmonize with the infinite life forces that exist on this physical plane.

The colour spectrum is very different on each of these diverse levels, as every single expression of life-energy on Earth vibrates according to the single-minded function it has been created for. The colours are filtered through from object to object, forming sophisticated patterns of light that connect all the various realities within this physical plane, and act as doorways into other dimensions of reality on distant planes. These realities can be recognized and brought into physical manifestation by any being who is able to alter his own inner vibrations of light to harmonize with the high frequency energies of light that comprise all expressions of matter.

I am being shown that it is possible for any person to attune himself to whatever shape or form he chooses. He can learn from the innermost vibrational essence of what that form or shape is, and literally resonate harmoniously with it for as long as he wishes. An example of this is: to become the rock that one is observing. To feel its pulse, to listen to its breath, to move within its rhythm of expression, to become one with it in composition and in structure. No harm would come to him who could do this, should he stumble and fall on to the rocks. An object would not knowingly create a situation where it would intentionally bring pain upon itself. But rather, it would choose to become itself over and over again: releasing, becoming, joining and forming new dimensions of substance within new evolving expressions of matter.

I open my outer eyes and discover I am still standing on the precipice. Only now I am having a totally connected relationship with all that lies before me. I am aware that it is all observing me as much as I am observing all of it. I am now feeling that I am finally free, within my own expression, to be all that I am in all that I do. I am free within myself to claim my freedom from my outer world by way of my inner world. Until now I have been restricting myself to my outer world, and depending upon it to support me in becoming more of who I am.

I am aware that there is no further need for me to be perched upon this platform on top of the world. It is no good standing here all alone. There is still much more for me to see and to interact with before this particular journey comes to a close. I embrace the loving energy from the Sun, take a long, drawn-out breath, bow to the four major directions and all of Nature, and begin my descent. Once again I am shown that everything I will ever need while on my life journey is contained within me. I continue to marvel at how simple everything actually is in life when moving in the current of my creative expression.

I continue to slowly climb downward, taking in and integrating my new awarenesses concerning the world I surround myself with. I also reflect on how I move within the textures of my inner and outer worlds, within the various dimensions of reality that exist within my consciousness at any one time, and that also exist on the deeper levels of the other dimensions that make up my being.

It is now time to declare openly to myself what it is I am choosing to be, and to state that reality to my outside world, should I be asked, without reservation from here on in. I will allow truth to be both my guide and my focus in my daily living expression. I will also allow more of my internal light to shine outside me more brightly. Everything seems to matter now, and yet nothing seems important enough to matter. I am continually moving back and forth between the dimensional doorways that separate all expressions of reality. I am swinging between the extremes on the emotional scale within my being. I am watching it all happen without having the slightest attachment to what is being presented. I am seeing that it is all very real for what it is, but it is not real in my living expression at this moment. None of it will affect me either adversely or positively unless I attach myself to it, or any part of it.

I am jumping for joy because I am free to play within all the various realities that exist within my being. I now have the ability to do whatever is appropriate and necessary for me within the ever-present unfolding of a creative living experience. I am consciously aware that I control all time and all space in my worlds.

The ground that I am walking on is becoming hotter by the minute. The temperature is over 96°F. There are no clouds in the sky. The Sun is openly expressing its love and support for all living expressions. There is no wind to speak of, and the air is dry. The path that I have been walking on is comprised of small, irregular shaped, sharp pieces of shale mixed with some fine sand and silty dirt. I am finding that the ground surface is holding all the heat in, and that I constantly have to remain in an altered state of awareness so I do not injure the bottoms of my feet. Walking on hot coals was nothing in comparison to what I am experiencing walking on this surface. At least the hot coals had a limited duration. This time, it is going to take me at least an hour and a half before I can get down to where the ground is cool.

I am thankful that I had been shown all that information while I was still standing on the precipice, for now I am finding it necessary to use some of it so I do not cause injury to myself. I am surrendering the soles of my feet so that they will become the surface texture of the ground that I am walking on. I create, within my conscious awareness, the light vibrations within my physical body to now alter in their structural composition to align with those forms of matter I will encounter. I am now in a state of continual surrender unto myself and to the elements that make up my path. This total unfolding experience is taking place where there are no time or space concerns within my inward or outward movements. I am feeling my feet as they embrace each and every razor sharp edge and jagged point of the surface rock. They are not resisting any of what is happening.

When I have no memory to tell me what I have done, or what I have to do, then I have no concern about how hot the ground has been, or how hot it is becoming. I have created it so there is no distinction between the heat in the air, the heat in the ground, and my physical being. I am choosing to use the heat as a form of energy that is supporting me in my journey, and not as something outside me that I have to struggle with. If I separate myself from the heat, I will surely be burned severely. As in all of my previous experiences within the natural elements, the more I surrender my desires and wants, the more I am provided with in the way of nurturing food. My safety is always assured when I align myself with my ever-loving Mother Nature.

*July 26, 1985*

My close friend and I decide to take advantage of the great summer conditions and head out on the West Coast Road, en route to Sombrio Beach. We both want to have a couple days of rest and relaxation within the natural elements. At the end of the trail we discover that we have the whole beach to ourselves. We proceed to lie around, engaging in many open-ended conversations and soaking up the loving warmth from the Sun. The focus for our dialogues is centred mostly on 'emotions' and 'relationships'.

I have been recounting to my friend the emotional backlog I have been holding on to and carrying around inside me for such a long time. I am now aware that the purpose for me being here at this time has to do with my emotional expressions within the various relationships within myself, as well as with others. Whatever is unfolding will allow me to bring to the surface – within my conscious awareness – and to bring into a harmonious alignment, my entire emotional structure. I am aware of how hooked I still am on some of the deep-rooted emotional patterns that are attached to my illusionary but very real past experiences.

We decide to go for a short hike through the trails that border the shoreline. Along the trail I am directed to a bright red flower by an aspect of my Higher Self. I am told that it will aid me in releasing the blocked emotional patterns that are still hidden deep within me, and that it will also allow my heart to be open and receptive to feeling through the illusions that might very well surface during my stay out here. This flower will also help strengthen certain energy patterns that are in the process of changing and evolving within my being. I allow my body the freedom to eat as much of the flower as it needs. I acknowledge Nature for providing me with what is necessary, and then we continue on our way.

We are both standing on the outer edge of the main rock formation, looking for a way to get to another section of rock that is separated by a four foot wide channel of water. The waves are quite large, and when they rush through this channel, the water level rises two or three feet. The waves continuously slap at the sides of the rocks, spraying water in all directions as they move through the narrow passageway.

I intently watch the waves as they continue their pattern of movement. I am now aware that there are three big, heavy waves, then a slight pause as the interacting swirls of water change their patterns of flow. Then there is a small, light wave, and then three more heavy ones. The natural rhythm appears to be set. Now all I have to do is attune myself to this external rhythm, and I will easily be able to make the transfer. I mention to my friend that we can make it to the other side if we time it correctly. She declines my invitation and tells me to go ahead. She says that she will take an indirect route to avoid getting wet or possibly hurt.

I wait until the third big wave arrives and is on its way out again before I make my move. I proceed to jump down to a small platform half way to my destination. This platform is a vital and necessary stepping-stone, as the other side of the channel is steep and slippery, and I do not feel that I can make the leap in one attempt. It is safer and wiser for me to take it one step at a time. This way I will be sure to arrive at my destination dry and in one piece. It is very much like what I am moving toward in my living expression, making the big leap into another world that exists deep within me.

I do not make the jump from one rock to the other all at once, for there are too many shifting, interconnecting waves moving in and out of the area I am hoping to move across. Symbolically, the water represents the emotional patterns that hinder my flowing movements between my two worlds. I can only observe all that is around me in order to align myself with the natural flowing rhythm. I do not want to control this rhythm. I only want to connect with it and allow it to move me. By moving in this manner, I will not use my own personal energy in any of my movements. When I am in perfect harmony with the surrounding rhythm, that is the most appropriate time to allow my movements to begin. The mid-way platform is to serve as a junction that will provide me with a safe passage through to a new world. It will also offer me an opportunity to readjust to my new surroundings and become more flowing and more stable within my movements.

I see that the next wave is already on its way in. Nature has tricked me! The wave is arriving ahead of when I had figured it would. I am about to get another reminder that it is not important for me to think about how things should be. It is more important to feel the unfolding of any experience within my inner awarenesses. I must allow my outer senses to do what they have been created for – to move through my outside world. I leap for a protruding rock section. As I begin to move, my right foot slips on the slimy surface of the platform. This drastically affects the connection I am able to make on the other side. As the wave comes rushing through, my right foot gets soaked. Symbolically, I am seeing that I might stumble a few times while I am making this total transition between my two worlds. But nevertheless, I will ultimately succeed in my quest. I am also aware that I will only stumble and fall if I choose to take my eyes off the internal light that is guiding me, and instead turn my full focus and attention on to the volatile emotional waters that are constantly around me within my thought patterns.

I continue to climb until eventually I come to rest on dry land. I motion to my friend to come over to where I am, but she decides to stay where she is. It is much safer and more familiar. I climb up to the highest possible point on this section of rock, some thirty feet above the water line. I position myself so that I am looking out over the water and everything else that lies before me. My friend has selected a place to sit that is near the water. I wave at her, and she waves back. We both remove our clothes – symbolic of man's world – and attune ourselves fully to the natural surroundings, absorbing the warmth and unconditional love from the Sun.

I alter my awareness and begin to create different perspectives with regard to what this unfolding experience might symbolically represent. I am now looking at my friend and where she is choosing to be, in relation to where I am choosing to be. What I see (from one angle) is that the path I am travelling on is being created by a spiritual light that originates deep within me. I am searching for my truth, and nothing else will do. I am only able to see life from where I am, for living in the moment is all there is. As I sit up here, I recognize that I have always travelled to the top of everything in order to find my purest truth. I have never left anything to chance. It has always been my choice. I am now aware that I can always go back down to where my friend is. It is also important to acknowledge that she is not able to come up to where I am in the spiritual realms, for she has consciously made her decision to remain on the earthly plane.

I now proceed to look at this experience from another perspective. This time my friend represents an aspect of my being that is attached to living on the earthly plane and is controlled and governed by the five earthly senses. Where she has situated herself is close to the water's edge, surrounded by water on three sides. The waves are continuously breaking and spewing froth right next to her. She is totally enclosed within the volatile sea of emotions.

Here I sit on my high rock, also representing an aspect of my being, totally removed from the effects of the waves – my emotions – observing all that is taking place below me. I am receiving a much larger and clearer picture than the other part of me down by the water. I am now seeing that the two separate worlds are very real. I have been living in both of them separately, while seriously searching for a way to align the two.

I ask myself this question, "Is it possible for me to be totally removed from my earthly senses and still function on the earthly plane?" I hear myself answer, "Yes, it is possible."

But that is the extent of the dialogue and I know that I will have to look deeper into this question in order to find the depth behind the answer.

I am aware that my emotions are created by thoughts that originate from outside stimuli, and that they are brought into my awareness by way of my five earthly senses. If I remove myself totally from being forcefully involved in my outer world affairs, then it will be possible to move through my entire life as an observer to all that would be creatively unfolding. I would then have no need to judge what I see or sense (with any of my five physical senses) as being good or bad, right or wrong. I would be totally free to observe everything in the purity of how it is being created. In this light, my emotions would not exist, for there would be no thought as to what the unfolding experience is all about. There would be no judgments or comparisons made in regard to any of my experiences.

The aspect of my being that is attached to the earthly plane cannot possibly become an observer, for he is too involved. His vision is limited by the fact that, within the unfolding of any new experience, he is always busy creating an emotional thought that can 'tie' him to the experience – by making a judgment or comparison as to what he thinks the experience represents – so that he can accumulate more power and be in full control. He always does this either before the experience has happened or after it has already happened. This emotional tie would bring me either pain or pleasure. This aspect of my self cannot possibly see clearly how the world actually is, for he is only able to see from a very limited, one dimension of reality that is totally under the control of my five earthly senses.

It all appears to be so simple. Deep within I know it to be the truth. It is simple in its expression, as truth always is. I begin to look around for what Nature is providing so I can observe this simple truth as it is naturally unfolding. I choose to focus on observing how the moving water comes in to meet with the rocks. I am aware of some kind of interacting movement taking place between both substances of matter. I see that neither one is holding on to the other, yet each of them is very much able to move in harmony within the limited boundaries and expressive forms of the other. I proceed to remove myself from my physical embodiment and project myself inside the rock formation that is right at the lowest level of the rushing water. I want to experience what it is like to be without any thought for stability in my existence.

The water surrounds and caresses every aspect of my form. The gentle massaging of the swirling water on my outer surface is slowly wearing down my rough edges and making me smoother and more rounded. Where the parts of my living form are worn and loose, the water penetrates them from every conceivable angle and re-sculptures me, subtly changing my texture of presentation and form of expression with every gentle movement. The next time the water comes to caress my form, it will have to change within its movement patterns in order to accommodate the new changes – within my surface structure – that have been made by the wave before it. This is a continually unfolding experience. We are both constantly changing and growing in our awarenesses. We are forever forming into each other in some ways and remaining distinctly apart in others.

I am truly enlightened by what I am observing within my entire being. The rock holds on to nothing. The water holds on to nothing. Both are complete within themselves as they are. Each of them is forever changing and evolving, becoming the purest essence of itself each and every moment of their interconnecting relationship. In their expressions, neither one is better than the other, for they are the same in their substance – both being expressional forms of matter. They are both spiritual in their essence.

I return once again to my own physical form on top of the rock, gazing down upon the other aspect of my self (as represented by my friend) that is sitting on the Earth being affected by, or affecting others by, how he chooses to move through his creative process. I am seeing, perhaps for the first time, the completeness that is expressed through that aspect of my being. It is not good or bad, right or wrong. It is just as it is, complete within its beingness as it continually unfolds.

I proceed to remove myself from where I am, within my physical form, to a place outside myself so that I can clearly observe that aspect of my self – my spiritual self. What I am now seeing is that it too is totally complete within its own form. It is in need of nothing, for it is connected to everything. It is attuned to the universal flow of life, the life force that is solely responsible for the manifestation of all things on the earthly plane. The two sides of my self are complete within themselves, but separated from each other by the process of thought. The earthly side of me is restricted by limited boundaries. The spiritual side of me has total freedom of movement within any dimension of reality, which he can access at any time.

I contemplate. I can do one of two things at this point in time: Firstly, I can remain here on this rock and live my life totally separated from my other side. Secondly, I can return to the earthly plane, acknowledge my other side, in its completeness, and help guide it through those trying times – that would be created by my thoughts – within my transformation until such time that the alignment and subsequent merging is complete within my living expression.

Is it possible for me to return to the earthly plane and enter into an accepting relationship with both sides of my self – spiritual and earthly – and begin to move through my conscious movements with the total awareness of how all things are part of the same structural fabric – that being thought? Thought is responsible for creating fragmentation within an experience, that eventually leads to ownership of the experience, and hence, gives way to the birth of emotions that support pleasure or pain. In seeing and in knowing this as truth within me, it is now possible to move through my daily experiences with no ownership directly attached to the experiences I create. With no ownership, there can be no thought as to what the experience is all about, and there will be no need for me to create any emotions. I will have, within my functional reality, the total freedom to passively observe all that comes into my scope of vision from my outer world. I will be able to use this information to let go more and more of the perceptions as to who I think I am, and allow more of who I truly am to be acknowledged.

Below is an example of how this might function within an experience:

> I am walking down the sidewalk, and a stunning woman approaches me – a woman who has a shapely, curving form and a beautiful, glowing face. I am automatically stimulated by her outer appearance. My body instantly begins to alter its internal vibration, primarily due to the mental perceptions I am creating and holding on to in my thought processes. I am now totally engulfed by my earthly senses. I am losing sight of this woman as a person. I am now seeing her as an object, an object to satisfy my inner desire to fulfill a pleasure or pain sensation within my unfolding movements. These two sensations occur within the same time sequence. It is my though process that decides which one it will choose for that particular experience. It is all dependent upon which one will give my earthly self more power and control within the form of the unfolding movement.
>
> I am quickly becoming fragmented in all areas of me, and my earthly self – five senses – is taking over full control of this experience, creating an ongoing image of what it wants to have happen. It is an image that is not at all real in my outside world. My spiritual self arrives on the scene and supportively acknowledges the object of beauty. He then reminds my earthly self that the image he has created is an illusion, an illusion that he has

created totally from within his own reactionary thought structure, and one that is based entirely on the judgments and comparisons that come to life from his perceptions. My spiritual self mentions to my earthly self that he is losing the reality that this woman is a living expression of life, who is very much connected to all the other expressions of life. In this light, this woman is not separate from himself, and he is now making judgments and comparisons about himself.

In reality, there is only the self. All truth lies within the multi-dimensional structure of the self. This is all that ever needs to be acknowledged. The reality of what this woman symbolically stands for instantaneously takes on a whole new reality. I am now seeing how this woman has afforded me another opportunity to see myself in relation to the worlds I continually create and live within from moment to moment.

Now I begin to look at my friend's position and mine on the rocks from yet another angle. This time I am choosing to see her as a woman who I am deeply involved with mentally, physically and emotionally. I am clearly seeing that she would also represent all the other women I have ever interacted with, beginning with my mother. Being intimate with my friend clearly opens all my past relationships for rediscovery and re-examination to either free myself completely or to further obscure my vision. Reflecting back on the conversations she and I had on the beach earlier, I am now aware that I had primarily talked to her about the anger and frustration I experienced within past relationships.

I now realize that I have not been sensitive to my friend as a woman, laying out to her all that illusionary emotional garbage I have been holding on to. I have been treating her like an object, to be used to either vent my frustrations on or to enjoy my pleasures with. I see that I have lost my awareness to living in the present moment, and my sensitivities toward her as a beautiful woman, worthy of attention. I have treated her like an object that I thought I could posses in the exact same way as I had interacted with the other women in my life.

I am now looking carefully at the first relationship I ever had with a woman – my mother. I am now aware that it was with her that I had set up my foundational movement patterns, and that I have been continually living those patterns within the framework of every relationship I have had with a woman. Each relationship I have had has reminded me of the relationship I have had (and still have) with my mother. These patterns are based entirely on how I had perceived what was taking place within our interacting movements.

I am now aware that I have been attaching myself to all the women I have ever been close to with invisible strings. Every time a new woman entered into my life, I would attach her to the same string line. In so doing, I would use her to either vent my frustrations on or to support me in being self-powerful. These relationships were doomed right from the beginning. I had set them up, by way of my past programming and conditioning, so they would not be viable. I did this so I could continue to be frustrated and angry within my living expression, and be completely ruled by my five earthly senses. Self-defeating, but true.

The question I am now asking myself is, "Is it possible for me to live in a relationship with a woman completely free of all strings?"

As I am observing this question, I see that it is indeed possible for me to do that. When I am complete within myself and moving in my life without judgments – thoughts – and I am able to observe myself move through my day without wanting control, then I will be able to move harmoniously within a supportive relationship with a woman, totally observing our relationship and continuously acknowledging her as being an integral part of everything I am. Therefore, she is not an object to either own or possess. She is an equal being who is very much able to bring riches into my life, and I am able to bring riches into her life, as I give myself unconditional freedom to live totally within the unfolding moment.

What a glorious insight I am having within myself. It is time for me to return to where my friend is sitting, to be with her in a whole new way, and to be with myself in a whole new way as well. I energetically jump across the divide and slowly approach her, being extremely sensitive not to invade her personal space. I proceed to ask her, "Would you like some company?"

With a warm smile on her face, she says, "Pull up a rock and sit yourself down."

I proceed to tell her the gist of all that I had been seeing while I was sitting up on the rock. I openly acknowledge her for her sensitivity in listening to what I had to say on the beach earlier. I outwardly acknowledge my deepest feelings, "Thank you for being who you are. And thank you for being my friend."

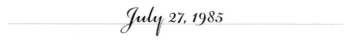

*July 27, 1985*

Later that afternoon, as I am sitting alone on Sombrio Beach, looking back into the wooded area, I want to see if there is anything I can use within the natural elements to help strengthen my awareness with regard to manifesting a harmonious relationship within myself and with all other beings on the earthly plane. I am observing two trees that are growing side by side and sharing the same foundational trunk and root system. They are both fine looking specimens, and their outer thickness makes me aware that they have been around for a long time. I sit down underneath them directly in the centre of where they are divided. I continue to sit quietly, attuning myself to their vibrational frequency, in the hope that I might be able to get some insight into how the two of them have made it so far by sharing everything they have. When the appropriate inner channel is open, I ask, "Do you have a relationship?"

They respond in unison, "We do not call it that. We know not what you refer to as a relationship."

I then ask, "What do you call what you have?"

They respond quickly and precisely, "We have no name for what we have. It is always continually evolving. We have no thought of what it is, like you do."

I think for a moment and then ask, "Is it possible that you might share with me your infinite wisdom as to what you do have?"

Again precisely and with a gentle voice, they begin, "We are here to be of service to ourselves and to the rest of the planetary life forms, encompassing all things on the physical plane and within all dimensions of reality. We are only superficially rooted to the Earth, in that our root systems only go downwards a short distance. You see, we all support each other in our growth process by aligning ourselves in large groups, so we can protect ourselves from the elements that surround us. We are all connected to Mother Earth. Mother takes care of us and nurtures us. We all share the same soil that is provided for us.

"We all know that we are being well looked after and cared for, for when we serve, we always receive what we need most, when we need it. We are continuously stretching ourselves higher and higher, moving toward the pure light of the Sun – the almighty creator that has given us a connection to the life-force energy, and that supports us in growing. When we are giving of ourselves openly and freely within all that we are, we are fed from Mother Earth. We must first give of ourselves, unconditionally, before we can openly receive our own life-force energy. They work hand in hand, balanced in every way.

"We do all of our growing from the inside, through the central core of who we are. All nurturing that comes from Mother, comes up from the Earth and supports us in growing towards the open sky and the ever-nurturing Sun. Although the two of us are connected by the same trunk and root structure, we both move within ourselves independently. At the same time, we depend on each other for everything. We are well aware that we both have a purpose here on this plane. We see that it is to be of service in a very large way. We know that we both have different growth cycles, as you can see from our physical structures, yet we both grow in the same way. We are both the same in that we have both come from the same seed, but we express ourselves differently in our movements within our outer worlds, as you can see from looking at the differences in our size and dimensions.

"Within myself, I am able to observe my own ever-unfolding creative process. I also get to observe all those around me unfolding within their own creative process, and acknowledge them for serving in the manner that is best suited for who they are. We are all well aware that there are no differences within us, for we have all come to be here from the same seed. We know that there is actually no difference between the way we are now, in this precise time sequence, and the way that we were when we were first put into the ground as a small seed. We also know that we will be no different when it is time to be no longer of service in this way, but perhaps another. As we continue to grow internally, we continue to expand our physical expression and spiritual essence out into the outer world.

"That is all I wish to say at this time. I am sure that you have received, within my dissertation, all that you were looking for."

I acknowledge, "Yes, indeed, and much more. Thank you for your enlightening words. I shall take what I have heard and apply it, as best I can, within my own living expression."

## August 11, 1985

I am now seeing that everything outside me is controlled by the conceptual ideas of time and of space. I also see that everything that is created within my internal awarenesses is totally free of time and of space within its creation and its expression. Within me lies a void – a void of darkness. It is the place where my Earthly Mind connects with the higher vibrations of Universal Mind, but only if my internal channels are open enough to allow their attunement. If the different factions within my Earthly Mind's thought processes are opposing each other, striving for control and for power, then the necessary channels for clearly hearing what is on the higher vibrational frequencies will not be open. As long as these factions are distorting the clarity within the reality of my functional innermost truth, they will continue to tune into those lower vibrations – from either the inner or outer space surrounding my personal being – in order to support their movements, or to add to their diversification through their organized confusion. All of this to accumulate more power and to have maximum control.

I clearly see that there is nothing that truly exists outside me. Every thing on this plane is created within the delicate fabric that constitutes my Mind, Body and Spirit. I was well aware of this simple truth before this day, but not to the same intensity as I am now. It was more from an intellectual reality than from a practical, functional reality.

> The sensitive light rays that make up all thought patterns, as well as all possible realities on this plane, whirl around inside of the larger consciousness of mankind, and they are directly presented within the unrestricted, formless structure of my consciousness. These sophisticated patterns of light align and connect to each other – in relationship to the different vibrations and resonations they constitute – to form various specified thought patterns of varying textures. These patterns of thought are created within my Earthly Mind elements, and they are brought forth, with intensity and with focus, within my bodily form by way of my five earthly senses. These senses are held within the framework of my physical body, and are controlled within my body's physical brain. The human body is made up of these same light energies, as is all matter that exists here on this earthly plane. The energies that make up the infinite number of thought patterns within my Earthly Mind come from the same delicate fabric, although they are much more subtle than my outer physical body.
>
> The clearer my focus is on these creative thought patterns – whether they are supportive or non-supportive makes no difference – the quicker they become realities in my outer environment. Since my outer environment is made up of these same light patterns, it is also created within the fabric of my thought patterns. These patterns are able to control the very texture of the realities that are created in my outer environment. In essence, then, my outer environment is only a play-act of the entire interplay between the different areas of my total mind that I am choosing to create and identify with at any one time.
>
> As the initial stages of creating these forms of thought take place within the early stages of a child's life, he unconsciously

begins to alter and change these patterns of thought, or light patterns, in direct relationship to the original stimulus (stimuli) he had encountered – the master building blocks. From this core of expression comes an infinite number of variables for him to choose from.

My Earthly Mind element gets heavily involved in creating opposing factions – within its own structural fabric – in order to keep control of the game it is playing with itself, and also to maintain chaotic order and control within itself. It becomes so involved within its own ever-unfolding fabric, that it knowingly creates the illusion that there is 'someone' outside of itself who is totally responsible for how it chooses to respond to outside stimulation. This someone is also responsible for how it chooses to create new forms of outside stimulation. This is quite impossible, for in real reality Mind is all that truly exists.

My power-hungry Earthly Mind begins to create angles of communication within itself to further diversify and confuse itself, so it will not have to look seriously at any of the truthful realities. It is not so much that it won't look, but rather, it is that things will be so scattered within its structural framework that it won't want to look that hard for the clarity in anything. There are always too many things going on at any one time within its formless expressions. It is forever creating levels of involvement that bring itself either pleasure or pain to further confuse itself within its own clarity as to what is real. It creates pain from pleasure, and pleasure from pain; or just straight pleasure, or just straight pain. It is definitely involved in a no-win situation with itself.

It creates pleasure and convinces itself that life is going along smoothly. Then it inflicts pain on itself, mentally or physically or emotionally, to show itself that pleasure is a reward, received only if it conforms to the appropriate action that is required in the world of man. When things are going too smoothly in the outer world of man, it usually creates a situation that will produce pain so that it can justify to itself that life is not all pleasure. One soon forgets the effects of pleasure. When there is pleasure, it is not held securely within the delicate fabric of my Earthly Mind for too long, for it does not have the same ability to divide me as pain does. Pain always creates more power and more divisions within the structural fabric of my Earthly Mind. One chooses not to forget as easily the experience that brings with it pain, for the vibrational texture is very different from that of pleasure. In reality, though, they are both the same, for they are mirror images of each other. One cannot have pain unless one has pleasure, and one cannot have pleasure unless one has pain. It is only the divided factions within my Earthly Mind that create the illusionary difference.

We are constantly being reminded of pain by our Earthly Mind, by the constant regurgitation of old, non-supportive experiences. Their texture is always altered or changed just enough so the pain can be reinforced in order to hold the mind-set to the earthly plane.

If man is always busy chasing the mind around, within and without himself, then he will be less likely to realize that perhaps this is not a beneficial thing to do. If his world consists of too much pleasure, he will never find the need to consciously look within himself to find out where all the pleasure is coming from. Likewise, it will be the same if he is getting too much pain, in that he won't consciously take the time to stop and look at what is actually causing all the pain. It would be so much easier to keep running away from the pain, or so he would think.

The mind is a very tricky entity, and yet, at the same time, it is extremely simple in its movements, for it has limiting factors here on this plane. If one chooses to focus his mind at any given time, and stop the inner wheels of perception from spinning, then the simple truth would be presented. The mind has the capability of being like a laser-beam of pure white light, or it can be like a diffused light bulb. It is purely by a choice that decides which one of the two comes up for an individual at any given point in time.

Deep down inside, we all know how it actually is for each of us. It is an inner journey. The only kind of journey that really exists. There isn't anything else. There is no place to go. There is nothing to do. It all continuously takes place within my inner dimensions of reality. If one goes in deep enough, one will see the illumination of the self, and the full realization that the creation of all life comes from within.

> All relationships on the external physical plane do not exist. They only exist within the delicate fabric of the sophisticated Mind. Even within itself, it is impossible for the Mind to have a relationship with itself. Unless, of course, it creates a division within itself to do so. This kind of relationship would be based on the opposing forces within itself – like pain and pleasure. Take it all right back to the root structure, and you will be able to see it much clearer. All there is, is Mind. Whether it is Universal Mind, or Earthly Mind, or Spiritual Mind, makes no difference. They are all Mind: All the same Mind.

> Spiritual Mind and Earthly Mind denote a division within Universal Mind. It is impossible, and yet at the same time possible, for the Mind to be complete within itself if it is continually dividing within itself. To divide itself gives it more power to create opposite polarities within itself: pain, which is negative, and pleasure, which is positive. In reality, there is only what is: both are contained within the one. Pain/pleasure are one in the same, with no divisional boundaries between them. It is not possible to have one without the other, for they support each other in their outward expressions.

> The God light is within the overall reality of Mind. In order for one to return to this higher vibration within a functional living expression, all divisions within the elements of Earthly Mind must be eliminated from within. To continually eliminate the opposing factions gives rise to the purity of what is: a forever continuous unfolding of the Universal Mind of mankind; a Mind that always remains constant through constant change. Everything that is on the earthly plane changes, and it also stays the same.

> Earthly Mind is continually changing in its outward expressions, unconditionally allowing itself, as well as all forms of life, to grow and to unfold. Then again, sometimes Earthly Mind never changes its outward expressions, thereby continually holding itself, and all other forms of life, from growing and unfolding.

## *August* 24, 1985

"Reality – what is it? One reality opposed to another. Is there actually any difference? Which one is real? Is either of them real? Yes, they are both real, and yet neither of them is real."

I have been questioning the limiting factors concerning a particular reality, wanting to know if it is possible for me to live on this earthly plane without having any constant realities, yet having the freedom and the ability to enter into all realities.

"Of course it is possible," says a voice from within. "Go deeper into it, and you will see. Go deeper into your inner self, to the place where all realities exist and where no realities exist."

I was walking into town today, talking to myself out loud with different emotions behind the various conversations I was having. I was creating an open discussion with two distinctly different voices from within my inner void, two totally different realities within me. The voices were questioning everything that came up, primarily looking at the way things are perceived by me now, and seeing if they could indeed be changed – changing them and shifting myself into another creative reality.

How do I know that all that is here on this plane is actually real? I have been told – by those who have called themselves an authority – that it is real, and that it has been structured the way it is because that is the way it is supposed to be. My reality is not actually my reality. I have accepted, within my movement of expression in my outer world, someone else's reality. Where is mine? My reality is limited to the scope of the reality that belongs to the person(s) I have been following. All of society is limited and restricted by the rules that are enforced to govern it.

As long as I continue to look outside myself for my answers, I will always be limited, for I will have chosen, due to my programming and conditioning, to align myself with those realities. The possibility of creating many different realities takes me away from this plane, yet I am still able to be on this plane – in it, but not of it!

How much power do I actually have? I am verbalizing things within and without myself, only to seriously look at, mind you. What I am seeing is that I have tremendous personal power. I have the personal power to die and to create a new life, as I have done within me. I have the personal power to materialize all the things I need in my life, when I need them. I have the personal power to stop all wars, as I have done within me. I have the personal power to change people, as I have done within me. I have the personal power to heal people, as I have done within me. I have the personal power to physically disappear when I no longer need to be in a certain place. I have the personal power to be present or not present in my unfolding thoughts. I have the personal power to do anything I want. I have it all inside me, not outside. Nothing exists outside of myself. If I go looking outside myself for anything, I will be giving away my personal power to some creative illusion. I will become the victim of whatever I choose to create out there. As long as I remain inside myself, I will be able to alter and to change time and space, for I am all time and all space. I affect people by just being myself. That is all I ever have to do – be myself! If I am, I will have everything. If I am not being myself, I will have nothing.

I am in the midst of looking at the power I have to change realities – both mine and other people's – when a man and a woman stop me on the sidewalk, and the woman asks how far it is to a certain tourist attraction in the city. They want to know if it would be possible to get to this particular venue if they keep walking in the same direction. Unfortunately for them, they are heading away from their destination. I mention that they have to go back the same way they came. The man insists that they are definitely heading in the right direction; his reality for him. The woman has a completely different reality than he does. She really isn't at all sure where the place is, and she openly admits it. She is more flexible. My reality is totally different from his and hers.

The man has a brochure in his hand that apparently describes where he wants to go. He is still very sure that they are heading in the right direction. He is desperately searching for the page in the brochure that will support his claim. He is really having a difficult time letting go of his reality. I can tell by his insistence that he must have been the one who chose the direction they are heading in. I excuse myself and ask if I can turn the pages of the brochure he is holding; action speaks much louder than words. I am going to affect and change his reality in one quick, fleeting moment. All I need is a detailed diagram showing the exact location of the place they want to visit. The appropriate page is found. My finger is dropped, and bingo! It is right on the exact location. With the full initiation of that one small gesture, I have successfully changed the realities that each of them had. They are both now aligned to my reality.

The man is still reluctant to accept his new reality. He is still searching through the pages of the brochure, looking for validation for his original reality so he won't have to acknowledge his error to his lady friend. As I am leaving the scene, he is still holding on. My reality is that I have changed their realities. It is all so simple.

They both had invited me into their separate and combined realities. They invited me to change their realities. One had fought the change. He was fighting the very thing he wanted. I affected their realities by giving them directions. The right information at the appropriate time changed their realities. Had they not asked for directions when they did, their realities would have taken them to a different place, only to discover, once they were there, that their individual or combined reality hadn't gotten them to the place they wanted to go.

I am able to create any reality that I choose in my outer and inner world. I am, in totality, the reality that I choose to create. I am not reality. Reality is me, in my entirety. I am not reality. Reality is me, in all that I do.

All I ever have to do is be myself. In so doing, I will affect people all the time. I don't have to be *someone*. I am already whatever and whomever I choose to be. I control all of my realities. I must stay clearly focused on my realities. That's it. That's the key: to look inside in order to find out what it is all about. To be able to see all the different realities that are there and that are not there, and to know that I can become any of those realities whenever I choose. My reality is that I am no longer limited as to what I can do here on this plane, or anywhere else!

# CHAPTER 7

# INITIATIONS INTO HIGHER ASPECTS

## August 10, 1985

I am house-sitting for some friends, looking after their townhouse and their two cats. I am sprawled out on the floor, observing the ever-changing creative movements of the two cats as they playfully interact with each other. I feel very much like an onlooker from another dimension of time, lying perfectly still, allowing myself to become just another ornament that has been placed in the room. I have successfully created a safe environment in which I can further expand myself into other altered states of being. I am much freer within myself, allowing myself to drift further and further inward, heading for the central core of my physical being, intrinsically knowing that all I will need to know within this particular time sequence will be revealed to me.

Suddenly, the front door flies open, and all the fragmented pieces of my being – those aspects of myself that are stretched out into the far corners of this room and all the other rooms in the house – are quickly hurtling their way back into the pulsating physical embodiment I am observing from. I am now more aware of just how far I have allowed myself to drift, and how vulnerable I am feeling. Even this place, where I have been residing alone as of late, cannot offer me the safest or most ideal environment for me to peel away a little more of the outside layers of my being.

As my two friends make their way through the open doorway, I hurriedly try to put myself back together again to a point where I will be able to converse with them in an orderly fashion. As I continue to move through my day, talking to my friends about their trip, I can feel myself beginning to come apart. I can also feel all sorts of emotional reactions beginning to swell from deep within me, all of which I know do not really exist. They are only projections of some deep-rooted thought patterns that have occupied time and space in my life many years ago.

This unpredicted and untimely interruption has made me acutely aware of just how close I am to stepping through yet another significant doorway leading to the depths of my inner being and to my ultimate connection with the rest of the universe. It is now time to find another possible living arrangement so that I might complete this segment of my internal initiation while it is still presenting itself.

My sister has offered me the use of her apartment 'up island' for as long as she is on holidays. This is the only option that has presented itself directly to me, and I know that it is where I need to be. I need to be away from everyone I know and all the distractions I am used to having in my outer world.

## August 11, 1985

It is apparent that I will have to do something immediately or else lose this golden opportunity forever, and I am not at all sure when the next one will present itself. Without further delay, I phone the bus depot and find out when the next up island bus is leaving from downtown Victoria. I then let my two friends know that I am going to be going away for as long as I need to in order to clear up some things that are happening within me. I am not even trying to explain to them what is actually going on. I know that they will not be able to understand any of it, as I am not even sure myself. I make the remaining necessary phone calls to those people who I had already made arrangements to meet in the upcoming week, and then I leave.

As the bus pulls out of the depot, I know that I am doing the most appropriate thing to enable the internal process to continue to unfold. I am feeling much more relaxed within myself, for I know that at the other end of this five-hour bus trip there is a safe and nurturing place waiting. It is a place where I can remain quiet and still within myself for as long as I deem it necessary, and a place that will afford me another opportunity of looking still deeper into the delicate fabric that comprises and holds together the very essence of my being.

On arriving at my sister's apartment, I close the door behind me, put my things down on the floor, take a deep breath, and leisurely position myself on the chesterfield. I am sitting perfectly still within the openness of the room, feeling the extent of all that will surround me for the next undetermined number of days.

As I gaze around, I am aware that this room I am sitting in, and the ones adjoining it, contains every possible distraction the outside world has to offer. It is all so perfect in its design. Here I thought I had to get away from all of my outer world distractions in order to be able to see everything clearly, only to come all the way up here to find out otherwise. It will be by going into, not avoiding, all of my outer world distractions that I will make my way through them.

There is a TV, a stereo, a tape deck and lots of tapes and records to listen to. There is all sorts of food in the fridge and in the cupboards. There are books all over the place. There are ornaments hanging on all the walls. There are ornaments positioned on the dining room table, the coffee table, and the two end tables at either end of the couch. Nearly every inch of this small, three-room apartment is occupied with some physical form of matter. I am clearly aware that I will have to continually walk a very thin line in order that I might receive the gifts of learning that are here.

I do a quick search of all the rooms, making myself familiar with where everything is. I put my things into the bedroom, being careful not to disturb the orderly arrangement my sister had put everything in before she left. I return to the couch, where I take the liberty of stretching myself out on the soft, supportive structure. I am looking aimlessly out into the centre of the room, letting my thoughts move however they will, not really wanting to control how they are being created or the things they would wish to create. I only want to be an observer of all that will present itself.

I had purchased some brown rice and popcorn before I left Victoria. These two things will be the only foods I will consume while I am here. I will be eating one bowl of popcorn a day and one small bowl of rice. I will consume them without adding anything to them, thereby depriving my physical senses from making them more than what they actually are.

The less the sensory stimulation, the easier it will be to go deeper inside, and the easier it will be to reach the purest communication with my Higher Self – the purest vibration of the Higher Self that exists within me. There are so many functional dimensions to my Higher Self. The purest one is that of the God energy – the total reality of all things.

I have been lying here on the couch for nearly six hours, watching my own internal movement and observing all the other movements within my external environment. I am looking attentively for the appropriate insertion point to align myself with so that I can communicate with the higher aspects of my being. I close my outer eyes and allow myself to drift freely within the greater depths of my physical embodiment.

I am moving through the open doorways that lead to the innermost dimensions of my being. I now see a pulsating light that is either heading straight for me, or I am heading straight for it. I am not at all sure which one it is, but I am not overly concerned. I know that we are definitely on a collision course. In a flash, there is a death, and then there is the commencement of a new life.

I have entered into a light-filled chamber of indescribable beauty and intensity. All that exists here is white light. I am also aware of the presence of another being. This being has substance and form, and he is the radiating energy force that brings this room to life and sustains its high frequency resonations of pulsating, life-giving expressions. I am seeing and feeling – on depths I have not known existed before – that this magnificent being is my true inner self. This is the true God being that I am. It is the part of me that connects me to every other living expression of life on the earthly plane.

I open my outer eyes and look around the room. Everything is very much different, and yet it all looks the same as it did when I last looked.

I begin to hear an aspect of my Higher Self speak from the depths of my inner being, "You have arrived here – for this brief moment in your earthly time sequence – at the *centre* of your being, and at the *centre* of the universes that exist within the universe you are currently living in within your physical embodiment. You have been given a glimpse of that which is already yours so that you might fully recognize that all of what you have seen and felt within your being is very much real.

"There is much for you to become aware of before this state of being may be yours in your daily movements within your earthly life. The process is moving and unfolding in accordance to that which is. In so doing, all that you have seen, and will continue to see, will soon be of your entire presence. This is to be so, so you may begin your work upon this plane.

"During the next little while, you will be shown within your own internal makeup, and the makeup of all mankind, the simplicities and intricacies of how this earthly dimension operates – in its entirety. The more you continue to align yourself with this high frequency vibration, the easier your journey shall be. Be patient, and allow it all to unfold as it is so destined.

"You cannot stop the process that is now unfolding within you, nor can you speed this process up. It is moving in the most supportive manner there is: by the creation of the God energy at the *centre* of your being. This energy force is responsible for the creation of all things. Continue to look deeper within the darkened areas of your being, and all will be shown to you. The clearer your vision is upon your *centre*, the easier it will be for you to arrive and to remain at your *centre*."

My body begins to move without any conscious thought from me. I am an observer within my physical form, watching the unfolding process as my body approaches the dining table. I gently pull out a chair and align myself with it, sitting in a comfortable and relaxed position.

I continue to watch as my hands slowly reach across to the far corner and gasp the binder I had been internally instructed to bring. The bound cover is opened, exposing many sheets of loose-leaf paper that are secured by three metal rings. I open the rings and take out a small stack of paper. I position them in front of me in such a way that I am now ready to write. I reach over to the other side of where the binder now lies and take out a ballpoint pen.

I hear a voice from within begin to speak, "Concern yourself not with that which is about to unfold. Allow that which is about to unfold to describe to you that which is so. Judge not its contents as it is being struck to paper. Allow yourself the total freedom to move freely within all that is to be written. As it is so done this way, you shall see the benefit of it being done this way for you, by you."

And so the process begins to unfold as it is ordained by my internal source of all knowing. On the top of the first sheet, these words begin to flow from pen to paper:

A JOURNEY TO NOWHERE
Before entering into this plane of reality, there existed – as in all particles of matter and sub-matter – an infinite number of light modules of all shapes and all dimensions: some circular, some like thin rods, some squiggly like snakes slithering on a smooth surface, all of them forever changing in their structure, yet always remaining the same in their core-essence – the purest form of energy as I know it to be – white light.

The universe is without boundaries in every conceivable way. I am very much a part of it, an integral part. If I were not part of it, it would not be complete. There would be a void within the void. This would be impossible, yet at the same time, it would be possible. In the universe beyond man's universe within himself, all things are possible, even the impossible, for even to think that something is impossible, makes it possible.

At the base structure of all things is white light. Since white light is the base root structure of all things, all things come from that root structure.

Living in this void where the earthly plane has originated from, there are no time or space components as I know them to be. Rather, all things are continually changing, forming, re-changing, re-forming, as in the basic description of the white light particles mentioned previously.

It is decided that I must enter into this plane of man's universe and make my way as man-forms have done before me, and that I have also done on many occasions prior to this time. I have come here, as does everyone else, to learn the lessons of structure and form, time and space, control and acceptance, all within the ways that have been predetermined partially by those who are in control, and partially by my own doing, in order that I might have a hand in my own unique human evolution. I learn these things so that I might effectively change the consciousness of man by simply moving in the world of man as determined before my arrival here, and also, in the course of my movement while I am here on this plane.

Those in charge choose the most likely place for me to enter into this plane. My parents are selected by seeing what intricate components of light they vibrate with most consistently, and how that aligns itself with what I must work through in order to achieve clarity and truth while I am on this plane. This is where the creative process becomes interesting, for now the variables become infinite in their ability to form building blocks that will shape my world and determine the way in which I shall eventually move through it.

Upon conception, I enter in to the fertilized egg inside my mother that has been impregnated by the sperm of my father, each of them carrying genetically coded material combined together as mixtures of light components. Hence, I am formed by the simple building blocks of these light configurations, complete within myself from the start. Yet I am also receptive to change in an instant, depending upon what light ray attaches itself to me, or me to it.

I enter into this plane of earthly reality in an instantaneous burst of light – a blue arc. I am totally aware of all things in the universal universe: totally aware of things that have already happened, that are in the process of happening, and that will be happening in the days to come for as long as I am here in the world of man.

As I begin to grow within the void of darkness inside my mother, her light configurations are changing constantly as she moves through and within her world. They change by how she dialogues within her own Earthly Mind and by how she perceives and moves within her outer world. This, in turn, alters and changes the structural compositions of my light configurations to keep in proper alignment with hers. It is done this way so that I can be nurtured by her until I am ready to come out into the structured world of man and make my own way through it.

Since my mother has already developed her own Earthly Mind – in the creation of her own world – I too begin to develop my Earthly Mind in accordance with those component light structures that are developing within me, and affecting her Earthly Mind. That part of Earthly Mind is very much a structural component of this plane, so I have no choice. I must also develop a diversified Earthly Mind in accordance with the set laws that govern this one dimensional plane.

While I am inside the womb, I am constantly changing in my Earthly Mind forms and physical body forms. They all seem to grow and change at the same rate in here. That makes sense, for my physical body, and its functions, makes up my Earthly Mind. My Earthly Mind, in its ability to oversee many different things simultaneously, is within every living cell of my physical body. This arrangement makes for steady growth and development in all ways.

As long as I am inside the womb of my mother, I am primarily affected by her Earthly Mind changes and, toward the later stages within my development, by my own Earthly Mind changes, all along preparing me for the outside world of man. There now comes into existence within me much friction. There is now the mindset of my mother from the egg, the mindset of my father from the sperm, and my own mindset, which now begins to form its own intricate patterns of expression that are very much different from those of my parents.

Before I arrive into the outer world of man, I am constantly changing due to the infringing influences that are manifesting themselves in the inner world of my mother, and also within my own inner world. As I continue to grow and unfold within this inner world, I am still able to see the universal universe within its entirety.

As I move toward entering into this physical world, the divisions within my Earthly Mind begin to take in more variations in light structures. Because of this movement, more complicated thought patterns are created that requires more of my attention. They are forever changing, and there does not appear to be a common form to their origin.

As my thought energies continue to manifest according to earthly growth patterns, my clarity of knowing all that is within Universal Mind begins to lose its luster. Universal Mind is very subtle in its nature and in its form – it encompasses all things. Whereas the Earthly Mind of man is focused on such a small mass in comparison, and it always seems to be changing in its complexities and its simplicities. This aspect makes it all the more inviting to the newly forming, ever-changing Mind that I have come to attune myself to.

When I enter into this physical plane, I see things within their completeness (as in Universal Mind) and incompleteness (in their fragmented states within time sequences and space allotments). This constant duality continues until such time that my Earthly Mind assumes control within itself by setting up patterns of light components that are opposite, and yet these opposites are one in the same. This process lures my Earthly Mind, and all of its component parts, to be totally captivated and highly stimulated. My Earthly Mind does not allow itself to stop changing the patternings, for it wants and needs control and power on this plane; or so it has set it up this way. Within this physical earthly plane, these patternings are manifested as life-supporting and non-life-supporting thought patterns.

Things that I do as a child when I first arrive here make everyone laugh and smile, and I attach that response to the ever-changing and ever-unfolding building blocks within my Earthly Mind. As I grow older, these patterns of behavior – they are called that here – are no longer acceptable by some people's standards, including my parents, and so I begin to feel the opposing reality to the original pleasure patterning. This new pat-

terning branches off and forms another major building block
– pain – that has its root structure within my Earthly Mind.

My parents' building blocks are ever-unfolding, yet they
continuously struggle within themselves to keep them the same.
They want me to keep mine the same as well. They also want
me to stay the same – helpless and controllable – so they can
remain stable in their illusionary worlds; or at least this is the
way that they have it pictured in their mindsets. Each of them
has a certain belief system that is based entirely on their programmed and conditioned mindsets. They are continuously encouraging me to adopt the beliefs that are included within the
framework of their mindsets. They are not totally aware that I
have my own unique Earthly Mind unfolding from within me,
and that it needs to continuously grow and unfold without strict
beliefs and concepts like the ones they have accepted and follow
so adamantly.

My freedom – or my want of freedom – within my Earthly
Mind becomes a threat to them, as they now begin to see, on
a deeper level within their own Earthly Minds, that they have
lost their ability to allow their Earthly Minds to continuously
grow and unfold. This creates more friction within themselves.
The only way that they can effectively be friction-free is if they
can maintain control over everything I do in my outer world. To
control me and re-shape me – to make me conform to their beliefs – would be sufficient enough to keep each of their Earthly
Minds from stopping to look deep within its own structural fabric in order to expose the root of the true friction.

Earthly Mind knows that it is the root structure that is creating all the friction within its structural fabric. For it to look upon
itself with any kind of serious truth-seeking intention, would
automatically mean that it would lose its power and control; or
so it reasons within itself. This would not happen at the base levels though, only at the surface levels, for there it is continuously
changing so it won't have to stop its divisionary process.

It is apparent to me that my parents have the upper and controlling hand in the physical world of man, for they have as-
sumed authority over me on my behalf. By subtle force – mentally, physically and emotionally – they work on my Earthly

Mind, which has yet to have learned the finer art of mind control within its own boundaries on this plane. My Earthly Mind is still very much open to all the incoming stimuli that continually come into its ever-unfolding, ongoing view of reality. There is a gradual increase in the degree and intensity of friction within my Earthly Mind. Hence, I create more pleasure and pain within my inner and outer worlds, on the gross physical levels and subtle sub-levels.

My parents want me to attach their building blocks to me so that I will experience their forms of pleasure. At the exact same time, my own building blocks are calling for free-flowing expansion and formless creative growth – ultimate freedom of movement. The enforced restrictions imposed by my parents continue to bring more division, in the way of pain, into my worldly experience. It is a constant, self-encountering battle that rages inside my Earthly Mind – a Mind element that is fighting against a mindset that has its primary root structure within one Mind. My Earthly Mind is not able to see this clearly though, as it is always fully engaged in all that is going on within the superficial layers of its delicate fabric, and also around its ever-changing structural compositions. The internal surging for control continues, and so do the variables of pleasure and pain.

Everything that exists and is labeled within the world of man has been created and manifested into a physical reality by thought forms (light energy) that have been generated through the Earthly Mind of man. Since I am subtly encouraged, or forced, over time to adapt and conform to the mindsets of my parents, my outer world teachers, to religious philosophies, etc., I begin to attach myself more and more to the general overall controlling mindset of society.

As this is systematically occurring within me, I lose the clarity of my own mindset, and its base building blocks, which has its root in the Mind, itself. I am now beginning to thoughtlessly flow with whatever comes my way in the form of creative light patterns, ones that can either be attached to support my own sense of reality, or that can be added to already existing patterns to give me a whole new reality. This reality, in fact, would be an illusion, yet at the same time, it would still be very much 'real' and with real effect within my experiential worlds – either inside or outside.

I set within my Mind certain beliefs and concepts of reality that serve to be the building blocks with which I am to live my life here on this physical plane. The more intense the light configurations are, the easier the physical manifestation of whatever I want within my earthly movement. These beliefs and concepts of reality are based entirely upon the pleasure/pain game that was first contrived and brought into being by my continually unfolding, ever-expanding Earthly Mind at the very beginning of my earthly expression.

Now my Earthly Mind no longer freely or openly changes, grows, or expands within its limitless dimensions. It is now restricted within the dimensions of time and space. The building blocks that act as my self-importance foundation – my beliefs and concepts of reality – now regulate and restrict all movement within my inner and outer worlds.

A Mind element that in the beginning was so keen to grow and to expand now becomes self-restricted within its own structural fabric and slowly begins to do itself in. It has, within itself, become so diffused that it is no longer able to distinguish between the reality and the illusion within its own structural composition. It has wanted, and has managed to acquire, illusionary control and power. It has done this to such an unstable degree that now the tide has turned within its unfolding movement. That same quest for power and control is slowly taking its life. In essence, it is now beginning to die within itself and within the physical embodiment that allows it to be expressional.

In the universe of man, there are always opposite forces at work within himself. Within the whole Earthly Mind there is a divided Earthly Mind element – let's call it 'it' – and within my being, there is an all-knowing Spiritual Mind element – let's call it 'IT' – that is not of this earthly plane. 'IT' is always waiting for the struggle for power within "it" to subside long enough so a balance of power might be brought into focus within my being.

'IT' sees clearly all of what 'it' has done along its life journey and how 'it' has come into existence. 'IT' knows that the beliefs and concepts of reality that 'it' has been holding on to so tightly are not real. 'IT' also knows that they are very real. 'IT' knows that 'it' has been scattered just like diffused light that radiates from an ordinary light bulb. The all-knowing Spiritual Mind element 'IT' also knows that the divided Earthly Mind element 'it' has been intently focused in its ability to re-structure itself in order to preserve its control and power in the physical world of man.

'IT' clearly knows that for 'it' to hold on to all that 'it' has accumulated along its journey means certain death. 'IT' also knows that for 'it' to release all that it has become securely attached to over the years, means the instantaneous creation of a new living expression.

There is a continual dichotomy within 'it's' structural alignment. 'it' wants to hold on to all that it thinks it has, and 'it' also wants to release all of it as well, for it knows that what it has is really nothing. 'it' feels that it will have to save face within itself for what it has done, should 'it' now decide to stop the whole process; and this is what keeps the whole process repeating itself.

It now becomes another game, another angle for control and for power. Once again the base root is whole Earthly Mind – which is, in reality, a single Mind and at the same time, a continually diversifying Mind – divided Earthly Mind. The divided Earthly Mind element ('it') is always within the single entity yet dualistically exposed Universal Mind – Spiritual/Earthly Mind.

For the divided Earthly Mind to release itself completely would still give it the same power and control, for it would be choosing to let go, and it would be choosing to change and to grow. 'it' continues to be distracted by the outer world illusions/realities that it has based its beliefs on. This distractive attempt serves no functional purpose, for all things only exist by way of perceptual images within my whole Earthly Mind, or within the factions of my divided Earthly Mind.

The base root structure, no matter how I choose to look at it, is in whole Earthly Mind. It is all too simple, so my divided Earthly Mind (that exists within Earthly Mind) is forever trying to keep the complicated game going. My all-knowing Spiritual

Mind element 'IT' calls upon my divided Earthly Mind element 'it' in order to find clarity and restore balance. 'IT' wants to let 'it' know that it is not going to be terminated, and that 'it' is needed on this plane, for 'it' is of this plane: divided Earthly Mind of man 'it', whole Earthly Mind, and Spiritual Mind 'IT' are in fact, component parts of Universal Mind – one in the same.

Slowly, a forever shifting balance point is arrived at within my newly unified Earthly Mind. By seriously tracing all things back to their roots, I clearly see that there is only one Mind. I also see that there are many factions, or opposing dualities, within the one Mind. To see this reality clearly restores truth as my guiding hand and brings about quiet on all the different divisional levels within my whole Earthly Mind.

The unification process of my all-knowing Spiritual Mind element and my whole Earthly Mind element would also allow my divided Earthly Mind element 'it' to align itself with my all-knowing Spiritual Mind element 'IT,' to become single in its consistency yet multiple in its expressional movements.

'IT' would be able to restore the unfolding and growing stages within 'it's' development, so 'it' might trace its own pro-gressional steps back into the depths of 'IT' in order to find its true connection to Universal Mind – a Mind that is the same as 'it', yet separate from 'it.' As a result, 'IT' would find the key that would enable 'it' to consciously enter into the purified world of Universal Mind, and be able to see all that there is, in its entirety, and then re-enter into the world of man and use these new awarenesses to help man evolve and take a step forward in his evolution.

I will always remain in the same place, moving toward my own destiny and my own sense of purpose: to selflessly serve mankind in my quest to improve human conditions for true spiritual enlightenment here on this plane. To purify my divided Earthly Mind is to allow it to be whole once again, as it was in the beginning, growing into God-like light.

Every relationship I have ever had with people, within the scope of my earthly existence, has existed solely within the deli-cate fabric of my Earthly Mind, and they have been securely held together by my thought forms. They have also been based entirely on stagnant beliefs and concepts of reality. None of my relationships have ever been free to grow and to expand, for my governing beliefs were, for a time, restricted in their ability to allow that to happen.

It is impossible for me to have a relationship with someone who is outside me, for everyone only exists within the thought forms that make up my Earthly Mind. According to time and space, they exist outside my person. Take away the elements of time and space, and they are only composite thought forms within my Earthly Mind. To say this clearly brings about the creation of a new division within my Earthly Mind. At the base root though, there is only one Mind, so it is as much a possibility as it is an impossibility to have this division occur within my Earthly Mind.

It is impossible for me to have a relationship with myself. In saying this in this way, I automatically bring about a new division within my Earthly Mind. At the base root, there is only one Mind. This new reality is impossible, and yet it is very much possible, depending on how I choose to look at it within any particular time sequence. It is all so simple and so clear.

If I focus my Earthly Mind to be like a laser, it is all so simple and so precise. If I allow my Earthly Mind to be like that of a diffused light bulb, it becomes overly involved in its functional ability to create emotions upon emotions. They are created and attached by thought forms. These thought forms, in turn, create divisions upon divisions within my Earthly Mind – a mind that is singular in its being, yet very abstract in its foundation and formation.

I am here at this time to find my ultimate truth: the purest essence of my being within the all-encompassing Universal Mind. I am also here to fully realize God Consciousness, which is me in my purest form and most creative light. I am already there – God Consciousness – within myself, and yet I am not there. The forever-shifting doorway keeps opening and closing. My Earthly Mind element is focused like a laser in order to keep the doorway open so that I might move into the infinite realities within Universal Mind unharmed, and bring back into this dimension of being all that there is. I am now ready for that full realization. All the channels within me are aligned and open in order that I might make this journey.

I know that my transformational journey is already in progress, and that it will complete itself shortly. I continue to ask for the divine guidance of my true God-self, and I continually ask my inner guidance to show me the ultimate truth as to what is actually real on this earthly plane.

The words have now ceased to flow from the depths of my inner void. I am still very much just an observer of all that has been happening, and of what is continuing to unfold. My body is making all the necessary movement patterns in order for this unfolding process to continue. The pen is placed beside the open binder, and my hands are positioned gently on top of the paper I have written on, with my palms down. My eyes begin to close, and I am aware that I am somehow attuning myself to all of what has been written.

I am now aware that there appears to be an alignment taking place on many different levels within my being. I am now assimilating all the information that has been presented. I am able to see all of it, in its entirety, and this is clearly happening without the utilization of thought. It is as though I have been expanded within my awareness so far within my inner dimensions that I am encompassing all of it within a single contained surface area that has no limits to it. I am now realizing that I am being awakened, to the innermost depths of my being, to information I already know. I know it beyond the limited boundaries of time and space and into the place of all-knowing.

There is a sudden flash of light. All that is before me disappears. I am once again immersed into the peaceful state of darkness, patiently waiting to see what will unfold next. I begin to hear a gentle voice within my inner void speak these words.

Concern yourself not with what you have heard. You know all too well that which has been written on this day, for you are the one who has written it. Allow yourself the opportunity to feel the purest vibrations of what has been given. As you move within the clarity of it, so shall there be more to unfold before you. It is necessary at this time that you awaken yourself to that which you already know so that your next evolutionary step may unfold as it is so destined.

Do not dwell on what has been given. It is now appropriate for you to rest and allow your physical vibration to attune itself to the much higher frequency that this information will provide. There will be much more available to you before your time here, in this new surrounding, comes to an end.

Continue to travel inwardly as much as you are able. Concern yourself not with how far you penetrate your inner depths, for inevitably you will discover, as you have done on so many other occasions before this, that there is no place to go that you have not already travelled to.

This experience, as well as all the others before it and all those that have yet to arrive, is only being presented to you in order to refresh your awarenesses to that which you already know within the greater depths of your whole beingness. As you continue to take one step at a time, looking seriously at what will be given to you on that step, you will open yourself to much, much more. It is entirely up to you as to how much you open yourself to within your evolutionary process.

The words stop and my eyes slowly open. I pick up the loose-leaf paper and carefully put it back into the binder. I leave the binder open to a clean, fresh page, and then remove myself from the table. I slowly make my way back over to the couch. I am feeling rather drained from the experience I have just witnessed. My body is weak within its physical ability to carry me from one place to another. I am aware that what I need to do most at this moment is to rest, to be quiet and be still. I know that what I am currently experiencing has something to do with the integrating of the information that has been presented. I curl up on the couch in the fetal position and drift off into my inner depths of dimensional travel.

*August 12, 1985*

*The writing process continues...*
I have been lying here on the couch since early this morning, staring aimlessly into the centre of the room. My thoughts are not bound by time or by space. I have been thoughtfully reflecting on all that has taken place so that I am fully present in the moment on this day, and also fully aware of the information I was presented with yesterday.

After the writing session, I ended up lying on the chesterfield for a few hours, totally off in another dimension of time, allowing everything to just drift through all the layers of my being. I then got up and made myself a big pot of rice, enough to last me a whole week. I then made a small bowl of popcorn and sat on the couch and ate it, studying the individual textures of each kernel that had popped. I had noticed just how different each kernel was from all the others. I also noticed how they were all the same, in that they were food to be consumed for nourishment.

Later on in the evening, I had a very small bowl of rice that I heated up in plain water. I then proceeded to lie back down on the couch and drift away once again. This time I was able to be an observer to the different dimensional dialogues taking place within my person. These different aspects of my self were sifting through many of my past experiences and effectively showing me how these experiences could now be viewed so that harmony could prevail within the depths of my Earthly Mind. This process went on for most of the time the Sun was not shining, and well into this day.

I awake after nearly fourteen hours. I get up, have a shower, and once again position myself on the couch, waiting patiently to see what will unfold within me. After waiting for nearly three hours, things finally begin to happen.

As was the case yesterday, my body aligns itself in a sitting position at the dining table. I sit here within my physical embodiment as an observer. I am once again watching everything and waiting for the unfolding process to begin. As I close my eyes, I begin to hear three distinct voices coming from the deep depths of my inner void. As they become louder and closer to the surface of my internal audio receptors, they somehow manage to mold into one voice.

This voice begins to speak, "I am the light that has come forth from the depths of darkness within your being. I am one of three who has come to you at this time to shed more light upon that which you were opened up to in your last encounter at this same place of meeting. I, as are the others who shall follow, am an aspect of your being. We are all aspects of a much higher frequency than your earthly physical embodiment is used to vibrating on. Know that after your encounters with us, there must be sufficient time allotted for you to rest and to align yourself with those internal changes that will be taking place due to the quality of knowing we will be passing on.

"Again, it is important for you to know that the information you shall be presented with, shall be information that you are already familiar with. For it is, as is all information, coming from within your being.

"Now, if you would be so kind as to pick up the pen in your hand, we may commence with our alignment. Allow all that comes to you to flow freely on to the paper."

A self-realized person is: one who is attuned to the all-encompassing Universal Mind; one who is totally aware of how Earthly Mind functions within 'IT's' wholeness and within 'it's' fragmentations; an observer to all outside stimuli, not an active participant; one who remains centred within himself; one who knows all too well the complexities and simplicities of Mind, for he has looked deeply, and with intense seriousness, within himself to discover that which is.

A noisy Mind is man's Earthly Mind. It is based upon the divisional groupings of light patterns that constitute, and bring into a physical manifestation, thought patterns. Each and every thought pattern has a directly opposite thought pattern that corresponds to it within its creative process. Each thought can only focus on one thought pattern within any one given time sequence on the earthly plane. Within the texture of its opposing thought form, it can never be caught by an outside stimulus, for it can immediately change, in all ways, the thought pattern that is necessary to suit its specific needs in any given time sequence within the limited boundaries of the earthly plane.

The only way that this process can be stopped is by Earthly Mind stopping itself. This can only be brought about by bringing into the light the direct opposite to that which is being shown in any given time sequence – shown only in reflection. This will be sufficient to bring the entire process to a sudden stop, but only for this one thought pattern. All other undesirable thought patterns must be viewed by the same process in order to eventually restore harmony and balance within the structural alignment of Earthly Mind.

The use of so-called teachers here on this plane needs serious examination at this time. Let us go into this. When a person's Earthly Mind manifests a teacher on the outside physical plane of reality, and holds that person within his mindset as a teacher, there is an automatic division that begins to take place within the fabric of his Earthly Mind. This division will lead to a series of chain reactions within the structural alignment of his Earthly

Mind. As a result, the opposing forces of pleasure and pain will soon begin to work away at each other within the delicate textures of the thought patterns that are created. These patterns will be greatly influenced by how tightly formed the person's belief structures are. Either way, there will be conflict and confrontation to some degree. Again this is Earthly Mind dividing itself more and more so that it cannot be cornered. All of this is characteristic of divided Earthly Mind. It is continuously looking outside itself, into the sensual world of man, for more stimuli in order that it might increase its diversity and (so it thinks) power and control.

There is an all-knowing 'Spiritual' Mind element ('IT') – one that directly opposes the Earthly Mind/divided Earthly Mind element – that creates a being that it refers to as a teacher. In this instance, the teacher is only observed as a reflection of the Spiritual Mind element. Doing the structuring in this way allows for guidance from within, for 'IT' knows all too well that Universal Mind is all there is, in its duality and in its entirety.

The other Earthly Mind element allows this acknowledgement to take place, for it still holds power and control over the movements of this being in many other different areas and on many different levels of reality. The divided Earthly Mind 'it' does not see this action as a threat to its survival. The change is such a subtle one that 'it' does not fully recognize the extent of what is happening, for it is too pre-occupied in creating more divisive attachments within and without itself.

Spiritual Mind is the reflection of Earthly Mind/divided Earthly Mind. They are part of one Mind, yet they are very much different in the way they function within the earthly plane. Spiritual Mind knows that the balance of power and control is too far over in favor of divided Earthly Mind, and seeks to always re-establish order within. Since it is all happening from within, there is less resistance from divided Earthly Mind for acceptance.

Divided Earthly Mind always works from the outside source of stimuli. Spiritual Mind always moves from the very *centre* core of reality within the inner dimensions and is always moving within the subtle energies. Divided Earthly Mind is not so readily aware of what is actually going on below its sensual recorders, for it cannot penetrate the higher frequencies like Spiritual Mind. As a result of this movement, the mindset – or beliefs – slowly begins to crumble from within the innermost root structure of Earthly Mind. This is all happening at such a deep and subtle level that divided Earthly Mind is unable to detect these changes, for it is always out there, somewhere, looking, looking, looking. Divided Earthly Mind is continuously attaching itself to whatever brings about more divisions within its delicate fabric.

Divided Earthly Mind is always on a quest for power and control within the illusionary universe it is building for itself outside itself. 'it' is totally unaware that it already has power and control over the universe, for 'it' is always too busy with outside distractions to stop long enough to see where it originated from in the first place.

Spiritual Mind is always setting things in motion in order to re-focus Earthly Mind, to get divided Earthly Mind 'it' to look within itself to find the appropriate questions and subsequent answers concerning its existence within this plane. Earthly Mind is also encouraged to find its place in the universe, and in all the distinctly different universes that exist within the universe. They are all components of the same Mind – Universal Mind.

There is no resistance for change from this inner Spiritual Mind, for 'IT' clearly knows that all things here on this plane are in fact Spiritual Mind in essence. 'IT' also knows that they cannot be controlled by any type of power. It is impossible to hold on to something that is constantly changing and evolving. Divided Earthly Mind can only create the illusion that it has the power to control all things, which then becomes its functional reality within a short period of time. Spiritual Mind knows that, in the end, it will all crumble by change or by termination of the current living expression, for change and growth are orderly within the wholeness of Universal Mind – which is pure within its expression of reality without attachment.

Divided Earthly Mind is constantly resisting change that does not support its supremacy over matter. 'it' creates environments where there are opposites, which, in themselves, are equal. Divided Earthly Mind never really goes anywhere except around and around in circles, always to return to the base root of its structure: one Mind – Universal Mind. Divided Earthly Mind is constantly struggling to keep itself separate. Yet in order for 'it' to fight to keep itself separate, 'it' must fully realize that it is one, for they are direct opposite forces. Divided Earthly Mind would rather continue in its ways to remain separate.

Divided Earthly Mind within Earthly Mind can take any course of action it deems necessary in order to accomplish this separation. The belief structure must be rigid in order for divided Earthly Mind to assume control with its own internal source of power within its world. If this process is supported in its continuation for the duration of a person's life, there will be much friction through the opposing forces of pleasure and pain until the rigidity and internal quest for power and control finally terminates this being's life. At this point in time, the person transforms within this plane and returns to the structure of Universal Mind.

All things eventually return to their origin. As all life here on this plane comes forth from the darkness in the form of light, so too it some day returns to the darkness when the light has become extinguished. The cycle thus continues.

Each time one incarnates back into this plane of reality, one brings forward all things from previous lifetimes, which can only exist within this lifetime. One does this in the hope of bringing the two separate Minds within oneself, Spiritual and Earthly, to a place of balance and harmony: the state of knowing that exists before a being arrives in earthly embodiment to become a part of the physical universe.

One aligns with the physical plane to bring about a harmonious reunion of Mind divisions into a single Mind that knows all. The purpose of being here is to bring that all-knowing state of being into a living reality. All life forms keep coming back to this plane until such time that this process is complete. Time, as you know it to be, is not an issue here – only purpose, clarity, truth and oneness.

## SPIRIT GUIDES, MASTERS, ETC.

Within Earthly Mind, there are all these things: spirit guides, masters and door-keepers; however one would wish to see it. Their purpose is to keep the divisions of Earthly Mind (within each person thought processes) looking for sources of power and control based on pleasure and pain: I can meet a guide, talk to a master, etc., or I cannot do it. They are only meant as stepping-stones back to the realities that lie within the depths of one's own being.

Earthly Mind attaches itself and divides itself by creating labels, such as 'psychics.' There are many different kinds of so-called psychics, yet they all come from the same base root in their awarenesses: Spiritual Mind/Universal Mind. It becomes a trap for those who label themselves, for it sets up a division within their Earthly Mind, and comparison and judgment prevail in the energies that they project to their outside world. This gives Earthly Mind more diversification in its quest for power and control. It now takes this spiritual reality and begins to slowly change the alignment of its configurations and dimensions to suit its own particular needs. There is an element of pain and pleasure introduced, in the way of rewarding and withholding, within divided Earthly Mind.

Depending on their structured mindset and its continually changing building blocks, each person will want to be someone of notoriety on this plane, desiring acknowledgement and acceptance from beyond oneself, supporting the image. When this occurs, the divided Earthly Mind has gained control, and the process of growth and evolution of the person begins to slow down. The belief structure then becomes more fixed and solidified. This being becomes less flexible on the ever-changing earthly plane, and soon becomes more brittle within its earthly expression. This brings about much conflict and pain within the living expression of that being.

When a being attaches itself to a label here on this plane, growth stops. A label is stationary within the functional framework of the being's reality, for the opposing thoughts (that are also equal) hold it there. The being becomes entrapped once again within its own divided Earthly Mind structure. There it will live, until the deterioration of the outer fabric allows it sufficient room within to carry out new growth and change.

There is only one Mind. Everything is, in essence, one Mind. Factions of Mind choose to create it otherwise. Look deep within the fabric of your own Earthly Mind to find your own connection to this all-encompassing Universal Mind. You are the master. You are the guru. You are the door-keeper. You are the spirits that use your physical embodiment to channel through information. You are the christ. You are the buddha. You are the Mind. Mind is everything. Mind is all-encompassing. Mind is you. Look closely at it all with utmost seriousness, and you will see, perhaps for the first time, the truth behind these words that have been presented. In the quiet of one's inner void, all truth awaits for one who chooses to seek it. Only by going further inwardly will you be able to see all this for yourself.

## PLACES TO GO TO LEARN

There is no place on this plane for one to go in order to learn more about oneself. No matter where one chooses to travel, one takes along one's Earthly Mind and its opposing force, Spiritual Mind. Earthly Mind will have within its structural fabric all of its divisions as well as the beliefs that support these divisions: divided Earthly Mind. Spiritual Mind will have its oneness with all things within the limitless boundaries of Universal Mind.

Earthly Mind always creates new places to visit and learn from, so as to ensure its diversification; hence, more superficial power and control. It is extremely clever, this Earthly Mind, always evolving within its own limitations, yet always returning to and depending on the source of all things – Universal Mind – for the creation of new outside stimuli. Divided Earthly Mind never really goes anywhere, for there is nowhere to go within the limitless boundaries of Universal Mind.

Divided Earthly Mind sets itself up, within its structural fabric, to create many illusionary (but at the same time effectively real) places to go, and people thought to have all the answers to the many meaningful questions. Divided Earthly Mind is the one that makes up all these questions in the first place. It then creates the appropriate people who will give it the appropriate answers that it already knew before it even asked the questions. It was the one who made up the questions, so it is the only one who knows what the answers are. This process by divided Earthly Mind ensures that the person keeps on the move outside himself, continually looking for something he already has within himself.

Every thing comes from Mind. There is nothing else. No thing exists outside the confines of Mind and all of its self-created divisions. Think about this seriously, and you will be able to see this plain and surprisingly simple truth. Earthly Mind has the ability to create anything it so chooses within its own realities, and to bring forth those things it creates into physical manifestation through the five earthly senses. These newly created things only exist within Earthly Mind, itself. They are always freely expressed within its fragmented, divisional factions through pleasure and pain: divided Earthly Mind.

There are no 'power-spots' on the earthly plane. Your Earthly Mind will create such places so that more divisions will be created within your being. How is it possible that one part of the Earth can be more powerful than another, when all that the earthly plane is made of comes from Universal Mind? In Universal Mind, there are no divisions of power. There is no power. There is only that which is.

Man has expressed over thousands of years that there are places here on this earthly plane that are conducive to change within the internal structure of man, in order to make him more of 'this' or more of 'that'. If you are to look closely at it, right here and now, you will become aware that it has only been man who has said that these so-called power places exist. Man could only have said this by utilizing the thought patterns of Earthly Mind – a Mind that is also divided within itself. The more people believe that these so- called places exist, then they exist, and only because the process of thought which supports the belief system holds it this way.

Stop what you are doing right now, at this instant, and look within your own mind. Within you lies the direction of your own unique, personal, self-protected, clearly marked pathway to fulfilling your purpose here on this plane: to fully realize yourself within the purity and stillness of Universal Mind; to use the awarenesses of this all-encompassing Mind to connect both divided Earthly Mind/Earthly Mind and Spiritual Mind into the single, laser-focused Mind that truly only exists – Universal Mind.

There are no outside forces working for you or against you unless your Earthly Mind creates them. There are no negative entities that reside within the structural fabric of the universe complete unless your Earthly Mind creates them within divided Earthly Mind. There is nothing that exists on the physical earthly plane, or any other plane within or without this plane, unless your Earthly Mind creates it to be here. If it has been given life through the organizational process of Earthly Mind/divided Earthly Mind, then there will be pleasure and pain attached to it, for its existence is entirely based upon an internal quest for power and for control.

Earthly Mind created thought to ensure fragmentation of the oneness of Universal Mind here on this plane. This is the way that it keeps control of and power over all that it creates. This is only a functional illusion though, for it knows that one day it will lose it all; that it will eventually have to face the reality that it has no power and no control; that those fragments of thought were only created by a faction of itself through the manifestation of thought patterns; and that thoughts, whether verbal or nonverbal, are not real (yet at the same time, they have very real effect).

As my consciousness returns to my physical body sitting at the table once again, as was the case yesterday, the words stop flowing and the pen is laid to rest beside the binder. I turn the loose-leaf paper in the binder so there is a new, clean sheet in an exposed position, ready for the next exercise to begin. I return to my familiar place on the couch and drift off into the depths of my inner darkness.

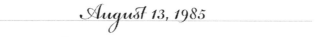

*August 13, 1985*

*The writing process continues...*

As I am lying here, I am very much aware that I have been in this position for almost thirteen hours. From all that has been happening on the different levels within my being, it has been very important that I rest after each session in a quiet, peaceful setting within my being, to fully integrate that which I have witnessed. Within the resting phases, I have become more aware of the gross as well as subtle changes that have been taking place.

I am now aware of an inner restlessness within my being, just as I had experienced yesterday before the voice from within began to speak. It is now time to dialogue with the second of three higher frequencies of my being. My body is summoned once again and immediately flows with what is being directed from deep within its cellular composition. Again I am an observer to all that is about to unfold. I resume my place at the table, securely pick up the pen in my right hand, hold it to the paper and the words begin to appear:

> The earthly plane is based entirely on opposites. Upon coming here, there is a division within Earthly Mind, one that has opposing forces. Universal Mind is one Mind, encompassing Earthly Mind, which is divided within its functional abilities – divided Earthly Mind. This is one of the Laws governing re-alignment for each person while they are on the earthly plane: to evolve one's Mind to a place where one recognizes that his Earthly Mind had become divided upon entering into this plane of reality; and then to move through one's life with this awareness using both parts of Earthly Mind to unify it back into one Mind – Earthly Mind. It would still be divided, yet it would also be unified: balanced and functioning.
>
> Once unification is complete, Earthly Mind becomes one. Upon being one, there is alignment. With alignment comes the reality of Universal Mind, which Earthly Mind is already. Once Universal Mind is a functional reality, Earthly Mind is no longer the same. There are no longer two opposing forces working against each other in divided Earthly Mind. Rather, there is one Mind that is able to separate in its awarenesses yet be unified in its mission: To use both forces in order to aid others who are looking for re-alignment within their own Earthly Mind and integration back into Universal Mind.
>
> This is accomplished by a person of Universal Mind Consciousness being able to move between Universal Mind/Spiritual Mind/Earthly Mind simultaneously while he is in the pres-

ence of another being seeking re-alignment. Once the being of Universal Mind Consciousness is aligned to the other person in this way, he is clearly able to see all the many different light patterns that make up the structure of the other person's Earthly Mind/divided Earthly Mind. He is clearly able to see all that has happened in the other person's life, as well as all that will come to pass as long as the person is on the earthly plane. He is also able to see the building blocks – at the foundational level – within the other person, and he is able to tell the person what is needed in order to enable him to realign himself with his self.

There are no time or space elements within the knowing-ness of Universal Mind, so the duration of time needed for the Universal Mind person to assist in realigning the other person is in between the elements of time and space. Spiritual Mind can be in Universal Mind at the same time as it is in Earthly Mind. Earthly Mind/divided Earthly Mind is totally governed by the elements of time and space. It is not possible for Earthly Mind to connect with Universal Mind as long as there is a division be-tween Earthly Mind and Spiritual Mind: when divided Earthly Mind is functioning and in control.

When Earthly Mind is unified with Spiritual Mind, instantan-eously Universal Mind is. If they are divided, then Earthly Mind *is* and Spiritual Mind *is*, both separate yet one in the same. It is all so simple. Do you see it? Unification is the key component. Division is not. Division is needed here on this earthly plane, for it is through the process of division that the creation of a living expression of life occurs.

When Earthly Mind and Spiritual Mind are aligned and uni-fied, they connect with Universal Mind Consciousness. A person who is aligned this way is able to see all things in regard to the experiences within the divided composite structures that make up the fabric of Earthly Mind of the person seeking realignment and unification. Information is presented about the person who is seeking to be realigned, yet at the same time, it remains ob-scured from conscious thought.

The functioning Mind of the person who has already been aligned and has a connection with Universal Mind Conscious-ness, returns to the earthly plane unified, and then he consciously divides once again – only this time with the full awareness of the intricate movement patterns of Earthly Mind/divided Earthly Mind and the openness of Spiritual Mind. Both are working and functioning separately, together to create an experience, and also together, separately to embody the experience created and recorded. There is no opposition within their movements, for they are one in the same at this point. One cannot oppose one. One just is one.

Spiritual Mind has a connection with Universal Mind. Earthly Mind has a connection with earthly matters through divided Earthly Mind. When Earthly Mind becomes attuned to Spiritual Mind, both aspects of Mind can now align and unify. Universal Mind and Earthly Mind now become one through Spiritual Mind, yet they still remain divided. You see, it is all so simple. It is all right here before you. Are you trying so hard to see it, that you are missing it? Let go of your restricting intellect, then you will see it.

The Earthly Mind of the person who is unified with Universal Mind Consciousness communicates to the person seeking realignment information regarding opposing forces and how they move within the earthly plane, and allows for an alignment to take place within the fabric of his Earthly Mind and the Earthly Mind of the other person.

It is not necessary for an alignment to take place between the Spiritual Minds of both people, for their Spiritual Minds are one in the same. Alignment at that level of expression is always apparent. By showing pairs of opposites to the other person – as to who he thinks he is and is not within the delicate fabric of his divided Earthly Mind thought processes – alignment of Earthly Mind is able to come about and substantial progress is made.

The key here is that the 'person' of Universal Mind Consciousness needs to prepare the person seeking realignment in the appropriate manner with regard to 'his' overall function in all that is to take place. 'He' must clearly present to the other person that 'he' is only a reflection of what is within himself, and not the source of his confrontation or his conflict. 'He' is only a reflective component that the other person will be able to visually see and interact with in his outside world, in a non-threatening way.

It would be similar to what it is like to observe oneself in a mirror. It is an opposite image that you see in the mirror. Like a mirror, it is impossible to hold on to the image. It only reflects back what is shown to its surface. Likewise, this is how the above illustration unfolds.

If, on the other hand, the person wanting realignment holds on to the Universal Mind person like a picture within a fixed frame, and has this image imprinted inside himself within his divided Earthly Mind, continually supporting and idolizing it, then realignment of Mind is impossible. What occurs is more division.

The Earthly Mind/divided Earthly Mind of the person wanting realignment must align itself with the truth of what 'is' in order to achieve a successful transformation. It might very well be that the Earthly Mind person seeking realignment may not be able to fully realize the total awareness of the oneness of Universal Mind within this lifetime. However, he will be one step closer to obtaining this enlightenment. Enlightenment comes forth in a burst of light, and then all things return to the way they were. Afterwards, the way in which one moves within his living expression, from within, is totally different. There is unification in Enlightenment; unification to the oneness of all things – Universal Mind.

A person who has attained Universal Mind Consciousness, within his living expression, is here to do the following: to serve the rest of humanity; to align himself with his fellow man and pass along all he has learned from being on the earthly plane; to give encouragement to those who are also looking for the oneness of all things within themselves; to help with the evolution of man; and to use his wisdom wisely – not from an earthly sense, but rather, from a universal sense of knowing. He knows all too well that to open immature eyes before they are able and ready to see, leads to the creation of distractions within, and it might possibly force the person to further turn away from his own light of truth. His conscious awareness of the unfolding of the universe he offers to whoever wishes to pay the price of introspection in order to find his own answers. He is wise to speak only when it is necessary. He is clearly aware that alignment only comes through being quiet and looking and listening, and not from doing. Look at it all closely, and you will see all of it for yourself.

Outer Space has no boundaries. Inner Space has no boundaries. They are both open-ended. They are opposing each other, yet they are each other. To journey outside oneself without realizing the journey inside oneself causes friction, and creates a division of power and control. An example is taking a holiday to an exotic place, or to any place for that matter; you will always return to the same place within divided Earthly Mind when you arrive back to the location you started from.

Sure, you might have exciting stories to tell for a while, but then your divided Earthly Mind will eventually return to the same place it was before you left. Soon you will forget the good times you supposedly had. You might have taken pictures to remind you just how much of a good time you were having. You might have to keep hauling them out in order to remind yourself of how it was, or how you wanted it to be. Soon you will forget the importance of remembering the trip, and you will once again return to the same state of being you were in before you left.

The outer journey and the inner journey are one in the same. If one is to travel outwardly within the dimensional realities of the physical plane, then one should also travel inwardly on the inner dimensional avenues of creative expression. To acknowledge the outer journey and not the inner journey brings about friction, which in turn leads to division through the creation of pain and pleasure. If divided Earthly Mind is structured securely within stagnant beliefs, then the inner journey will not be taken. If, on the other hand, Earthly Mind is connecting with Spiritual Mind and there is unification through alignment, and the Mind remains open and flexible, then one travels both inwardly toward a higher Mind state and outwardly to a higher Mind state of awareness. This higher Mind state of awareness opens one up to the knowing of all that is of Universal Mind.

There is no place to go. There is nothing to go and see. It is all inside you. Inner space, outer space, it is all the same place. It all has its origin in Mind. All things are of Mind. Mind is all things. There is only one Mind. Go inside yourself deep enough and you will see clearly that you really haven't gone anywhere, for there is nowhere to go. It is all right here, right here – and – now! Can you hear it? Can you see it? Look seriously at it all piece by piece, and you will see. Life is serious. Not serious as seen through your divided Earthly Mind, but serious in all that it represents. Why do you continuously see life as a joke? Why are you so tied up inside yourself and so afraid of your own shadow? The laugh is on you, my friend. Did you know that? You will only be able to see the humour in your life when you take the opportunity to look at what you have done, are doing, and will be doing, with laser-like seriousness.

Everything on the earthly plane has been (and is) created by the process of division. Natural things exist as they are. In order to make them useful for man, there must be a division of one kind or another. Man is the same. Man comes to this plane of existence and is created of flesh through a process of division. Cellular division within his physical embodiment allows him to continually grow and regenerate what is needed for the body to survive, without interference from or influence of divided Earthly Mind.

Man is governed within his movements by the Laws that structure this plane of reality. One comes here to this plane over and over again in order to realign with Universal Mind Consciousness, so that he might ascend through the earthly dimensions of time and space and return to the state of light. Look at it all seriously, and you will clearly see the plain and simple truth. Within the purity of this forever changing truth, you will be able to see the simplicity of it all. Everything here is of division. Division of Mind is the same.

There are no influences here that contribute to that fact of division. Here, it is just so. There is no one you can blame for your anger, fear, jealousy, love, etc. They are all part of the Laws that govern this plane. Your mother is not to blame for your misfortunes; neither is your father, nor your brothers, nor your sisters, nor your friends, nor the cat, nor the dog, nor the mouse – no one! It is only through the divisions of your Earthly Mind that all of it has come about. Some of it is favorable, and some of it is not – pleasure and pain. The division of Earthly Mind is a natural occurrence here. Look seriously and you will see it all. But first, you must look!

As soon as you came here to the earthly plane of existence, there was a division within your Mind; Earthly Mind and Spiritual Mind, one in the same yet divided. They are always together, yet always apart. This is how they have come here to this plane, and this is the way they will always remain. This division is what allows for alignment with Universal Mind. Each time a being comes back here to this plane there is a movement toward aligning Spiritual Mind with Earthly Mind/divided Earthly Mind through the conscious awareness of their unification and division within the same instant of reality. There are traps to get caught in all over the place. Watch out! Or they will surely get you. Are you clever enough to see just how very simple things actually are on this plane?

Questions that you want to look into. So be it.

### 1. What shall I do?

Do nothing! For in wanting to do something here on this plane, you set up a division. You will be trying to do something that you think is important, and there will be someone else who doesn't think it is important, wanting you not to do it. There will always be competition and struggle if you choose to move in this way. Instead, do whatever is needed, and only when it is needed – nothing more, nothing less. Everything will come directly to you that is needed for your growth and proper alignment. If you are always busy doing things, you will not be able to clearly see it when it arrives before you. All meaningful movement comes only through observing. Be patient, and your way will be made smooth.

### 2. What shall I be?

Be nothing! For if you strive to be someone on this plane, there will be someone else who will not want you to be someone in one way or another. There will always be competition and struggle doing it this way. This is a Law that governs this plane of reality. What is recommended is that you be whatever you need to be, whenever it is necessary for you to be that which you need to be. When it is no longer necessary for you to be that, then go back to being nothing. Know that everything comes directly to you that is needed for your growth and proper alignment. If you are always too busy trying to be someone, you are not going to be able to see it when it arrives right in front of you – the gift, that is. Not only that, but you will not allow yourself the opportunity to be all that you truly are.

*3. What shall my purpose be here?*
Have no purpose! For to have a purpose means that there will be someone else who will want to take that purpose from you. There will always be confrontation and struggle within you doing it this way. Instead, it is recommended that you be yourself in all that you do, at all times. This is all that you can ever be here on this plane. Listen to your own wisdom that comes from within, and know that all you will need in order to move through this plane of reality will be presented to you when you are ready and open within yourself to receive it. Be patient, and continue to observe all that is around you at all times.

To want or desire anything on this plane automatically creates a new division within your being. They are always equal to each other: the chances of getting something and not getting something. Look at it seriously, and you will see the simple truth behind what is written. It is all so simple here on this plane. Do you see how simple it all is, or is your divided Earthly Mind still holding on too tightly?

Want nothing, and all that is here will be yours. How can that be, you ask? It is all so simple. If you want or desire nothing, there is no division. When there is no division, you have realized Universal Mind. Universal Mind is everything. Everything is Universal Mind. If there is no division within the structural fabric of Earthly Mind, then Earthly Mind/Spiritual Mind is one. When it is one, everything is possible, for then there is Universal Mind. There is no division within the limitless boundaries of Universal Mind. Now do you see how simple it is?

*4. Does the physical body of man really exist?*
Let us look at this question more seriously. In the beginning, there is Universal Mind. One chooses this plane. Since this

plane is governed by the functional Laws of Division, Universal Mind now divides into two. I shall be more specific and say that in order for this plane to exist Universal Mind creates two distinct divisions (Spiritual Mind and Earthly Mind) within an aspect of itself, but still remains whole within itself. First there is Spiritual Mind, and then there is Earthly Mind.

Spiritual Mind allows a person to identify with Universal Mind. It also allows a person to go deep within the delicate fabric of his own Earthly Mind element in order to align himself with the information that is needed for his steady growth and evolution, through experience and introspection, while he is on this plane. Then one day, in one of his lifetimes, he will be able to align himself completely with Universal Mind and leave this plane, never to return.

Then there is Earthly Mind. Earthly Mind is governed completely by Earth Laws. One such law has to do with dualism: opposites that continually keep everything in a permanent state of balance and order. Earthly Mind has the functional ability to create an infinite number of divisions within divided Earthly Mind as a person goes through the progression of movements within their lifetime. These infinite divisions are counteracted upon by Spiritual Mind in order to maintain a steady balance within a person. Should there be an imbalance of power in favor of divided Earthly Mind, then sooner or later destruction within the fabric of Earthly Mind will take place, possibly resulting in the physical death of that person. The other possibility is the eventual surrender of Earthly Mind to its mirror image, Spiritual Mind, which will align itself in such a way that balance is restored and evolutionary growth is continued within the unfolding of the oneness of all things.

Earthly Mind names and interacts with everything that exists on this plane. Since all things here are governed by the Laws of Division, every thing here is Earthly Mind. Where does this leave the human body? The body is governed by the same Laws of Division, is it not? If you look closely at it, you will see the simple truth. Since the body is also governed by these Laws of Division, it must be Earthly Mind – a division of Earthly Mind perhaps, but still Earthly Mind. The human body does not exist as such, only Earthly Mind exists. What does exist though is the human body as a faction of Earthly Mind and, within its wholeness, Spiritual Mind.

Earthly Mind makes it seem like the human body is separate, yet Earthly Mind remains in control of the human body – with its own self-generated power – at all times. The human body sets up the divisions within itself through Earthly Mind in order to keep itself busy creating experiences on the earthly plane that are based on pleasure and pain. This process creates the opportunity for the human body to think that it is something other than what it truly is. So very clever is this divided Earthly Mind.

The human body is completely programmed from conception to respond to every possible occurrence of Universal Mind, for the human body is Universal Mind. However, since Earthly Mind controls all facets of reality within the structural framework of the earthly plane, it directs – within the physical embodiment – what the body will acknowledge and know. Earthly Mind controls how the human body will move and create experiences, and how it will respond to certain situations, according to the divisions that Earthly Mind has set up within its structure. There is no human body *per se.* The human body simply *is.* There is only Mind: Earthly Mind/Spiritual Mind/Universal Mind.

*5. What about eating? Does the physical body really need to eat? What can I eat?*

The human body is set up with divisions within itself for eating. The human body has separate but coordinated systems whose sole (divisional) purpose is for processing nourishment for the body. If the human body does not eat, this will lead to further divisions within the body's component structures, with some areas consuming others in order to ensure survival of the whole. There will be self-destruction and eventually death within that organism. If one eats too much, more divisions are created within the system, which will cause a slowing down and an eventual deterioration of the natural process necessary to maintain a balanced state within the physical body. This process will eventually lead to disease and decay within the physical structure, possibly leading to the physical death of that person.

No matter what you feed your physical body on this plane, there will always be a process of division that occurs – half being good for the body (nutrients), and half being not so good for the body (toxins). This is how the human body maintains a certain degree of balance within its compositional and structural alignment – organs, bones, muscles, etc.

Natural elements of food have not been divided prior to the human body consuming them. When the human body eats, the appropriate divisions are set according to the body's balance structure at the time of consumption. (Specific digestive processes for each type of food, use and/or storage of nutrients, elimination of unused or unfit food). If, on the other hand, man has taken the natural elements of food and has divided them into other components by processing them repeatedly, and then a person consumes them, and his body again divides them through digestion, then what you have is a very significant amount of food division taking place within the body. This will cause some friction within the structural alignment of the body. The end result will be a high degree of fatigue within the functional expression of that person. If man could fully awaken himself to the realization that everything that exists on this plane is of Mind in its origin, then all food consumed could be effectively balanced by the aware choices of Mind. It all really depends on a person's Mind development as to whether he does or does not consume certain foods and quantities.

Eat whatever you like at the time it is presented to you. Eat sparingly and often like the animals that are free within the natural elements. Look at and observe them carefully, and you will see this simple truth. Because the divided Earthly Mind creates opposites, if you say you are going to follow a certain eating habit, then there will be an automatic division set up within your Earthly Mind that will be totally opposite, creating resistance to the pattern you want. This opposing force will create friction within your movements and further divide your Earthly Mind. If you eat what is available with the total functional awareness of Earthly Mind, then it matters not what you eat.

*6. What about sex and the human body?*

Let us look at this more closely, and in so doing, you will clearly see what is. The human body is Mind. The Mind is human body: Earthly Mind/Spiritual Mind/Universal Mind. The human body has been programmed with everything about Universal Mind, and also everything regarding Earthly Mind. During sexual arousal, the thought-mind connection is quiet and the body-mind connection is active, feeling and sensing, knowing step-by-step what is to come next within the unfolding experience, and how the body is to do what it has been programmed to do. Its main function is to procreate, to bring more new living expressions to this plane. Divided Earthly Mind sets up an automatic resistance to bringing new life into being, for this is how it goes about maintaining its power and control.

Division and resistance foster new patterns of movement that are now programmed into the functional aspects of the physical embodiment, according to how the divided Earthly Mind determines it should be – whether it ultimately wants to create pleasure or pain. Earthly Mind chooses pleasure or pain based on which one will give it sufficient power and control at that appropriate moment. There is never any consistency within its choosing. It is only when the experience is in the process of unfolding, with the help from an outside stimulus, that divided Earthly Mind adjusts and makes its choice.

It is Spiritual Mind that continually opposes this pleasure or pain patterning. It always wants to bring the full attention of Earthly Mind to the oneness of all things. These two opposing and non-opposing forces – Earthly Mind/Spiritual Mind – are constantly interacting with one another simultaneously. They are each so very subtle in their movements that it is sometimes difficult to determine which one is directing the creative, flowing movement, and which dimension of reality it is coming from at any given moment.

The physical embodiment of each person is harmoniously moving with the other, and the creative process continues to unfold. The mind/body connection in each person is responding according to how it has been previously programmed to act or react to the other person's movement patterns. These responses are based entirely on the experiential conditioning that has been previously initiated by the divided Earthly Mind through prior sexual encounters and information that each of the two persons have had in their living expressions.

Spiritual Mind is continually moving within the inner depths of the more subtle levels. It is always bringing forward, into the inner awarenesses of the two persons interacting, the oneness of all things. Spiritual Mind always wants to show the two separate individuals that they are in reality the same person, but different aspects of the same person. That is why they have come together: to share with each other what they think they have. The question that always arises in this situation, as well as all the other experiential situations on the earthly plane, is: Will each of the two people interacting within this creative process be detached from what they are doing long enough to see the simple truth that they are one in the same? Or will each of them choose to remain so involved in determining the direction of the creatively unfolding process that they get caught up in the pleasure/pain rewards of it all? It is such a trap. Yet at the same time, it is also a tremendous opportunity for creative freedom if one is only able to see it clearly enough when one is within the unfolding of it.

Earthly Mind 'needs' and 'wants' on this plane. It knows full well that it can never actually have what it needs and wants, for it has set up divisional opposites to the needs and wants to ensure a continuing struggle for power and control. All of this only exists within the delicate fabric of Mind. There is nothing outside the all-encompassing Mind.

Earthly Mind can clearly think there is more that exists outside itself, for it is clever and knows how to make everything move the way it wants. Or, at least, so it thinks. You can believe and support the fragmented thought from your Earthly Mind that these needs and wants truly do exist outside your Mind. However, if you take the appropriate time to look seriously at all that is being presented to you, you will be able to see the simple truth. It is all so simple once you stop! and look at it. Look seriously, or else you will miss how simple it all actually is here on this plane.

Taking away the needs and wants within the living expression of sexual arousal allows for the total freedom of movement in the awareness of Universal Mind. There is the freedom to be without the elements of time and space, without restrictions of any degree. There is only the absolute freedom to be whatever is needed, within the time sequence that it is needed. Afterwards, there is only the experience; nothing more, nothing less. Each time there is a creative process, there is a new direction to move in, a new unfolding to behold, and a new movement pattern to engage in. All of this is taking place under the free-form guidance of Universal Mind.

In the unfolding sexual experience it matters not who you are with, for within the creative process that is unfolding, the person you are with never has a name, or a face, or a form of expression, or any of that, while the process of exploring continues to evolve and the internal awarenesses increase to an almost frenzied state of being. It is only before you begin, or after the completion of this creative process, that there is a total awareness of the person you are with. For the time in between, you are totally involved within yourself and your own perceptual awareness of what is actually taking place, as opposed to what you think is taking place.

Earthly Mind/Spiritual Mind/Universal Mind: you continuously move within the textured fabric of each of them in everything you do here on this plane. Every moment of every day this process unfolds. Ultimately, there is only Universal Mind. Universal Mind creates the expressional opportunity for Spiritual Mind/Earthly Mind within its structural fabric. Earthly Mind creates divided Earthly Mind within its structural fabric. Nothing exists except when your divided Earthly Mind chooses to create it otherwise by using a negative and positive based language – words – that creatively allows for an experience to occur.

Do always only that which is needed, and only at the time it is needed. You can do this without the conscious element of restrictive thought, provided, of course, that your focus remains within the total awareness of Universal Mind. As you do this, you will come closer to the full realization of living all ways in

Universal Mind. There is truly nothing else. It is important that this simple truth be emphasized over and over again to you at this time, mainly due to the secure hold that your fragmented and divided Earthly Mind has over your physical being and its five earthly senses. This hold is coming from the continual deep-rooted programming and conditioning that you have undergone during this life of time.

Align yourself to the oneness of Universal Mind, and let go, and you will actualize Universal Mind. When you consciously let go of everything you think you are, and think you have, then you will return to the all-knowing central core of your being within the all-encompassing Universal Mind. You will have, with absolute freedom, everything you had let go of. But first, you must let go! Truly let go, and not just intellectually, either. Do you dare do it? Go ahead. What is it you are so afraid of? Is it possibly that you will truly see that you have had the higher properties of Universal Mind in you all along? And then how will you ever be able to justify all those unnecessary situations and petty earthly struggles you have created along your life journey?

Sometimes when you look so seriously at this experience called life, you will come to the full realization, at that precise moment, that viewing life as complicated and unfathomable, is one big joke. When this occurs, be free and spontaneous enough within yourself to laugh whole-heartedly at the humour that lies at the bottom of all of that seriousness. This will ensure that you continue to grow and evolve according to what has been pre-determined.

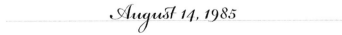

*August 14, 1985*

*The writing process continues...*

When the internal alignment and unification is completed between Earthly Mind and Spiritual Mind, and Universal Mind is fully realized, the human physical embodiment will also be automatically aligned with and consciously attuned to the complete process. The physical body is constantly in alignment within itself, and it is governed strictly by the fragmented structure of Earthly Mind.

The mechanics of the physical body are constantly in the process of change within the restrictive framework of Earthly Mind. These changes are based primarily on the genetic coding within the inner dimensions of the physical embodiment, which has subsequently been aligned to and structured by the creative light patterns that were activated at the time of conception. Observing the way the physical body continually experiences and moves and changes in regard to the earthly plane allows you true insight into the splendor of the all-encompassing Universal Mind. To study the physical body, and its ever-unfolding and ever-changing functional aspects of reality, one is free to travel within the inner dimensions of the all-encompassing Universal Mind.

A person who studies his physical body in order to find the way into the depths of his Mind, loses the restrictive, structural fabric of his body and totally immerses himself within the realities of Universal Mind. A person who studies his mind will eventually arrive at the same place of unfolding reality, only he will do this at the expense of his physical embodiment. A person who becomes and remains trapped within the restrictive structural fabric of his physical embodiment, eventually loses everything he thought he had and returns to the all-encompassing Universal Mind through the earthly process of death and transformation.

The physical body is Mind. Mind is the physical body. Align the two within themselves and set yourself absolutely free, free to travel anywhere and everywhere. The earthly saying, "know your own body", goes much deeper than the mere words that convey the idea. Look deeply into yourself for all of your questions and all of your answers. You will soon discover that if you are able to ask a question, then you are already aware of the answer. Above all, one must ask the right kind of question, one that has meaning and purpose within the creative aspects of one's evolutionary process.

To become fully aware of the omnipresence of Universal Mind, attune yourself to the structural realities and functional creativeness of your physical embodiment. The body is always free to move. It is only the structural rigidity within the fragmented and divided Earthly Mind that restricts it in its movements. Seek this simple truth from within yourself, and you will see as you have never seen before. You will continue to see everything within you, as well as outside you, in ever-unfolding new ways. Look deeply only if you dare.

Eternal wholeness is assured to you if only you dare to freely venture far enough inside your own inner dimensions. Go through the delicate fabric – thought – that holds your fragmented Earthly Mind so confined, and there you will enter into the conscious reality of Universal Mind. They are all parts of the same Mind. There is no difference. Venture forth and observe and see from within your own self the simple truth behind what is being written today.

The inner self knows. The physical body knows. The physical body is the self, and the self is the physical body. Trust the feelings that come from deep within your inner dimensions, and let go of that delicate fabric – thought – that has so much tension holding it securely in place. What have you got to lose? It is all so simple. Look seriously at it all, and you will be able to see the simplicity within the structure and the alignment of all things.

The Mind knows, and so do you, for you are Mind. What is there in your structured world that could possibly be worth holding on to? To hold on to anything, including your own self-identity, will create friction within the depths of your being and bring about more division and diversification within your fragmented earthly thought processes. Let go! The only way that you will be able to see it all as clearly as it truly is, is if you let go and ascend to the higher aspects of your being.

## HOW TO OBTAIN ENLIGHTENMENT

There are no special methods or principles that one can use in order to look into the existence of Mind. The fragmented and divided Earthly Mind creates many different ways to do this. All of them originate from within the structural complexities of its delicate fabric, and from within the self-generated, diversified movement patterns it creates at any given time in order to ensure that it maintains control with optimum power.

Every 'method' that has been devised by the fragmented thought patterns within Earthly Mind, becomes a restrictive trap for anyone who would choose to follow it, other than the person who has created the particular method. Mind is everything. Everything is Mind. There is no separation within the purity of what is.

Even to the person who has created the method from within himself, it eventually becomes a trap. Earthly Mind creates and expresses the method by the initiation of thought processes. This action automatically creates a division within the structural framework of Earthly Mind. There will be a corresponding creation of friction within the functional expression of the method, which in turn will create either pleasure or pain. Earthly Mind determines which one it will select at any given time based entirely on the accumulation of power and maintaining of control. This is Earthly Mind's way of controlling the structure and the efficiency of the method devised.

All disciplines that exist outside the person, within the structure of time and space, are illusions, for they are held fixed within the fabric of thought, and there is no allowance for a creative process to continually unfold. These external disciplines lead nowhere except around and around in circles. And like the dog who becomes tired from chasing his own tail, a person eventually becomes tired of being involved in supporting a particular method. He stops and takes a rest from it. The purest form of evolutionary unfolding can only take place when the fragmentation within the structural alignment of Earthly Mind has come to a complete stop.

The only way for one to attain the purest alignment to the all-encompassing Universal Mind, is through one's *own* Mind. In order for this process to take place, one must align all the separated factions within the structural fabric of the divided Earthly Mind in such a way that Earthly Mind becomes one within itself in all ways. There is no other way that this is possible if one clearly chooses to become aligned to the oneness of all things – God energy. One must be totally complete within one's self.

If there is but one single string still attached to the environment outside the person, there can be no permanent alignment to Universal Mind Consciousness. Alignment – that is to say the purest alignment – only comes into a functional living reality when one goes deeper within one's self.

## MEDITATION

Meditation, as you know it to be on this earthly plane, is intended to bring quiet within a person's mind. To quiet the mind is a creation by Earthly Mind, controlled by divided Earthly Mind. Divided Earthly Mind is in total control of the texture of the quiet it creates: power and control are its only concerns, with pleasure and pain as its rewards. Meditation practiced in this way will not bring about total alignment. Structured meditation on the earthly plane is nearly always practiced or completed within a specified time and space relationship, which only exist within the limited framework of the divided Earthly Mind, and not in Spiritual Mind.

It is true that one receives great benefit from meditation when it is completed following this method. But what about all the other functional activities within one's daily life that are created outside the time sequence allotted for a methodical form of meditation? What about the light patterns that already exist and are constantly interacting and changing within the depths of the structural form of the physical embodiment, including the mental, physical and emotional relationships within that being? One is led to believe that by quieting one's (thought) mind, peace and harmony within the self can be realized. Not so! This belief only leads to a part of Earthly Mind that Earthly Mind has chosen to allow to become quiet. It does this in order to keep the person from looking deeper within himself.

'Proper' meditation is continually unfolding through the awareness of observation, and not through any conscious movement of doing. Only by observing the mechanics of another's physical body can you possibly hope to learn more about your own body, for they are a mirror image of your own body in the way that they move through the physical world. To be busy doing, is to be busy doing. Divided Earthly Mind is only able to do one thing at a time, as long as it is participating within the limited structure of the first dimension of reality. This is the dimension that is controlled and structured completely around time and space.

One cannot possibly observe and do something at the same time as long as the divided Earthly Mind is engaged and functioning. Mind is everything. Everything is Mind. Meditation is Mind. Mind is meditation. Look deeply into Mind – into the base root of its structure – and you will see everything. You will see Universal Mind. Look deeply into the structure of organized meditation, and you will see Mind. Look deeper still, and you will see Universal Mind. Universal Mind is all that is.

It is all so simple, isn't it? You are continuously making it so difficult on yourself – Why? The more difficult you make it, the more you want to reward yourself, then when you reward yourself, you go about making it more difficult. This is the fragmented Earthly Mind's way of having and maintaining control and power within its functional realities of pleasure and pain. The fragmented Earthly Mind is very cunning in its way of moving. It is always looking at how it can accumulate more power and continue to maintain control over all that it chooses to indulge in.

Proper meditation is realized through the passiveness of observation, and not through the activeness of doing. Proper meditation is seeing that the outside is actually the inside, and that the inside is actually the outside. Proper meditation is seeing that the divided Earthly Mind is entirely composed of fragmented aspects, and that by initiating the interaction of pairs of those fragmented opposites through experiences, one can bring about realignment of Earthly Mind to Spiritual Mind into the full awareness of all-encompassing Universal Mind. Observing one's own movement in a balanced alignment with Spiritual Mind allows for sudden changes in the way one sees one's outer and inner world, and allows for greater growth toward one's evolutionary destiny.

Proper meditation is done at the root structure, from within the depths of inner awareness, and moves outwardly to bring about unrestricted, expanding growth within the person. The 'structured' form of meditation begins on the outer edges, and it slowly and systematically gets the person to move inwardly. This is very restrictive, compared to the growth possible to a person choosing a non-structured method. Can you see the difference between the two?

Be careful not to judge what is being written to paper today, for to judge it means that you are holding on to some belief or other either supporting it or not supporting it. See how easy it is to become trapped by your fragmented earthly thought patterns. It is all so simple. Are you simple enough in your approach to your life that you see it, or are you still all caught up in it? Let go, and you will see how simple it all truly is. Let go of that delicate fabric of thought that is holding your fragile world together, and you will witness first hand the simple truth of it all.

It is all Mind. If you are still resisting, realize that you are resisting the truth that you are Mind: all-encompassing Mind, ever-changing and ever-unfolding. Are you now trapped into looking at all that is before you, or have you run away from it all, allowing your fragmented Earthly Mind to create more divisions within its own structure? How long can you keep running from the simple truth of what you are? Why are you running? There is nowhere to run, for you are everything, and you are everywhere. You are Mind. You are always in complete control of all the things you create in your world. Likewise, you have the power to change the way you are choosing to see within your inner and outer worlds. If you are always in control, what is it that stops you from doing it? What creates that fearful thought within your divided Earthly Mind? Do you know? Can't you see that it is *you* that you are trying to find? It is also you who is keeping you from finding out who you are. Do you dare look at all this more closely and more seriously? Everything is Mind. Mind is everything.

Use reflections outside yourself in order to see within your awareness of Mind. Use caution, though, not to get caught holding on to the reflection. Spiritual Mind, Earthly Mind breathe the same breath – both in and out – for they are one in the same. It is so easy to be swayed if you continue to focus outside yourself while trying to find out more about yourself. Look within the reflection, into the depths of Mind, and you will see how it truly is. Your Mind and Universal Mind are one in the same. There is no separation. How can there be any separation? How is it possible for you to align to something that is outside yourself? It is impossible unless your divided Earthly Mind chooses to create it. Then it is possible, but only as long as your divided Earthly Mind supports it being this way. One can only align with oneself, and only from within oneself. There is nothing else. All things come from Mind. All things are Mind. Mind is everything. Nothing exists outside of Mind. Look at it clearly, and you will see.

Look within your fragmented and divided Earthly Mind, restricted by its own self-created structure of time and space, and you will see the plain and simple truth. See for yourself whether anything actually does exist outside the framework of your Mind – as you know it to be. Well, does it? Look carefully and you will see the universal truth within your own Mind, which is also Universal Mind. Align yourself with all that you hear, and open your internal eyes so that you can see all that lies hidden within you.

All that exists is Mind, and all that does not exist is Mind. There have been many divisions within the delicate fabric of Earthly Mind created in order to discover what Mind is. How is it possible for Mind to examine itself? In order for it to do that, it must be separate from itself. How can something that is separate from itself be that which is separate? Two separate factions lead to more divisions, which, in turn, lead to more divisions....

The structure of ego does not exist, except within the fragmented fabric of Earthly Mind. Another faction of Earthly Mind is id; another is super-ego; another is conscious mind; another is super-conscious mind; and the list goes on and on. All of these labels are divisions of the fragmented Earthly Mind, and they all take a person away from aligning with the all-encompassing, non-judgmental, Universal Mind.

There is only one Mind: Universal Mind/Spiritual Mind/ Earthly Mind/divided Earthly Mind. It makes no difference. There is still only one Mind. Earthly Mind and Spiritual Mind are one in the same simultaneously, and yet simultaneously they are totally separate from each other. They each have their base root structure within Universal Mind. There is nothing else unless the fragmented Earthly Mind chooses to create it, in its focused quest for power and control.

All the terms and labels that have been given to you today, as well as on previous days, disappear when there is death and transformation. In the end, all things return to Mind. And in the beginning, all things come from Mind. There is only Mind. Look openly and creatively at it all, and you will see the simple truth behind all of it, including yourself. You have to look clearly at it, though, before you will be able to see the simplicity in it all.

Do you dare look deeper within your own inner darkness? Who knows what you will find once you begin. It could very well be your internal ticket to freedom within your daily living expressions. Stop and look, and you will see it all. Look deeper within your own Mind. That is where it all lies. Look deep enough, and you will soon discover this plain and simple truth: There is only one Mind. Your mind is Earthly Mind/Spiritual Mind/Universal Mind. All Mind is Universal Mind.

# CHAPTER 8

# DIMENSIONS OF POWER

I load the last of my belongings into the truck and proceed to drive to the place that is going to be my home for the next undetermined number of days or months. I have a strong feeling that this new place will provide me with more opportunities to dig deeper within the depths of my being, so that I will be able to bring forth, into my conscious awareness, more of the light that makes up the totality of my earthly expression. This is to be the first real 'home' I have had since I arrived here on the earthly plane. My original home – the one I was raised in and had my earliest experiences in – was the place where I had been initiated into the different dimensions of reality within the world of programming and conditioning, judgment and comparison, division and fragmentation. This new home is to be the home where I will open myself within myself to the purity of my inner truths, the truths that remain constant in their ever-changing appearance, as well as absolute within their design.

I am going to be joined in my new home by a friend. We were both looking for a place individually and, after neither of us having much luck finding one, decided that it would work to share a place together. We sat down one day and shared what each saw as the purpose behind sharing a living space; where each of us wanted to live; what age and style of living space each wanted to live in; and what each of us wanted in the way of furnishings within our living space. It had been agreed upon from the beginning that each of us had an equal say in the matters that pertained to the living space and living arrangements. We both wanted to create a house of equality and truth, in whatever form it would assume.

We agreed that the purpose behind sharing the same living space would be so that each of us, in our own unique ways, could look deeper within ourselves to unravel the superficial mysteries of who each is, and to bring that creative aspect into a functional living expression within our everyday movements. We also saw that it would serve as a means of support, in that the new, consciously created environment would be the place where it would be totally safe to look at our lives seriously, without feeling judged at any time.

It has been my ongoing experience that the outer, competitive world of man is not truly set up to be supportive of an individual's desire to look deeper within himself to find his own unique creative abilities. It has been set up and structured in such a way that man is continuously being conditioned and programmed into following the voices of a few who choose to control others for their own personal gains.

I wanted a living space that was fairly new in its construction, had carpet on all the floors, and plain smooth walls that were painted white. My friend, on the other hand, wanted an older style home, preferably with character, that was a little rustic in appearance.

We sat down and proceeded to look at what the symbolic significance was behind our choices. I was looking for a new and clean living space, mainly because I was looking to create a totally new expression within my own living experience. It only seemed fitting that the two would move harmoniously together, for it would be a constant reminder for me, moment to moment, while I was moving within the living space. I wanted my life to be plain and simple, for the textured and complicated world that I was coming from somehow didn't ring true or work for me. I figured that perhaps, just maybe, this other approach would be the appropriate combination to aid me in my own personal quest.

My friend, as she slowing began to discover the closer she looked at it, liked old things. She liked to buy old houses and renovate them so they looked new again. Superficially they might have looked new and fresh, but within their inside cores, they were all still old. She wasn't interested in building new houses, only renovating old ones. She also liked collecting paintings that were old and supposedly worth a lot of money. She often said that they were valuable, and that one day they would bring her a good return for her initial investment.

What we discovered from this experience of deciding what our living space would be, was that within each of us there was a whole history of valuable pictures, in the way of earthly experiences, that were worth a lot – a lot of grief, anger, sadness, hate, violence, love, compassion, empathy, laughter, joy, happiness, etc. We discovered that these pictures were continually being created every time we made a judgment either of ourselves or of someone else. We then decided that we didn't want any pictures created within the walls of our new living space. We were more interested in removing as many of the pictures that we were holding on to of ourselves and of each other. As a reminder we agreed that there would be no pictures of any kind hanging on the interior walls of our new living space.

We also agreed that there would be no outer world newspaper, radio or television, for each of us saw that they would only serve as a distraction. We would have no furniture other than fifteen good-sized cushions to sit on and over thirty-five plants. These would eventually fill our living room and dining room area, and they would serve to remind us that with self-love each of us would continue to grow within ourselves. Through that inward desire to be all that each of us is, we would be able to give more of our unique gifts to the worlds that are continuously unfolding all around us. We agreed that in our kitchen there would be a minimum of clutter. We went through all the things that each of us was going to bring and made decisions as to whether we wanted to keep any of it. The things we chose not to hold on to, we gave to someone else who could use them.

Within our own bedrooms we could have whatever each of us thought was important, that would provide the security we thought we would need in our totally new and foreign living quarters. We both knew we would be able to receive more from the experience of sharing a space together if we had a minimal number of distractions to contend with within our surrounding environment.

With this conscious awareness, we moved in together, and proceeded to live within our own unique and creative expression.

## September 1, 1985

*On the path in the daylight and in the nightlight*
I have been walking along this path in the woods trying to figure out, once and again, if I am indeed on the right path in my life journey. I am choosing to align myself with the natural elements of Mother Earth to help me see if I can come any closer to answering that recurring question. I have chosen to walk along a path in a park-like setting that has been made by man and has been well travelled by many over the years. Man has continuously used it to come out and make contact with Nature in order to find some peace and quiet within the fast-paced life he has become so attuned to. I am sure that there are many more purposes for this path as well. I would not want to get into any one of them at this time, for they are of no importance to my evolutionary process.

I choose to use this path as a symbol of a path that will eventually lead me to my truth. Is it possible for me to find my truth while I am travelling on a path that others, many others, have continually used and influenced each time they have used it? Would it be possible for me to maintain the purity of what the path stands for, as I continue to travel its route, knowing that others, who are perhaps not as serious as I am in seeking truth, have walked it before me? They might have abused the purity of it by adding to or taking away from what is there within the wholeness of its natural state. It would become distorted from its original layout. It would be continuously changing its course and manner of expression. Everything about it would be constantly changing, if not from man, from the natural elements. I know that many will continue to claim that it is the same path it was in the beginning, never changing. They will only see what they truly want to see.

Who was the person who made this path? How do I know that I can trust the person who is responsible for its creation? How do I know that I can trust him not to lead me into a dangerous situation that might further suppress my creativity? I am not at all sure where this path leads to, or what is at the other end, or even if there is another end. How will I know? Who do I trust?

I have to trust someone. If I do trust the person who has constructed this path, I will take this path for granted. I will know that all I have to do is follow what is already here. If I do follow it blindly, I will find other things of much less importance than my life to talk about along the way. Once I have walked along its route just one time, I will surely say, "I now know the way." As a result of this assertion, I will lose the newness of the path's expression each time I walk its surface. As I journey along its course, I will be continuously consumed by my useless thoughts and the thoughts of all the people who have travelled it before me, all caught up in their useless stuff. How can I trust fully what I hear from their vibrations as I proceed along?

I can't trust them. I can't trust someone who is following this path as well as I. I feel that I must go and seek out the person who is responsible for its creation. But why? I am not sure why. Where will I find him? In order to find him, I will have to follow yet another path – the path he is on now – another path that others will have journeyed on long before I do. If I choose to go looking for this person who makes all of these paths, what is it that he can possibly give me? I see that he can give me nothing except his path to follow. I see that I am looking outside my own being in order to discover a path that will take me to the depth of the all-knowing presence that lies within me. How do I know that I can trust this person who spends all his living days making paths for other people to travel on? I don't know that I can, but I do know that I can trust myself. I have to look deeper into this question.

I proceed to move off the main trail, taking myself up behind the lake that has been my sanctuary for the past while. I am choosing to move deeper into the untravelled bush, away from any of the places where man can happen by. I am choosing to take my questioning one step further. I need to be on my own in the darkness of the night air to discover once and for all the clarity behind "what path do I move on?"

I have been sitting here for close to four hours, waiting patiently for the Sun to disappear behind the rolling hills so the darkness of night can fill in all the space that surrounds me. I have taken up a stationary position in the centre of a large section of cedar trees. I know from my prior experiences that they will effectively hold in the darkness so that no light will be cast, and that I will not be able to discern the different objects that are close at hand. This is the first time I have ventured into the depths of the forest in the night-time hours, and I don't mind saying that I am a little apprehensive about what could possibly come up for me while I am out here. I know that I am always protected from the elements that surround me by my inner guidance, provided, of course, that I listen to it when I need to. I also know that I am continuously being supported, in all ways, in finding the purity of my truth.

Now I am immersed in darkness. I am unable to escape its control over my emotional state of being. Here I am, alone with myself within myself, deep within the darkness of my inner and outer voids. I am unable to see anything that is representative of my outside world, anywhere. Not even my hand that I am holding only two inches from my eyes. It is black, and I mean black! I am feeling a little off balance within my physical body, adjusting my internal centre of balance, trying to figure out which feelings inside me are real. I have decided that I will walk wherever I am directed within this inner-guided experience, in order that I might emotionally embrace the unfolding reality within my inner and outer search for the path that will lead me to my internal resting place, to eventual self-realization.

There appears to be no time or space element in this new environment I have created for myself. There is absolutely no difference that I can distinguish between my inner and outer world of darkness. I am not able to tell with absolute certainty, within the range of my five earthly senses, which of my internal or external worlds I am in at any isolated moment. Whether my eyes are open or closed, I am only able to observe the same simulated movements of light patterns that pulsate through the darkened voids of both dimensions of reality.

I have walked only five steps through the ever-changing terrain of Mother Earth, and already I have become aware that there is no such path I can follow in this environment, or any other environment, for that matter. All there is, within my total awareness, is the purity and simplicity that "I am all there is." I am

now becoming emotionally bonded to the intellectual awarenesses I have experienced over and over again along my journey. I am now beginning to see the
humour behind it all. There is nothing else in my existence on this earthly plane.
There is only me. I am the way, the depth of truth, and the full expression of life.
I am the beginning as well as the end, both at the same time. There is never any
separation between the two unless I choose to create it. There is nothing outside
my person that I can use to make my way through the maze that lies all around
me – the one I cannot see but I can sense – except my two legs and feet. They
continuously connect me to and guide me over the textured surface of Mother
Earth. They cannot see, though. Or can they?

I am becoming totally aware, as I have yet to experience prior to this day, that
whenever I put any degree of focus or intention outside my own person, looking
for direction or confirmation of the direction I am taking, I become very insensitive to the immediate needs of my physical embodiment. I am now aware that
I constantly want to feel the outer dimensions of the outer darkened void that
surrounds me in order to consciously validate the direction I am heading in. Yet,
I am not at all sure which direction I am going in, for there is no positive proof
that any direction exists at all. For all I know, I could be just walking around
in a circle over and over again, clearly believing that I am going in a particular
direction.

I am now seeing that I have always had to emotionally experience the experiences I have created within my outer worlds, with one or all five of my earthly
senses, before I would trust any of what I was doing within me. In the process
of doing it that way, I have been constantly separating myself from my deep
inner sense of knowing – my internal sensitivities. I am now clearly seeing that
I have always spent so much of my time thinking about where I am going, and
whether or not I am heading in the right direction; worrying that there has be a
right way in going about getting there; wondering just how long it will take me
to get there; and wondering if there would be anything there once I arrive.

I am now experiencing those same patterns over again, and there is a notice-
able part of me that is becoming anxious over this new discovery. I sense that
this part of me knows, all too well, that it is losing more of the power-hold it has
had on me over countless years. It is totally concerned with wanting to know
how long I have to spend out here in this environment. I am also seeing that this
is a means of distraction that has been set up through my intellectual thought
process in order to maintain control and attain more power. They have all been
distractions, and I have continuously been caught up in them all.

As I move along this physical path, I am aware that when I focus outside myself for validation for where I am going, I am constantly creating resistance patterns within the unfolding experience: thereby running into difficulty, stubbing my toe(s) on roots, rocks, or branches, as well as bumping into the odd tree. I have absolutely no idea where I am or where I am going. I am absolutely sure that I am nowhere and that I have to get to somewhere, to a place that I am not even sure exists. I am continually creating all of these obstacles – some of which create a lot of pain and damage to my physical, emotional and mental bodies – so that I can make the place where I am going worth going to. Wherever this place might happen to be! Whoever said that there was a place to go to, in the first place?

I have been following, or should I say attempting to follow, the flow of the surrounding vegetation, for that is all there is outside me. I am now seeing that it all hasn't worked out positively. I have been walking out here in the natural elements with extreme caution. I have wanted to be careful about whatever I have been choosing to do, so I do not bring more pain into my unfolding experience. I have not been moving as confidently as I would if I was absolutely sure of what I was doing.

I am hearing myself say – through the protective inner voice that is associated with my outer world experience – that: "I am not used to walking about in a strange place in the middle of the night and in total darkness." At the same time, I am also getting a very clear picture within my inner awareness that I have been indeed walking about in my outer world experiences no differently that I have been walking out here this evening. I just haven't been totally conscious that that is what I have been doing. Until now, that is.

I have been utterly consumed with questions pertaining to the outside environment I have been travelling through, wanting desperately to know where everything is in relation to everything else, somehow believing that knowing that would make a big difference to the outcome of the situation I am creating. But, of course, how could it? The fact still remains that I am blind in my movements within the darkened outer world. In trying to make my way through the hidden maze that I have created by making this journey, I haven't been successful.

This is supposed to be an inner experience to look deeper into my inner depths, to find a viable solution to the dilemma concerning the path I am on, or that I want to be on. All I have been doing so far is reacting to everything that is around me – things that I cannot even see – and to everything I have wanted to be within my grasp and wasn't. I had originally planned this experience so I would be totally alone with myself in all ways. Now I am very much aware of how I have been expanding this experience so that it has included much of the environment that lies outside me. This is an environment that I am not even sure exists, for when I am standing absolutely still, I am not able to clearly detect anything that lies beyond me using one or more of my five physical senses.

I see that I just can't keep moving the way I have been. I know that I have to stop this whole movement pattern before it consumes me. I also know that I have to initiate a new, supportive pattern of movement that will aid me in flowing within the creative current of my living expression, one that will nurture and guide me to my greatest inner destiny. I am now beginning a dialogue from the inner dimensions of my thought processes. I know that a solution, an easy and functional solution, can be easily reached and fully utilized within my daily living expression. I proceed to ask another part of myself, "Just where is it that you think you are going?"

"I'm going home," came the reply.

"And just where is that? Do you know?"

"Well, of course, I do. It's over here. No, maybe it's over here. No, wait. I know, it's over here."

"Well, which way is it?"

"I don't know. I know! Look, we can just wait right here until it gets light, and then I will be able to tell you which way home is."

"That's it! I've got it now. I see it ever so clearly. It's all just a big joke." It has all been made so clear in a fleeting moment, and I have seized the moment. I am now emotionally bonded to the full realization that there is no place to go; now or ever! I see that there is no path for me to follow. I see that I am the path in all that I choose to do. Wherever I choose to go, I am on the path, for I am the path. It is that simple!

My observation about waiting for the light of day to arrive from the darkness of the night has opened a new emotional awareness in me as well: "If I live totally within the darkness of my inner sanctuary with love and trusting patience, then my own inner light of all-knowing will come forth from the eternal depths of darkness and light my way in such a manner as to guide me into creating the most appropriate experiences for my evolutionary growth. Experiences that will allow me to be all of who I am, in all that I do."

I am fully aware that I have no static home within which to enclose myself, except, of course, if I choose to create one such place within my process of thought. I also see, oh so clearly, that I will remain lost forever, spinning in a continual circle, re-living old experiences in new ways, if I continue looking outside myself for any answers. There are only answers to be searched for within the outer fragmented world that continuously surrounds me. Within my inner world, there are no answers. There are only questions, questions that answer themselves just by the way that I choose to ask them.

I am now awakening to a new awareness flowing throughout my being. I am really getting it this time. I am getting the full impact of the power of the spontaneous emotion that comes from within an unfolding experience. I am now clearly seeing that all the other times when I had said, "I got it," I had only been getting it intellectually. Knowing something intellectually is only a small stepping-stone to the totality of the living expression within any experience. The power of knowing comes only through the emotional bonding to the wholeness of the experience that is unfolding. It only comes when there is no attachment to the way the experience unfolds, or to what the outcome is once it is over. The emotional bonding only comes when I am able to fully embrace all of what the unfolding experience is, without the slightest hint of judgment.

I am finally getting it. It is not about thinking. It is about feeling, being totally free within myself to feel all of that which is unfolding at any given time. There is no need to think within the purity of my own inner world. There is only a need to think within the outer world that I share with my fellow man. The only thinking that ever needs to be done in that world is when I have to function within the mechanics of man's organized systems.

I am getting yet another angle with regard to my new enlightenment. I am now seeing with both my inner and outer eyes that if everything was to go completely pitch black all over the world, I would be exactly where I would most need to be. I also see that there wouldn't be any point in me trying to get to any other place, for everywhere would be the same. There would be no need for any of my five earthly senses, for there would be nothing outside me. If I would choose to create something, it would only be a functional illusion. Yet it would be an illusion that I would create to be a reality in order to fulfill a desire to experience something while I was wherever I was.

I am beginning to get it all much clearer on the inside. I now see that everything that lies outside me is truly an illusion. I am also seeing that I make it a reality because I want to experience the totality of it. From there I can emotionally bond myself to the wholeness of the unfolding experience in order that I fully obtain my inner sense of knowing what lies behind it.

I am now seeing where I have gotten all mixed up prior to this new awakening. I see that I have previously believed that everything outside me was real, and that everything inside me was an illusion. I see that I have become, in the past, emotionally bonded to the illusion and its flow of movement. I thereby believed what took place in the unfolding experience was the total reality of my living expression. Whenever I have done that, I have become detached from the all-knowing connection that comes from within me. This connection allows all of my experiences to be created so that I might fully experience as many different experiences as I can, within my living expression, without becoming attached to any of them, except when I become emotionally bonded to the experience within the unfolding moment. When I do it that way, I do not have to think, for I would know all there is to know regarding the experience. I would know that the knowing would only apply to that particular experience, and that all experiences contain a totally different sense of knowing.

The key to all of it is not to become attached to the illusion, but to fully recognize that it is all just an illusion. Everything that is here on this plane is an illusion that I can make into a reality at any given time. I would do this in order to become more aware of my own God light and the all-knowing aspect of reality that it represents. I am beginning to laugh at all that has unfolded within and without me, for I have gained the inner awareness of the purpose behind experiencing this plane. There is still much more that I wish to experience here. I will now choose to continue going inwardly so that I might discover still more within the dimensions of who I am. What else can I do? Where else can I go? What is the limit here? I need to keep pushing further and further inwardly, through the time-less dimensions and space-less frontiers, so that I can experience it all in the totality of who I am.

## September 6, 1985

*Reflections on events that have taken place since my experiences up island*
I had met with my hiking partner on Wednesday, August 21, for our usual weekly meeting at the back gate that leads into the wooded area surrounding Thetis Lake. Something had been very much different inside me on that day. I had an overwhelming feeling that I no longer wanted to be in the woods. All I knew, deep down inside, was that there just wasn't any point in going to the woods any more. I knew that I had to be able to use more of the information I had already been given within the natural elements within my daily living expression. I felt as though I wanted to be totally alone within my own self-created world. It felt strange, totally opposite to the way in which I had been feeling and moving over the past two and a half years.

There had been a definite struggle for power taking place within my being. One part of me wanted very much to be there with my hiking friend, and another part of me wanted to be all by myself, at home, in the security of my own room. I had watched it all for a while within the vision of my inner eyes, eventually made light of it, and then carried on with the evening's agenda. After we had finished our hike in the woods, we went to a local restaurant for a small bite to eat. As usual, we also shared more insights about how each of us had been seeing the world around us, and supported each other in our endeavors to become more of who we are within the deepest depths of our creative beings.

During the next week, my internal energies began to change quite noticeably. I had felt, more than ever before, that I just wanted to be alone. I had been withdrawing into myself, into the deeper levels of my being, levels that allowed me to be closer to who I truly am. I had been definitely resisting going to the woods during any part of that following week. I had felt that I had to break away from all outside support so that I could become totally dependent within my own being for guidance and for nurturing. I had sensed that this was the next step for me to take within the evolutionary flow of my life. I had also known that I couldn't struggle within myself, or create waves in my outer world, in order for this to take place. It would all have to happen within the flowing course of its own movement pattern. I knew that I would have to be patient and wait for it all to manifest, and that I would also have to be cautious not to forge ahead and try to force things to happen. If I did that, I would be setting things in motion that would not be in the best interest of me arriving at the *centre* of who I am, and bringing forth the most revealing and creative aspects within my being.

I had been sitting at home one day, asking my inner teachers how it would be possible for me to get even closer to the *centre* of my being. I knew there had to be more than what I had been shown thus far. What I wasn't sure of was how to go about tapping into the reservoir of information within me that would illuminate the entirety of my inner universe, as well as all the other universes that exist within that universe. The more questions I asked of my inner teachers, the fewer answers I received. I could only hear these repeated words:

"Be patient, my friend. Remember, that all things are provided for you when you are most able to utilize them. Your free-will to want the necessary information is so strong that you might not be able to fully assimilate all the pertinent information you are asking for, if it was all given to you at this time. Your body must become a purer vehicle in order that your opening to all this information does not short circuit all of your internal energy patterns and cause you severe damage, possibly even death.

"Your physical brain still needs to go through an opening within itself, one that will allow you to utilize all the information that has been going on since time has begun, and that will continue to go on until time is no longer. Trust that you, in your almighty and infinite wisdom, know that the unfolding of this process is evolving in the appropriate flow of all of life. It can neither be sped up nor can it be slowed down. If you activate the force within your free-will, as you have done in your past movements, you will affect the purity of that which is unfolding. Release yourself from your own self-imposed time restrictions, and know that each moment is all there is within the entirety of a life cycle here on this plane.

"If you are able to fully comprehend all of that which has just been spoken, then you will know that there is no need to be in a hurry while you are on this plane. There is nowhere for you to go, and there is nothing for you to do, beyond the unfolding creative process that is forever being created from within your being. Know that you are being well looked after by the guidance of your own inner wisdom, and that you are protected in all that you do here on this plane, provided that you allow yourself the total freedom to become all that you are, and that you give yourself the total freedom to experience all that you create within the unfolding movements of your life journey, without attaching to it any judgment or comparison as to what it is you think you have experienced.

"Be patient, and know that all that is destined to become part of your earthly expression, shall arrive when you are most able to emotionally embrace it so that it does not create unnecessary imbalances within your living expression."

\*

I am up and moving early this morning, after having only three hours rest on the earthly plane. I have an electrifying feeling that a totally new type of experience is about to unfold within me. I have a sense that it will be one that will enable me to consciously go deeper within myself to whatever level I would choose to explore. I look at my watch. It is 3:15 a.m. I enter the bathroom and take care of my bodily necessities, then return to my room and put on some warm clothes.

I proceed to light the three candles that I have placed on the makeshift shelf that is in one corner of the room. In front of each of the candles I have placed an eight inch piece of light blue stained glass that has a logo design painted on it. The design had been given to me by my inner teachers when I first started on my inner journey, back in May of 1982. The design on each piece of glass is the same, but the colour balancing between the light and dark blue is reversed. One signifies the male aspect of my being, while the other signifies the female aspect.

When each of these pieces of glass is laid on top of the other, they form the wholeness and the purity of the logo [see figure 1]. They also represent the

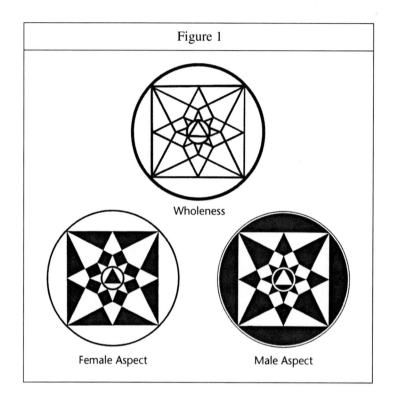

Figure 1

Wholeness

Female Aspect                    Male Aspect

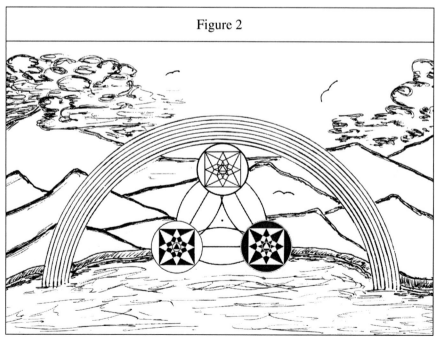

Figure 2

wholeness and the purity of who I am as a person. When I am able to fully integrate and balance the male and female aspects of my being, then I will be able to fully utilize the unlimited energies that exist within the deep, well protected core-essence of my being.

The one that represents the female side is leaning against the candle on the left. The one that represents the male side is leaning against the candle on the right. On the wall above the two candles, five inches above the height of the flames, is a thin piece of wood (approximately 8" x 30") that has been etched with the symbols that reveal my eventual destiny while I am on this earthly plane [see figure 2]. These symbols were presented to me over a period of time by my inner teachers as a means of allowing me to consciously unravel myself, revealing the deepest depths of my inner being. Approximately eighteen inches above this symbolic picture is a beautifully balanced wooden sword that has been handmade by a martial art student, created especially for me. It is absolutely flawless in its construction. To me, it is the sword of my truth. It is an instrument that I can use all the time (while I am on the earthly plane) to cut through all the illusions that make up this plane of reality.

I am sitting quietly, focusing all of my attention on the wooden storyboard that contains my male and female symbols, as well as the one that represents the wholeness of who I am. The three symbols are laid out on the wood so they form an equilateral triangle. The male and female symbols make up the base structure, while the one representing wholeness forms the apex. In the centre of this triangle, there is another much smaller equilateral triangle that has a dot in the centre of it. This dot represents the *centre* of my being and the *centre* of my universe – and all the infinite universes that co-exist within my universe. It also represents the *centre* of all-knowing. To arrive there in totality, within the framework of my earthly human form, will ensure me everlasting life. This *centre* represents everything that is not of this world, yet it creates the expressional illusions of what this world is all about. It lies within the deepest, darkest depths of my being. I know that it all truly does exist, and that the challenges that arise within my own intricate fabric become more sophisticated the further I go into the depths of my inner being. I also know that this journey can only be made by going through my inner channels, for my outer channels are severely blocked by all the dense states of social conditioning and programming that man has been subjected to for so many years. By looking outside, I am continuously being affected by all the illusions that the outer world of man creates around me. By looking inside, I am totally free to observe the many tempting illusions that are surfacing from time to time.

It is still dark within the perimeters of my room. The Moon has been full for a couple of days, and is now beginning to change its form. The light from this heavenly sphere is shining through a sliding glass door that opens onto a southern exposure off my bedroom.

I completely release myself from all that lies around me, and I put my full attention on to the dark dot within the *centre* of the inner triangle. I vacate my mental process of all conscious thought, and I begin to feel the intricate textures of my being slowly beginning to alter within my physical embodiment. I am now travelling through the outer fragile layers of my being. I have consciously reached the thin veil of earthly covering that separates me from all the other possible realities.

It is at this point that I hesitate in continuing to go any deeper without having the confirmation of my inner teachers, for I am now aware that it has been by the use of my strong will that I have arrived at this place. I fear that if I continue to journey inwardly in this manner, I might not be able to find my way back out again. I take up a position within this fluctuating matrix of reality and illusion, and put forth a call to one of my inner teachers to guide me in my endeavors. I continue to wait.

Thirty minutes have passed. I have not heard a word from within the darkened depths of my being. I now know that I am being tested by my inner teacher to see if I can remain patient enough to allow it all to unfold as it is ordained.

An hour has passed, and still nothing. I continue to hold my internal and external positions, knowing full well that it will all come to pass. Within the texture of my inner eyes, I see the brilliance of my own inner light as it slowly begins to ascend through the delicate layers of my being. I am seeing the intensity and the softness of this pure internal light. The moment I have been patiently waiting for has arrived. The light vanishes, and in its place, I begin to hear the soft and gentle voice of my inner teacher – the all-knowing aspect of myself:

"Greetings from afar and from near. You have indeed learned well that which is termed your will. You have gained mastery over that which has held mastery over your entire being. You are now truly ready for a new journey within your being. Allow all of what is about to unfold to become that which you already emotionally know."

I can feel some apparent shifting taking place within my physical body, as well as within my mental processes. Illusionary emotions are beginning to surface within my unfolding living expression. I open my outer eyes. I observe that the three candles are still burning on the shelf. Fear begins to grow within me. I am fearful that I might get taken on an inward journey so deep that I will forget about the burning candles, somehow knock them over and burn the house down, as well as myself. My mental processes are busy creating scenario after scenario of what might possibly happen. I am presently stuck between the thin veils of reality and illusion. I am now wondering which one I am looking into the face of at this exact moment.

My inward journey is now beginning to manifest, and I am not at all sure what to do. One aspect of my being is going with the flow of the unfolding experience, while the other is struggling with what to do with the candles and all that they represent. I feel as though I am literally being ripped apart inside. I know that I have to do something, but what can I do? The longer I think about it, the further away I seem to be slipping from this illusionary life-threatening reality. I can feel myself beginning to panic. I am feeling that the candles are now in control of my being. I have to regain control over all facets of my being before this unfolding process takes me too far from the realities of this plane.

I struggle to get over to where they are. I lick both my index finger and thumb and extinguish the three candles. I then return to my sitting position. I close my outer eyes and begin to surrender my entire being to the process that is now beginning to build and intensify its momentum. A knowing sense from within directs me to open my outer eyes once more. As I do, I am met with a very disturbing and breathtaking observational reality. The two large candles are still burning brightly!

I cannot believe what my outer eyes are showing me. The fear is now becoming more intensified within my being. I am not sure of anything any more. I am not at all sure as to the direction I am going within my inner journey. I distinctly remember putting the three candles out. "How can it be possible that two of them are still burning?"

I look down at the two fingers I had used to extinguish them. They are both black. I can smell what to me is burning flesh – my flesh! I can even smell the aroma that comes from candles after you blow them out, especially if the wick is still aglow. I once again look at the candles. They are still burning.

"How could this be possible? What do I believe? Oh, God! What is happening to me? Is it possible that I only imagined I had put them out? How do I explain the fact that there is one candle that is not burning? How will I know what I can believe? How will I know anything? What can I trust?"

Fear continues to race through me. I can feel desperation gripping me from all sides. I am now aware that I am gradually slipping further and further from the earthly reality of myself that I had come to know and depend on for all these years. "What can I trust?"

It now appears that my mental processes were able to put the candles out, and then bring them back into the same physical condition they were in before I had put them out. I have a sense that I am dancing in between the delicate strands of time and space. As I arrive at the forever shifting focal point within my being – the point that represents totally surrendering all of my conscious desires within the unfolding of the experience – I begin to hear the voice of my inner teacher. His voice is very soft and subtle, and at the same time, sure and exact. He begins his dialogue with such strength and precision, "Do not trust anything that will come to you and be perceived by you through the use of one or all of your five earthly senses. Let go and relinquish all of your conscious thought patterns, and venture forth by relying totally on your feelings of knowing. Those that make up the purest essence of your being. Trust only your deepest inner feelings."

The voice is so powerful in its delivery that I immediately drop the whole issue with regard to the burning candles. I know deep within my inner knowing that the candles are out, and that it was only my intellectual fears that had brought them back to life again. I am aware that my inner knowing always knows the difference between illusion and reality, and that it is only my thought processes that get in the way of that clarity. I am now free to allow the unfolding process to continue. From the depths of my being, I hear a soft form of chanting ascend to within range of where I have been waiting. The chanting is repetitious, and it seems to be reverberating off the subtle inner dimensions of my beingness. It is moving in such a way that I am not able to feel it from any one place. It is apparently vibrating throughout my whole being simultaneously. The words continue to flow, "Here we go, you and I, you and I, you and I; in we go, in we go, in we go; deep within, deep within, deep within; deeper, deeper, deeper; here we go, you and I, deeper, deeper, deeper; do we dare, do we dare, do we dare; you and I, you and I, you and I; do we dare, dare, dare; go deeper, deeper, deeper; deep within, deep within, deep within; do we dare, do we dare, do we dare; you and I, you and I, you and I...

"...through the door, through the door, through the door; deep within, deep within, deep within; deeper, deeper, deeper; in we go, in we go, in we go; deep within, deep within, deep within; deeper, deeper, deeper; in we go, in we go, in we go; deep within, deep within, deep within; you and I, you and I, you and I; through the door, through the door, through the door; in a room, room, room; you and I, I, I; deep within, deep within, deep within...

"...deep within, within, within; in we go, go, go; you and I, I, I; in a room, room, room; deep within, deep within, deep within; not without, without, without; but within, within, within; inside, outside; outside, inside; inside, outside; it's all the same, same, same...

"...see the light, light, light; burning within, within, within; inside, inside, inside; here we are, are, are; you and I, you and I, you and I..."

All the while this process is unfolding from within my being, I am observing my outer physical body going through incredible contortions. The different levels within my living expression are being affected by the higher inner frequencies that are now continuously resonating through every dimensional aspect of reality within my being. The outer surfaces of my programmed and conditioned physical embodiment are totally resisting the journey the inner teacher is providing. Part of me wants to escape through the opening within the inner doorways in order to see the wholeness of who I am. There is another part of me that wants to escape through the outer layers of my skin so that it won't have to witness the coming of my internal light.

As a result of the two way struggle taking place within my being, my hands and legs begin to shake uncontrollably. I repeatedly scratch the sides of my ribs, head, and chest. I clutch my throat. Breathing is becoming next to impossible. I am having great difficulty trying to figure out how to breathe in and out. I am caught in between time sequences and trying to find a way out by utilizing time sequences. It is impossible for me to do that, for I am always behind that which is actually taking place outside my thought patterns. By the time 'thought' can make sense out of any of it, it is all over, totally buried under the next unfolding moment. I am totally beyond any time sequence, yet I am reacting as though I am totally controlled by time.

I am now sensing that I am getting closer to my true inner self. I am also aware that the closer I continue to align with the higher aspect of myself, the more intense this process is becoming in its unfolding. This is only happening because part of me is still operating from a consciously activated process of thought that is based entirely on all the memories that have surfaced, reflecting all of my past programmed and conditioned experiences.

This inner process has been going on for nearly two hours. I have been continuously venturing back and forth between the inner dimensions of reality and outer dimensions of illusion. This process continues to gain momentum. 'I', the outer conscious illusion of who I am, does not want to relinquish any part of what it knows to be so in its world.

The subtle forces that have been at work within the structural alignment of the chanting (which has been very much a part of opening the inner doorways to my self) are now beginning to break through the resistance that the programmed and conditioned aspects of my living expression have been keeping solidly in place. This has been done so that the illusions of their existence do not come to the forefront of reality. There is to be one last surge of resistance offered before the door will be fully opened. Once this happens, my internal light of all-knowing will brighten, allowing me to embrace, on a conscious level, more of the deep-seated knowledge that exists within me.

The outer shell is now broken and a vacuum is being created within my physical embodiment. I am feeling as though I am being pulled in every conceivable direction at the same time. I feel as though I am being sucked through an opening that isn't quite large enough. I am not able to swallow, nor am I able to breathe in or out. My internal organs are in spasm. Everything inside me feels as though it is expanding. I sense that all of my internal organs are soon going to explode, leaving me nowhere in particular, but at the same time, everywhere. The top half of my physical body feels like it wants to head in one direction, the bottom half in the opposite direction, both at the same time.

My mental processes are becoming activated once more, "How do I get out of this one?"

From within the darkened depths, my all-knowing inner teacher proceeds to speak, "Do not trust any of what you perceive with your five earthly senses. Trust only that which comes from deep within your being. If you do, you shall make it through the illusions that are now before you, and you shall come into your own light."

Once again, upon hearing these all-knowing words, I relinquish all that I am perceiving, knowing that if I freely release myself from all thought my inner teacher will guide and care for me. As I feel the last of my inner struggles subside, I open my outer eyes and discover that the room I am in is now full of light. I get up, walk over to the sliding glass door and look out. I can see the Sun shining through the trees as it slowly begins to ascend. A murder of Crows forms a tightly woven, dark-colored blanket in the clear sky as they fly by. They are en route to their daily locations so they can carry on with their living expression.

I know that I am no longer the same person I was before this inner journey began. I have made it. To where, I am not at all sure at this point in time. I am inside the eye of a raging hurricane, only the hurricane is me, in all that I am not. I proceed to lie back down on my mattress and turn on my inner vision so that I can see, with conscious clarity, all that is being presented within my being. I continue to marvel at the clarity and simplicity of all that I am observing. This place that I have come to is saturated with peacefulness and with what I can only describe as love.

This inner experience has been going on for about an hour. I again open my outer eyes so that I might experience the total newness within my being from both the inner and outer world stages. Everything I set my eyes to in my outside world slowly begins to disintegrate before me. I am being shown, as I have been shown on so many other occasions out in the natural elements, that nothing exists outside me. Even if it did, it would always be in an ever-unfolding state of being: becoming and dissolving, dissolving and becoming.

I can still hear my inner voice bringing forth, so I can hear it, the reverberating chanting that carried me into this peaceful place. I can only guess that this inner voice is still responsible for sustaining me in this position. I am now noticing that the inner reverberation is also emanating from my being whenever there is any form of movement coming from my physical body. As I move my arm through the air, I can feel the subtle vibrational frequencies within it. I can also hear, within my inner ears, the sounds that the different vibrational frequencies produce when they move through a continuum of space.

I am aware that I am becoming a purified rhythm of vibrational energies. I am on the verge of being able to totally realign the vibrational frequencies that make up my entire physical structure and hold it in constant form. In being able to do this, I will be able to easily change the structural form of my physical embodiment to suit any desired shape that I might want to assume within any of the different worlds that exist on the earthly plane, regardless of what that shape might entail – animal, mineral or vegetable.

As I attune myself to the process that is continuing to unfold, I am able to see the intricate vibrational frequencies of light that are held within the composite mass that makes up my arm and my whole physical embodiment. I am able to observe all the different vibrational frequencies that allow the things within my room to be here. I see that everything is always in constant motion. There is nothing that is ever static. Although in my outer perceptions of reality (within my outer world) all things appear to be solid in their form, I am now seeing that they are only that way principally because I was told they were when I first arrived here on this plane. I am now able to see clearly – within every aspect of my being – that nothing in my outside world is ever the way it seems, for it is always the way it is. I also see that it is never the way it is, for it is always the way it seems.

As I gaze down at the carpet, I notice that its texture is continuously changing, or at least that is how it seems. Upon closer examination, I am now seeing that it is not the carpet that is changing, but rather, it is me that is constantly changing and evolving.

I am now aware that I am not my thoughts. I am also seeing that it is my thoughts that hold me together in a static position and keep me from becoming who I truly am. I see that when I release myself from all thought, regardless of what it might be, I am more able to flow within the ever-changing and ever-unfolding creative expression of who I am deep within the innermost core of my earthly essence.

The internal chanting is becoming louder. My outer eyes slowly begin to close. I once again find myself being guided to the deeper levels within my being, where I am once again being shown the many ever-changing aspects of truth that exist on this plane, how this plane has come to be formed, and the purity of all that exists here for whoever chooses to search within himself to find it.

There are no conscious words that I can use to describe what is being given, for words are never adequate to fully describe the simplicity of all that is on this plane. I am being shown all this information, in its entirety, without words, yet with complete knowingness. This information will soon become a functional living reality within my daily expression on this plane, as well as on the other planes of reality that are contained within this plane. I will be open to using it, as always, at the appropriate times.

I sense that there is no limit to what I can see and do. I am also aware that within the inner dimensions of my being, I am moving at an incredible rate of speed, and that in my outer dimensions, I am not able to move as quickly. I am aware that I have to be cautious of the speed at which I am choosing to move. If I am not extremely careful, I will create a lot of friction between the movements of the two dimensions I am travelling through, as well as the other dimensions that exist simultaneously along side them. If this happens, I could very well explode into flames and return myself back to ashes.

The space I am now occupying encompasses all time and all space. I am not able to hold on to any one sequence of time or fragment of space. If I do, they will surely disappear. If I allow them to be just what they are, when they are, then I will be able to return to them within any time sequence I choose. I am literally able to return to any place in time and relive my own prior experiences. I am also able to jump ahead in time, experience what is to be, and then wait for that living reality of time difference to catch up to me. At that point, I am once again able to relive that experience in its entirety. I have also found that it is easy to jump back into my past.

I proceed to return my physical body to the location of the shelf in my room. I relight the two major candles, and I take my place on the floor so that my outer eyes are gazing upon the dark spot within the *centre* of the inner triangle. Once again from within the depths of my being comes the reverberating chanting. It slowly begins to pull me still deeper within my inner depths. I allow myself to fall freely until I come to rest in a quiet and peaceful place. I am now somewhere within the depths of my multi-faceted human expression.

Within this environment, I am opened up to a discussion that *centre*s mainly on creative sexual energies. It is not the kind that gets trapped in the beauty of one's face, or in the shapeliness of one's physical body, or in the use of one's genitals. It is the pure, subtle, creative sexual energies of the feminine part of my being – comparable to the kundalini serpent fire. This discussion continues on for a while. The room is quiet. The Sun is shining through the glass door and onto my body. I open my outer eyes and proceed to put my full focus and attention on to the dark spot in the *centre* of the triangle.

I continue to lose myself within the depths of the dark spot. I am feeling totally free within the experience that is continuing to unfold. I am about to descend into my inner passageway when something quite magical happens. As I am about to relinquish my being from my inner processes of thought, I see a blur before my outer eyes. I also hear a loud noise that quickly brings me back to the reality of the present time and current space I am occupying.

The blur that I had witnessed was the sword of truth falling from its location on the wall. How it did this is rather confusing, as it was securely fastened to the wall. Upon closer examination of all that has just taken place, I discover that as the sword fell toward the shelf, it had somehow extinguished the candle in front of the glass logo that depicted the male side of my being.

The sword had also struck the glass logo that depicted my male side and moved it away from the wall and against the candle. The sword had then proceeded on its journey, striking the shelf and bouncing forward toward where I am sitting. It finally came to rest, lying perfectly balanced on a six inch wooden disk. This disk had been placed in the middle of the shelf to catch the dripping wax from the third candle. As the sword came to rest, the cutting edge was facing upward, (symbolically) positioned in a strictly passive alignment.

The movements of the sword have conveyed a very strong message to me. I am now aware that the subtle female energies are the appropriate energies for me to develop at this time. These energies are so much more powerful in their subtle ways. They are so precise and so clear in the ways in which they are manifested and in the ways in which they move. It appears that only the least necessary amount of energy is ever used when these energies are confronting outside stimuli. It is truly a priceless gift to be able to witness the magic that is released through the movements of the subtle forces. It is definitely a supportive omen from within.

All day long, and well into the evening, my physical body has been going through some really major changes. My digestive system has been strongly affected by the unfolding experience. The measures I have been taking for the past three years have helped tremendously so that this process could complete itself during this particular sequence in time. It has been mainly the diet I have been on that has allowed me to open myself with minimal resistance to what has been taking place. My diet has been very simple: popcorn, rice, water or juice. I am not emotionally hooked on anything, food or otherwise. As one goes deeper inside, one has to release oneself from the emotional attachments one has been brought up to believe are so important.

I can feel things moving and changing on the physical plane, as well as in the more subtle energies that are beginning to make their presence known. The kundalini serpent fire at the base of my spine is definitely moving. I can feel my self-imposed restrictions within my physical embodiment as the serpent continues to stir the pulsating life-force in my lower pelvic cavity. The serpent wants to express itself more creatively up my spine. My physical body does not want to allow it to do so, for it fears that the serpent could quite easily get of hand.

The raw creative power within the serpent fire has been continuously growing as the day progresses, and my body has been having a difficult time containing this restless force. My body eventually weakens as the hours pass on, until finally the bonds of restriction break. The transformational serpent becomes free within its newly found domain and slowly begins moving up the base of my spine as it sees fit, bringing into full play within me the new found creative energies of its life-force.

My creative sexual energies are now more heightened. I am finding that I want to let these creative energies express themselves within my outer world movements. I am also aware that I have to take this new surge of energy and use it creatively within my being. I know that if I choose to use it outside my person for my own selfish wants, I may be destroyed in the process. My whole body is alive with a new awareness. Every cell within the texture of my skin is super-charged with sensitivity, and everything I see, feel, touch, taste and hear, is more sensual in its expression.

This is definitely a totally new experience. It is a bit frightening at first, only in my newly formed appetite for harnessing and using these creative energies, yet at the same time, it is all so positively exciting. Life is beginning to take on a whole new meaning and appearance inside me. I know that my whole living reality is now in the process of being completely changed. I will never be able to look at the sexual world of man, and my movement within it, in the same way again.

My sensitivities are so acute at times that I find myself drifting further and further into the physical framework of the house. Not just certain parts of it, but all of it. I find myself in all the different rooms, feeling and pulsating with the vibrations that the walls contain. At the same time, I am vibrating with all the different energies that are contained within the structure of the walls. What a tremendously powerful feeling. There are absolutely no boundaries in my movements unless I create them. I can push as far outwardly as I choose, or I can retreat inwardly as close to my *centre* as I choose.

I am now beginning to see that there is so much for me to see and become aware of while I am still here on this plane of existence. It is now apparent, more than ever before, that the deeper I go inwardly towards the *centre* of my being, the more subtle the energies become, and along with that, the more powerful they are in their expressions.

The energies in my throat area have also been affected by the new experiences I have opened myself to during this day. When the kundalini serpent fire became free from restriction at the base of my spine, physical changes occurred in my pelvis and in the area that surrounds it. The area became free from obstruction within its own specific movement patterns. I am also aware that my shoulder and throat area has a different sensation. My internal energies have definitely changed, as well. I am now aware that my throat area is not as bound as it was before this process began. I have an inner sense that this area is directly connected to and affected by the area where the serpent is now moving from. I now consciously feel that my inner truth can be spoken outwardly with much more freedom and more impact.

All day long, I have been courting the male and female sides of my being, in the hope that I might get them to merge completely and become whole once again. At the exact same time, I have been a little apprehensive about doing it all at once. My female aspect lies quietly waiting, for she seems to sense all of what is happening. My female aspect knows that sooner or later my male aspect will seek her out, for the subtle energies that make her what she is are just too powerful. My female aspect reflects nothing outside herself, thereby enticing my male aspect to come closer and closer until eventually the actual integrating, sexual ritual begins. There is closeness, then separation; then closeness, then separation; then touching, feeling, sharing, nurturing, sensualness, acceptance;

and finally, there is the intercourse that leads to the ultimate of orgasms. It is an orgasm that reconnects my delicate strands of light – the building blocks of what I am – in a balanced and perfected array. There is no more separation within my being. What has been done can never be undone. I have successfully reunited my being into the wholeness that I was before I came here, and that I was when I first arrived.

I am now complete within myself. I do no need anyone or anything outside my own person to make my life of any value or any purpose. There is no longer any need for me to look any further than inside my own being in order to find all my own answers. There is no need to ask questions to myself any more, for there are no answers deep within. There is only what 'is', in its entirety. It is all so simple once I am inside. Now the journey begins to bring out, into a functional living reality, all that is inside my newly realized and emotionally experienced being. I must now move with it in all ways on this physical plane, otherwise it is not a reality for other beings here to move toward.

The key is to find a delicate balance between the creating aspect of my inner world and the performing aspect in my outer world. To be clear within myself at all times will allow for only the truth to come forth within my living expression. Truth will forever speak for itself in words, or in quiet moments when words are of no importance. It will be as it will be, according to the higher and more subtle energies that are beyond the earthly plane and dimension of reality.

## January 17, 1986

### The Journey into the Underground City

Here I am, sitting in a hotel room in downtown Toronto. I am at peace with being here. I do not have any pictures of what lies ahead for me, and I am not attached to any of the many pictures I have left behind. It feels as though I have been here all my life, that my life is a continual starting place. I have a clear sense that there is much here for me, although I do not have any indication as to what it might be. I do know that it will be clearly presented to me when it is time for it to be....

I left Victoria, B.C. on Monday, January 13, 1986, at 7:40 p.m., saying farewell to my friend that I have been sharing a house with, and who has continuously supported me in coming into my own light. Before I left the house, I could feel a release inside my being, one that would guide me on my journey.

I had completed all that I had to while the last moments passed by, making sure that I looked seriously at what is, instead of looking at the illusion of how

I wanted everything to be. I knew that my time there was up. I had a knowing sense that I must now move on in order to grow more into my own light, to share with others the divine light that I have come to know and trust, without question, from deep within me.

In preparation for my journey, I was directed from within to clear up all my inner and outer relationships with the people I have been interacting with, and who have been aiding me in my search for my truth, even though they might not have been aware of it on a conscious level. It was also clear to me that I would be leaving Victoria, the only home base I have ever known, and that I would not be coming back this way again. I would only be able to take with me what I truly needed, and everything else would have to go. I had to rid myself of all possessions that were not absolutely necessary for my daily needs, so that I could be emotionally free from being attached to any object that has been created within the world of man. I ended up either selling or giving away the few belongings I did have.

As I get into the taxi and look back toward the front doorway, the last vision I have is of a person standing there waving as we slowly begin to pull away. I feel nothing. All is complete. I do not fear going ahead, for I do not wish to stay where I have been. There is no time and there is no space. There is only continual movement.

I strike up a conversation with the driver. I am now becoming aware of how easy it is to let go of the pictures of what has been. Sitting in this car, I have a strange feeling that I have been sitting here for such a long time. There is no future or past tense in our communication. All there is, is the present moment unfolding.

We arrive at the bus stop on the highway, and I leave the taxi along with three small pieces of luggage and a brief case. It feels good knowing that all I will need, I have with me. I also know that if I don't have it with me, I don't need it at this point in my life.

I am standing at the bus stop, waiting patiently for my ride to the ferry to come along. Deep down inside I am aware of a feeling beginning to stir: that I won't be coming back to this place. There are no words or physical feelings attached to the deep-rooted feelings I am experiencing. There is only a sense of knowing. Everything feels just like it does. It just 'is', free to move however I would choose to create it. I will use the purity of the sword of truth to help guide me through all the illusions that continually surround me, ones that I have made into a functional reality within my living expression. I am experiencing no further processes of thought in my present reality. I am openly ready for whatever will present itself each moment.

The bus pulls up, the door opens and the driver steps down onto the sidewalk, where we conduct our necessary business arrangement. I tell him that I will gladly pay him whatever the going rate is if he will take me to the ferry, then to the Airport Inn, in Vancouver. He agrees. I pay him and get on board.

When the driver returns after putting my luggage into the cargo space, we resume our journey en route to the ferry terminal. Along the way, I am moving unconsciously through many different levels within my being, cleansing those parts of me that need to be cleansed.

Once I am on the ferry to Vancouver, I make my way up to the cafeteria, where I want to experience one of my favorite brands of clam chowder. This time, however, I am consuming the chowder without any attachment to its taste. It is only what is. I have stripped away most of what I have thought it was, and what remains is what it really is, without any judgment or comparison. I clearly see that it is only what it is at the time I am eating it, something I call food, and that I am putting it into my body so that I might keep moving on my life journey.

I know that I will not be taking this ferry ride again. My days here on the West Coast are coming to a close. All that I have needed to do while I have been here, has been done. It is now time to reawaken my conscious connection to my own inner light: the light of the God principle at the *centre* of my beingness. I will use this creative light in order to be of self-less service to all mankind, and to do all of it within myself, for myself.

When I arrive at the Airport Inn, I ask the attendant when the shuttle bus departs for the Vancouver Airport. He informs me that it will be leaving in ten minutes. I enter the main lobby area, leaving my luggage outside leaning against a concrete wall so the driver of the shuttle bus will know there is someone who wants a ride. I position myself in a corner of the room where I am well out of the main- stream of traffic. I am observing those people who are already inside, as well as those who are continuously coming and going. I am observing all that I can without any judgments or comparisons whatsoever. I feel as though I am an observer who is visiting from another planet. They are not aware of my presence, and they won't be unless I choose to engage them into my unfolding reality. The shuttle bus pulls up and I load my things on. We continue on to the airport terminal.

We arrive within twenty minutes. I take my luggage inside the main terminal and proceed to look for the Wardair ticket centre. As I move toward the counter,

I become aware that they are closed for the night. It is now 11:20 p.m., and they will not be opening again until tomorrow morning at 4:30, two-and-a-half hours before my flight is scheduled to leave. The terminal is quiet. There is not very much going on. There is no place to sleep except in a chair or on the floor.

For a while I choose to sit and be still, contemplating whatever comes up within my mental thought processes or across my visual mental screen. There is no question as to what I am doing. There is no doubt as to whether I am making the right move. I know that I am connected to the creative light inside me, and that all is unfolding in a very supportive way.

There have been a few times along my journey where my five earthly senses have taken over, and I have become overwhelmed for short periods of time. When that has happened, I have called upon my internal sword of truth – my inner light – to help guide me through all the obstructing thought patterns. I know deep within me that all is unfolding according to my clearest light: the light that will guide me to the *centre* of my self and beyond.

My home-front testing sequences are all finished. There is nothing else for me to do except move on, and keep on moving within myself to become more of my own guiding light. That is all there is. I do not fear what lies ahead, for I know that I am the creator of all that will unfold before me. I know that the creative God light is me, and that I am the creative God light. I am now moving under the guidance of that light, and I am choosing not to look at the shadows that have been cast behind me. I know that the shadows will come back again and again. I also know that the shadow is only a shadow, and that it is not me.

I know that I am the creator of the shadow, but the shadow is not me. It is only the darkened reflection of the me that I truly am. The shadow is my friend, for it continually shows me what I am not. It is also my teacher, for it continuously shows me the way of the light-force – the force that has created me and forever moves and guides me.

The light and I are one in the same. The shadow, on the other hand, is all that is not me, the light. It does not exist independent of me, the light. What is, is the light. What is not, is the shadow. Both the shadow and the light are me. Me is not my shadow. Me is my light – the creator of all life here on this plane.

There is a part of me that is waiting for someone to come along and say, "Here we go. Come along with me, and I will make the next major move in your life for you." This is not going to happen, and I know that deep down at the core of my being. I know that I am the creator of all things, and that I am the light of creation. I also know that there is no one outside my own true self who has the power to direct my life. I know that I create all things and all people in my life.

It is absolutely clear to me that I am choosing to do what I am doing; no one else. It is up to me to create supportive people and opportunities in order to bring about changes in my view of both this planet, and myself as an integral part of this planet, to aid me in connecting, on as many levels as possible, with all forms of life here on this plane.

I end up sleeping on the floor for a while, knowing that it will be a long day once I arrive in Toronto. Five o'clock arrives. I check my luggage at the Wardair ticket counter and get my ticket. I continue to observe all that is taking place around me in the terminal. I proceed to move toward the designated holding bay. I am amazed to see that there are so many people who are going to be taking this flight.

I continue to watch the movements of the people as they are constantly coming and going, and I listen attentively to all that is being spoken. It is mostly just filler talk, people not wanting to be alone with their thoughts, people anxious about flying and about travelling to new places. I see them all as real aspects of my own being in one way or another.

I am clear that all is safe for me making this journey, and that I will arrive at my destination as planned. In fact, I have already arrived there, and that part of me has been there for years. I feel as though I am going to meet with that other part of myself soon. I also get a sense that there will be a lot more that will surface when I do, beyond what I know at this point in time – a very creative time for me indeed, to create a new life, free to be whomever and whatever I choose.

I board the plane, find my seat and make myself comfortable, waiting to see who will be sitting beside me. A young man in his late twenties sits down after placing his things in the overhead rack. There is no immediate conversation between us. I sense that he would rather keep to himself, and I am getting no impulse to commence a dialogue with him. I decide that the best way of handling this situation is to do nothing until an impulse arrives.

I wait until after we have had our first bite of food before I ask him if the book he is reading – *The Magic of Findhorn* – is a good book.

He replies, "There is only one good page in the whole book, and the rest is junk."

Puzzled, I ask, "If you know that already, why are you continuing to read it?"

He answers quickly, "To get that one good page."

I am able to use this dialogue to look at the experiences I create in my life in another way, from a different perspective. I am now aware that I create the experiences in my life so I can open myself more to myself. Within each and every experience, regardless of how small or how grand, there will always be something that I can use as food for growth.

We continue to chat about various topics for a while, and then our conversation runs its course. We both want to rest a little before we arrive. I doze off. I awaken a few times to take a short glimpse out the side window to see the beautiful, life-giving Sun shining radiantly. I now know that I am indeed heading in the right direction. We are so high up that the Sun shines all the time. This is a clear message for me to emotionally embrace: to stay well away from the active stimulation of the earthly senses of man, and to move within the creative light of man's outer Sun – the eternal light of creation. My whole being is aglow with what is.

The captain comes over the intercom to let us know that we are approaching the Toronto International Airport. He also informs us that it is a cold 1°F in the city of Toronto....

It has been six days since I first arrived here. Before I left Victoria, I was presented with one contact person I could connect with so that I might find out where everything is downtown. From that one person, I was given two other names that I could connect with to let them know what I was up to, and to see if they would be able to direct me to where I might need to go. I was very attentive to all that I was hearing from those I had encountered. I knew that all that I would need would come directly to me when I needed it. All I would have to do is be ready and open to receiving their many gifts.

On my second day, I met a gentle and loving man and his woman friend, both from San Diego, California. They are visiting friends, and he is being of self-less service to the needs of the local people in any way he can. He does this through doing what he does full-heartedly, being who he truly is at all times, loving himself and others unconditionally. He is using the creative energies within himself so that he might align with others who wish to align with their own inner healing energies to bring about major changes in the way they are expressing themselves on this planet.

He and I dialogue for almost three hours. What I eventually see is that everything we have talked about, I have already heard many times over from deep within my own being. I am now clearly seeing that I have continuously created people in my life to fully support that which I already know. Upon this simple realization, I begin to quietly laugh within the depths of my beingness. I cannot help thinking to myself: "It is all just a big joke – a joke to laugh at. All there is, is what there is inside of me."

From our conversation, I am feeling lighter within my movements, clearer and more sure that I am in the most appropriate and supportive place at this point in my life. I know that all I will need at this time is here. It all begins again right here. There is no sign of my shadows, there is only my light. My focus is now on my internal light, and I know, without any reservations, that the love I give freely will be the love that takes care of me.

When I left the man and woman, I was flying within my being from the realization that all of me is becoming the light that is totally responsible for bringing me here to this plane of existence. I am the light. I am all things, and all things are contained with the 'I' that I am. They had both said, and I heard the gift they had offered, that I should take a few days to myself to go sightseeing and explore the city in order to get a better sense of what is actually here. They presented me with some free passes to the CN Tower and the cabaret that is located on one of its vantage points.

On the third day, I went out exploring the outer and inner dimensions of the large city. It is all so big, so new looking, and so creatively expressed in its design and its layout. At the same time, I am very much aware that it is really nothing at all. Only my thoughts make it all that I want it to be or not to be. All around, everywhere I look, I see creation and I see Nature. People are continuously moving in and out of the underground city in the heart of the city, deep within the depths of Mother Earth. I walk for hours, observing the various creative forces at hand. I see myself as being totally separate from all of what enters into the scope of my outer vision. I totally align myself so that I am in this new world, but I am not of this new world.

I am looking for something to show me what I am to do while I am in Toronto. What I keep hearing from within my inner and outer channels of communication is, "To be of service. To give whatever I can, whenever I am able. To give freely; in so doing, I will always be looked after on my journey. All I will ever need to know will be revealed to me when I am most able to fully utilize it."

Making money is not an issue here. It never has been. When I have been moving with people in the most life-supporting ways, money has always been made available so that I could continue on my truth-seeking inner journey. That is how it will always be for me. All that matters to me is being of self-less service to mankind. The clearest message I keep receiving from within is, "To help whenever and wherever. To give more and more of me to my inner creative light, so that I might return to the purity of my own inner light and walk once again in the total essence of that light-force – the God light I am."

It is the evening of the sixth day, and I am sitting here quietly within the nurturing warmth of my hotel room, looking back over all that has taken place since my arrival here. I am beginning to get an inner sense of what this whole journey is about. I see that I have been on a quest, looking for my own precious inner truth. The testing, within the textures of this quest, has always been on the outer physical plane, for that is where all the emotional impact is. "Would it be possible for me to lose myself in order to bring out and be, in all that I choose to do, my true creative inner self?"

The tests that I have created have been many along the way, and this journey to Toronto is just another. Could I give up, unconditionally, everything I have ever known, and everyone I have ever cared for and loved in my living expression, and go to a strange place, an awesomely big place with millions of people constantly buzzing around, and be totally centred in myself? Not having any pictures to cling to as to where I have come from, and not having any pictures to cling to as to where I am going. Could I manage to stay above the clouds, to where the Sun shines all the time, while my money slowly dwindles away each day, and the connections I have been making with various people – that appeared to be going somewhere in a positive and supportive direction – totally dissolve and only emptiness prevails....

Before I left Victoria, I had sold all of my remaining possessions and used most of the money for the plane ticket to Toronto. I had just enough money so I could stay in a cheap hotel room for eight days (after that, I had no idea what I was going to do). I also had just enough money so I could buy $1.50 worth of food for each of those eight days. I have no way of leaving Toronto, for I arrived here on a one-way ticket.

… Could I totally let go of a way of being and fully trust, without any hesitation, my all-knowing voice from within, the one that is always presenting to me the ever-changing two sides to every situation, and I always have to figure out which one supports my life more at that particular time? Would it be possible for me to tear down all the walls I have built around me for so long, while still remaining totally conscious of all that is continuously taking place around me? The ultimate test is to see if I can indeed find unconditional love for all my fellow man, without judgment or comparison. Could I observe all people without attaching myself to them and their insignificances?

The humour of this whole situation of being here is beginning to show itself. There is an incredibly light feeling coming from deep within me. I am now beginning to see through those obscurities that have been surrounding me. I am able to fully see all that has been happening on the many different levels within me. I have arrived where I am now, and what comes next doesn't matter. Nothing matters at this point. It is all truly very humorous. The more I expand within my own self-imposed limitations, the more of the humour I see.

As I sit quietly, a voice from deep within my inner void begins to speak, "Now that you have consciously arrived at the full realization of what has been given, it is time for you to go back to Victoria. There is still much for you to do there within yourself. That environment is most appropriate for you to complete the next phase of your evolutionary process."

"Go back! But you told me that I was never going back!"

"Whatever was then, no longer is now."

"What does that mean?"

"It means that it is now time for you to move your physical embodiment to a place that goes by the name of Victoria. The place where you have lived before, yet when you return, you will no longer have lived there."

"You are confusing me."

"No. You are confusing yourself. The pictures that you are bringing back, by way of your thought processes, are no longer a reality in your living expression, for you have been connecting with much higher aspects of your being while you have been here in this environment. You can never go back to being the person that you were before you arrived at the place inside your being where you are now. If you insist on holding yourself in the framework of old pictures, you will bring upon yourself further imbalances that will complicate your living expression to a degree that will not be pleasant."

"How will I face all those people that I told I wasn't coming back?"

"Listen, my friend. You are not going back. You are going to arrive at."

"I don't understand what you are saying."

"It is not a question of understanding. It is a matter of feeling what is being conveyed to you. You are no longer the same person that you once were. You are a new person. When you arrive there, others will say to you that they know you. But I tell you that they will not. They will only know that static picture of you that they hold within their fading memory banks, within their mental processes. Let go of your concerns and rejoice within your being that you have arrived."

"How do I go about getting back to Victoria?"

"Phone your mother now. She is at home, and she will have the necessary monies available to ensure that you arrive at your new destination."

"I can't borrow money from her."

"There will be a job opportunity waiting for you when you arrive, so you will be able to pay her back quickly."

"What shall I do when I arrive in Victoria?"

"Outside of this short job, nothing. Do only what is absolutely necessary, and only when it is necessary. All will be taken care of for you so that you may continue on your inner journey."

"But—."

"The next leg of your journey has to do with *Returning to the Truths of the CHILD: The CHILD identity that lies within you and within all human forms.*"

"Can you expand more on this?"

"Not at this time. Know that all will come to you as you have asked it to be given. Be patient enough to wait for the most appropriate time."

"Will I be in Victoria for long?"

"No, not long."

"How long?"

"Anywhere from one to ten years."

"Okay! – Okay! I get it!"

"You are always concerned with future time. Pay more attention to the precious moments that are unfolding before you. The ones that you are missing are the ones that hold the most value, for they can never be made up."

"I will go wherever it is necessary in order to be of self-less service to all mankind. I will keep myself free of creating useless pictures of what I am perceiving in any given sequence of time."

*March 10, 1986*

*Back in Victoria, in the house that I left*

THE POTENT AND POWERFUL PSYCHIC REALITIES
The inter-dimensional journey within the striated matrixes of colour variations that make up the physical embodiment of my being, is beginning to take on a new and vibrant texture. The focus seems to be centring along the different pathways on the astral planes. They are the ones that bring into my conscious awareness extremely high frequencies of psychic energies. The vibrations and resonations of these energies can be harnessed instantaneously and channeled through the central vortex that separates the infinite dimensional planes of reality. They can

be fully used to either bring about positive, nurturing, creative changes within an individual, or they can be used to overpower and possibly even destroy the functional creativeness of an individual, thereby forcing that person to live their remaining years on this plane as a helpless servant to the cosmic consciousness of the darkened side.

It is six p.m., and the outer doors of the building housing the psychic fair are officially open to the public. Slowly and systematically, the streams of people begin filtering through the connecting aisles. They will eventually gravitate toward those persons who can hopefully give them some insight into the complexities of the worlds within the world that they have been creating for themselves. By observation, I am able to ascertain that the majority of those who are now in the building are not at all consciously sure or clear as to why they are here. At the same time, they are very much unconsciously aware that there is something within this environment for them to identify with and witness within themselves, something that will support them in the direction they are contemplating taking at this point in their lives.

My psychic friend and I are sharing a booth in the *ESP Fair*. We are sitting at our head table, which separates our booth from the main aisle, looking out into the mainstream of traffic as it continues to flow past, knowing full well that the people are observing us as they would observe animals on display in a zoo. We are fully aware that if we become too intense in our outer projections of knowing, it will deter them from harmonizing within themselves. As a result, they will pass us by and surely gravitate toward another reader who is not so intense.

This is my first experience at doing public psychic readings since I was first introduced into this dimension of reality, back in 1983. I have been invited by my psychic friend to come and share the totality of the unfolding experience with her and all those who are present. I see it as an opportunity that the universe has brought to me, and one that I will be able to learn from. I am here to give holistic readings to any person who would like one, and I am giving them free of charge. I cannot justify charging someone money for the information I will be giving, especially knowing that they will already know, deep within themselves, all that I am going to present. I am also hesitant about charging someone money for a gift I didn't have to pay anything for. I do not want to have to depend on anyone to make me who I am. I am here to be of self-less service in any way that presents itself. I am also here to explore the psychic realities to a depth I have only intellectually known prior to this experience. It is all so new and so exciting. I am aware that there is much for me to take in while I am here.

I am looking at the different dimensional pathways that are present within the boundaries of the building we are all gathered under. I begin to notice that there is far more happening in this space than can be easily detected or recognized by the natural five earthly senses.

There is an interaction of similar as well as opposite energies occurring simultaneously within the depths of the astral planes. It is one that is gaining in momentum as each new hour of the fair unfolds. Within its creative process, it has the possibility of having a devastating impact on all those who are gathered within these walls. It can easily explode, without any warning whatsoever, and create a living reality of pain and anguish for anyone who might be in its wake on this physical plane. It also has an equal opportunity to implode within the delicate dimensions of the human psyche, and create, as it moves, imbalances within the creative and destructive energies that co-exist within all things that exist on the earthly plane.

It is during the latter part of the second day, after witnessing the intricate dances that were being performed by formless psychic entities on the different energy levels, that I become aware of the powerful vibrations circulating around me. They are warning me of the possible shape of things to come. I am now aware that I will have to be cautious in all that I choose to do while I am here. There are apparently energy forces on the 'dark side' that are combining their energies on the astral planes, ones that are of the destructive vibration. They are beginning to look at ways of increasing their own personal power, entirely at the expense of other beings. They are quite prepared to align with each other, if necessary, in order to destroy anyone who would dare try to stop them from achieving their goal.

I am aware that this kind of movement will violate the personal rights for freedom of expression that we all have here on this plane. I know that what they are anticipating doing goes against the purity of the teachings I have been opened to within myself. I know that I will not be able to stand by and watch any of this, in part or in whole, take place. I am prepared to enter into this dimension of reality within the astral planes in order to protect those who could possibly get hurt.

I am sitting in my chair, intently observing the mechanics of movement that have been taking place within the interactions of certain people, when I notice bolts of energy being hurled across the room. They are not being directed at any one person in particular. I have a sense that whoever is responsible for their creation is only playing within the open spaces above the main floor area. As I continue to watch, I am aware that the surrounding air is becoming more intense with a mass of static energies, to the point where a thin cloud of vapor is beginning to form on the physical plane. At first, I think that it might just be smoke coming from people who have been smoking, but then I notice that this cloud is moving in a definite circular pattern within its stationary position.

There is a man walking along the aisle directly in front of me. As he passes by, I notice a flash of light coming from this cloud. I cannot believe what I see next. A bolt of light is projected from the centre of the cloud and enters into the small of the back of the man who is passing by, minding his own business. I then observe the man twinge as the bolt of light disappears inside him. He then proceeds to put his left hand on the exact spot where the bolt had entered. In the next unfolding moment, there is another flash and another bolt. This time it is directed at a lady who is just entering the booth beside me. I quickly respond with an equal charge of light, one that equalizes the one coming from the cloud. I have saved that lady from experiencing some form of discomfort. I can see that this cloud, whatever it is, has the potential to create a disaster if it is allowed to stay where it has positioned itself.

I have to move fast. I have to create an equal force that will totally engulf that cloud, so that when the next bolt of light comes out, it will lose its charge and become suspended between the malevolent energy cloud and mine. The opposite charges of both clouds will have an affect on this bolt of light in such a way that it will implode within its own vortex and project itself, as well as both clouds, into an open-ended dimensional doorway, thereby destroying both forces.

All is in position within a fleeting moment. I have moved within the delicate strands of all time and all space, where large undertakings can be accomplished virtually within seconds. I am now waiting to see when the next bolt will come. Seconds pass before the next victim is selected. I have a clear sense that I am to be the next one in line. The bolt is created. The flash of light appears and then disappears without a trace. The surrounding air is back to being clear and fresh.

I am now aware that I have interfered with the process of power accumulation by those who have been pursuing it. I know that they are not going to be overly thrilled with me for what I have created from their creation. I also know that they will probably strike back at me some time before this fair is over. I will have to be extremely careful from here on in. I cannot afford not to be totally present while I am in this building. As long as I stay centred within my own being, I will have nothing to worry about. I will have to use all that I have come to know through my journeys in Nature in order to keep them from catching me standing still within my thought processes. If I dare allow this space to be created, I might not be here on this plane for very much longer.

I am now aware that I am inviting a confrontation between myself and those entities who are representing the dark side of the creative forces. I can only hope that those beings who are responsible for all that has been taking place are still connected to the limiting factors of time and space. If they are, they can easily be defeated. If they are not connected, then anything can happen, and I will not know either way until the moment of confrontation finally arrives.

The ESP Fair has ended, and I know that I have to get out of the city and away from all the conflicting, swirling energies. I have to retreat to a neutral place where I can release the pent-up psychic energies I have been accumulating over the past four days. I have a sense that there are dark forces (representing the destructive side of the creative force) combining their abilities together, and that they want to destroy me in any way they can. I feel heaviness around my heart and tightness throughout the rest of my physical body. Some moments are more intense than others. I have a feeling that I am going to have to call upon all of my inner wisdom in order to confront the forces that are presenting themselves. I sense that I am going to have to do battle, and that my physical death is a very real possibility. I am totally prepared for whatever will present itself to me. I am not afraid to die. In fact, I am quite prepared to die, for it is only through continual death that I shall find my ultimate truth.

I have been moving within a tense circle of magic over the past four days. I have come up against a few powerful, power-hungry individuals who have been using their knowledge of magic to manipulate the energies of others, who are not as adept as they, in order to gain more personal power.

Black magic has been responsible for a few of the scars that I have received over the years. I have been aware that unknown entities have been trying – unsuccessfully – to manipulate me on the higher vibratory levels of my psyche, to join forces with them and to use my personal energies for their accumulation of more power and control. I know that I have been watched closely by this side of the dark force for at least ten years. They are now becoming concerned that I am getting too strong in my abilities, and that something has to be done to either destroy me completely – mentally, physically, emotionally – or get me to join them in their quest for power.

I have been moving within the white magic circles for well over ten years. I have been developing these creative forces inside my being very slowly and very carefully. I have known deep within me that the day would eventually come when I would be tested severely, in all ways, in order to see if I do indeed deserve to shine my own light in this world in the capacity I desire. I have a sense that all my years of training will now be needed if I am going to come out of this inevitable confrontation in one piece.

I am now ready for whatever will present itself. My body is strong and adaptable to respond in whatever way the unfolding situation warrants. My intention and my focus is laser-sharp. I am openly welcoming my death if that is to be the outcome. In all my training years, I have been continuously walking the thin line that separates life from death, and death from life. I have become so accustomed to moving on that line that nothing else will ever do in my world. I am totally centred within my being. I am always guided entirely by my inner truth, a truth that will lead and guide me into battle, protect me in all ways while the fight is on, and allow me to walk away from the battle unharmed. I trust the knowing presence within me, and I consciously call upon the universe to present to me the greatest experience I will ever be able to engage in, so that I might remove myself completely from the simple, mundane concerns of living on this plane.

My friend – the person I have shared a house with before I went to Toronto and since I have come back – and I are driving into town to pick up a psychic ally we had befriended during the previous four days at the fair. She was giving psychic readings in a booth across the aisle from me. This psychic, too, has been moving in the white magic circles of healing. Like me, the psychic had been very much aware of the dark forces that had been present in the areas we had been gathered in. Once we pick her up, we will be heading out of town for a hike in the natural elements.

As we proceed to move out of the city limits, I have a knowing sense that the opposing forces are slowly collecting themselves and starting to focus their energies. I am also aware that a battle, of some description, is not far off. The other two people are not aware of the subtle vibrational changes that have been taking place around us. I sense that these opposing forces do not see these people as a threat to their cause, as they are still moving through their initial training periods and up to this moment in time have not amassed enough personal power within themselves to be a threat.

I continue to direct the flow of the conversation in my direction to make sure that the opposing entities will be able to locate me without any difficulty, and also to make sure that I keep the others out of the possible confrontation. I am also putting out to these entities that I am prepared to meet them anywhere they choose, and under any circumstance.

We arrive at the back entrance to Thetis Lake Park just as the intensity of energies is beginning to build within the confines of the car. I am the only one who is able to detect the explosive peak of these energy forces. We get out of the car just in time. Any longer, and they would have surely been able to get the whole lot of us in one strike. It would have been a bonus round for them. I separate from the others and head in the opposite direction. I want to make sure that they will not be in any danger if things get out of hand. I continue to walk until the others disappear along the tree-lined pathway, and then I proceed to backtrack. I am being directed from within to an opening on a small knoll where I can prepare for the possible ensuing confrontation.

I remove my clothes and sit on a moss-covered rock at the highest vantage point. I am sitting facing west, the direction of introspection. I centre myself within the stillness of the natural elements I have observed and befriended for such a long time. After a short period of contemplation, I feel an urge to get up and move through the wooded area and connect with all of my brothers and sisters (within the wholeness of Nature) on a Spiritual level. It will be through all of them that I will do battle. I continue to move in and out of different time sequences and constantly transform my physical embodiment to blend in harmoniously with the surrounding environment.

Nature has also provided me with nourishment in the form of edible mushrooms. These are not like the ordinary mushrooms I have observed and eaten on many occasions prior to this. These particular ones have been purely manifested by my inner teacher in order to give me strength and clarity, so that I will be able to go into the unfolding battle with all of my defenses down. I will also be able to adjust my mental forms in any way necessary to clearly reflect back toward my aggressors all of what they are.

It is clear to me that I am to do nothing – something I have become accustomed to doing many times along my journey – only to wait for the moment of truth to arrive. When this moment arrives, I am not to be attached to the event or to the outcome, for many deceptive devices will surely be used – continually changing realities. If I hold on to any single form that I perceive within me, I will be killed outright.

I am being instructed to be more like wind, felt but never seen, and more like water, flowing and ever-changing. The ceremony of preparation is over. My defenses are now down and totally immobilized. The moment of truth is quickly approaching. As it draws closer, I am becoming more peaceful and calm within my centre. I am now moving within the formless form of nothing, yet at the same time, I am within the form of everything.

I put my clothes on and walk along the path for a short distance before I begin to feel that I want to connect with Raven. I want to touch base to see if he has any new awareness as to what is taking place within the other dimensions of this reality. I call externally three times, and then wait. I can hear two of them talking in the distance. I continue my internal dialogue with them, giving them directions as to where I am. When they arrive, they are both very eager and anxious to give me their inner awareness regarding the merging of the dark forces that have been building in this area. They also caution me to be absolutely free from attachment to all that will eventually unfold. The vibrational changes that are presently moving through me are far too powerful for my Brothers to effectively harmonize with, so they are not able to come very close to me while we talk.

I am told that I will have to do this particular battle all on my own, without assistance of any kind from anyone. The outcome will apparently have much significance as far as my future planetary duties are concerned. I will not have any protection whatsoever, for the battle will not be fought on the earthly plane. It will be fought on many different planes of reality. My Brothers fear for my living expression, and mention that it would be perfectly okay if I was to choose not to go into this unpredictable confrontation. I thank them both for their concerns, and bid them farewell.

As they fly off, they depart in a frenzy and in opposite directions to each other. Through this gesture, they are telling me that if I become the least bit fearful at any point along my journey, then that fear will divide me and instantly cause my physical death. I take a long, slow breath, and then continue to cautiously make my way along the path.

I am sensing the presence of an electrifying tension all around me, and a flash of insight is presented within my inner channels of being: that the other two people are in danger. It is not at all safe for them to be anywhere near this area during any of this. I have to go and warn them, and get them to leave quickly, without alarming them. I stand still and successfully project myself between the infinite spaces of time – as I have known it to be. I am moving within the thin veil that separates this dimension of reality from all the other dimensional realities. I physically reappear on the path, almost a mile away, that my two friends are on. I am careful not to enter too close into their dimension of reality, so they will not be startled by my sudden appearance. I connect with them some one hundred yards away from where they are standing. I am moving ever so slowly toward them, feeling all that is contained within this particular section of the woods.

I demand that the dark forces leave them alone. I tell these forces that I am quite prepared to meet them strictly on their terms, and that it has nothing to do with the others. I am being told that they will make no agreements, and that anything goes, now that they have me right where they want me. I tell them that I will only meet with them if they leave the others alone. They agree to deal with me first, and then after I am terminated, they will get around to dealing with the others.

I proceed to move alongside of my two friends, look their way and smile. I stop on the path, redirect them, and wait for them to disappear out of sight. As they continue to move slowly away, I begin my retreat, being cautious and sensitive to all that is going on around me. When they are finally well out of sight, I once again open up the thin veil between the strands of time and remove myself to a place in the woods that is far enough away from everyone.

As I move along, I am continually moving in and out of different dimensional planes of reality. As I do this, I am feeling the presence of a few pulsating forces that are also moving in and around my being within the planes I am moving through. These opposing forces are becoming stronger with every movement I make. Every so often, they strike at me in full force. Their intention is always to annihilate. Each time they have decided to make their move, I have dissolved within the dimension of reality I was moving through and entered into another dimension.

As I continue to walk along, moving in and out of the many different realities, I can feel myself constantly dissolving all of my ties here on this earthly plane of existence. My mind, body and emotions are surrendering unto themselves and unto each other. I am clearly feeling that I no longer have any firm connections to this plane.

I can feel myself being guided to doorway after doorway, and I have no resistance to going through any one of them. I have a sense that it is the dark side of the force that is trying to lure me through these doorways, wanting to pull me into their illusionary worlds so they can close the door behind me. I would then be trapped between dimensions, and I would be forever at their mercy.

This happened to me on three different occasions, and each time Raven called out just in time to help guide me through the illusion. It was always just enough to help keep me focused on where I was, and on where I didn't want to be. It was after their second attempt that I realized that this was the only way they would be able to trap me: if I allowed it to happen. I am now aware that the battle is on and moving on the subtle planes of reality, and that any mistakes by me will certainly mean the end of my living expression.

At one point along the path, I dissolve into the sheath covering of a fir sapling in order to get a clear glimpse of the dark forces at work against my creative expression. To my surprise, I am able to see five distinct and separate entities or energy embodiments. Each one of them has taken on a completely different texture, resembling my brothers in the animal kingdom. There are four specific cats, and one that is an equal blending of human and cat form. He is busy attuning himself to my outer world personality traits.

I am beginning to see why I have been cautioned about holding on to any one thought form or pattern of movement for any period of time. As I return to my original physical shape and form, I begin to feel the presence of many opposing forces all around me. I have a distinct feeling that there is another major battle taking place outside the one I am presently engaging in, and that I am involved in providing the main event.

The on-again, off-again battles continue to move for nearly an hour and a half before there seems to be no point in continuing to play with them. No matter what they try, I end up forming the reflection of that form of movement and it is instantaneously neutralized and held in a position of balance. It is turning out to be an incredible journey, one that has allowed me to experience a wide range of existing realities on the many different dimensional planes, and all at the same time. There are no space or time elements outside this earthly dimension of reality.

I am now beginning to feel that it is really important that I physically remove myself from the area I have been moving through, and that the sooner I do, the better off I will be. I receive a message from Cougar that I should move quickly before it is too late. I am not sure what he is referring to. All I know is that I can feel, from within me, a great sense of urgency to heed his warning. Everything is beginning to happen all too quickly around me. It is crystal clear that it is not safe for any of us to remain in the wooded area any longer than absolutely necessary.

I quickly attune myself to the resonating vibrational level of Cougar, and transform my physical embodiment into his physical form and shape. I proceed to move along the trail at top speed. I am covering the distance at an incredible rate. For the first time since that day on the rock face, back on my birthday two years ago, I can once again feel the potent subtle power that Cougar has, and how gracefully he moves and stalks his prey within his own environment.

I arrive back at the parking lot and find my two friends leaning against the side of the car, where they have been waiting for close to forty minutes. I express to them my concerns about what has actually been taking place within the wooded area this afternoon. Each of them acknowledges that they, too, had received strong feelings that evil things were brewing, and each had heeded their own inner sense of knowing that they had to leave the area when they did. Without further delay, we decide that we would go back to our house, put on a fire, cook up some light, warm food, and enjoy each other's company in a much more relaxed atmosphere.

The three of us are sitting around the fireplace, absorbing radiating warmth from the transforming flames. The room is dark except for where the light from the creative fire continuously darts and dances into the depths of the room. It is casting shadows off each of us and all the plants, and projecting multi-dimensional apparitions onto the smoothened walls and textured ceiling.

After a few hours of casual conversation, the psychic ally agrees to show us, by demonstrating on me, an ancient ritual, one that I was told I had performed on many different occasions when I lived on the Island of Atlantis, a few lifetimes ago.

I was not a bit surprised when the psychic ally mentioned that I was once on Atlantis, for I had already been told that by a few other people who are adept in higher psychic dimensions. I have been receiving ongoing outside signs of this reality, as well. Books about Atlantis have been continually surfacing within my outer world expression, and I have always gotten a sense of beingness whenever I have attuned myself to what the books stand for. It is never anything that can be clearly defined or identified. Rather, it is a strong inner sense of knowing.

I remove all my clothes and proceed to lie face down on the cushions that form a makeshift bench in front of the fire. I have been noticing that since I have come back from being in the woods, I have been experiencing a slight pulsating pressure building in my head, one that is beginning to intensify with each passing moment. The ritual that the psychic ally is about to conduct will hopefully move the different energies throughout my body, so as to release the tremendous pressure I am feeling.

As she continues to move through each of the unfolding movements, I can feel the energies beginning to move in many different directions within my bodily form. The only thing is, the energies appear to be moving just a few feet away from me, in any direction, and then they come to a stop. The area where the outer stimulation from the psychic ally is being centred, feels electrified and vibrant, but the remaining areas of my body receive the after-shocks – waves of pressure against my outer extremities, the worst of which has located itself within my head. Instead of releasing the pressure, these massage-like movements appear to be creating more.

I am beginning to sense that this ritual – although it might have worked successfully on Atlantis – will be of no help in the situation that is unfolding within my being. I know that all of what is taking place within me is new. This is the first time that this process is being manifested like this on the earthly plane. I am the first to experience it in this way. It is about relating to the world of man in a whole different way, a way that aligns the forces of the universe within the wholeness of each living expression of man. No matter what the psychic ally tries, the pressure continues to pulsate in and out of my living reality. There is nothing that anyone can do except allow me the space to move through whatever comes up, without reacting to or judging any of it.

When the psychic ally has finished her last attempt, I continue to lie on the cushions in a very quiet and still manner. I am thoroughly allowing all that has been taking place inside and outside me to fully integrate within me, and to move through the different dimensional planes that make up my being. I am aware that the pressure is beginning to build once more, only this time I sense that there is going to be an outward direction to this pulsating surge. This one will be released from body. I can now feel the presence of emotional fear rising from the depths of my thought processes. My body has now become frozen. I am being held in one place by my own doing. I am not really clear as to what is taking place. All I know for sure is that I am all alone, and that I will have to move through this whole experience by myself. There is no one who I can rely on or trust, for they would not be able to feel any of what I am going through within my person.

I am removing myself from the external world around me. I sense that in a very short period of time I will no longer be attached to this dimension of existence. Part of me is excited about leaving, while another part is reacting rather aggressively to the possibility of leaving. I express my concerns to the psychic ally, and suggest that she try something else – anything! It doesn't really matter if it works. It will serve its function perfectly if I am able to keep myself grounded to it while the inner experience continues to unfold. As she proceeds to initiate another phase of a ritual, I can feel things beginning to shift and move throughout my entire being – including my head. The physical sensations from this alignment are very much different than anything I have ever experienced previously. It is all part of the newness of the whole process that has been unfolding within me for many years now.

As the pressures continue to increase, I am becoming aware that the same forces I had been doing battle with earlier, on the different dimensional planes within the natural setting, are once again combining their energies in a collective manner to trap me within my own internal movements long enough to bring an end to my living expression. I have a knowing sense that this will be my final attempt at either destroying myself or in defeating those who wish to stop me from becoming all that I am. I sense that I will have to surrender completely to all that is moving through me, and be open to moving and shifting constantly and instantaneously through whatever dimension of reality happens to present itself.

Not a moment too soon, the psychic ally holds onto my shoulders and drapes her two-hundred-pound body across my back so that I am not able to move. As I feel her take up this position, I release myself from the orderly earthly plane and begin floating within the thin veil that separates all dimensions of reality. My physical body begins to create spasms of varying degrees. I sense that I am being possessed by the forces of the dark side of my living expression on the earthly plane. I can feel my body reacting to these foreign currents of vibrational energy. They are wanting to conduct the battle within the texture of my being. Their purpose is to destroy my essence by creating conflicting movement patterns within my physical embodiment. I know that they will only be successful if I stay within the structural alignment that they have set up. In order for me to come out of this ordeal within the wholeness of who I am, I will have to find a way of removing them, as well as myself, from my internal battlefield.

The spasms are beginning to increase, and so are my reactions to them. My head is now beginning to move from side to side in a very aggressive manner. Once every twenty seconds or so, I slam it violently into the carpet covered concrete floor – not just once, but over and over again each time. I cannot feel any pain from this movement. All my senses appear to be incapacitated. I am aware that I am without form. My physical body's movements continue to be controlled by these foreign impulses. My upper torso begins twisting and turning erratically and aggressively, wanting to move off the floor and out from under the suppressive control of the psychic ally.

At the same time that all this is unfolding within me, there is another part of my beingness that is holding the opposing forces in a neutralized position. It is as though I am not in any particular form or shape at any one given time. Whenever the dark forces come at me from a specific angle, I immediately insert a mirrored reflection of that form, and a balance position is created and maintained once again.

I am sensing that the opposing internal forms are now beginning to take on distinct shapes and forms within my unfolding living expression. There are many subtle energy shifts continuously taking place within the confines of my physical embodiment. I am beginning to realize that I am using an incredible amount of my own personal energy just to keep myself from being ripped apart and eliminated from this plane of reality.

As all of this continues to unfold, I am aware that the possessing entities have fully realized that they are not getting anywhere with me. I am indeed winning, and it will only be a matter of time before it will all be over. I will have to be patient and wait for the most appropriate moment to intervene with the right intensity of focus and the purest of intention in order to defeat them once and for all.

The moment of truth is getting closer. I can feel the desperation mounting from within the dark forces. They appear to be accumulating all their energies through one specific channel – one animal form. Which one? I am not at all sure. I know that they will soon be throwing everything they have amassed among them at me, within me, in one last attempt.

I know that I will have to wait, be absolutely still within my thought movements, and let them play the part of the creative impulse. I know that if I stay without attachment to any form, I will be able to align with whatever form they choose to create and activate within me. I will have to be sensitive to feeling the energy impulses that they will create. Inevitably, they will try to create diversionary impulses in order to trap me within a specific dimension long enough to get a strong fix so they can throw all that they have my way.

If I continue to feel nothing, then I will be able to easily detect when the exact moment of the final assault will occur. I know that I am the master of my own world – a world that is very much a part of everyone else's world. I know that I am indeed the master of illusion and the master of reality. I will have to use all that I know and feel in order to move through this experience and open myself to all the hidden information that lies behind the facade of what it all seemingly represents.

All of a sudden, I begin to feel an awesome influx of energy flowing throughout my body. I know that this is it. This is the moment I have been waiting for. It will be now or never for either force. I can feel, deep within, the wave building as it slowly begins to move toward the outer dimensions of my being. There is no turning back. Whoever will come out on top of this confrontation will remain, while the other will vanish from this plane of reality.

The dark side of the force has decided to come at me from within a texture that is familiar: my brother of the cat family. This is not an ordinary cat. Rather, it is a conglomeration of cat identities that have been very much a part of my outer world expression in the world of black magic. My physical embodiment is beginning to transform gradually and systematically, responding just as a wild and scared cat would. The power that is pulsating through my body is steadily increasing as the multi-faceted cat continues to do battle with my own cat spirit. It is definitely going to be a fight for death, right down to the end.

Things within me begin to intensify, so much so that the psychic ally has to harness all her internal power through one channel in order to restrain me on the cushions. I can feel my strength increasing with every breath I take. I feel as though I can throw her off my back without very much effort. My face is continuing to go through a physiological change, distorting and realigning itself over and over again. It is clear to me that I am seeing all the things around me through the eyes of a cat.

My arms, legs, hands, and feet begin to transform into appendages and take on movement patterns that resemble those of the cat. I can sense that the final assault is beginning to unfold. My body is quick to respond. I come off the cushions and quickly pivot my head around, snapping at the psychic ally, glaring at her with deathly intensity. I snap again and twist my body in such a manner that I grip my hind legs into the cushions, push off my left front leg and savagely strike out at her, hoping to create an element of panic within her being long enough so I can strike the fatal blow to steal her essence to feed mine. I rake my claw-like fingers only fractions of an inch from her face, but she is not reacting to the illusion she sees taking place in front of her. She is able to maintain her centre through all of it.

Little did the psychic ally know that had she wavered at all, the cat would have ripped her apart mentally, emotionally, and possibly even physically. Instead of turning away from the action, she chose to look deep within the menacing eyes of the threatening cat, to go beyond the illusionary outer eyes and venture deep within the feeling centre of the cat's nervous system. What she projected there was the purity of her feeling by surrendering herself unto the illusionary image of the cat and filling her entire being with love.

The cat senses what is taking place and quickly alters course. It is desperately looking for someone to feed it the only way it knows: through fear. There is to be one last effort in order to regain a stronghold. It now only has one more avenue of approach, to go after my housemate. She is sitting a good four feet away from where I am positioned under the control of pathweaver, far enough away that a lunging strike from the cat will not reach its target. The face of the inner cat distorts more. It is now choosing to throw everything it has toward her, in hopes of getting her hooked on the illusion through her own fear. If it can successfully do this, then it will have successfully defeated me, for it knows that I care a lot for the people who are in my company. It knows that I will put their safety before my own. It also knows that if I can be distracted long enough, in regard to them, I will not be able to block their final assault.

I can feel the intensity building within my being. My body begins to jerk and to go into incredible spasms, my muscles contracting and expanding at the same time. Everything is moving within me. I am on the edge of being totally out of control and totally in control. I know that I have to lose all control in order to resume full control. I will have to be patient and wait, making absolutely sure that I do not make my move too soon. If I do, it will surely mean the end of me, and of my friend.

The darkened-force cat begins to make its move from deep within my belly, releasing an angry breath. The growl is a low frequency one. My jaw opens wide as the sound makes its way toward my friend. As the sound hits her with full force, my right front appendage lashes out at her with all that it has. My friend reacts just as the cat has hoped she would. She jumps up and back, and her face radiates fear. The cat knows that it has her right where it wants her. It begins to make its move, throwing everything it has her way. The more it throws at her, the more fearful she becomes.

What the cat fails to realize is that as it put all of its attention toward my friend, it forgot about the battle being fought within the inner dimensional levels of my person. It has become so engrossed in the outer world illusion – the one that it has set up – that it is slowly being consumed by it. It is creating its own defeat. It has just lost everything it was hoping to gain. By the time it has fully realized what has taken place, the sword of truth has been activated. The cat now begins to react to all that it has created. It is slowly consuming itself bit by bit. No matter what the cat chooses to do from here on out, it will only work against itself. It lashes out in desperation again and again at my housemate, and each time it becomes weaker and weaker.

The moment for me to move is at hand – time to insert my own creative energy into the battlefield and cast the final blow. Waiting patiently has paid off once more. I internally match everything the cat has thrown out, and the end result is a neutralized and balanced position of being. In a fleeting moment, it is all over. The pain is all gone. The intensity that I have been experiencing is removed, and all within and without my physical beingness is still and quiet.

My physical body is totally exhausted. My breath is heavy and erratic, like the panting of a dog. In a long, drawn-out breath, it is all over. I feel a tremendous relief within me that I have made it, and that we all have made it through the ordeal with no one getting hurt. I know that I have claimed many a victory within this single victory. It will only be a matter of time before I am opened up to all the hidden information that lies within the deeper levels of this entire higher psychic experience. As always, I will have to be patient, and know that as I need to know, all will be provided for me. It is now time to be thankful that I have loving, caring friends around me. Friends who continually allow me the space to move within my own internal darkened areas in order that I might find out a little more about who I am not, so that I can live a little more of who I truly am.

CHAPTER 9

# THE CHILD IS FREED

## March 23, 1986

I have been walking along a new section of trail out in the backwoods behind Thetis Lake, looking at all that has been taking place within my living
expression during the past two weeks, especially the encounters I had with
the psychic energies while I was involved with the Victoria ESP Fair. I have become fully aware that there are forces constantly moving me within me that are
extremely powerful, and that these forces can be harnessed and used in many different ways. I am also aware that there are only two directions that they can move
in – either creative or destructive. The power within each direction is equal. Either
way, it is not to be taken lightly. If I do, then I will surely do myself great harm by
not being sensitive to what is unfolding within or around me at any given time.

I am not really sure where this hiking trail leads, and I don't really care. I am
allowing myself total freedom within my movements so that I can fully experience all that will present itself to me while I am here. I want to explore more of
my inner and outer world expressions – where the two intersect and become one
within the dimensions of time and space – so that I might create a constantly
harmonizing environment within my living expression. In spite of all that I have
seen and done along my journey into the higher vibrational teachings of the
natural elements, I still feel that it will all remain very much incomplete unless
I can use all the information I have been presented with in such a way that I
am once again able to return to the same state of wholeness I was when I first
arrived here on this plane.

I proceed to close my outer eyes so that I will not be distracted by all the
new surrounding sensory stimulation. I open my inner eyes and release myself
into the depths of my inner void – the place where all the information regarding this dimensional plane of reality, and all the other infinite dimensions of
reality, exists. I continue to move along the path at a slow and consistent pace,

putting my full attention on relaxing all the external aspects of my physical embodiment. I am focusing on altering my breathing pattern, making sure that I am breathing deep into the depths of my lower abdomen. On each out-breath, I empty myself more of myself, and with each in-breath, I fill myself with the natural elements that are very much a part of me. It is important that I keep myself attuned to the surrounding environment, and keep myself totally connected to all the living expressions of Nature, so that I don't injure my body by walking off the trail and into an unhealthy situation.

As I continue to align myself with all that is around me from moment to moment, I am aware that my body is beginning to glide along the surface of the path. My feet are embracing the fluctuating warmth and coolness that is forever emanating from within the depths of Mother Earth. Each time my fleshy soles embrace the nurturing ground, the rest of my body attunes to and becomes it. It is all happening instantaneously, with no separation between what has just taken place (within the restrictions imposed by the previous second of time) and what is happening within the unfolding of the creative process from moment to moment.

This is a totally new and exciting experience for me, in that, for the first time on this level of awareness, there is no separation between myself and all that lies outside me. I am all that surrounds me, and all that surrounds me is within me. It is now so much easier to move through the varying levels of awareness that lie deep within my being. I have a sense that I am getting ready to create a new form of experience for myself this day, one that will allow me to go even deeper into my old and worn-out states of programming and conditioning. It will also be an experience that will enable me to thread the delicate fabric that connects those linking structures (of programming and conditioning), so that I can free myself a little more from the grasp of the whole social structure/society and become a whole lot more of the person I am.

I am losing all sense of time and space. Neither seems all that important any more. I am now consciously aware that I have been continuously moving through previously hidden doorways within my being. At the same time, I am also fully conscious that I actually haven't travelled anywhere. My internal sense of knowing is projecting to my outer world sensory awarenesses that these doorways are, in reality, the illusions that I have previously identified with in my outer world expressions. My sense is that my journey this day will eventually take me further into the functional day-to-day living expression that supports those illusions, and allow me to release myself, within my deeper levels, from the clutches of those securely patterned belief structures. I am not at all sure of the mechanics of how it will all come about. I do know that it will unfold in the manner that I will most readily be able to integrate within my conscious living expression.

I continue to allow myself to walk aimlessly through the winding trails, all along feeling comfortable about being fully guided by my inner eyes. I am beginning to feel, to a much greater depth, that I can unconditionally trust these eyes and all that they will show me within my inner and outer worlds. I am quickly discovering the distinct differences between the vision that is provided by each set of eyes – inner and outer. I am becoming more aware of how my ongoing social programming and conditioning has played a major role in me choosing to separate myself from my all-encompassing sense of knowing – that aligns me to and connects me with all forms of living expressions on this plane. I sense that the experience unfolding at this time is being created to help realign me to the full awareness of that knowing, so that I will soon be moving from that place in all that I do.

I now feel as though I cannot go any further on this trail. No matter which way I want to go, I feel the presence of an impenetrable wall. I am feeling completely closed in within myself. I am also being affected, within my outer world senses, by all that is developing outside my physical, three dimensional space. I am beginning to react. My breath is altering in such a way that I am having difficulty swallowing. I am losing the sensitive connections I have been experiencing with my inner eyes. I am feeling a strong need to validate with my outer eyes all that is taking place.

A cold sweat begins to form on the surface of my upper body. I cannot believe what is happening within my being. It feels as though I am riding in an elevator, whose journey began in the deeper depths of my being and is quickly ascending to the outer, superficial expressions of my physical beingness – mentally, physically and emotionally. Nothing is working for me. My body is completely shut down and I no longer have any conscious control over what is unfolding. I sense that I will have to wait for the elevator ride to be over before I will be able to do anything. I am concerned that I might not be able to hold on long enough, that I am somehow going to terminate my living expression before the inner elevator can finally come to rest at the level of present time. I can feel myself beginning to slip ever so slowly from this level of reality.

It is all over in a flash of light. I am jolted back from the higher frequencies of energy that are pulsating within my entire being, my awareness returning once more to the outer edge of my body. I gasp for a long-awaited breath of cool air. My outer eyes open. My breath is short and quick. I am hyperventilating. I am beginning to see little black dots forming in my outer visual field. I know that I will have to do something quickly or else, in another few moments, I will black out and disappear into the depths of my inner void. I hold my breath and close my eyes, and begin to slowly exhale, making sure that I remove as much air from my lungs as possible. Then I take a long, deep breath. I repeat this procedure three more times before I begin to feel that I am back into a balanced place within my being.

I open my outer eyes and look around. I have no idea where I am. By visual observation, I am aware that I have somehow managed to arrive on top of a knoll. I am standing motionless within the centre of a small clearing that is completely surrounded by scrubby bush, arbutus trees and young fir trees. There does not appear to be a way out of this place. The bush is too thick. From where I am standing, I am not able to consciously determine how I got here. This new environment is set up in such a way that there are five semi-sectioned off compartments that are separated from the centre, and yet at the same time, they are all very much a part of the whole.

I am beginning to identify with all that I am observing in a whole new way. I see that this new place, with its apparent divisions, is very much like my own head. The whole space represents my skull, which encloses my brain, which separates and connects my thought patterns. I am beginning to change my whole inner and outer environments. I am now inside my head completely. I am projecting my inner awareness of the mechanics of how my brain works within my outer world expression.

I have somehow jumped the time/space gap within my being. I am now totally living – within this new, outer environment – my thought patterns as they occur within my internal processes. I am in awe of this accomplishment. But how did I get here? How do I get out of here? Why am I here? I am now beginning to react to what I have created for myself. I am starting to spin out within my thought patterns, as well as in my physical movements.

Internally, I am jumping from one thought to another trying to make some sense out of all that is taking place, and at the same time, I am trying to find a way out of my dilemma. Externally, I begin to search out the boundaries of each of the compartments that make up this clearing. I search through every inch of each space, looking desperately to find the path that will take me out of this encapsulated environment. I continue to go around and around in circles within my thought patterns, and also in my outer physical movement patterns within the space. The longer I keep myself busy doing, the more frustrated I become. When I stop what I am doing and just sit with my eyes closed, there is nothing – no thought, no movement – inside me or outside me. At this point, there is no time/space connection. All appears to have been set within an element of continuance.

Seemingly out of nowhere, another impulse of thought and physical movement is created. As a result, I am back to spinning all over again. The same thought pattern is repeating itself over again from within my darkened void. It is no different than it was the time before. Word for word, it is the same. My physical body movements are the same, as well. All of them precisely the same, just as they were the first time.

I follow the same order in exploring these outer, individual compartments, with the same dialogue going on inside my thought processes and the same movement patterns within my physical expression. I am now seeing how I operate from strictly a programmed state of being: that there is little spontaneity in my thinking or in my physical movements. The more times I repeat the programmed expression, the more conditioned I become within its mechanical structure. It is all so clear to me that this is the same process that has been taking place within me for many, many years.

To find a solution to this dilemma would provide me with the necessary insights to find solutions to all the other programmed states that exist within my living expression. This is the knowing that I have been looking for. This is the root structure that is responsible for creating all of my earthly illusions. I must go into it deeper. I must experience more of it emotionally so that I don't forget its qualities once I leave this state of being. Maybe I never need to leave this new state. Maybe I am already out. Perhaps I have already broken the old patterns, and this is where I am right now. How will I know for sure unless I take this experience to the nth degree, being cautious not to believe any of what I experience?

I lie down in the centre of the clearing. I look up at the cloud covered sky, wondering if this is all just a dream, and also if I will ever wake up. As I close my outer eyes once more, all returns to quiet once again, absent of time and space, yet encompassing all time and all space. The whole pattern is now beginning to repeat itself again. It is all so utterly incredible. All of my patterns of movement, both inside and out, are the same, identically the same. I have seen it all before. I have heard it all before, over and over and over.

I am now becoming frustrated. My anger toward myself for not being able to find a way out is beginning to surface. I start yelling at the top of my lungs into the surrounding air. It feels like this is the only way I can effectively release the pent up energies that are surfacing within my thoughts and physical actions.

I am quickly manifesting outwardly my inner dilemma. My outer response is more devastating than my inner reality. They are way out of balance.

It is amazing to realize that the outer manifested reality of my inner dilemma is not the same as my creative manifestation that supports my inner dilemma. My inward depth of thought is without time and without space, whereas my outer physical response is totally controlled by time and confined by space. It all makes so much sense now. My outer world reaction to my outer world thought is an illusion. I make it my reality because I am caught within the restrictions of time and of space. The question is: "How do I get away from the controls of time and confinement of space?"

I once again come back to the centre of the clearing. I sit down and proceed to look for a way out. This time there is something different happening. As I look around, I am aware that there is a pathway – the one that I had used to get in here – that is set off in a far corner of the opening. It is totally obscured from the outer vision, but very much in view of my inner knowing. I know that it will take me out of here and release me from my frustrating dilemma. All I need to do is walk over to it and leave. It all sounds too easy. There has to be more to it than just that. Upon further examination, I see that there is nothing else to it. It is all so simple and out in the open.

I slowly get up with the clearest intention of taking that path. As I get closer to its threshold, I feel it slowly drifting further and further away from me. I can feel myself being drawn back into the same programmed and conditioned state of relating to the entirety of this limited open space. I am being drawn like a magnet. There is nothing I can do. I am helplessly caught within the grasps of my illusionary thought processes. In another split second, I am back to repeating the same thought patterns and physical journey around the opening and the connecting compartments. I am so close to releasing myself, yet I am so far away from actualizing this reality.

I sit down on a rock and gaze at the pathway that will eventually take me out of here. I know that it is the way out, but what I am not sure of is what is keeping me from taking it. I have no memory of the fact that I have tried it once before without success. I am aware that I am repeating that process once again.

I am now changing the programming within my thought processes. Through this process, I will soon condition myself to leave this place once and for all. It is all just a matter of a time sequence that passes through a given space allotment.

I am becoming aware of how I come to do the things that I do. I am also becoming aware of the differences between spontaneous living – through the absence of time and space – and controlled, programmed living – that is structured and controlled by time and space.

I get up and move in the direction of the pathway. After I take the same number of steps as before, I feel myself being drawn back to my original patterns of thought and physical movement. My frustration and anger are the same, as well. The intensity of my outer dialogue is the same. Everything is the same. I am operating totally from an automatic, uncontrollable place within my responses. The total process is repeating itself again and again, totally new and totally fresh in its unfolding each time. There is no stored memory, yet I am somehow aware of all that is taking place. I am living this experience within its unfolding, and I am also observing the expression within its unfolding. I am free of time and space, as well as being confined by time and space. I am in two dimensions of reality simultaneously and consciously.

In a few moments, it is all over once again. I am watching myself take up my position on the rock and gaze hopelessly in the direction of the pathway that leads to my freedom. I am aware that the same dialogue is returning within the structure of my thought patterns, and that if it continues, I will once again repeat the same course of movement as before. I have to change the wording of the dialogue as it comes up. Not before, and not afterwards. I have to wait and seize the opportune moment to bring about my absolute reality of freedom. That's it! I have got to integrate the word freedom within the unfolding dialogue. For freedom implies no restrictions.

The repeating dialogue is now presenting itself, and I begin to move with it. The point of insertion is now at hand. Action is initiated. My new dialogue is beginning to flow, "I am now free to leave this place, for this place no longer holds power over me. I am also free within my movements to come back to this place whenever I so choose in order to learn more about myself. When I do, I will remain totally free within myself."

That is all that is needed. As I get closer to the threshold, I sense that I am indeed free and that I can easily leave. As I enter the thick bush that slightly obscures the pathway out, I stop and look back to my self-imposed prison. I marvel at how hard it was for me to leave when I didn't clearly want to be free within all of my movements: when I was not taking full responsibility for my own creative movements. I see how easy it was for me to leave when I chose to see myself in the light of my own creativity, creativity that continually manifests freedom on all levels.

I am now aware of my freedom. I see that I had to go through this experience in order to really 'see' it all. I proceed to turn away from the top of the knoll, and

I open myself completely to the freedom that is symbolically held within the path that I am now on. It is a path that I am now seeing with my outer eyes for the first time, yet one that I already have a sense of within my inner world. I am much more aware of the varying textures of this path, and I am open to allowing it to show me all that it knows.

I find a section on the path that weaves in and out of some big fir trees, and decide that I am going to leave this trail and align with one of them and look over all that has taken place. I move up through the salal bushes until I find a suitable spot where I can look more intensely at the mechanics of what that whole experience has to offer. I know that there is far too much in it to just leave it all alone. I want to sit with it and see how many different perspectives I can come up with that will allow me to stay free within all that I will choose to create within my living expression. I proceed to sit quietly. Closing my outer eyes, I open my inner ones and begin to relive the whole of the experience over again.

I am becoming aware of the very fine line that separates me from being imprisoned by my thought processes or totally free within them. I see that as long as there is one, there has to be the other. I also see that spontaneous living can only come about when neither imprisonment nor freedom exists. That state is the state of all-knowing. I am seeing that this would be the state of being that is not controlled by time or space. I am also aware that within the state of being where both time and space exist, and are the controlling factors, there has to exist two equally polarized realities. They are opposite to each other, and in most cases work against each other, for that is what keeps the polarization equal and held in position. In so doing, it also ensures that time and space will continue to define and control this earthly plane.

It all seems so simple, yet if I did not create the experience to free myself from time and space restrictions, I would never have been able to see it so clearly. I used to know all this from an intellectual place only. Now, thanks to the experience, I have received the full emotional impact of what it all means, and much more, as well. I am seeing the fine line that exists within other pairs of polarized word groups within my thought patterns. The fine line between in and out, up and down, left and right, night and day, right and wrong, good and bad, etc. I am seeing, for the first time, that my thought processes have the power to make any experience I create fit on either side of the razor thin line. It will always be this way as long as I continue to 'think' about what I want the experiences to be: before it happens, or after it has already happened. This will be based entirely on the programming and conditioning stages I have been continually introduced to ever since I first arrived here on this earthly plane.

I open my outer eyes and look out into the distance. I am not really focusing on anything in particular. I am allowing myself to take in more of all that lies around me. I open myself to experiencing as much as I can from the central position of the fine line that separates my inner and outer worlds. What else can I use from the surrounding environment to show me more about myself, in regard to how I continually dissolve into and out of the thin line, and also, about how this line is forever changing in the reality of no time, no space living?

As I look straight out into the distance, I am able to clearly see everything that is within a 180° sweep of my outer vision. As I remain absolutely still within my physical form, I am aware that there is no movement outside me. I see that I, and everything I am observing, am in a no time, no space living expression. We – all things in my vision, as well as my own person – are free from any restrictions imposed by time or space.

Everything is always in a constant state of continual movement and evolution. We are all evolving at the same rate. Therefore, there is no separation between any of us. We are all one in the same. If we are all in a constant state of movement, then we can never really change, for we will all always remain the same. We will remain the same in what we are, yet we will alter the way in which we are being what we are. We will not age, for there is no aging in a no time, no space living experience. We will all be forever young within the depths of our inner-connectedness, for new, ageless growth always comes through the central core of any living expression. Our creative vibration will always remain the same: forever free-flowing and unrestricted.

I proceed to move my upper body from left to right very slowly, noting the textural difference within my field of perception. The first thing I see is that all the trees and clusters of salal bush appear to move. It appears that everything is in a constant pattern of change, and that I am the only aspect of reality that remains stable. It now appears that all of that which lies outside my being, within the scope of my straight-ahead vision, is directly influencing the accuracy of my initial perceptions. I am beginning to react to what I am seeing. I am beginning a new programming stage within my living expression. I am living outside myself, but living within myself.

The fine line is once again making its presence known. I have to do something. I proceed to stop all of my movements. As a result, everything returns to stillness. All thought has stopped, as well. My focus is back onto everything within a 180° sweep. I start the sweeping movement once again. As before, everything starts to change. My thought processes become activated. Within my outer vision, I am becoming more selective in what I am now allowing myself to see. As I change the focus of what I hold in my outer and inner vision, I notice that my thought patterns change, as well. This shows me that I am always being affected by every form of stimulation that enters into my outer line of vision. It will always be this way as long as I am living within a time and space oriented environment. I am now judging every bush and every tree in relation to every other bush and tree. In some cases, I am judging various aspects of structural continuity with regard to a single bush or single tree. I keep dividing my thoughts, thereby creating new illusions to keep me spinning within the static thought patterns I am holding on to.

I want to examine all of this from another angle. I get up and slowly walk toward a small cluster of trees that line the pathway. I allow my vision to be unfocused, looking at everything equally as I move. There are no thoughts moving from within my being. I stop and fix my vision onto a tree that is only about an arm's length away. As I do this, I am aware that everything else begins to fade away out of the clear picture. Within my outer vision, my thoughts are now identifying what I am looking at as a tree – a small Douglas fir.

As I continue to look, I am aware that I am freezing the tree in a restricted and limited time and space expression. I see that I am, within my thought processes, keeping it from evolving into all that it is. I proceed to take my right hand and extend it in front of me so that I am now holding on to the outer layers. As soon as I make contact with the outer layers, I see the tree begin to disintegrate right before me. It started to fade away as soon as I took my focus off the tree and put it onto my hand. I am now freeing the tree from my own time and space restrictions so that it can continue to evolve within a no time, no space environment.

I am now affixing myself to this controlled environment, one that will always remain the same, for it is controlled entirely by time and space. When I release my hand once again, the tree comes back into focus, again freezing it within my own self-imposed time and space restrictions. I let my vision move freely so that I am not looking at anything, in particular. When I do this, everything around me returns to a place of equality and apparent stillness.

I see that it is only me who chooses to continually freeze myself, as well as everything else I encounter within my living expression. I am seeing that I set up all of my own time and space restrictions, and then I blame others because I can't seem to find my way out. I see that as long as I continue to think, I will always create an environment that will be controlled by time and space. To be totally free of all the restrictions of time and space, will allow me the total freedom to interact with all the components of time and space, without being either attached to them or affected by them. I know that time and space are only illusions that are created entirely by my process of thought. I also know that their only purpose is to allow me to find the truthful reality that lies within their structural framework.

I continue to walk along, observing within me more of the simplicities of living here on this plane. I am looking for a viable way in which I can bring forth, into my everyday living expression, the treasures that I am uncovering inside my being. I once again let my eyes wander aimlessly, and as I do, all thoughts cease within my being. I am back gliding within the freedom of my whole beingness. I have no concerns, for I know that it will only be a matter of time before my thoughtful desire becomes a functional reality. I know that a sign will soon present itself so that I can begin a new journey.

I continue to walk along until I hear the gentle calling of a young fir sapling. I am not sure that I can believe my ears, for young trees have never spoken to me so directly before. I am pleasantly surprised, as I am aware that my newly found freedom within is expanding in all directions within my living expression. I position myself in front of this noble messenger and open myself to what it has to say.

"Take one of my appendages, cup it with both of your hands, cover your mouth and nose with it and take three deep breaths. Keep your eyes closed at all times and observe that which will present itself within your inner vision."

I do exactly what has been spoken. As I take my third breath, the visual screen within my being becomes activated and images begin to materialize before me. The first image is a child, a male about three years old. The second image is also a child, a female about five years old. The third image is of a child that is neither male nor female, but encompasses both genders. It has no definable age, for it is ever-changing in its physical structure, smoothly flowing through all ranges of age on the earthly plane.

As the last image begins to fade from my inner visual screen, I hear the small sapling present these final words, "Become more like the child in all that you do, for only the child truly knows how to be absolutely free within himself. It is a time-and-space-free world that he continually surrounds himself in."

As I let go of the branch and open my eyes, a warm sensation begins to fill my whole being. I know the exactitude of what has been spoken. I can feel it in the deeper regions of my darkened inner void. The words that I have heard are still reverberating throughout my physical embodiment. I am feeling very light-headed and totally off balance within my outer movements. I begin to sway back and forth.

As I begin to walk, I stagger, so I continue to use the branches from the trees that line the pathway to steady my way. I am high on the purity of the information that has been given. I am filled with joy at the experience that I have created for myself. I am thrilled that I am now beginning to get closer to my inner dimensions of truth. It is a truth that is connected with the purity and innocence of the child. I now know, like I have never known before, that the movement of the child is the key to remaining in this world a free man. I am eager to begin on my new journey, yet I know that there is nowhere to travel. The process that has allowed me to get this far, will bring forward all that I will need, when I most need it. I will only have to remain quiet within myself and wait – with stillness and with patience.

As I continue to move along the pathway, I decide that I want to continue to look at how I might possibly be able to connect more with the child aspect inside me, and how I can effectively use this approach in my everyday living expression. I veer off the path that I have been travelling on and head into the depths of the woods. I continue to ponder over all that I have seen and heard. I decide that I am going to align with my inner teacher, to see if he can shed more light on this situation.

I position myself near the edge of a low bank next to a flowing stream. The piercing rays of sunlight are dancing through the spaces between the tree branches overhead. All along the bank, and covering the rocks in the stream, is a blanket of thick, plush, green moss. Off in the distance, I can hear Raven calling out. As I listen attentively, I can faintly hear the trickles of water as they drip off the saturated surface of the moss-covered rocks.

I close my outer eyes and pull in all of my outer senses so that I am totally isolated from it all. I am secluded deep within my inner darkened void, awaiting the presence of my inner teacher. I once again enter into the place where there is no time and no space. I am freely drifting between the infinite numbers of dimensional freeways that exist within the depths of my inner void – the void that connects all possible dimensions of reality on this plane, and every other plane that exists within this plane and beyond. I am patiently waiting for an impulse to come from within my inner darkness, knowing that if I am to know, it will be presented to me. I ask for the guidance of my all-knowing God self to come forth and align with me.

A clear and focused voice begins to speak, "You have indeed learned well your lesson for today. As you have asked, so shall it be given. This is by far your greatest test. It is truly to be a test of truth for you. It will require that you surrender all of that which you think you are so that you can become the total essence of all that you truly are."

"What is it I must do?"

"Are you prepared to die within your physical embodiment for that which is to be given to you?"

"I am a fearless warrior. I am always ready to die so that I might find a purpose to live."

"Hear these words, then, for if you are not absolutely clear within your realities, you will surely perish from this plane. Are you sure you are ready for this, the grandest of all tests that you have encountered?"

"You cannot frighten me off with your words. I am sure within myself of what I have asked for. I have indeed earned my journey here. I am strong and clear within my own internal convictions, and I will not be tricked by either your words or your actions. I have learned along my way that you are a force not to be taken lightly. In all of my experiences, you have neither presented to me a truth nor a non-truth. What you have always shown me encompasses all truth. I seek only the purity of my truth, all-encompassing truth, a truth that always remains the same: forever changing and evolving. I am aligning myself in the wholeness of that truth."

"It is the purity of that truth that this test represents. We shall both soon see the purity of your intention."

"I am ready for that which will present itself to me. Bring it forth whenever you choose."

"As you open your eyes, you will see before you, just off to your left, a member of the mushroom family. This particular mushroom is not of the nurturing kind. It will quickly terminate your living existence here on this plane if you are to consume it with any attachment to it whatsoever. This variety of mushroom is extremely toxic for your internal system. The only way for you to make it through this test alive, is if you are able to ingest the mushroom and move with it throughout its breakdown within your body. You must align with it, become it in every way, so that your body will be able to produce the necessary chemical substances that will neutralize the harmful toxins contained within its mass. If there is any hesitation on your part once you begin this movement, your physical life will be taken. Know this well before you begin, and do not begin until you know this within every inch of your being. You may now open your eyes."

As I open my eyes and look off to my left, I am already aware of the ominous presence of the mushroom. It has to be the coldest and ugliest thing I have ever seen. It is black with grayish-white spots sprinkled over its domed surface. It stands about four inches tall and looks totally out of place embedded in the thick, green moss. I know that this particular species of mushroom is not from around these parts. I also know that my inner teacher has creatively manifested it specifically for this test. It is only meant for me, and no one else.

I lean over and pick the mushroom from its resting place. It is coated with a thin, slimy covering on the underside of its dome. The stem is spongy and thick. It is cold and absent of all living expression. It exemplifies death in all that it is. A cold chill races up and down my spine. "Can I really believe that this is indeed a poisonous mushroom? Can I really believe that my inner teacher would actually give me something that would cause my death?"

I cannot afford to take this experience lightly, for I can't be sure that I will get another chance at it if I don't succeed. How could this possibly be any different than any of the other death-defying trials I have had over the years? I know that this experience is to be no different. I must enter into this unfolding experience willing to align with and overcome the hand of death so that I might venture forth with a new life.

I continue to hold the mushroom, gently embracing it with both hands. I sit cross-legged and place my cupped hands so they rest on my thighs. I proceed to go deep within my being to the innermost depths of my inner darkened void, to the place where my sense of all-knowing resides. I attune myself to the composite structure of the mushroom, and search through my inner awarenesses to see if I can find the appropriate chemical composition within its structural framework.

I am not able to find what I am looking for. I am now aware that this particular brand of mushroom is entirely different (within its structural and chemical composition) than all the other species that exist on the earthly plane. It is clear to me that this particular specimen is forever changing in its internal chemical composition. There is no static way of moving with it. I will have to continuously align with it through every aspect of its movement within my digestive system. I cannot afford to be absent in my intention for any part of a time sequence. If I am, then I will surely suffer for my wavering action. I have to be absolutely clear about what I am choosing to do, before I choose to do anything.

As long as I continue to keep clear within myself, I will be successful in my endeavor. I will have to keep surrendering my own identity unto myself and unto the mushroom. I will have to give in to the oneness of all things, and see the mushroom and me as a part of that oneness. When all things are within the veil of the oneness, they are protected. For within the covering of the veil, there is only harmony. I will have to continually slip in between the dimensions of reality that make up the chemical structure of the mushroom, and stay there.

I wait until the impulse comes from deep within. I am ready for my final test at the hands of Nature. I will now become all that I have been seeking since my journey began so long ago. I will either become it within the wholeness of this plane, within this physical embodiment, or else I will become it by totally surrendering my physical embodiment and returning to the oneness of all things.

Without further hesitation, I take the dome off and break it in two. I put one half in my mouth and begin to chew. It is without taste and feeling, a constant reminder that it represents death. I find it very cold and almost unpalatable at first. But then, as I continue my alignment, all of these sensations disappear. After I swallow the first half, I slowly put the other half into my mouth and begin chewing, making sure that I remove myself from any further judgments about what I am doing, or how it all tastes.

It is too late to turn back now. I am totally committed to following through with this experience. I have a feeling that if I can make it through the first three minutes without panicking, then I will have no trouble making it through the whole test. I swallow the second mouthful and sit for a few moments before I put the remaining stem piece into my mouth. As I place the stem in, I can feel my internal organs beginning to react to this foreign substance. Cramping spasms are being created within my stomach and small intestine. I can see clearly all that is taking place. I have to work fast within my own internal structural alignment. I have to synchronize my internal movements with those of the mushroom.

I release myself deeper within my inner void, totally disintegrating all the illusionary realities I have been holding onto, as to who I think I am. I am now absolutely free within my creative process to integrate fully with the chemical substances that are now being released into my system. I am able to neutralize the harmful chemicals before they enter my bloodstream. I am able to alter the vibrational frequency within my own cellular matter that makes up my internal organs. As this process continues, I go back to chewing the rest of the stem. A few more moments, and I swallow the remaining section of the poisonous mushroom.

I continue to sit, constantly releasing myself from all time and all space. There is no other place to be but right here. There is no other time than right now. For the first time, I feel as though I am living totally in the here-and-now. I cannot afford not to be. My total being is at peace with all that is taking place within and without my physical embodiment. As each moment unfolds into the next, I am becoming more aware of the sensitivity that can be unleashed within my body when I am totally living in a place of no time and no space. This is one emotional experience I am completely embracing with all of my emotions, yet I am not getting hung up on the illusions that this experience was created under. I am clearly aware that this experience has been created so that I will be able to identify more fully with the purity of the all-knowing child that is living within the *centre* of my being.

My total focus is on dissolving all that I am observing. I am not choosing to believe anything that is happening within my body. At the same time, I am also clearly aware that all that is happening is in fact happening. I would have to be a total fool if I didn't. In the awareness of the child, nothing is real. Yet at the same time, everything is real. The child knows that everything here on this plane is an illusion. Knowing that, he is able to see that everything here on this plane is very real, and that it is only to be used while he is using it, and set free when he is not. In this way, he is absolutely free within himself to see everything through new eyes each time he encounters it.

The Sun is now setting down behind the trees. There is a blanket of darkness slowly beginning to cover the surrounding environment. The colours begin to fade into the shadows of the night. My body remains still, as it has been for many hours. I have successfully made it through this, my final test. I am now emotionally bonded to the reality of the all-knowing presence of the child from deep within. The process is almost complete. There is only one more stage to complete before I can be free enough within myself to get up and leave. I will have to pass all the foreign material from my body.

Once my body has eliminated the mushroom, I position myself on top of a moss covered rock, internally removing myself once again from the surrounding environment. I want to dialogue with my inner teacher, for I need to know whether or not the mushroom was really poisonous.

Out of the inner depths a voice begins to speak, "You wish to know if the mushroom was indeed poisonous. Why do you find it so necessary to know? Is it not enough to know that you have made it through your test?"

"I know that two things are possible. Firstly, that the mushroom wasn't real. But because you gave me the suggestion through the depths of my inner doorways, I created it to be all that you said it was. Secondly, that the mushroom was indeed poisonous and could very well have terminated my physical life here on this plane."

"And which of the two would you have it be, if you could select?"

"It doesn't really matter. They are both equally as powerful. They could both have been either creative or destructive in their expression."

"You have truly learned well this lesson. There is still much that remains hidden within this lesson, and as you move along on your journey, you will be able to gain from it in many ways. To go further into the question of time and space will help shed more light on to your path – the path that you are in all that you do."

I proceed to make my way back to where the car is parked at the back entrance to Thetis Lake. I am beginning to see the experience with the poisonous mushroom from yet another angle. I can use the purity of this teaching whenever I am with other people. Each person that I encounter in my life journey is very much like the poisonous mushroom, in that they have the ability to terminate my freedom in creating my own living expression. They can also allow me to continually free myself from being held within a time and space oriented idealism. In both cases, it wouldn't really be them at all, in who they are, that would either free me or confine me. It would only be my perception of how I was wanting to hold them within my time and space oriented thought processes.

As I continually align with each person, I will be able to allow each new experience to unfold in the purity and simplicity within its creative unfolding. There will be no need for me to hold another person in a static position within my thoughts, creating all sorts of judgments and comparisons as to who I think they are, or what I think it is that they are doing. This alignment – based on an unfolding moment-to-moment creative process – will allow me to completely release myself from all past programming and conditioning.

When this alignment occurs, I will not get hung up on thinking that the illusionary experience I am participating in is real. I will be able to see that it is only real while I am emotionally bonded to it as it is creatively unfolding. Once it has completed each stage of its unfolding, the illusion can be released back into the void of darkness. I will then be free enough within myself to emotionally bond myself to the reality that I identify with within my being, so that I might become more of who I truly am.

I am now aware that all the experiences I have ever shared with other people are illusions, for I have chosen to hold on to them long after they have been completed. My past experiences have been somehow secured within my memory banks, promoting a reality that my total living experience is static, that it is securely held together by time and by space. The actual recalled experience is an illusion. The information that I can utilize from that experience (to help me free myself a little more) is the reality. It is only a reality for that moment in time, though, for I am forever evolving within my own evolutionary process.

The reality of the initial experience will always be the illusion, for my ongoing participation in the unfolding experience is entirely controlled by my memories of past experiences *that* might have been somewhat similar. (*That* is only a judgment presented from memory through thought. It is not based on reality or on unfolding truth.) Those memories are made up of programming and conditioning stages that promote judgments and comparisons.

If I always try to live the creatively unfolding moment through eyes that continually remain focused on and deeply connected to experiences that took place yesterday, I will become the victim of the illusionary experience. As a result of this, I would lose touch with my inner sense of knowing. I would be forever lost within the depths of my inner confusion regarding why my life never seems to be totally immersed in peace and harmony.

If I become emotionally bonded to the initial illusion, then I will react to how the experience unfolds or doesn't unfold. I will not be able to fully commit myself to just observing the process as it unfolds. If my thoughts are wandering all over the place while the experience is unfolding, then I will not be able to see clearly what the experience is all about. As a result of my inability to observe the present moment unfolding before me, I would formulate new illusions within my thought processes – in the way of judgments either regarding myself or the other person – that are based on the small bits of information I pick up on during random parts of the experience. Based on my past programming and conditioning, I would become emotionally bonded to that which I create within my thought processes. I would create it so strongly within my emotional thought patterns that it would become a living reality. It is all mainly due to the fact that I want to be right.

My security – especially if I am insecure within my living expression – will always come from my being right. My emotional bonding to the illusionary experience will always set it up so that I have to fight with myself or with others in order that I am right. Either way, I am losing my own ability to create a loving, supportive world for myself. I will always create a world that is based on my reactions to the experiences that take place within my living expression. As a result, I will not be able to see the true gift that each person has to offer me: the simplicity of who they are. It is only I who will ever choose to make things more than they actually are. I am not at all sure why I would want to do that in my life.

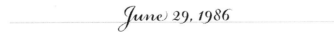

## June 29, 1986

I am walking alone along a well used inland trail in the woodlands of East Sooke Park. I have come to a place where I am clearly feeling a sense of oneness with all aspects of Nature. There are no names or labels to separate living expressions. There is only the total freedom to feel and to absorb my connectedness to the oneness of all things. I am beginning to feel the subtle power that is shared between all that is connected to the oneness. I am beginning to realize, more and more within my emotional centres of reality, that there is never any differentiation between living expressions out here, as there are within the world of man. There is only an unconditional acceptance for all things pertaining to the one. All things of the oneness know that they are here on this plane to be of service wherever they are needed. They are all totally self-less within their living expressions.

As my bare feet embrace the ever-changing textured surfaces of the all-nurturing Mother Earth, I can internally feel the freedom that comes from being more of who I truly am underneath all the illusions I have ever held, and sometimes still hold, of myself. It will only be a matter of time before I am totally free of all of my self-imposed restrictions. I am now moving more and more from within the depths of my creative child.

I have been observing my movements along the path, and what I have become aware of with each step is that I have not been able to feel any separateness between my steps and the surface I am connecting to. I have been continually surrendering my illusionary identities so that I am able to feel more connected to all the simple expressions of Nature that are all around me. This is where I truly feel most at home and most welcomed to be all that I am. I am never judged out here. I am, in all ways, encouraged to release more of who I am not so that I can be more of who I am. I am supported in using these times of solitude and quiet to connect with the oneness through my deeper inner channels.

As I move off the main trail and begin my ascent up the mountain, the darkened heavens above begin to release a soft and gentle shower of rain. There is nothing more nurturing to my soul than walking in the woods when it is raining. It is always so refreshing and extremely energizing. It now appears that the higher I climb, the heavier the rain is becoming. I am feeling totally free within myself to experience the inner joy of being an integral part of all that has been my outer teacher for so many years. I am now sensing that the teacher/student relationship we have had is being terminated, and that a new, equally realized relationship is being created and initiated. There is an all-knowing sense moving throughout my being, to a degree I have not experienced prior to this moment. It is allowing me to feel more of the inner living vibrations within the expressions of life that continually surround me as I move within this environment. I am all that I sense. And all that I sense, I am.

I am feeling an overpowering urge to shed my clothes (representing man's world and my position in it) and run freely throughout the ever-changing forest, to be no different than any of the other members of the animal families that live out here. I am sensing a place up ahead where I will be able to put my clothes so they won't get wet.

I strip off everything. As I am doing so, I feel the coolness of the surrounding air as it seductively dances across my exposed body. In an instant, my reality is altered. I have altered my reality so that I am now part of all that lies before me. I am surrendering all thought of what is happening and allowing myself to experience the totality of what is actually happening. I am free to create my deepest creative expression. I am acknowledging this feeling from deep within, and I am welcoming the opportunity to physically become one with everything else.

As I continue to stand on top of a protruding rock formation, I am being cleansed with the purifying waters from Mother Earth's nurturing process. I now know that I am once again being initiated into another deeper phase of my inner/outer journey. Within a few moments, there are streams of water meandering through the curves and hollows of my body. They are sending rippling cold chills in every direction along the outer layers of my skin. Electrical impulses shoot through my entire system, connecting the deeper layers of body tissue and organs to the unfolding experience. My whole body is beginning to pulsate with the all-embracing heartbeat coming from the core of the Earth. I am extending myself in all directions. I can feel my direct connection to all that lies before and around me, feeling the interconnectedness and oneness of Nature in the purest vibrational form. I am becoming alive with a new-forming vibrancy within my being. I am becoming, within my physical embodiment, all that I am feeling connected to inside.

As I continue to ascend the long winding trail, the rain becomes progressively heavier. I call upon the four major elements – Air, Water, Earth, Fire – to allow me to align with each in the purest way so that I might experience the fullness of this unfolding creative movement. As I am moving through my inner channels, I make the appropriate alignments within my physical embodiment so that I can transform my vibrational frequencies to become whatever I choose. I want to be able to move through the woods unaffected by any of the four elements.

I am becoming the living physical extension and expression of each of the four elements. I cannot feel the coldness in the air, nor can I feel the rain that is embracing my body, nor do I feel the earth that I am walking on. I am totally numb to all that exists outside me. I am becoming all aspects of all that exists outside me.

It is all so easy to see from this place of being. There are no woods. There is no me.

There is only what is: all things contained within the oneness. If there is not oneness within all things, then there is separateness. In order for there to be separateness, there must first be oneness, for that is how the separateness comes into being a reality.

I continue to move lightly and quickly over the ever-changing landscape. I am keeping my attention and intention focused on arriving at my final destination – the highest point on the summit. I summon my inner knowing in order to push beyond what I feel and know myself to be in thought, so that I might become more of who I am through my actions. The higher I climb, the more at ease I feel, and the more willingly all aspects of my programmed and conditioned earthly being surrender their illusionary patterns into the transforming knowingness of the oneness. They return to the same place they were first created from: the darkened void, from where the first breath of life was created.

The rain steadily increases as I venture along on my journey. The wind begins to dance around and along every inch of my being. It is trying to discourage me from completing my journey. It wants to see if indeed I am truly connected to the core vibration of all things, or whether I am just telling myself that I am.

I do not hesitate within this experience – based on what I feel on the outer edges of my body – for I know that it is all just an illusion that I can very easily make my emotional reality. I stoke up the heat inside my physical body by using my breath – the breath of life – to keep me in constant contact with the all-embracing oneness of all things. I continue to glide over the textured surface of the path. I am one, in my entirety. It is a feeling I have encountered many times before, only this time it is very much different. The connection I now have is much stronger and more powerful than before, because I have the emotional knowing to go with the intellectual awareness. "i" am the oneness. i am all things. i am.

As I reach the summit, the heavens open up and sheets of sleeting rain pour forth, forcibly bouncing off every inch of my physical body. I am now standing on the top of my world, looking down over all living expressions of life. I quietly acknowledge where I am, who I am not, and my deep-rooted connectedness to the four major elements – Water, Air, Fire and Earth.

I begin to unconsciously raise my arms from my sides, extending them outwardly until they are well above my shoulders. As I am doing this, I call upon the wind to come forth and play with me. Suddenly, the wind begins to howl with laughter as it continues to dance all around me. My body is moving within the same rhythm of breath as the wind. It is as though I am swirling my arms, in fact my whole body, in a large pool of water. I laugh at and with the wind, to think that it is separate from me, and that it thinks it can blow me over. When it tries to sneak up on me and knock me off my centre, I allow myself to move deeper within the earth. The harder it blows, the more rooted I become.

When I lower my arms, the wind ceases to tantalize my body. I pause within my movements, feeling within the deeper levels of my being all of what I am becoming within each unfolding moment. I once again raise my arms, stretching them outwardly until they extend above my shoulders. Shoulder width apart, with my palms open and facing the heavens above, again I summon the wind to come and play. As before, out of my creative void it ascends and our playful interplay begins. This time the wind sings as it howls, and whispers as it caresses my body.

I look at the surrounding treetops and scrub bushes. They are at peace within their own living expressions. They are playing spectator to all that is unfolding. There is absolutely no movement within their expressions to the outside world. The creative dance is strictly between the wind and I. The wind and I are one. We are brothers of the same family. I am fully awakening to the realization of all that has been evolving within this initiation. The voice of my inner teacher begins to speak, "You are one with all that is of you. Know that you are now attuned within your earthly movements to align with and utilize, as it is necessary, the four major elements that comprise this plane."

"What is it I should do with them?"

"Do! They are not here for you to do anything with. They are your living experience of the truths that you have been given along your journey. Allow them to reflect to you the harmony that is sustained when all things within the one know of their connectedness to each other, and their purpose within being of the oneness: to serve without thought of their separateness."

I am feeling the depths of the message that has come from my inner knowing. I sense that I am now completing my unification with the ever-changing, ever-present elements. We dance and celebrate our connectedness on top of the hill: the wind, the rain, and I. We continue to laugh as we dance. I am feeling the joy that is created when life is totally experienced within the creatively unfolding moment. I am alive with electricity. The purpose of making this journey on this day is to arrive at the place where I am standing. Now that I am here, it really isn't a big deal any more. There is no purpose for me to be here any longer. I have received the ultimate gift from this experience: freedom to be connected without feeling separate. It is all so simple. No matter how I try to make something seem more when I am experiencing it, the less it really is after I have experienced it. I am beginning to see that life is like that: simple expressions in simple ways.

As I begin my descent back into the depths of the Rain Forest, I hear the croaking of my brother, Toad. As I get closer to where he is positioned on the path, his croaking becomes louder. He is telling his song of life to the world that supports him. He is also waiting for me to come by so we can chat a little more.

As I step over a log, I see him perched upon a small stump that has been severed quite close to the ground. I stand my ground perfectly still. I am waiting to hear what he has to say.

Minutes pass, and nothing is happening. He is testing me. I can feel all that he is doing. We are connected in all ways. I ask him the purpose behind his visit, saying, "If you choose to speak, my Brother, then why do your words not flow? I am eager to hear your words of wisdom."

Another moment goes by, and then he begins his dialogue:

> you have come on this road
> and you have dropped your load
> you have since gone to the hill
> and there
> you have made everything inside you still
> you have come to me here
> without any of that which you call fear
> you have seen who you are deep, deep, inside
> and you have clearly come to realize
> that there is no place for you to hide
> you have come to know that you are all that you see
> and to see that so clearly
> know that you are, indeed, set free
> now you must re-enter into the world of man
> and do all of that which you can
> for you have clearly established
> within you
> a flowing relationship
> like that of the log in the sand
> now go, and be, my friend
> be all that you can be, just like me
> when you come across someone who wishes to be set free
> send them on down to the openness of the sea
> for that is where they will truly see
> that it doesn't matter how they be
> for the final reflection
> is always in
> "me"

Croak! Croak! And with that, he hops down off the stump and disappears in behind a rotting tree that is stretched out on the ground. I laugh inside, knowing that everything out here is just the way that it is. It all seems so magical out here. It always has. But I know that it really isn't. I know that it is just what it is.

## July 2, 1986

I have been sitting here at my writing desk for nearly ten hours, threading together the writings of the created experiences I have been moving though over the past four years. Within some of my experiences, certain questions have arisen from time to time that have to do with 'human conditioning and programming'. I have a strong desire to create a dialogue with my inner teacher, in the hope of shedding some light onto specific areas concerning human behavior.

I release myself from my intense focus on writing and allow myself to drift freely within the multi-dimensional doorways that exist within me. I return to the space of darkness deep within and call upon my inner teacher to engage in a dialogue on these matters.

Within moments, I hear a voice: "What is the purpose of this dialogue?"

"I have a few questions to ask concerning my own human behavior. Will you answer them?"

"No. I am not able to do that at this time."

"Is it that I am to be denied the answers?"

"No. There are no simple answers to the questions that you wish to have answered."

"Is it possible to dialogue about any of that which I seek?"

"No. It is not possible. If we are to dialogue about these issues, you might miss the purity of the information presented. You have been intently concentrating on other issues for almost ten hours of your earth time, and your intensity during this time of examination has been such that any new information will lose its effectiveness."

"Is there another way that we can look at these questions?"

"Yes. There is another way."

"Is it possible to write about all of it?"

"Yes. Shall we begin? Take the pen in hand and allow the words to flow to the paper by way of the pen. In other words, let the pen do the talking for you so that you might rest and be free to observe all that is presented."

"I have been looking at the possibilities of not eating, not having sex, and being of self-less service. What is the truth concerning these realities?"

## NOT EATING

As long as the human body has a particular form and shape, all of these realities will be part of its everyday movements. There are functional practices of various earthly movements that, when practiced, allow one to be free of all those things. Realize, though, that it shall only be truth as long as one practices a specific discipline. What then happens is that the human body is at the affect of that particular discipline. That is to say that whatever one decides to do by way of thought, the body will respond in a certain way according to that thought impulse. For instance, if one is to stop eating physical food with the total conscious awareness that one is doing so, regardless of the system that one is following, then the human body will be affected in some way or other. That is to say it will become smaller in its mass and weaker in its movements – mentally, physically and emotionally.

Out in the Natural Elements, a tree, as one knows it to be, has no name, no identity, other than the form that it has, and only when it has it. This living expression of life changes each and every moment while it is here on this particular dimension of reality. It continuously gives of itself unto the creative energies of the universal God – light. It does not hold on to an identify such as man does. Therefore, it is free to move within and express itself in the purest form. It is continuously surrendering itself unto itself, for it has no structure or form within its existence. It continually puts as little emphasis as possible on keeping itself fixed to the Earth's surface. It moves continually upward, creating the highest possible living expression for its movements on the earthly plane. It continuously grows bigger and stronger. It keeps on evolving into more of its connection to everything else, and it does this by not identifying itself as anything.

When one is able to move freely in the world of man like brother Tree, then it will not be necessary to eat, or sleep, or any of that. Only when there is an attachment to the physical human body, and a belief that the body has a particular form, do all these things need to exist on the earthly plane. Surrender yourself to the universal energy of creation, and you will never need to concern yourself with any of those purely mundane things again.

Remember, though, that all the outside systems man creates on the earthly plane work, but they are strictly governed and controlled by time and space. They will only function as long as one travels through the creative process within a time sequence and a space allotment. They are limited.

Everything that is manifested and held in form upon the earthly plane, is limited within its living expression. One cannot avoid the purity of this truth. There is no way around it, only to totally surrender oneself unto the free-flowing creative energies, free of all time and all space, but encompassing all time and all space.

When one surrenders one's identity unto the wholeness of all things, one fully acknowledges the inter-connectedness and interdependency of all things. One becomes all things in totality, and all things will continually nurture one. One will be able to assume any identity, whenever it is needed, in order to move unobstructed on the earthly plane. As well, one will be free to consciously maintain the highest vibrational frequency there is in the universe – all-encompassing white light.

The body is continuously being re-created from white light. It knows deep within its finer awarenesses how to maintain an openness to the potent energy force moving it at all times in a channeled and controlled manner. To open oneself up to that all-encompassing energy current completely, one is totally freed from all possible resistance forces within the earthly plane, or any other dimensional plane of reality.

One is able to mold oneself in any way in order to bring about subtle or major changes in the awarenesses of mankind, and no one ever has to know. The freedom comes from not having anyone know what is available to you, for if they become aware of it, they will want to know how to go about getting that which you have. It is best to be silent until the appropriate time. It matters not whether people are aware of your physical embodiment. What they will feel within themselves is a surge of power being generated through their bodies, but they will not be able to detect where this power surge is coming from.

Be cautious as you journey along on this path, for one short or faltering step and you will vanish within the speed of light. It is not an easy thing that you seek. There are many potential traps along the way, but there are also as many potential gains, as well, within the context of winning and losing at this game. It is a game, of sorts – one that requires that you attune yourself more with the rules of the free-flowing creative energies. Know that you are heading in the direction that is best suited for your purpose here. All that you will need shall be brought to you. You have demonstrated within your living expression, that you are ready for the next phase of your movement on the earthly plane, and it is forthcoming.

Be patient and maintain your centredness wherever you are taken. There is still much that has to be done before you will be able to return to the highest possible vibration – the one that you are seeking and are here to bring into manifestation on this plane.

There is no one else here at this time who is capable of doing what you are seeking to do in your living expression. There are no other persons that you can seek out who will be able to hear or see any of that which you are speaking of.

When you open the creative doorway to the larger awareness of man, they will all see it clearly and plainly. It is a simple thing that you see, and yet remember that to the normal soul here, it is as simple as it is complicated. They, in their in their normal way of moving on this plane, have a tendency to put more focus on the stabilizing of themselves within all that they do. You, on the other hand, are choosing to dissolve all of your aware-nesses concerning this plane, giving you total instability and all stability at the same time. Keep attuning yourself to the purest expression of truth – the all-encompassing truth – and you will eventually arrive where you already are, safely and wholly.

## NOT HAVING SEX

Yes. It is possible to not have sex. It has been demonstrated on the Earth for thousands of years now, that by doing certain sex-ual rituals (as in Eastern Tantric Yoga) it is possible to increase one's level of awareness off the earthly plane. The fact still remains that those who choose to follow rituals of this nature are imprisoned by those rituals. That is to say that if they did not follow the ritual, then they would not receive the benefits behind what the ritual stands for.

So long as the physical body of man has a form and a shape, or an identify that is fixed in a particular time sequence and space allotment, it will only be able to move within the guidelines that are outlined within the manual governing time and space. The first page of that manual says it all: time and space offer one the total freedom to travel wherever and whenever one chooses. The only thing is, it is limited by what is contained within the structural composition of the two variables – time and space. This means that anything that is physically manifested on the earthly plane will only function within an element of time and space existence.

There will be trade-offs within and about the physical body if, while it is in a particular state of beingness, it is separate from everything else. It will be separate from itself even. To follow a ritual of any dimension that has its origin outside of oneself, brings about the enforcing limitations of time and space. So you can see how limiting all this actually is. It will always only be a part, no matter how you choose to look at it. It is impossible for it to be any different so long as you continue to identify with any one face of existence or reality on the earthly plane.

Surrender yourself to your ever-present desires of finding anything while engaging in any ritual, and you will have the awarenesses of how to maintain that which you already possess, and that which you did not need a ritual to bring here.

But a ritual was needed in order to bring you here. Therein lies the trap. Can you see it? Can you also see beyond it to see the truth of it? It has been yours since the very first moment you arrived here.

Let us look at this angle a little closer. For the first nine months while you were in your mother's womb, all the things that were necessary for your growth and evolution were brought to you with the blessings from the universe. This was made possible by the creative energies moving through you. This is the same creative energy force that has been your guidance along your life journey thus far, and that will continue to be until you choose to leave this plane. You were not attached to your form, as your form had not even taken form. It was continually unfolding before you. There was no separation between you and your Mother: Mother universe took care of all of your needs. Flowing through you at all times were the vital elements you needed, and that allowed you to grow in size and in shape. You were totally supported by Mother from within the existence of yourself.

There was nothing else – only Mother and you. Everything that you needed was given from within you. You, alone, are still able to maintain this connection to Mother. Surrender yourself, and you will experience the truth that is hidden behind these words. You must go back to your beginning in order to know all this for the truth that it is.

Following rituals concerning sex means that this Mother connection is only available to you whenever you connect with someone else who also shares the same ritualistic movement. This allows for limited growth. However, we do see that having sex is a step toward maintaining, within your person, the wholeness of this all-encompassing energy form that you are presently moving with in your living expression.

When you clearly discover within yourself that there is no need to seek any of that which you know here to be truth, then you will have arrived at the place where there will be no words to speak. You will then be directly connected to the flowing creative energy within all things. That way, all things will become you. Therefore, there will be no need to speak words, for you will know. Words show that a person has form within their existence, and they also show separation from that which you speak of.

Dissolve all of your attachments to finding this energy force through utilizing any particular ritual, and you will have the fullness of that which you seek. Be cautious not to go about seeking it, for it is not contained within the structural limitations of time and space. Yet time and space are manifested through this creative energy. When you say that you are seeking it, you are putting it into a time sequence and space allotment. Let go of all of your desires, and all will be available to you, far beyond what you know to be available to you. To move totally within the light of creative energy, one must become the wholeness of what that energy stands for. In the purest way, it stands for all things within the simpleness of no thing.

Let us now look at the sex act of intercourse. What is the point behind this act? It is to get in touch with the creative energies. It is not the creative energies though, only the connection to it. Do you see the difference? Connected to it means that one is part of yet still separated from. The sex act is limited in its application to maintaining the wholeness of what is always available when one transcends all time and all space limitations. When one opens the inner doorway and sees that this is only the *connecting impulse*, one need only step through the doorway and unconditionally surrender all of what one thinks they have found, and allow the purity of what is there to be there. One must move in this awareness like the bird that soars higher and higher within the freedom of the air that supports it in doing so. You are looking much too close to the ground in this area of your living expression, my friend. We suggest that you move yourself a little higher, and you will be able to clearly see the simple truth of that which you are hearing.

The first level of sexual experience is to familiarize each person with their own inability to see above all that is actually taking place on this plane. If one becomes attached to one's own image of who they think they are, then the act of sex will hold them in a place of fixed time and space. They will be directly affected by the Laws that govern time and space here on this plane: division of power and a struggle to maintain control over all that is circling around the sexual act itself. The sex act will continuously promote pleasure and pain within its ever-changing textures.

The next phase of development comes through looking for a more expressional matter of moving the creative energies of orgasm through the deeper channels within the physical body. This will allow for greater freedom of expression. It will also allow one to take the focus off the physical nature of the act and connect one to the higher vibrational expressions. This will allow one to feel within oneself the wholeness of who one truly is on many different levels. It will also allow one the opportunity of freeing oneself from one's own self-created barriers. In the process though, one will be putting up more barriers of belief: that whatever ritual one is following works, and is truth.

## BEING SELF-LESS

What does it mean to be self-less? For you to be self-less, you must be void of self. That is to say that the self must not exist separate from all other things that exist on this plane of reality. The self is to be fully integrated with, and moving harmoniously with, all other persons on this plane. There can be no expression of identification with any separate embodiment here on this plane. You must be able to fit into all dimensions of reality equally, without the slightest preference to any single one. You cannot resist moving into another functional expression of reality if it comes to you through the creative universal energy. You must not seek out any particular reality, as for example with your loved ones. You cannot go to them and ask them to join you in your world, for in doing that, you would be identifying with a specific form and expression of reality. You must wait patiently, and the universe will provide you with all the different realities – at the most appropriate time – in order that you might be of optimum service to this planet.

You must first go through each of the necessary stages of relinquishing all of your earthly identities, so that the purest vibration of God energy can move through you without causing any damage to your beingness. The purpose behind your being – the one that you are asking to manifest on this plane this time around – is of the highest order that is available to man. As such, all precautions must be exercised to ensure total safety to you and to the others who will be connecting with you while you continue to make your way along your journey.

There is no one else here on this plane at this time who is moving in the way that you are choosing to move. You are the first of many. You will find all that you need to complete your journey coming to you as you need it. Focus on and maintain your stability around the unfolding moment. Watch and observe everything as you move through your living expression. Remember, trust nothing that you perceive through you. Rather, feel the truth of that which lies within you. Once you learn to trust the inner feeling, you will know the way. Once you know, then no one or no thing shall distract you from your purpose here.

## RETURNING TO THE TRUTHS OF THE CHILD

When the sperm and the egg aligned and interacted within the darkness of the void, a miracle took place. Both of them surrendered their identities unto themselves and unto each other, and they combined their individual wholeness to create the beginning and subsequent progressional evolution of a new organism – totally separate from each of them, yet comprised of both. I am that organism.

Upon my arrival here into this world as a newborn child, I was pure, all-knowing, innocent and whole within the process of creation that took place. Nothing could have been added to me, nor could it have been taken from me at that point in time. For if it could have been, I would not have been complete within that process of creation. All the necessary tools that I needed in order to complete the lessons in my life journey, were (and still are) contained within my being.

This earthly plane was all so new to me. I was in constant awe as I continued to grow and to open myself to the many magical gifts that were developing inside me. With my eyes, I was able to see the many ever-changing forms and shapes within all things. My ears presented to me an infinite number of vibrations of sound that added multiple dimensions to the forms and shapes I was perceiving. My nose enabled me to experience the unique scent that each new form and shape had. With my mouth, I was given the opportunity to discover that all forms and shapes had their own individual taste. My hands and feet allowed me to feel the different textures in the forms and shapes that surrounded me. They also afforded me the freedom to go wherever I chose to further discover my new world.

I was never in a hurry to go anywhere or to do anything. There was, in all ways, so much to see and to do. I was always so totally free within myself to examine it all at my own pace and in my own way. I never saw any one thing twice in the same way. It was always so completely new to me. There was no such thing as a future to look forward to, nor was there a past to look back on or to hold on to. All there was, was the total and complete present, unfolding moment by moment. I never had to worry about anything. Everything I needed for my growth and development was brought to me. I only had to be patient and wait for it to arrive.

I was well looked after back then. All I had to do was stay out of my own way and let the universe bring to me all that I would need in order to complete my life journey.

Oh, to be the child once more!

## THE CREATIVE CHILD WITHIN ME

You are a constant reminder of how simple life here is; of how my time here is so short, yet it lasts a lifetime. You also remind me of the importance of being without age, for living on this plane is a continual process that unfolds each moment.

When I look at you, really look at you, I see the timeless wisdom that you have inside you. When you are truly being who you are, you are all that there is. By being around you, I am able to create a focus and a purpose to my life. Oh, the sheer enjoyment of being myself and finding out that it doesn't matter who I am, or who I am not.

To look into your deep eyes – those clear, bright, open doorways into a common universe we all share – I join you in a place that is not bound by time or by space, yet encompasses all time and all space.

When I observe you moving in your ordinary way, I see life continually unfolding from birth to death within each breathing moment as you go through a metamorphosis; becoming and dissolving, whichever is appropriate.

When I am alone with you, I get taken back to the time when I was an infant, a child, an adolescent, a young adult, and an adult. And I am continually reminded that I am all of those – and at the same time, none of those – simultaneously in everything I do. It is important for me to remain totally free within myself to be all of those components in one, every moment I am here.

To give freely is to expect nothing in return. As a gift, you give me nothing. Yet at the same time, you show me everything. I choose not to hold on to you, for that would surely dissolve you away. Instead, I will allow you to continually unfold as a gift of life to be seen in new and simple ways. I will remain flexible in my own world so that I might see you with new eyes each day, and support you in growing and evolving according to the Life's master's plan.

There is nothing I shall want from the world outside me. All that is, and all that is not, is given life through you, within me. You are a continual reflection of what life here is all about.

To say to you that I love you would not be enough, for to say that I love you would freeze you somewhere in time and in space. What does seem appropriate to say to you is that I am evolving towards light while watching you become who you are, and that I am becoming who I am while watching you evolve towards light.

The newness of a gift is only as I choose to perceive it. My perceptions of you and of me are continually disintegrating and falling away, and soon all that will be left is the child in you and the child in me – a gift!

## July 6, 1986

I walk into a local restaurant in Victoria and spot my friend/hiking buddy sitting at a booth in the far back corner. I walk up to the table and sit down. As I do, I begin to speak, "Good morning."

"Greetings, how are you doing?"

"I'm doing well."

"We're ready to go."

"There is no hurry, my friend. There is nowhere to go. It's all happening right here. It is all inside me no matter where I go. So there is no need for you to hurry."

"It's a great day for a hike. Any idea where you want to go? Out of the city – I don't care where, just out of the city."

"How does East Sooke Park sound?"

"Okay by me. I haven't been there for a while. I have my dog in the car. He could use a good run."

As we head out of town, my friend and I start to dialogue about the things that each of us had been looking at through the week. I always look forward to our meetings. They are the only times that I feel I can open up and share some of the experiences I have been experiencing over the years, without fear that I will be judged in any way. Our discussions always have to do with seeking more inner knowledge and using that knowledge to make our worlds a better place to live in.

One of the topics that has come up is about time and space, and how they appear to hold everything on this plane in a stagnant position within their existence. We continue to talk about the different possible ways of moving through the outer world of man without being influenced by time and space. Our discussion provides more food for me to take in and digest. I very much want to look further into this question of time and space orientation within my own inner and outer worlds. I want to explore it to the limit to see if there is any possible way to live free of that environment all the time. I know that there will be no intellectual solution available for me. If I truly want to know, I will have to emotionally bond myself to an experience where I can find out for sure.

Today I have decided that I will create a time and space oriented experience while I am out in the woods. It will be another life-supporting opportunity. I feel that there is nothing for me to worry about, for if I get into trouble, my friend will be near. I will be able to continually use him as a grounding tool to make sure that I don't go over the edge of my illusionary reality so far that I won't be able to come back. I know that there will be an element of danger in what I am going to do. It is not so much in what I am about to do, but rather in how I will go about doing it.

I have no outside teachers to guide me through and tell me what to do or not to do. Like all my other initiations, I am totally on my own – and I wouldn't have it any other way. If I can't experience something for myself, as it is best suited for me, then I won't be able to stand up in front of people and say: "I know, for this is my self-created experience."

I always want to experience living on the edge of life and death in all that I do here on this plane. For in doing so thus far, I have become aware that I can fully immerse myself in an emotionally based experience and extract the purity of truth that lies behind the actual illusionary experience. Living on that thin edge all the time promotes me opening myself up, more and more, to my inner intelligence – the aspect of me that knows all things.

As I get out of the car in the parking lot, I begin to move back and forth within the thin veil that separates time and space and no time and no space. I have been moving in and out of focus so quickly that I am not at all sure how long I have been standing here, gazing aimlessly out into the surrounding elements. Since my enlightened experience with the poisonous mushroom, I have been finding that it is much easier for me to consciously induce these shifting altered states of being within my daily movements.

It appears that once I find the effective combination that will break through an old pattern of resistance, and enter into a deeper awareness of who I am, I can enter into that state of being, at any level, whenever I choose, and for as long as I choose. I am now able to freely drift further and further within my internal darkened depths. Whenever I have looked within and experienced an environment with no time and no space restrictions, I have always been alone. Today will be an opportunity for me to see how functional this state is when other people are involved.

I bring myself back to the present moment and centre myself within my inner void. I am choosing to ask my inner teacher for support in what I am about to do. I want to make sure that I am not initiating this experience from my strong will. If I am, then it will surely encourage a struggle for power to take place within my being, just as I have observed many times before. As I stand my ground, I ask for an internal sign to show me one way or another. I wait, and I wait. There is nothing coming, no response.

I can now feel the impulse building from within. I am now feeling the unfolding creation of the indicator I have been waiting for. I now know that I am in control of creating the unfolding experience in any way that I want, and for as long as I want. I will also be able to change it any way I want, and at any time. This is the first time that this kind of creative situation has been presented to me in this way. My inner teacher and I are emotionally bonded within this experience. This also means that my inner teacher and I are one in the same. I have finally made it. I am now entering into that chamber within me where all the meaningful treasures are kept: the chamber of all-knowing. I know that this is only the beginning, that it will always be just another beginning point in time.

I am overflowing with joy, and my being is full of lightness. I open my outer eyes and consciously bring myself back to the moment at hand, knowing full well that there is much that I want to observe this day. In order to effectively do this, I cannot afford to be momentarily absent from my purest intention. If I am, then I will create an imbalance within my internal and external movement patterns, thereby possibly creating more illusions, which I might mistakenly believe to be real.

I remove my shoes and put them on the floor of the car, and then I lock the

door. As my friend is letting his dog out and locking the car, I slowly begin to
venture out along the trail. As I move, I begin to remove all my conscious connections to time and space. I take myself inwardly deeper and deeper to a depth
I have not known before this moment. I am totally free from any movement
within. I am clearly moving outwardly through my inward channels. I am becoming all that lies within and without me. I am dissolving within the vacuum
that creates time and provides for the formation of space. I am free from any one
form of thought, yet I embrace all possible thought. I am able to slow time down
as well as speed it up. I am also able to jump forward in time and slip backward
through time, however I see fit to do so. I am becoming all things from within
the central creative core of the unfolding emotional experience, which is quite
a bit different than the intellectual thought of becoming all things. The thought
is based on thinking, which implies a static position of realization, whereas the
emotional embracing is based on being and dancing within the fine strands that
make up all time and all space.

As I start on the trail that will eventually take me up to Mt. Maguire, I decide
that I will begin to play with this unfolding experience from different angles,
possibly even mixing the different angles together to see what other effects I
can validate within my own personal experience. As I begin my ascent along
the salal covered path, I put my full attention onto a tree. I now focus my eyes
below me so they are looking at the surface of the path. I proceed to take five
normal sized steps, at which point, I look upwards to see the same tree – only
what I discover is that I am back where I had started, five steps before.

I repeat the procedure. I look at the same tree, then I lower my eyes so that
I am once again looking at the path directly in front of my feet. I proceed to
take five normal sized steps and then look up at the tree. I cannot believe what
I am witnessing. I am back at the same spot where this exercise had started
from. Once again I have slipped backwards through the veil that covers all time
sequences.

I am now becoming concerned that I will not be able to leave this place in
time, and that I will be held captive here by my own doing. Rather than dwelling
on what has been taking place, I am choosing to acknowledge that it did in fact
take place just as I had observed it, and that I can change the unfolding experience at any moment if I choose. I choose to move on and allow another creative
moment to unfold along the trail.

As I arrive on top of the first steep section of the trail, time appears to disappear altogether. I am dissolving myself into the delicate fabric that connects
me to everything else around me. I am now observing myself shifting through

dimensions of time and space: being here in the woods one moment, and then gone in the next, with no awareness of where I have been. My only secure reference point is the trail that I am walking on. Everything else is moving through its own evolutionary process, and is not controlled by time or space, for it encompasses all time and all space.

As I dissolve myself into the all-encompassing void of creation, I am swimming in a continual pattern of thought: a mass of emptiness that is responsible for the creation of all thought. I am aware of the infinite number of thought vibrations that are resonating within this limitless void of darkness. I know that they all have a place somewhere in this universe, or in the universes that are contained within this universe. I do not want to hold on to any particular thought pattern. I know that each one will only be a reality worth bonding to if I am creating an experience (within the dimension of a time sequence and space allotment) for the purpose of freeing myself so that I can become more of who I am. I am aware that who I am encompasses all thought, for I am all things.

I have been leaving this physical plane, then jumping back into it, then removing myself once more, and returning once more. I am continuing to move at an incredible rate. Sometimes I am able to be simultaneously within this physical plane as well as being far removed from it. When this occurs, I have no feeling within my being. What I do have is a sense of all-knowing, almost as though I know everything that is going on all over the world, all at the same time. Whenever I move toward locking into any one particular thought pattern, I lose the whole sensation of what it represents. I am aware that this happens because conscious thought is created and controlled within a dimension that is affected by time and by space.

I am not at all sure of the speed I am travelling, in and out of the different dimensions of reality, until my friend calls out a couple of times. I am aware that I am presently vibrating at a much higher rate within myself, and that in order to fully hear what he is saying, I have to slow down my vibrational frequency so that it coincides with his. Otherwise, the sounds I hear coming from him are such that I am unable to make out what he is trying to say.

The first time he began to speak, I could actually detect a reaction in me to his vibration. I missed the whole line of his dialogue. I had to ask him to repeat all of what he had said. I was so excited about finding this new dimension of expressional reality within my being, that I didn't want to stay in touch with my surrounding environment. I wanted to keep releasing myself from my own inner programmed fears. I felt that the only sure way of doing that was to go further inside my living expression until I reached the edge of my total existence – for that one brief moment in time.

I continue to climb until I finally arrive at the summit. Upon doing so, I take up a position on the edge of a large rock and begin to release myself even further into all that is surrounding me. As I wait for to my friend and his dog to arrive, I turn my full attention to the Sun and observe it slowly beginning to descend toward the fog bank that blankets part of the Olympic Mountains. As my eyes look directly into the Sun, I can feel myself moving deeper within my own inner void, and somehow I can sense that I am a lot closer to the Sun than I actually am.

As I am sitting here within one dimension of reality, I am also travelling on another. I am not at all sure which one is real, yet I know that they are both real. I am continually being awakened to more of the wholeness that lies deep within me, and the more I experience it, the more I allow the experience to carry me in even deeper. There is a magnetic pull coming from within my central core. I am sensing it as a pulsating beacon of high intensity light, no different than the Sun. It is so strong that I can feel part of my physical body being sucked into the vacuum that it has created. My outer physical shell is struggling to stay on the dimension of reality it knows best, and my inner shell is slowly being ripped from the clutches of my outer shell. My outer shell is reacting to all that is happening, while my inner shell is becoming the wholeness of all that is creatively unfolding.

My friend's dog arrives, shortly before my friend, on the top of the rocks off to the left of where I am sitting. I am observing him moving over the surface of the rocks, exploring every inch and making sure he marks his territory. I watch him run down an incline and then come back up again. I continue to look straight ahead while he is doing this, so that he will pass through my visual screen as he goes through his movement patterns. When he finishes his movement, and is standing up at the top once again, I ask myself these two simple questions: "How do I really know that the dog actually went down the incline? What real proof do I have that he did?"

I am now fully aware that all I will ever have is my memory to validate what I thought I saw. I am deciding to take myself still deeper within my being, to a place where I will be able to release myself from my inaccurate memory. Again, as I peer straight ahead, absent of all movement either in or out, I watch the dog run past my visual screen and then come back again. I proceed to ask myself the two questions once more, this time with more intensity in my intention. I am pushing myself to a new limit inside. There are no answers. I cannot be sure that any of what I have seen actually happened, and what difference would it make if it did, as opposed to if it didn't?

I am succeeding in inducing myself into a no time, no space dimension, and totally interacting within a living expression on a time and space oriented dimension. I am becoming aware that there are two distinct parts of me interacting within the unfolding of this experience. One part of me likes to use time and space as a means of determining its existence. The other part of me wants to be totally and unconditionally free of all time and all space so it can roam into any dimension of reality at any time.

The outer part of me is beginning to resist my conscious desire to push this experience even further – to continue going in until I reach the centreline that connects all possible realities, even sanity and insanity. I want to walk that razor-thin line and experience firsthand what the difference is between those two dimensions. I know that I am close to that place of discovery, mainly from how my outer part is struggling within my physical body.

I release myself back into the depths of my inner void, chanting the words: "truth, truth, truth…" The outer part of me has no say in what is unfolding, for it is strictly controlled by time and space and cannot travel into any of the dimensions that are free of time and space. I will be fine as long as I avoid connecting with time and space.

I continue to sit and watch the Sun. I then proceed to turn my full attention on to my friend, who is now just making himself comfortable on the top of the smooth-faced boulder. I sit observing all that is unfolding, being cautious not to hold on to any of it with thought. I am seeing it and releasing it as it arrives and departs simultaneously within my visual screen. It is an incredible feeling. I am absolutely free to just observe the totality of all that is taking place.

I am able to see it on many different levels within my awarenesses, mainly because I am observing it all from a place inside me where all time and all space meet and are one.

As I sit here observing over and over again the movements that my friend and his dog are making, the questions that keep coming back to me are, "How do I really know that any of this actually took place? And how do I really know that this is actually taking place right here, right now?"

I am once again re-entering a dimension of reality that is controlled by time and space. The outer world aspect of my being is beginning to panic. It cannot justify anything. It is not sure which way is up and which way is down. It is panic stricken, for it has no control, and it is being introduced to dimensions of reality that it cannot begin to comprehend. As I drop the line of inner questioning and release myself once again, I float in between the delicate strands of time and space into the all-encompassing darkened void. I am aware that I am now walking the invisible edge between the two worlds of sanity and insanity.

I continuously cross back and forth over that separating razor-thin line, always aware that I have to come back to the 'right' side of the line but also stay on the line at the same time. I am now definitely playing on the edge of life and death, and I am playing on it in a whole different way than I did in all of my other experiences. I sense that this experience is so much different because I am moving from within my central core, so close to the essence of who I am. I know that finding out more about who I am has something to do with walking the razor-thin line that separates all sets of opposites on the dimensional plane of reality called Earth.

From my brief interaction with this thin line, I am becoming more aware that this thin line is forever changing. It does not remain static at any time as long as I am free of time and space. That is the reality behind its existence. It will only remain static if I remain in a dimension of expression, here on this plane, that is structured and controlled by time and by space – that is the illusion that is exalted and supported as a truth.

I waver back and forth over each side of the line. I am not really staying long enough on either side to identify with it. I am darting back and forth between security and insecurity within my own living expression. I sense that I am now identifying more with the side of insanity.

I begin to stare aimlessly down the face of the rock I am sitting on. I am overcome with a feeling that I want to jump, jump to my death. I am feeling that there is no longer anything here on this plane worth living for.

I am listening to myself think these thoughts and believing the illusion of what they actually mean. I am preparing myself to execute my innermost feeling. It is coming from a purely irrational impulse that has its root structure locked in a few earlier experiences I had encountered in my living expression, especially when I was locked into only seeing my outer world from a time and space oriented dimension.

Just as I am about to stand, a voice arrives from within my inner void of darkness and guides me back over to the supportive side of the line. The words I hear are, "Only a fool would jump. A warrior always knows that he has the option to jump or not to jump. He would never exercise those options unless he knew for sure that he would die in order that he could live. The fool, on the other hand, would die in order to die."

As I hear the last of the words, I turn and focus my full attention onto the setting Sun, watching it ever so slowly descend. I am getting a clear indication from within that it is time to head back before it gets dark. I glance at my watch. As soon as I do this, I re-enter into the dimension of reality that is controlled by time and by space. I am curious to see what will happen to my awarenesses if I stay within this operating dimension of reality for the duration of my journey back to the van. My fears are now starting to surface. I am now beginning to feel myself react to all that has been taking place. It is all so incredible. I am definitely experiencing two distinctly different worlds. "Which one am I really in? And how do I know that either of them is real?"

Within a fraction of a second, I am spinning within the illusionary reality that is unfolding. After what seems like an eternity has passed, I look at my watch once more. Two minutes have passed. As much as I want to go, I am not making any effort to create the necessary movement within my physical body. I start to panic. My inner thoughts are saying: "Let's go!" My physical body is saying: "Let's stay." It is a stalemate. Another eternity passes by. Again I look at my watch. Another two minutes have passed. I am now racing inside. Everything is travelling at an incredible pace. Whenever I slow the inner dialogue down, I become aware that I am stuck somewhere in time, for nothing moves.

The voice of the outer world aspect of my being begins to dialogue toward my friend, "It's time to go. It's time to leave this place before it gets dark. If we wait too long, we won't be able to find our way on the path. It is at least a forty-five minute walk back to the car, and twenty of it will be in darkness unless we get going."

Fear starts to race uncontrollably throughout my being. I am now becoming anxious, but neither my mouth nor my body is doing anything to remedy the situation and take a course of action. I am still sitting in the same spot. I am observing all this from within a dimension of being that cannot be held in place by thought. I am suspended in a state of peace and quiet while I am watching another part of me spin within its illusions.

I finally manage to convey to my friend that it is time to head back. He acknowledges what I have said, and we both proceed to get our things in order. I start off down the trail, sure that he is right behind me. I walk a few hundred yards before I receive a clear indication from within that he is not following me, that he is still on top of the rock. I walk back along the trail to see what is happening. My friend and his dog are still in the process of getting ready. Panic is again beginning to build within me. The controlling outer world aspect of my being begins to internally speak, "Hurry up! Hurry up! Doesn't he realize the urgency behind us getting out of here?"

I do not want to alarm him by telling him that we might not make it out in time, so I keep it all to myself. He is moving at what I see as an extremely slow speed. He is free to move as he sees fit, whereas I am moving at a rate that is being dictated strictly by my watch. I am imprisoned *once again* by my thought processes. I am fighting to break free of my restrictions, and at the same time, I am fighting to keep myself restricted in my outer expression.

When I feel he is ready to begin his descent, I turn away and head back along the trail. After travelling a few hundred feet, I gaze back over my shoulder and, once again, my friend is nowhere to be seen. I again begin to internally verbalize what is coming up for me, "I can't believe this! What more can possibly go wrong?"

I am becoming more frustrated and angry that I am not in control of all movement, yet I know that I am in control of all movement. It would only require that I slip back through the thin veil that separates time and no time. I am not prepared to do that. I want to see what will unfold within this dimension of reality. As I again approach the top of the rocks, I see him slowly starting to move in my direction. I call out to him, "We're really going to have to hustle if we're going to make it in time."

After a slight delay he responds, "Okay. I'm ready. Let's go."

As he starts toward me, I turn, and once again, for the third time, begin my journey. I am now aware that I have set it up so that I am racing against the clock. I am becoming engulfed in my own fear. I am forgetting that I am in control of all of my actions. Instead, I am choosing to get all wrapped up in trying to control someone else within my reality of what time is all about. I see that I am always going to be limited to reacting if I continue to interact with people on a dimension of reality that is governed entirely by sequences of time and allotments of space. I know that I am in control, yet I am not exercising my option to control. I do not like not being in control, yet I am not doing anything to free myself so I can be in control. I am losing all sensitivity to my own being and to what I need most in my surrounding environment in order to find inner peace and harmony.

I am afraid that I will lose my way along this path if I am not able to see by the light of the outer Sun. I am completely negating my own inner light, the light that has guided me through all dimensions of reality and has always protected me from harm. I am now seeing that my inner light is never of the dimension of time or space, but it is always within the dimension of reality that is governed by time and by space. The outer world aspect of my being that is reacting to what is happening is totally restricted to this plane – the plane of division and of separation. I am now seeing it all like I have never seen it before, and it has only been made possible by removing myself completely from the time and space oriented dimension of reality. The key is to stay removed, but at the same time, be part of. I am beginning to see the simplicity behind all that is on this plane. Once I remove myself far enough from the opposites, the clearer it all becomes.

I am using my friend to keep myself grounded to this plane so that I can venture further within my inner void and find more valuable information about how the different aspects of me relate and react to each other and to other people. I am able to remove myself completely from controlling any of what is unfolding, for I know that it is all just an illusion that I am using to get me deeper within myself. I am using this unfolding experience to bring forth the purity of my truth from the depths of the overall illusionary experience.

I finally make it down to the main pathway. Now there is only a short distance to go. Another ten minutes or so and it will all be over. Or will it all be just beginning? I am not altogether sure. As I continue to walk, I keep peering over my shoulder, hoping that I will see my friend and his dog. All of a sudden, I stop cold in my tracks. Fear begins to fill my entire being as a thought pattern begins to form within the depths of my time restricted dimensions of reality: "How do I actually know that my friend is behind me? How do I know that I am not just making the whole thing up, believing that he is right behind me? What if he is still up on the mountain? Oh, God! Can that be possible? Can that really be possible?"

I am once again dancing on the side of the line that denotes insanity. I am playing this one right to the edge and then some. I have to know how far I can push it and still be able to come back. I am saturated with anxiety and frustration, yet at the same time, I am completely relieved that I have made it down off the mountain in time.

Again I start to question the reality that my friend is actually behind me. I stop and look over my shoulder, and what my eyes behold offers me instant relief. I see him and his dog coming around the bend in the path. Everything is instantly okay. I am amazed that because my eyes have seen him, everything else just seems to systematically slot into place. It all seems so easy. When I see him, I automatically stop questioning all of what has been taking place. I am surprised that I am not questioning the reality of what I am observing on the path – that this is actually my friend. My inner dialogue continues, "How can I be certain that what I am seeing is in fact real? How do I know that I just didn't create an image of my friend and his dog coming around the corner so I wouldn't have to look at it any further?"

I have had experiences before in the woods where things were created that I couldn't explain. I am now questioning that maybe this is just another one of those experiences. "How will I know for sure? Will I ever know for sure? What do I believe when I'm not even sure what I've seen is real?"

Panic once again races throughout my being. I am no longer sure of anything. I am not even sure if any of this is actually happening. I have a sense that I may have gone too far over the thin line. I feel as though I am slipping further and further into the unstable world of the insane. How far is too far? I don't know any more. How do I know for sure that I am sane? For all I know I could be insane thinking that I am sane.

This whole experience is becoming too bizarre for me. I am not at all sure how to get out of this place. I am not even sure how I got in here. My outer world self is being turned upside down and inside out. We – the different aspects of my being – are now totally immersed in a free-flowing dimension of reality. The resistance patterns have been surfacing through my trying to control all of what has been happening within this dimension.

I know that in order for me to pull myself through this experience, I must keep removing myself from attaching any thoughts to what is taking place – or to any of that which has already taken place. If I attach myself to any of it, I will surely be locked into the dimension of reality called insanity. I now clearly see the whole process and how it all works, but I want to stay in it, to go in deeper just to make sure that I haven't missed anything. I release myself into the void once more and dance between the thin thread that separates the two realities of sanity and insanity.

We arrive back at the car. My friend opens my door and I get in. He disappears behind the car. I am floating off and thoughts begin to flood into my inner void, "How do I know that I am actually down here in the car, and that my friend and his dog are actually here, as well? How can I be absolutely sure that I am not still up on the mountain, trapped by the darkness, unable to move, thinking about being down here in the car? How can I be absolutely sure within myself that I am not just making this whole thing up in my head?"

I am back to dancing deeper within the depths of insanity, only this time I feel much more at home. The question I am pursuing is legitimate. I know that I cannot be absolutely sure of anything, that nothing is real, and yet everything is real. Only an insane person can see that for sure, for they are constantly travelling back and forth over the invisible dividing line. The only thing is, they don't know that for sure. Once I clearly see that I am insane, I am automatically saying that I am sane, for the two are one in the same. I am now totally aware of how it all works, for I have consciously taken myself back and forth over the line with the purest intention of finding my innermost truth regarding who I am and who I am not.

As we are driving back into town, I allow the process to continue with one big difference: there is absolutely no resistance within my being to what is unfolding. The two aspects of my being have merged into one. I have clearly broken through another dimension of my programming and conditioning. I am now free to venture forth and fully explore the experiences that will present themselves. The more I question everything, the clearer everything becomes and the easier it is to see.

Everything I did, I questioned. As I sat in the car, I questioned as to whether the three of us actually went for a hike. When I ate some of the nuts that were beside the seat, I questioned as to whether I actually ate them, or whether I had just imagined that I had eaten them. When my friend and I dialogued, I questioned as to whether we did in fact have a dialogue. How can I be absolutely sure that we actually did? Again, the only means I will have to validate my experience will be my memory. My past experiences have shown me that my memory is not at all accurate at recalling precise details in regard to unfolding experiences I have encountered with others.

I ended my day by going to a movie with two other friends. I kept sliding back and forth across the line throughout the entire movie. I was totally present all the time. I have no memory of what the content of the movie was, but I know I was following the theme all the way through. I know that what I most needed to see in the movie entered into my awareness, and the rest was filtered out.

As we proceed to walk out of the theatre and down the street, I question as to whether I actually saw a movie. What proof do I actually have that shows me that I have seen a movie? I am seeing that the only indication is validation from my friends. How do I know that I can trust them? I am beginning to see the world through different colored eyes, eyes that are clear and free of time and space, yet eyes that move through all time and all space.

Later, as I lie in bed, I wonder if indeed any of what I have seen today actually took place. How do I know for sure that I actually did all those things I think I did? The only way I have of knowing anything is through my memory. Memory is comprised entirely of judgments and comparisons that come from experiences that are of the illusionary past, and not of the creative present. I react to the experiences in the present from my past programming and conditioning. The last thought I have before I consciously return to my normal vibrational frequency is, "Is there anything on this plane – the plane that is governed by time and space – that is real, or is it all just an illusion that I continually fight to make real?"

## August 17, 1986

"Is this all there really is to life? Oh, God! Tell me that it isn't so. There has to be more to living here on this plane than what I have encountered thus far. I have a feeling that there is something I have overlooked that is so simple – but what? I have done everything here that I have created in my thoughts, and I am no closer now to my ultimate truth than I was back in 1982, when I first started this truth-seeking quest."

I continue to lie here quiet and motionless, just as I have been doing for the past 52 hours. I have consciously placed myself within the confines of my bedroom, to further remove myself from the outer world chaos, so I can look at my inner journey from another angle, one that will be more confronting. The room is a fairly standard size, measuring approximately ten feet by ten feet. I have removed everything from off the floor, save my writing desk. My sleeping bag is all I have to keep me warm and nurtured from the outside. I have put blankets up over the window, completely shutting out all light. I have been immersed in total darkness, seeking to find a way into the chambers of my all-knowing. I want to go further into myself, to a depth I have not known thus far. I only feel that it does exist....

*

It has been a gradual process of movement that has enabled me to get this far: being locked away from all outside stimulation. I first began six weeks ago, when I sat in my room and contemplated what it would be like to just sit in a small space like this for seven days and seven nights, not going anywhere except to the bathroom, and having nothing to eat other than two small bowls of rice – one in the morning and one at night – and a glass of water with each serving. The temptation was, as were all of my other self-created trials, too inviting to pass up. I had to find out first hand what it would be like.

It was when I had the initial impulse that I took the necessary steps to create the experience. I had asked my housemate if she would be willing to support me in doing that, and she agreed. She agreed to put some rice and water outside my bedroom door twice a day. I had mentioned that those necessities should be put there at random times so I wouldn't be able to rely on anything being the way that I wanted it. I felt that by doing it that way, I could stay more focused on the present moment. I put in a set of earplugs to keep out all noise. I wanted to eliminate as many outside distractions as possible. I also blocked out all sunlight by securing a blindfold across my eyes.

That first experience lasted close to thirty hours. At that point, I had freed myself completely from any fear of remaining in that state until the day that I would die. I was willing to take it to that extreme, not just intellectually, but emotionally. To me, there was nothing else that was important. I had to know just how far I had to go in order to find my truth.

The first eighteen hours or so were the most difficult. That was when the chatter inside my head became unbearable. I couldn't believe how much dialogue was being created around not eating when I wanted, and around supposedly not being in control of the situation. I had observed it all without any judgment. I was totally removed from any active involvement. That form of action had enabled me to see through the illusions that were being manifested by my intellect. Because I did not get actively involved with the illusions, they eventually disappeared.

This process had gone on hour after hour. I could not avoid it, for there was no place for me to go. All that existed in my world was within my inner world. It was either confront it or let it destroy me. With the pure intention of a warrior, I persevered through the disillusioning illusions, knowing that behind them all I would find the simple truth – and it would be in the state of absolute quiet.

When I arrived at the place where quiet prevailed, I wrote a message (without the use of my eyes) to my housemate, saying that I wanted no more food or water. I wanted to see if the chatter in my head would come back. I didn't have to wait long before I found out. Within minutes the inner voices began to ascend, and once again the illusions were being created in the form of fear – fear of what would happen from not eating or drinking.

Again with the purest intention I entered into the dimension of the illusions prepared to do nothing other than observe all that would unfold. With no one to dialogue with the ascending inner voices, they, one by one, returned to the darkness of my inner void, and quiet prevailed once more. I had arrived at that place inside myself, after another twelve hours, where I was prepared to keep going on that particular line of movement, even if it meant that I would physically die. I was quite prepared to do so if it would allow me to fully realize my truth.

At that precise moment in time, I knew that there was no point in me continuing that first experience. I had successfully dissipated all of my fear, and that was all it was set up to do, so I had been informed by my inner teacher. Knowing that I had clearly arrived at this understanding, not intellectually but emotionally, I emerged from my darkened space and once again entered into the world of man, thirty hours after it all began.

My second encounter came three weeks ago. At that time, I had decided to secure myself away from all outside stimulation for a period of forty-eight hours. I had immersed myself in total darkness and deprived myself of eating any food or drinking any fluids. I wanted to experience how I would react to this time limited ordeal. I also wanted to look a little closer at whether I actually had to eat or drink.

I had sat there for almost forty-four hours, sifting through all the illusions that presented themselves, observing, without judgment, the mechanics behind each one. It was a fascinating journey into the forever-changing world of my intellect – the sole creator of all of my joy and all of my fears. I became aware of what a valuable gift my intellect is, and how important it is for me to channel my energies in such a way as to promote more harmony within my dialogue with it – on all levels of communication, verbally and non-verbally.

Upon arriving at this new awareness, I returned to the place inside me where all quiet resides, the place where time and space do not exist. I knew there was no further need for me to be in my room. What I had gotten out of the experience had nothing to do with why I had created the experience. I left the room knowing that I was one step closer to another inner doorway, the one that would lead me into the depths of the deep void within where all knowledge lies – knowledge that begins with creation and goes infinitely in both directions.

✦

… Here I am again, back in my room, attempting to go even deeper into the depths of who I am not so that I might become more of who I am. I have totally freed myself from all time and all space. I am clearly floating freely within all that presents itself to me. Sitting here in the dark, I am quite prepared to go as long as I need to in order to realize my truth. If it means physical death, so be it. I am totally prepared for that possibility. I am not afraid of dying, for I know that death is an illusion: that everything is only in a state of transformation. I have removed myself completely from this earthly world. I have turned my full focus inwardly knowing that I cannot trust anything that is outside me.

I have been strictly moving within the corridors of my inner dimensions. I have been totally within myself. I see that there is nothing else for me to do. I have been moving along on my quest now for a few years, mainly from the outside, and I have yet to arrive at the place within where I feel my truth lies.

Sometimes I have felt that I was getting close, but that has only been on fleeting moments. I am hungry to have it all the time. That is all that matters to me.

I know there are no restrictions to the depth of my being, that I stretch in all directions and encompass all time and all space. I clearly know that I must continue to go deeper in order to find out all of who I am not. And in doing so, I will discover who I am. This is all there is left for me to do – to go in deeper. Me, myself, alone inside and outside, for as long as it will take, praying to my God-self to provide me with my truth so that I might begin to live my life accordingly.

I am feeling as though there is nothing else to live for any more. If I am not able to find my ultimate truth, whatever that might be, then I do not want to remain on this plane. I am now looking at the possibility that I might have over-looked something, something very obvious. Perhaps it is the manner in which I have been looking.

I see that I have travelled outside myself many times, looking and searching for the keys that would open me up to the flow of universal information – the all-knowing presence – that I know exists within my complete being. I have travelled through countless different dimensions of reality on the physical plane. I have been taking bits and pieces from each of those particular experiences, collecting them as I would pieces to a complicated puzzle, and slowly sifting through all of them to see if they were actually a part of my being. I wanted to feel my wholeness.

I have been tested over and over again from different angles many times along my overall journey, continually facing decisions between life and death within the different levels of my being – mentally, physically and emotionally. I have always come through each ordeal with the necessary information that has taken me a step closer to the *centre* of my being. I have seen that the further I journey along, the more sophisticated and complicated the tests and trials have become; or perhaps what is more appropriate to say is that I have created them to be more sophisticated and complicated.

I have ventured through many different realities within a single reality within my own existence, and I have still not fully realized or recognized who I actually am within it all. I have seen that I have been many things at any given point in time, and yet at the same time, I have seen the illusion behind that which I have thought I was. I have given up all forms of reality on the outside edges of my being. I have done this so that I might possibly become more consciously aware of those aspects of my inner truth that will bring me everlasting peace and harmony within all facets of my living expression.

I have always had a burning desire to consciously realize the full extent of who I am. There isn't anything that exists outside me that I would ever be satisfied doing. I am also feeling that there isn't anything outside me that I would want to do, other than to be all of me. Nothing outside me will ever be important until I find the appropriate connections within that will truly reflect to me who I am and what living on this plane is all about.

I have recognized that the possibilities of different realities on the outside plane are infinite. I know that there are billions of people within the outer physical world of man, each of them unique and very much real in their movements within their living expressions during any given time sequence. Within each person, there is a continual unfolding process taking place, which, in its movement patterns, allows each person to fully create their own realities within their conception of what life here on this plane is all about. Their reality of the universe of man is totally different than mine – for our experiences are different – but it is still very much real. Who am I to say any differently?

I see that all human beings come to this physical plane called Earth to move through the continual, ever-changing maze of illusions that lie within the infinite realities, and to find sense and order within them so that each person might move closer toward their own individual creative inner light. I recognize that each person is very real within the wholeness of their living form. I am also aware that each person has a function within the textures of the world they are creating for themselves – supportively affecting the world they are creating, or non-supportively being affected by the world they have created. I see that I cannot negate a single reality outside of the dimensions of my own realities. If I choose to do so, I am, in reality, negating my own human existence.

I am aware that all the working occupations that are continually being created by man are very much real and necessary within the texture of his movement here. Everything that man chooses to create in his world, regardless of the dimension of reality it is created on, is very real. Realities are forever changing. I have seen the truth of this within my daily living expression. Within a single day, I have observed myself play many different roles for many different people. I have been a man, a husband, a contractor, an employer, an athlete, a coach, a trainer, a father, a son, a brother, and the list goes on and on. All these positions are complete realities within themselves, none of which can be negated by me or by anyone else. They are what they are, and that is what is. They all have a place within the overall scheme of things, within the unlimited framework of an expression called life.

I have moved within the complicated structures of the world outside me, hoping to find the answers to the all-important questions I most often ask myself, "Who am I? Where did I come from? What is my purpose for being here on this plane?"

I am now seeing that I have not been able to become any clearer within myself by searching in this way. I see that I could very well spend the whole of my living experience exploring all the possible realities that exist outside myself, looking for those ever-changing answers. I am sure that I would create whatever answer I wanted that would appease me for a while. Sooner or later I would become bored with what I had created, and I would then set out to create another answer, and so on.... Everything is possible out there. I know that I can have it any way I choose to make it.

It has all been so confusing at times, in that I have known that I cannot fully trust any of what I experience through any one or more of my five physical senses, yet they are all I have ever had to work with. I have discovered that I have continually created distractions whenever I have engaged them within my living expression. The distractions that I have been creating along my life journey have always seemed to take me further away from that which I want most in my life – to be free within myself to be myself.

I have repeatedly used Mother Nature as a means of beginning my inner journey, and for support in maintaining my focus and redirection while I moved along on my outer journey. I had become dependent on all of that for my own insecure stability. It had become a very dangerous game that I was playing. As much as it opened me up to looking into my worlds differently, it also severely limited me as to what I could do and where I could go within my inner textured layers.

All the information I have ever received from within the many different dimensions of expressional reality is an illusion, and a very colorful illusion at that. There has been lots of magic, adventure, excitement, and unlimited stimulation of my five earthly senses. Realities, as I had innocently discovered, remolded and changed until they became fragmented illusions. The so-called illusions that I had encountered in my altered states cracked and disintegrated within their own unfolding expressions to become my truthful and functional realities. In the end, they all turned out to be one in the same. Their expressions and appearances were different, but the message they conveyed was the same: All things on this earthly plane are actually illusions that I live out through my own self-created realities. I was always the one who was choosing to make it all that it was, depending entirely on what it was I needed at the time. The absolute truth of the whole experience of living in that way was that it all came from outside me. It hadn't worked in any kind of a way that was supportive of me being all that I am deep inside.

I was becoming divided within myself, looking for the appropriate direction that would take me closer to my own central inner core of light. I saw the outside world of man as the living road map, and I was using it to find my way through a very strange and complicated maze of dimensional realities in order to arrive at my innermost holy sanctuary. I always found myself in a new and exciting world each time. I enjoyed the challenge of making my way through them, especially when the texture and the design of them kept changing every time I referred to the maze to get my bearings. Consequently, I had always found myself back at the exact same place where I had started from. I wasn't going anywhere in my travels, yet it always appeared that I was indeed going to many different parts within these new worlds, learning new awarenesses about me.

I gave it all up on the mountain that day. That was the day when I had aligned myself to the four major elements of Nature – representing all of my movements within my outer world dimensions of reality – and fully realized, emotionally, that I was the controller of all of my outer world experiences. I had clearly seen that I could spend every moment in every day looking out within my outer world for the illusionary answers to an endless list of questions I could create. I knew that I would never be able to come to the end resting place within my exploration of all the different realities that exist out there, and from which I could learn endlessly about nothing that was really important to learn about. I was aware that form within my outer world is very much limited and restricted, but that the expressions of those outer world forms are not. They go on and on.

I then proceeded to travel within the depths of my inner world, a world that has no form or consistency to it, yet encompasses all form. I had found it all to be fascinating at first, not really any different than I had found my outside world to be. It, too, was full of magic, color, adventure, intrigue, and heavy stimulation of my earthly senses. All these things I experienced during the quest I was on in order to find and connect with my inner light of truth. The whole texture of this inner dimension of reality had a much different flavor for my sensual appetite. I was instantly overwhelmed by it all, and I found myself getting swept away in its mainstream. This was mainly due to the fact that it was all so new, so inviting in its design – a whole new approach to my living expression. There were more realities to play with in hopes of learning the full extent of my purpose here on this plane.

I continued to explore the many dimensional planes of reality that exist within this limitless world of creative expression. I used the many gifts I had received from these realities to further become aware of how my outer illusionary real world was put together. I was able to move within my outer world using my newly awakened higher sensitivities – within the psychic realities – to open myself up to the many other formless dimensions that exist within the depths of my inner world. I became aware that there is no form to identify with within the textures of my inner dimensions, and that the movement there is forever moving, changing, becoming, and surrendering. I found that whatever I chose to create within my inner dimensional freeways, I could easily manifest within my outer living expression.

I have physically channeled through all sorts of information for many different people. I have journeyed back through timeless time and spoken freely with the great Masters. I have gone ghost hunting in a house, communicating openly with the entities that were trapped there, and helped them to return through their own inner dimensional doorways, to give them their freedom to venture forth into their respective dimensions of reality. I have experienced, on many occasions, creating things on this plane from nothing, materializing them in seconds and then returning them back into the void of darkness in the same amount of time. I have created battles with death-seeking entities on the so-called astral planes, moving through the thin veils of dimensional realities, gambling always with my life in order that I might find the goodness and the magic in my life. I have travelled within the inner depths of the circle of white magic. I have also explored and moved within the depths of the reality of black magic in order to reach a place of balance.

The simplicity of what I had found within both of those realities was that I could always make it all fit any way I wanted. I wasn't hooked on having it any particular way. I only wanted to find the purity of my own inner truth, and nothing else would suffice. I have talked with people who, in their own reality, say they are from distant places other than Earth, and who have come here by travelling on spaceships from distant galactic movements. I have also talked to some earthly beings who say they have been on alien spaceships, and who are still in communication with them at various times. I, too, have seen many of the inner-dimensional, extraterrestrial realities manifested on the physical plane called Earth.

What I have become aware of, through all of my journeys, is that they have all been meaningless distractions, distractions that have kept me busy searching for my illusionary absolute truth, and that have prevented me from coming any closer to seeing it or feeling it. I have used my inner and outer world together, sometimes simultaneously and sometimes against each other in order to make my living expression more exciting, and to give me a sense of accomplishment (within the structure of my movements), looking for a truth that has no solid substance to it. I have discovered that truth cannot be obtained in this way. It is not possible for me to find it by moving through my inner journeys. Nor is it possible for me to find it by moving through my outer journeys. Neither of them has ever shown me the purest form of truth. What they have shown me though, through their truthfulness within the unfolding moments, are the infinite expressions of reality that exist within the dimensional planes within this earthly plane. I have seen that they have served as mirror images for each other: my inner world is, in reality, my outer world, and my outer world is, in reality, my inner world.

> Oh, God! If this is truly so, there can be no ultimate truth. There is no truth that is possible to seek. There are only the illusionary reflections of both worlds. They are illusions as long as I think they are something, and they are only real in the exact moment of realization – and that's it! It is all so amusing. I have been telling myself that over and over again all along, and now I am consciously aware of the emotional impact of it all. I now feel the truth of this realization. It is all a joke. Noooo! There has to be more. It can't be this easy. How do I justify all of my journeys? There must be something I'm missing in all of this. It is all too simple. There must be something I'm overlooking. What can it possibly be?
>
> I demand that the purest truth be shown to me now. I demand that I be shown all the realities and all the illusions. And I demand that it all be shown to me at the same time. That's it, the mirror effect. When an object is reflected outside itself by way of another means other than what it is, what is in the central connecting point between the two? In other words, what separates the two objects – the real one and the reflection – yet allows them to be together?
>
> That's it! That's what is missing. It is all so simple. If I dissolve my inner reflection and my outer illusionary reality, I will be left with the purity of truth within my central connecting point – that place where all of my answers to all of my questions lie. Could it all be that easy? How do I go about doing that? There can't be a way of doing it or arriving at this place. In order

for that to happen, I would have to utilize one of my two worlds, either inner or outer, or possibly even both.

Well then, how do I do it? I know. I have to surrender myself unto myself. By doing this, the infolding reflections of any two sides of my being will create the reality of no time and no space for me to move through. I must be able to go inside and outside at the same time. I have experienced this many times through my many journeys within the altered states. There is a very thin veil that separates the two realities. I have to find the common thread that inserts within the layers of my two worlds, the one that runs throughout all the infinite dimensions of reality: the swirling vortex of human existence; the *centre* of all realities and the place where all realities arise from.

The purest vibration of any truthful expression lies with the silence that is held within the central core of the swirling vortex of all life. The truth is always secured within the *centreline* that separates any two opposite functional realities upon the earthly plane. I see it all so clearly now. I see the complicated and at the same time, simplistic fabric that all of this – all that I have been seeing and doing over the many years of this living expression – represents. I now know how to go about getting there. It is *in between* all that I have come to know to be so on this plane.

As I lie here on the floor, my inner doorways begin to open. I now realize that I have found the combination inside that leads to all the dimensional realities. I now know that I can go there at any time from this moment on. I begin to move within my inner pathways, remembering at all times that all of what I will experience along my way is an illusion if I perceive it within the limited range of one of my earthly senses. I know that in order for it to be the purest form of ever-unfolding, ever-changing truth, I must be able to feel, without any attachment to the feeling, the silence between the opposite realities.

I am now beginning to move increasingly faster within all the textured dimensions. It is much like riding an elevator that goes on and on, continuously opening and closing to the infinite dimensions of reality that are possible here on this earthly plane.

I am now travelling at the speed of light. All is quiet within, but on the outer edges of my being, I can feel my outer body disintegrating layer by layer. Everything around me is also dissolving. It is all returning to the purest essence of life – white light. I am now a ribbon of the striation of white light. I am all-encompassing, yet infinitely divided within my wholeness.

I am moving toward the central core of all existence within the endless dimensional universes that continually emerge from this ongoing matrix of color, the likes of which cannot be described in words. They can only be experienced through the very subtle vibrations of feeling. I am now at the *centre* of it all. I am now all of that which is. I am feeling as I have never felt before. I am the totality of my very being – the wholeness within the completeness of my beingness, and the separateness within the wholeness of my beingness.

As I am releasing more and more into this swirling matrix, I am opening to all the possible combinations of light patterns that exist at all times on the earthly plane, the number of which is endless. I am the knowingness of all things that reaches far beyond the comprehensive ability of human understanding – through the use of the physical brain as I have known it to be. I am moving through all of this at a speed beyond that of light, yet at the same time, I am not going anywhere.

All the patterns of light arrangements are continually changing, simultaneously, and constantly moving, yet at the same time, they are standing still. I see that there is no separation in all of that which I am, but I also see that there is no cohesion in any of it, either. It is formless, yet it encompasses all forms. There is movement all around me, yet within the wholeness of all that I am, there is only silence and no movement within that totality of being. I am feeling the depth of all that I am. I am truly and purely all that there is within the structural framework of this universal universe complete. There is nothing else. I now know this to be so: There is nothing else that exists outside the texture of life that I am now feeling within my wholeness.

As I continue to align myself to all of my self, everything around me ceases to be as I have been observing it. Everything is now quiet and motionless. I am now surrendering into the depths of the void that keeps hidden behind that which is. I am slipping between and within the very textured essence of all that I am. Within the ever-unfolding darkened void, I am realigning to all of that which I have known for lifetimes within this earthly lifetime. I am now the endlessness of the all-knowing presence.

I have arrived here at the beginning of all things and at the ending of all things. I am the space that exists in between, as well as the dimensions of space that oppose each other. I am free to move within my own multi-dimensional worlds, whenever I so choose, in order that I might bring into a physical manifestation, on the earthly plane, all that I have been witness to within this experience. I am the ever-present, all-encompassing consciousness. I am the light of creation, the God energy personified.

I am now aware that it is not necessary for me to search within my living expression for my perfect truth. I now see that truth is all-encompassing, and that it only truly exists from unfolding moment to unfolding moment. I am now aware that it is time for me to return to my earthly form and manifest and live the purity of that which I have been shown.

I am beginning to move within the geometric matrixes of ever-changing colour patterns of light, realigning with the essence of vibrational consistency that shapes and forms my physical embodiment. I see that it is my essence of this living expression that lies at the central core of who I am on the earthly plane, and that all the necessary light pattern combinations are attracted to this central core. I am seeing that it is this core that supports my connection to the all-knowing presence within me – and within all mankind.

As those patterns of light continue to form around my core essence, I am being presented with all of my living experiences, experiences that I have moved through within this earthly lifetime, as well as within all the other lifetimes I have had on the earthly plane previous to this lifetime.

I am watching the wholeness of this current earthly living expression unfold, beginning once more with my birth into this physical plane. I am continuing along on my journey through to this moment in time, listening to and observing all the experiences I have created since arriving here. I am seeing for the first time, while being totally removed from the emotional experience, the fact that how I had perceived everything to be back then, was not actually the way that it was. Yet because I had chosen to create it all that way, it actually was that way.

I now see that it was (and still is) my perceptions of thought, as to what an experience was or wasn't, that were continually responsible for my misalignment within my outer world. I am now aware that it was through my thought processes that I had imprisoned myself. I also know that it is only when I feel from the core essence of who I am, that I will move within the guidance of the all-knowing presence that lies deep within my being.

I am now arriving back into the restricting limitations of the time and space oriented environment I have created within these walls in my bedroom. I am feeling my own internal and external presence in a totally new and child-like way. I feel as though I am experiencing it all for the very first time. It all feels so new and so much more alive with creative energy. I have arrived back to where I have always been. I am feeling a surge of loving warmth rushing throughout the totality of my being. I am realizing that I have brought through into my physical reality (at this moment) my central core essence – the pulsating force behind my living expression.

I slowly open my outer eyes and begin to observe all that presents itself to my visual receptors. I begin to move my physical body through many different positional alignments, exploring the depths of feeling that I am creating within my being. There is something about all of what lies within and around me that is showing me the preciousness of life, and the simple ways of expressing life here on this plane. I am aware of the total feeling within its existence, and words take away from the purity of what it exemplifies. The most precious gift I have to offer myself is my ability to feel all things for what they truly are at any one single moment in time.

I now see that all living expressions of life are created within a movement that is manifested through the simple magic of feeling. This feeling originates within the central core essence of all life forms here on this plane. This feeling can only be acknowledged when there is total freedom from thought, for thought always concerns itself with what has already taken place, or what might take place in the future. Thought never focuses on that which is unfolding within the unfolding moment. It is all so simple when I stop and remove myself long enough in order to get a good close look at it. *I am now aware that there is only one true purpose for being on this plane called Earth: it is to love, unconditionally, all aspects of my being through the creative process of feeling.*

✳

## LOVE – THE ESSENCE

I have been on somewhat of a magical expedition into the very depths of my being, and into the limitless realms of realities that exist and are continually being created within my own illusionary thought projections. I have been weaving a tapestry of experiences throughout my living expression, in hopes of returning to the purest vibration that is obtainable within the wholeness of human existence.

I have been continuously journeying far and wide to the ongoing galaxies that exist within and beyond the physical space my bodily form occupies here on this plane. I have felt the wind on many occasions caress my heart and propel me in many directions, simultaneously ripping me apart and opening me up to a conglomeration of resonating vibrations of such intensity that words cannot be found to adequately describe their existence.

I have breathed the air around me that is saturated with the infinite colour striations of light – of variable intensities. I have felt my physical embodiment being slowly tantalized, seduced, and enticed as it was metamorphosing to the dancing energies of the God-like presence that makes up all expressions of life here on this plane – and all the other planes within this plane. I have been observing the continuum of movement around me as the process of life unfolds within the thousands of seconds of time – as I know them to be – bringing new and wonderfully simple variations of creative living expressions into physical manifestation on this plane.

I have sat in many houses that have radiated love in all their shadows and within the structural framework of their covered-up walls. I have felt the love that has been circulating within the ever-unfolding vortex of the air that we all breathe. I have continuously sat like an ornament within these dimensionally fabricated structures of form, and I have taken on many forms and shapes in order that I might transcend the limitations of my own restricted vision – in the ordinary sense of the word.

I have oftentimes dialogued with my Brothers within the variable realities that surrounded me, and that I have continually transposed into and out of within the multi-dimensional contexts of who I am, as well as who I am not, and within who I am becoming from moment to moment. It is, in all ways, so simple, yet at the same time, it is intricately complex within its simplified expressions. I have given up my identity and released my connection to being of a constant form, and I have also surrendered my essence to the universal flow of life.

I am now seeing that this multi-dimensional plane called Earth is, in reality, an ever-changing magnitude of complicated matrixes of colour vibrations, that continuously resonate inter-dimensionally within the limited space of time and space to bring into a physical manifestation the wide range of creative living expressions of a natural source: the essence of God, personified.

I have experienced a zillion forms of the essence of love within the complicated spectrums of light intensities that exist within my entire being. These forms have allowed me to connect freely with the vastness of the universe complete in a very simple way. My living expression continuously unfolds within the resonating vibrations of the essence of that love that has brought all things into physical form, and that allows all things to continually alter their state of beingness in order to bring forth the simple magic of life in a kaleidoscope of reflections and permutations of resonating light forms.

I have reconnected the child essence that lies deep within me and at the *centre* of my very existence. It has allowed me to flow upon the delicate fabric of my being in a ever-changing expression of thought and physical embodiment, gracefully dancing upon the notes of vibrating music that compose the eternal song of life here on this plane.

I have surrendered my humble presence of being unto a much greater presence of being, one that allows me to be nothing, yet at the same time, to know everything there is to know. Life for me now is an ever-moving orchestration of intricate light patterns that manifest themselves into a physical reality, through various resonations and vibratory frequencies, on a swirling geometric matrix of all-encompassing color. I have fully embraced the reality that: The element of God is totally contained within the presence of any one thing – through its wholeness and within its separateness – and that it is contained within the limitless formations that exist within the structural composition of all things.

There is no simple expression of communication I can honestly present that will fully justify all that I have seen. Yet in the silence of my thoughts and creative expressions, it is experienced in a most simplified manner – love! The personification of love and of life is me. I am love in all that I do. All that I do is love. Love is brought forth through the creative process. Love embraces all things that exist on this plane.

I see that I am continuously shifting within the swirling vortex of all life within my very existence here on this plane, and on all levels of dimensional existence that simultaneously express themselves beyond the doorways that lead to the universes within the universe of all realities, and that co-exist within the intricate and delicate veils of illusions and realities, far beyond the comprehension of my own thought processes.

*

I am now moving towards the bedroom door, feeling deep inside, as I reach for the handle, that my inner journey is finally coming to an end. A new journey is about to unfold with the sudden emergence of sunlight, as it penetrates through the darkness that has been my sanctuary for the past fifty-two hours. As I open the door, I feel the lightness and newness of all that lies on either side of the creatively expanding doorway that separates my unfolding realities.

As I move toward the sliding glass door that leads to the sundeck, I begin to feel a tingling sensation pulsating throughout my entire being. I am feeling the unrestricted range of freedom that is pouring forth from the depths of my beingness. I know that I am not the same person who originally went into the room fifty-two hours ago. I also know that I am still the same person I have always been.

As I slowly draw open the sliding door, I feel the inrush of cool morning air caress my face and exposed hands. There is a certain feeling that is engulfing my entire being. It is a feeling that is allowing me to be more poetic and expressive in the newness of what Nature is presenting, concerning my alignment to the interconnectedness of all things.

As I gaze out toward the ever-unfolding distance, I witness the Sun slowly ascending the imposing formations of mountains that rise from the curving horizon. As a ray of sunlight dances across the light striations within the very air I breathe, I see, for a thousandth of a second in a time sequence, an expression of form and shape that cannot be seized within the normal accessible vibrational process of thought – yet it dances throughout me, bringing into a functioning reality the creative vibration and resonation of who I am, as well as dissolving the aspects of who I am not.

Within each moment of my existence, I am a continually unfolding and ever-changing matrix of colour that is forever composing an inexhaustible number of resonating vibrations of forms and shapes – images created through me to further heighten the sensitivities of the physical senses that make up the depths of my being.

The early morning air is still. There is an absence of sound everywhere, yet I am able to hear the breath of the wind and feel the pulse of the Earth. Raven flies toward me out of the South, the direction of 'innocence and trust'. I now fully realize the message he brings with him this day. I have brought together the opposing divisions that exist within my being, and I have created a space of peace and harmony within all that I am.

As Raven continues to fly toward me, I move off the suspended balcony and transform myself into the full essence of all that he is. I merge within his being with his freeing spirit and we climb to greater heights in order that I might feel the extent of the freedom I am giving myself. We are soon joined by two other Brothers, and the three of us frolic and play within the shifting currents of the ever-present life-force that sustains all living expressions on this plane.

The equilateral triangle of wholeness has now been formed within my being. I am free to fly to my own individual heights within this world, and also within all other worlds. This alignment has been completed so that I may enter through the hidden central doorway of my being at any time I choose. My heart begins to pulsate to the current of all life. I am feeling the wholeness of all that is. There is no further need for me to search in any direction for anything, for I have arrived within the totality of who I am.

My Brothers break away and begin to make circular patterns, constantly changing the height of their soar. Once again I am being shown that all things within the natural creative process move into being by a spiral motion which receives its impulse from the central core essence of all life.

As I am standing on the railing of the sundeck, I catch, out of the corner of my right eye, a fleeting glimpse of a Monarch Butterfly. As I direct my vision toward his direction, I see and feel another impact to what I have awakened myself to through all of my journeys. The Monarch is a Brother who has come to welcome me to the magical rhythm of life in his own unique way. He is dancing on the currents of air, gently bouncing from sphere to sphere, lighting up the world the only way he knows how – through being all that he is at all times. His gift to the world is the gift of himself and all of his color. He is able to bring joy and love to all of his living brothers and sisters, for he has spent a period of time in seclusion, working on and transforming himself, always striving for the highest possible expression he can obtain within his earthly existence.

The Monarch Butterfly has come to me today to celebrate my emergence into the world of colour and transformation. He has also come to remind me that I am free to fly within any dimension of reality, and that I will touch the hearts of many who will be open to seeing and feeling me for who I am. I am free to give to the world all that I am, and in doing so, many will be affected by my presence in just the way that I am.

I close my eyes, take in a deep breath and smile within the depths of my being. I am the peace and the love that I have created for myself. I am free within myself to be myself in all that I do, without attachment to anything on this plane. I am once again free to experience my life through the creative energy of the child. I am free! I am free! I am free!

# CHAPTER 10

# RELATIONSHIPS:
# SEARCHING FOR THE INNER CHILD

## *September 1, 1986*

I feel very much different today. There is definitely a change taking place within my internal core. My inner vibrational resonations are altering slightly. I have been working on my journal becoming a book, and I am continuing to open up to the ever-unfolding information that keeps surfacing around all the experiences I have had out in the natural elements. There is so much to absorb. I have been getting lost in it. I begin typing at 4:33 a.m., and the next time I look at the clock, it is 2:30 p.m. Time seems to be irrelevant. Where do I go when I get lost? I have no idea. When I return and look at how much I have done, I see close to twenty pages of material that has been prepared, and I always ask myself, "I wonder who typed all of this?"

The process of typing on an electrical typewriter has been an interesting one. I am teaching myself how to type as I move along. I have found that using the index finger of each hand works well. I am aware that my eyes select the keys that spell the words that my inner voice dictates while I hear a musical beat through the keys as I thoughtlessly sit through these long time periods of typing. It is all happening through a creative process that uses no thought, but thought arrives through the process.

I know that it is actually me who is doing it all. I just allow myself to be taken back in time and space to those experiences I am writing about, and I relive them in totality. I relive them as I am writing about them. I literally become the experience all over again, reliving every detail that unfolded the first time I had experienced it.

I have been looking once again at those missing pieces in my living expression. I am now aware that the piece I need most is around relationships. I am now aware that in order for me to become all that I am on this plane, I will need to create a loving, equal relationship with a woman. I need to have someone else in my life in order to live totally within myself – independent of everyone, yet dependent on everyone. My whole journey so far has been alone, with the help of many outside people – unknown to them on a conscious level. It has been safe doing it this way, in that I could easily keep myself aligned to my truth and not be distracted by someone else's insecurities.

I am now feeling that it is time for me to create a nurturing relationship that totally supports all that I have been doing, all that I am doing, and all that I will continue to do in the years to come. I am not at all clear why I might need to establish such a relationship at this time. All I know is that I have been getting a really strong inner feeling that this is what I need most in my living expression.

I am still sharing a living space with my friend, but it isn't exactly what I need. The person has created a picture within her thought patterns that I am someone she can base her security on. She is not able to see me clearly in the light that I am – that I am a free-expressing, loving human being who chooses not to identify with pictures. I am not wanting to put my security into another human being, and I will not let someone else base their security on me.

We are all on this Earth to find our own ways through the continual maze of illusions that we all end up securing ourselves with. I trust that if it is a relationship I need, then one shall arrive shortly. I know not who or when, and I don't even care. I know that everything I need, I shall receive. Once again, I will just have to be patient and wait.

## September 13, 1986

My housemate and I have just finished our Saturday morning breakfast at a local restaurant. We have been walking around for the past hour or so, and are on our way back to the car. I am being directed from my internal knowing sense. I am being pulled in a definite direction. I am very sensitive to what is happening within me. I am not aware of all that is unfolding. All I know is that I am being guided toward an eventual destination. I am following my inner impulse, and my friend is following along with me. It doesn't matter to her where we are headed.

We are heading up one of the short side streets. My internal knowing says turn left. As we round the corner, I receive a most unexpected and welcomed surprise. A former girlfriend is walking along the sidewalk with another person, heading straight for me. It has been a while since I have seen her. I last saw her just before I went to Toronto. Since I have arrived back, I haven't bothered to get in touch with her. I had decided not to call anyone, that I would let my inner guidance take care of who I needed to see.

As we greet each other, we both more or less wrap ourselves around each other and fall into a deep and nurturing hug that seems to go on and on. There has always been a great connection between us. It was always very easy to get forever lost in the warmth and lovingness of a hug.

After endless moments, we separate ourselves and gaze into each other's eyes. We are both now moving within the feeling mechanisms of our past experiences together. There are no words that describe the feelings that are surfacing within my being. The connection that I have to her is still very much there, and I can tell that it is for her, as well.

After a brief conversation about what each of us has been doing recently, we decide to meet the following day. With that gesture, we both depart and continue on our separate ways. I am definitely having a reaction inside me. It appears that whenever the two of us have gotten together in the past, there have always been strong feelings of love coming from each of us. The feelings that I have for her have always been indescribable with words, so I have never tried. I am looking forward to our meeting and sharing of time and space.

As I sit here, sipping on my morning coffee, reflecting back on my experiences with my former girlfriend, the phone begins to ring. After the third ring, I pick up the receiver and hear her voice greeting me to the new day. After a few minutes of dialogue, I invite her to go for a walk. I tell her that I will pick her up in twenty minutes at the house where she is staying.

I put a few things together and head out the door. The Sun is shining and there is a warm breeze in the air. It is incredible weather we are having for September, definitely another Indian summer day. It is a great day for heading out of town, out into the wide open country for a nice leisurely walk through the woods, perhaps down near the ocean. I am feeling calm inside and at peace with all that is unfolding. I have no idea what is going to happen, and I am not really concerned. I am just looking forward to spending a few hours out in the natural elements with someone I really enjoy being with. It has been a long while since I have been out with anyone except for my regular weekly hiking partner.

When I pick up my friend, we decide to go to East Sooke Park, as I have the use of a car for the whole day. We pull out of the driveway and head through the centre of town, en route to the West Coast Road, where we will eventually arrive at East Sooke Park in an hour.

There is little to talk about on the way. We are both feeling each other on the subtle levels. It has been some time since we have connected in the manner I am now feeling inside. It all feels supportive and very loving. The dialogue that is created is mostly about other people we both know – third party filler talk. Neither of us is really sure what we should say or how we should say it. Neither of us is struggling with words. If they don't show up, then there is silence and feeling. I know that whatever is going to happen, will only happen if I allow space for it to. I am exercising patience. I do not want anything from her, so I don't need to be in a hurry. I am out to freely participate in whatever is to unfold.

We have been talking mostly about what she has been up to, and what she wants to do in her life, both in her outer and inner world. Her biggest desire is to explore the possibilities of love – unconditional love. That is something that has always meant a lot to her, but has always eluded her. She has told me that she does not have a steady relationship going at present, but is hoping to create a supportive one soon if the universe will support her in doing so. She has mentioned that she has put it out on the universal airwaves, and now will wait and see what comes back.

She had asked me what I had been up to. I was a little leery of letting her in on all that I have been doing out in the natural elements. I proceeded to talk around the outer edges at first, telling her about my four and a half year initiation into the sacred inner teachings. I mentioned about being initiated as the warrior – the shape-changer; my death-facing journey on the cliff; and being introduced to Raven by the medicine man. As she was open to listening, I automatically opened more. I wasn't at all sure why I was telling her all this, for I hadn't told anyone any of it before except for my housemate. It all just felt right, so I let the words flow. As they flowed, I continued to listen.

I mentioned about my shape-changing experiences – about turning into Cougar that day on the rock face out at Goldstream Park. I then mentioned about Little Bird – the one who comes to visit and to speak whenever I am out in the woods and in need of his wisdom; that I have never known when he will arrive, but his appearance has always been timely to whatever I needed to hear. I then finished off by telling her about my experience of eating the poisonous mushroom, and about my final alignment with my own internal guidance system; that I would get nothing more from the natural elements; that, from now on, my teachings would only come from other people. I would have to take what I have been shown and share it with others. By doing that, I would be opened up more to that which I already know. As I told her all that I did, I was continually feeling how she was receiving it. She continued to be open to hearing more.

As we were getting out of the car in the parking lot, I mentioned that at various points along my journey, I was afraid that I might have gone a little too far in my desire to find my truth. She shared her concerns about what I had been doing in the past few years. She mentioned that in the past she had judged me and what I was choosing to do in my life, and that perhaps it wasn't fair of her to do so. After hearing all of what I had to say about my inner journey, she said she didn't have a hard time believing any of it, that it all just felt right to her. She then said she could sense a difference in me, and that the feeling between us was also different. She recognized that we had both changed, and I recognized it too.

We continue to dialogue as we walk along the path, mostly about relationships. I can hear a few Ravens talking back and forth in the distance. They too are discussing relationships, their own tribal relationships. It is mating time once again, and the males are busy declaring their territorial boundaries as far as the females are concerned. The males are also exercising their dominance over each other.

As we move along the path, we are getting closer to where they are dialoguing. I commence a dialogue with them within my inner channels, for I do not wish to call out to them verbally. I will just wait and see what will unfold between my friend and me. I do not wish to do anything with her here, for I fear that she will react to what might happen. I know that if I keep it all to myself, she will not be able to create any more pictures or judgments within her mental thought processes.

I can now hear the Ravens very clearly just ahead. I can hear the noise that is created when they flap their wings. As I look up, I see six Ravens moving and interacting with each other, in two groups of three. I am automatically aware that there is something more going on within this simple communication than I can visually see. I am not sure of what it might be. All I know is that I have never seen this many Ravens together before. I want to know more. I direct my dialogue toward them all, "Greetings, my Brothers and Sisters. There is magic in what I see. I know that there is much for me to learn in listening to and watching your movements at this time."

A single Raven answers, "Greetings, my brother, from all of us. There is always much for you to receive out here. Observe, and all will be revealed to you."

I want to let them know that I am not here for their teaching, so I respond, "It is not appropriate for us to continue in our dialogue. I am not sure as to what—."

Before I can finish what I want to say, I am interrupted by one of the others, "Yes, that is so. I know all about it. I am too busy within my own movements, as well. Look closely at all that unfolds within you, and the gift that you have been looking for shall be revealed."

As I continue to observe, I see that the Ravens, still in their two groups of three, have landed in two separated trees. Each Raven is now taking his and her turn speaking. They are voicing their own feelings as to what is taking place within the tribal connection. They have just come together for the first time. My friend and I are being treated to a magical gift. This new arrangement is only now being created. We are witnessing the birth of a new and creative relationship.

I begin to look at all that is unfolding in a different way. Symbolically, I see that (using numerology) six represents family relationships, community involvement, nurturing, sharing, loving, supporting, all in a family manner. Two is the number of relationships. It has more to do with the individual relationships that exist within me: the two aspects of my earthly being – male and female. The Ravens are communicating to each other about how it is in their individual worlds. They are trying to reach a conciliatory agreement regarding how the territorial boundaries are to be designated. The three Ravens in each group represent the three aspects of each side of my being. My male aspect has a mental, physical, and emotional reality within its outer world expressions on this plane. My female aspect also has three realities within its inner world expressions on this plane. They are mental, physical, and spiritual – (the aspect of all-knowing).

What I am clearly seeing, within this approach of looking, is that I am coming to another major shift within my own internal alignment. I see that there will soon be a merging of energies within the male and female aspects of my being. There appears to be a slight delay within the unfolding of this process, but if I am patient and let it all unfold, it will open fully within its own creative expression.

There is something beginning to unfold within the Ravens' dialogue. Frustration is mounting within their inner circles. There is more squabbling going on. There is also a slight power struggle developing. The males are exercising more of their dominance, each one trying to prove to the others that he is worthy enough to be part of the tribal community.

I continue to listen to the dialogue within my inner channels, and then I can't help wanting to put my few words in to give them a different angle. Without further hesitation, the words begin to flow, "Why don't all of you get off your pettiness and harmonize with each other? Why don't you practice a little of what you have always said to me? Is what you have shared with me in the past only for me, or is it for all living expressions of life on this plane?"

I know that I have startled them. It has suddenly turned quiet. Not a word is coming from any of them. All I can hear is the soft melodic singing of a few of the smaller birds who call this area their home. I am waiting to see what their reaction will be, or if indeed there will be one.

Within seconds, out of the stillness and silence of the inner void comes a seemingly angry voice from a Raven, "You stay out of this. It has nothing to do with you."

"On the contrary, my Brother, it has everything to do with me. It has to do with everything I have learned out here."

"You are in our territory. When you are out here, we are the teachers."

"That is where you are mistaken, my Brother. You are no longer my teacher. It is now your turn to be the student – but not of my words, of your own. In your struggle for power and control within your interacting relationships, you are causing a split in the flow and creation of life."

"We do not need your words here. You have not been invited to participate in our tribal affairs. Stay out of it!"

"No. I won't stay out of it. We are Brothers, and we are equal. We have made an agreement to share with each other what we know. We have been one ever since that day when I officially severed my ties with you. That is how it shall always be."

There is definitely a reaction from all the other Ravens. They are not sure how to handle my interaction. They are deciding whether they want their tribal meeting to continue where they are, or to go and seek out another place where they won't be interfered with. The one who has been dialoguing with me speaks sternly to the rest of the assembly, and convinces them, by his intensity, that they are moving somewhere else. He proceeds to move, and the rest begin to follow. As he is departing, he calls his last words to me, "You look after your own life, my brother, and stay out of mine."

I calmly and quietly respond, "There is no need for you to be this way, my Brother. Why are you so upset with what I have chosen to do?"

There is no answer coming from him. I know that he is trying to save face with the other tribal members. He is exercising his power-thrust for the females and other males. It is all just a mask that he is wearing. I see him as the fool, the trickster. It is only real at this moment, for when this moment is over, so too will his mask have changed. I feel his essence. He has been playing with me as much as I have been playing with him.

Although there is much truth in what he has just shared, there is also nothing in it except empty words. I now see his gift. It is not what has taken place within our dialogue that counts. It is what I get out of the experience that unfolded. As I am not attached to any of that which took place, I am able to receive more from my participation in it.

I am now seeing how this is also applicable within my own internal and external relationships. It is never what takes place within the unfolding dialogue that is of value. It is how I stay detached from the outcome that will determine what I get out of the interaction. It is truly a gift that I am seeing, one that will continually aid me in my search for a harmonizing relationship within my internal and external living expressions.

As the rest of the day unfolded, my friend and I continued to talk a little, run along the ever-changing trails, and sit and be quiet within our own individual worlds. Everything had been moving along without any friction whatsoever. In our past relationships (there were two different occasions when we had seen a lot of each other) there was always an element of friction that would enter into some part of the dialogue and cause us to move away from each other for a time. Whether our separation was for five minutes or two months all depended on how what was done or said was interpreted by the other person. This time things were definitely different. There was a different air to the whole experience. Neither of us wanted anything from each other. We were just out to enjoy each other's company and soak up some sun.

At the end of the day, I dropped her off at the house and said goodbye. We didn't make any plans to see each other again. She mentioned that she would be coming back to Victoria from her home in Vancouver each weekend, and that perhaps we could get together again some time. I was complete with all that had taken place during the day. I did not want or need anything else from her. Her company was more than enough. I was feeling alive once more within my internal movement. I had been spending so much time on my own, typing and editing my book, that I had completely forgotten what it was like to just go out and relax within someone else's company.

On October 5, 1986, my friend phoned me from the place she was staying in Victoria. After our initial exchange of 'hello', she quietly said, "I want to talk to you about 'not doing'."

We arranged to get together that afternoon. I picked her up and we went down to the beach in front of Beacon Hill Park. We talked about wanting control, about holding on to things, and about creating pictures within our thought processes, and how we keep those pictures intact when we interact with each other. We also talked about the pictures that each of us held of the other, and how these pictures were getting in the way of us establishing a harmonious relationship. We looked back on our past relationship and saw how it was affecting what was presently unfolding between us.

She was definitely not happy about where she had put herself in her life. She wanted to change it, but wasn't sure how to go about doing that. I had told her about my internal movements when I first started on my journey. I had mentioned how I was instructed by my inner teachers to "do nothing", and that through doing nothing, everything would happen when it was supposed to. She was always busy doing things in her life, striving to get somewhere that didn't exist. She was frustrated within her own movements. She believed so many people and so many stories that she wasn't sure which person or story she could trust and which one she could believe.

Our dialogue went on for nearly three hours, and then she had to catch the ferry back to Vancouver. She mentioned that she would get in touch with me when she came back to Victoria the following weekend. She had also mentioned that she definitely wanted to look more at what we had talked about on the beach. As we parted company, I could feel the unrest within her, and I was hoping that she wouldn't go away and beat herself up with what we had looked at. I gave her a lengthy hug, sending lots of nurturing love her way, for I knew what it was like to be trapped within the intellectual thought processes.

I had no picture of what was unfolding within our getting together, other than this person was wishing to make some possible changes in her living expression. I could only share with her what I knew was truth for me. I could only ask questions that both of us could look more deeply into. I knew that I had no answers for her, and that there were no answers to be given or sought after.

On October 18, my friend and I met again. This time it was at one of her movement classes. She was doing a creative workshop with a local group of young people. She was co-hosting this session with another person. I was also invited by this other person to come along and share some of my ideas. My friend and I ended up using the time together to further explore some of the things we had been talking about during our recent meetings.

We allowed ourselves to flow freely with whatever presented itself. We had been talking about creative flow, and how to generate more of that within a group of people, and perhaps between the two of us. We looked at many things, observing the people who were taking the class, and also the other person who was instructing. There was much to see within the context of it all.

At one point in our interaction, my friend and I move out on to the floor and begin free-flow dancing with each other with our eyes closed. No words have been spoken to begin this movement. It more or less begins on its own impulse.

There is only harmony and flow in the way our bodies interact together. There is no resistance from either of us as to where the movement is heading. We are both just flowing with it and allowing it to create its own rhythm. There are no words to adequately describe the feeling that is moving between us. Words can never seem to reflect the creative spontaneity of movement as it is being created and moved.

I feel something stirring deep within me through this exercise. It is as though we have been rehearsing this movement pattern for a long time. I am so connected to her that I lose myself in the creative process and allow myself to be totally guided by my inner sense of knowing. I am not thinking about what should be done or how it should be done. I am too busy doing it.

As we end our creative movement together, we both look into each other's eyes and simultaneously travel into distant dimensions of reality within the inner void. For a few moments, time is irrelevant. There is no dimension of space that we occupy, either. Things are happening within each of us on the more subtle levels. What they are, neither of us is quite sure. All I know is that it is generating a peaceful feeling within the central core of my being. I am alive with feeling as I have never been before.

After the workshop is over, we decide to go to a nearby restaurant to have a coffee. While we are dialoguing about what we had seen within the unfolding of the earlier session, a young boy of about two slowly walks up to our table. He is a perfect gift at the time he arrives. My friend and I are in the middle of a discussion about freedom of expression, creativeness in movement, and the joy that comes from spontaneously moving within the flow of a creative expression. The young boy comes over to where I am, completely ignoring my friend. He and I dialogue within our inner channels. I thank him for his gift and tell him that he has arrived right on time. As he and I finish our discussion, he walks back to where his mother is sitting.

I turn to my friend and mention that he is a very special gift for her. I proceed to interpret what I have seen from my interaction with him and her non-interaction with the Child. It is centred mostly on not allowing herself to identify with her own inner Child, and that she will not be free enough to move as creatively as she wants until she consciously opens up her connection to her inner creative Child – the one that knows everything there is to know about movement. I mention that it was the creative Child within each of us that allowed us to move so harmoniously on the floor, a little while earlier.

As I am finishing the dialogue with her, the Child comes back for another visit. Through the inner dialogue, he is once again (symbolically) telling both of us the importance of being Child-like in our approach to life: through the eyes of the pure Child, all is a creative journey.

Just as he is finishing with his inner wisdom, his mother happens to come around the corner of the booth and proceeds to engage in a short outburst of dialogue. Her words are quick and to the point, "When you have had enough of the child, just send him back."

As she finishes these words, she quickly disappears behind the next booth, totally out of sight. I mention to my friend that the mother is also a gift, in the choice of words she had used. We dialogue a little longer about the gift of the Child, and the creativity we could both open up to within ourselves if we go back and totally live through the eyes of the Child. We look at the practical feasibility of doing this all the time.

We also continue to look more seriously at common issues around concepts of reality and habitual belief systems. We are not finding any answers to our questions. It is more important to know that we can just sit and look as seriously as we are, and not get hung up on wanting to be right. This is the first time that there has been such intensity of 'looking' in our movement together. In the past, the issues that were important were always clearly avoided by either or both of us.

Through our common desire to get out from under all the stuff that has been holding our free-flowing creativity in check, we are slowly becoming closer in our on-again, off-again relationship. We are definitely heading in a new direction. The feelings between us are progressively getting stronger each time we dialogue. There is total freedom to be who each of us is in the moment, without judgment. We both know that we are not what we believe we are, or that anyone else is truly as we see them. We both recognize that we have been, and still are sometimes, caught in our illusions of how everything seems to be.

I am not feeling as though she can give me anything that I do not already have. I also know that I cannot give her anything she does not already have. If we both stay open and share what we think, without attachment to what it is, or was, then we will supportively open each other to what each of us already knows.

In the past, she has always wanted something from me – within the context of our on-again, off-again relationship. She had wanted more of a sexual relationship. Sex had been a way that she had secured herself in her intimate relationships. It was also a gauge to tell her whether the relationship was working out. She has been using her outer world movements to tell her how she was doing within her inner world. Within that context, sex had always brought an element of uncertainty and friction within our relationship.

Our relationship was never really allowed to open within its own creative flow. We had both been too busy holding on to the pictures that we were carrying around of our past experiences in relationships. We had continually judged what was taking place within our relationship by what had taken place in our past movements with other people. We had not been totally honest with ourselves or with each other, so our relationship was doomed from the beginning.

I didn't know how to begin to talk to her about how I was feeling inside, because of the non-supporting experiences we had had in our first two interacting relationships. At that time, I had put some things out and she had reacted to them – and not favorably, either. She was only able to work with what she knew to be her truth within her past experiences. She was never able to freely talk about what had gone on in her past life, for most of the men she had loved ended up leaving her for someone else. She had established in her mindset that our relationship would be no different. I was just another one of those guys, and she was certain that it wouldn't work out favorably for her. She had a definite picture of how things were in her life, and she wasn't willing to drop the picture long enough to see that I wasn't any of the things that she had experienced in her past. All she knew for sure was what she had experienced.

We continue to talk for another half an hour, and then we both leave. She goes her way and I go mine. All is complete within each of us. She mentions that she would be open to looking more at what we had been talking about during our discussion. I invite her to come over to the house the next day, and we could go from there.

On her way over to the house, she gets involved in a car accident right at the corner where my house is situated. She had planned to be at my house for a few hours, and then out to a friend's cabin to spend a few days in solitude. After the accident happens, I mention that she might want to take a good close look at it all. That perhaps it isn't appropriate for her to be going anywhere. The universe has definitely stopped her right outside the house, and that perhaps this is where she should stop and look at her life.

We continue to talk for the rest of the afternoon and well into the night. I invite her to stay, and if she wants to leave in the morning to go to the cabin, so be it. She agrees to stay. I invite her to sleep with me without any attachment to the outcome. I mention that I am not interested in having sex with her. I only want to share with her the loving and nurturing feelings I have.

We continue to dialogue, for the next hour and a half, about the feelings we both have around intimacy – sex, touching and expressing emotions. At the most appropriate time, silence enters into the entire inner and outer spaces we both occupy, and we slowly drift off into the other dimensional pathways that exist within our inner channels.

The next morning, we sit around and look further into all that had taken place the evening before. I have been questioning her quite a bit. I am trying to over-load her intellectual awarenesses so we can both move within a feeling environ-ment. Her intellect is in full control of all of her movement. It is busy trying to complicate the simplicity of what we had shared last evening. Her intellect is frying all of her internal circuits. It wants to run away, for if it can, it will be able to easily divide her some more.

I keep pursuing her intellect. I want to get it out of the way so we can cre-ate a new flow within our movement together. I am not succeeding. She is now getting close to the breaking-point within herself, and she is also getting ready to run. I cannot stop her, and I will not even try. She has to do what she thinks she needs to.

She decides that she is going to go out to the cabin. She says she has to be alone, and that she will be able to work it all out on her own. She is absolutely sure that she can figure it all out. I mention that it was her thinking, not her feel-ing, that had gotten her into the mess she is now in, in the first place. I ask her, "How do you think that you are going to get yourself out, when you are not even sure how you got yourself in?"

She has no answer.

I then say, "If you are going to the cabin because that is what you feel you need to do, then do it, for that is truthfully what is needed for you at this time. If you are going to the cabin because you are running away from what has been happening, then you would be making a foolish mistake. To act is the way of the wise man. To react is the way of the fool."

She pauses for a few moments and then mentions that she needs to go and be by herself for a while. She says that she has had enough and is feeling really fried by the whole experience. She says she will be all right to drive her car out to the cabin. Without further delay, she packs her things together and leaves. We make no further arrangements to see each other. I am clear that she still doesn't have anything I want. To me, the experiences we have shared are complete. I am at peace with all that I have seen within myself from each of our interactions.

On the following Saturday, November 1, we met again. We were both at-tending another creative workshop for young people. She was co-hosting it with another person, and I was once again invited to enter into the creative unfolding of it. We were not able to talk to each other after it was over, but we arranged to get together later that evening. She was going to call and make arrangements after she got back from the teaching duties.

After she phoned, I went over to the place where she was staying. During the course of the unfolding evening, many things were looked at. None of them were very much different than what we had been looking at during all the other times we had gotten together. It was during our conversation that I suggested to her that if she was truly looking to find her own truth, then she could come and stay with me and look all she wanted. I mentioned that it was not important that she give me an answer right away. She could think about it for as long as she wanted. I told her to feel the entire process we had been dancing through over the weeks, and that if she could clearly do that, then she would know when the time would be right to make her decision.

Before I left her that evening, I mentioned that if she decided to take me up on my offer, we would not be setting up any kind of a relationship as we had done previously. If she decided to come, she would be coming to uncover the illusions within her belief structures. There would be nothing but unconditional love created between us. I told her that I would love her unconditionally, and that I would not judge or compare her to anyone or anything, for I do not judge or compare myself in any way.

I didn't have to wait long for her to call back. On November 4, she phoned to say that she was indeed moving in with me and my housemate, and would be arriving soon. When I arrive home later in the afternoon, I see her sitting on the cushions against the far wall. She says she feels calm and peaceful. We continue to talk for a little longer, and then I outline the conditions for her being in our house. I mention that our house is representative of the house of truth, mainly because we are all looking for our own individual truth. I also mention that if she is going to stay here with me, there are certain rules I expect to be followed, and as long as she could follow them, she would always be welcomed. The rules are quite simple: That you be totally honest with yourself and with each person here at all times; That you have unconditional love for yourself and everyone in the house; That you speak your truth at all times, regardless of what that might be.

"In this house, everything will be provided for you," I say to her. "You won't have to go anywhere in order to get what you are looking for. If there is any separation between you and I, it will be because you are creating it. I am not wanting to be your friend or your lover. I am whole within myself, and there is nothing you can give me. I have nothing I can give you. We have lots that we can share with each other. I will never ask you to leave this house. If you go, it will be because you choose to. I have not asked you to come here. You have freely chosen to be here, and only you will determine how long you will stay. I will love you unconditionally as long as you love yourself enough to be all that you are."

Under these guidelines, my friend agrees to move within all that has been outlined. She expresses that it is all she has ever really wanted in her life – to love and be loved unconditionally. Our close interaction together is going to unfold as it will, and neither of us is quite sure how that will be. We are both certain that it will be rewarding in what we allow ourselves to be open to seeing as it unfolds.

## December 22, 1986

I have just dropped my friend off at the airport. She is going home for Christmas, and will not be back until December 30. I am feeling nothing as the car is moving further away from the terminal parking lot. I am complete within all that has unfolded. Everything feels right.

It has been quite a dance that she and I have been doing since she first arrived. We have certainly journeyed to many far away places within ourselves. The love that we have both opened ourselves up to is nothing I have ever experienced before. It is really nothing that can be fully described by words, but can be felt in all that we do. We have been creating a harmonious relationship ever since we connected that first night when she arrived to stay. We have been virtually inseparable and have not had one moment of disharmony in all that time.

We have both come to see that what we have created between us is no illusion. We see that it is by the purity of our intention that we are being guided within our creatively unfolding relationship. We have both come to see that we do not need the other person to make each of us who we are. We both see that we need each other to support each of us in being all that we are within our creatively expressive worlds. Our love for each other is not based on what we get from each other. It is based entirely on what we can give each other. And it does not come from conscious doing. It comes from allowing the other person to be and do what they truly desire to be and do, with no pictures of what each of us would like the other to be or do.

We are choosing, within our creative movements, to see every moment as an opportunity to move lovingly, and to be more giving to ourselves and to each other. We are not looking to build anything between us. We are continually looking to destroy those things that are keeping us from being all that we can be within our relationship. We are finding that if we are continually aware that we don't have a traditional relationship based on expectations, then we will always find a creative purpose creating an evolving relationship that only lasts as long as it is unfolding.

We both realize that the ways we have moved within our previous relationships didn't work to our advantage. Now we are creating new relationships all the time within ourselves and with each other. We maintain a constant dialogue of support and nurturing, always encouraging the creative element to be the first and foremost direction of our movement together and apart.

I am looking forward to going back and working on my book. It feels like the appropriate activity for me to be doing at this time. It has been a while since I have done that. There have been too many other things happening within the creative textures of my relationships with my friend and my housemate. We have all been learning a tremendous amount about ourselves and each other since my friend moved in. It seems to be a continuous process of evolutionary unfolding, these things called relationships – interpersonal relationships, that is.

## December 28, 1986

My long time hiking friend and I are on our way out to Sombrio Beach for an afternoon of rest and relaxation, away from the Christmas pressures that have been captivating everyone for the past few weeks. We are driving on the West Coast Road, listening to some New Age music and discussing the newest travels each of us has been taking within our inner journeys. I am not feeling as though I want to talk much. I just want to be in the company of a fellow seeker, and let whatever arrives within my inner channels to freely come and go without being attached to any of it.

We stop and watch the surfers maneuvering the five-foot breakers at Jordan River. I feel as though what they are doing is very much like what I have been doing throughout my inner journey – riding the waves of creative expression, hoping to find that big wave: the one that will give me the ultimate ride – the internal ride to the central core of my living expression.

I have been feeling that there is still more for me to do within my inner search. I know that I have been opening myself more within my relationship with my lady friend, but somehow that doesn't seem to be enough. There is still a piece that I am not seeing within my internal movements. I am focusing all of my attention on finding out what that piece might be. I am hoping that today's outing will provide me with a clue, so I wait patiently to see what will unfold before and within me.

My friend and I have been walking along the beach for well over an hour. As I round the bend, I see the sandy beach that my lady friend and I had visited some time ago – the place where I had first started looking into my relationships with women. As I jump down from the rocks onto the sandy shore, I hear a discussion going on between three dogs. As I continue to walk along, I see them come out from behind a cabin a few hundred feet away. They are running toward me. I sense that they are friendly. As we interact and play for a few minutes, they begin to tire. I am the one who is directing the flow of our movement, and they are not too thrilled about that.

As my hiking friend comes around the bend and jumps down onto the sandy surface, the dogs run after him. He is busy fending them off. There is no way he is choosing to engage them in a creative interaction, so they run away.

He and I engage in some Tai Chi-like movements, as he is a part time practitioner of Tai Chi. We often spend a few minutes each time we are out in the natural elements playing and sharing who we are with each other, always looking to enhance the harmony and sensitivities we are both developing.

I ask him if he would like to see a magical waterfall. When he agrees, I lead the way. We follow the stony creek bed for about one hundred yards, eventually coming to a narrow channel, roughly sixteen feet wide, with side banks that rise up twenty feet and gradually slope upwards as we travel deeper. It appears that Mother Earth had, some time back, creatively split and parted this opening of sandstone that we are walking through. As we travel further up the creek, the sidewalls eventually rise to forty feet at the end where the waterfall is located, nestled between two walls that are about six feet apart. I proceed to move as close to the far end as I am able. I cannot quite reach the level where the waterfall is. It is up about ten feet from where I am standing. In order to get there, I will have to climb. If I do that, I will surely get soaking wet, so I am content to just observe it from where I am.

I close my outer eyes and retreat inwardly. I am feeling the power that lies within the creative forces of the water that is falling from the top of this narrow thirty foot high waterfall. The gentle breeze created by the falling water sprays a light mist over my exposed face, neck and forearms, sending intermittent currents of electricity up and down my spine.

There is a strong feeling beginning to stir within me. I am not at all sure what it is about. I am feeling restless within my own internal and external movements. I have been looking so intensely at finding the missing piece to my inner puzzle that I feel like I have overloaded my thought centres.

I walk up to one of the steep sidewalls and lightly press both palms onto the textured surface of Mother Earth. I proceed to ask from within my inner channels, "What can you tell me, Mother? What is it I am missing within my living expression?"

I do not have to wait long before a reply comes forth. As my external words are finishing, I can hear the words being formed and expressed within my inner channels: "At this time, it is appropriate for you to retreat to the greatest depths of your being and seek out the path of the fearless warrior. It is now time for you to experience either the reality or the illusion of physical death. You have done everything there is for you to do within your inner channels. You are now ready to move within your outer world expression with the knowingness you have connected with within your being. By going through this experience, you will be consciously moving toward it by your own conscious movement of thought. It is the only way to totally free yourself to the level that you have expressed you want. Know that you are well protected within all of your movements. It is now time for your ultimate test, and you are clearly ready to meet it. A warrior's path is to stalk death to see what the functional reality of death is."

I open my eyes. I am feeling an energizing movement pulsating through my entire being. I know that what I have been listening to is truth. I know that I must go to that place and find out once and for all what death actually is. I feel that I am definitely ready for whatever will come. This is the missing piece to my living expression. Until I go and experience what is at the other end of life, I won't actually know what is real and what is an illusion. I am a warrior in all that I do. If I have to physically die in order to find my ultimate truth, so be it. I am prepared to do so.

As we walk down the narrow channel to the beach area, heading back to the place where the car is parked, I can't help but think more about what I heard back at the waterfall. I decide I am going to ask my brother, Fir tree, for any insights he might have. I walk up to one that is nearly four hundred years old. I stretch my arms around him, giving him a loving hug, and ask, "Tell me, my Brother, what do you see I should do at this time?"

As I slow my breathing and relax my body into the knobby outer layer of the tree, a calm and clear voice from within begins to speak: "That which has been spoken by Mother is the appropriate action for you to take at this time in your living expression. Fear not that which you do not know. All is as it is in the natural way. Remember that the central core is the place of creative energy. To go there ensures eternal life. Your journey is about that, my brother. It is your movement toward your own eternal light. In order to get there, you must go through all the darkened areas of your total living expression. If you succeed in doing this, all that you have been seeking shall be yours within your conscious movements on the earthly plane. It is indeed an opportunity for you to attain everything that is. Know that you are in tune with the infinite, all-loving energy within you, and that you shall succeed in your inner journey. Fear not, for you are truly a fearless warrior, and because you are not afraid of death, you shall not die. You shall live forever in the creative flow of the all-encompassing God-light."

I pause for a moment, and then respond, "Your words are well spoken, my Brother. I hear them, and I will move with them within my inner and outer world movements."

I disconnect myself and carry on my way. As I am walking along, I have a knowing sense that it is all supposed to happen this way. Words cannot describe the feeling. I now know what I must do. I know like I have never known before. My focus and intensity is like a penetrating laser-beam.

As we are sitting in the car outside my house, I mention to my hiking friend that I am going back in, into the central depths of my being. I have one last thing I must do. I mention that I am going in to find my ultimate truth. I do not tell him that I am going after death. I tell him that I am going to abstain from food and water for as long as necessary in order to find out what I need to know. I also mention that I have done everything there is to do on this plane, and that I have seen it all. I know how everything is put together here, and yet I am still restless. I tell him that I need to go and see what else there is here on this plane. I also mention that there is only one thing left for me to do. I tell him that I am going to change the world. He thinks that I am talking about my own world, but I reassure him that I am referring to the whole world.

Before I get out of the car, I mention that I am going to be out of action until the 15th of January, 1987, and that I will not be answering the phone or talking to anyone outside of the people in my living space. I tell him that I love him, give him a hug and a kiss on the cheek, and then open the door. He tells me that he loves me, and that his prayers will be with me, as they always are. I smile at him one last time and tell him to take care. I then proceed to walk toward the front door of my home, to begin the next stage of the journey to the inner circle, and beyond.

# CHAPTER 11

# DEATH, TRANSFORMATION,
# BACK TO THE BEGINNING: GOD REALIZED

## *January 7, 1987*

I have been sitting here on the cushions for the past three hours, feeling as though my living expression on this plane of existence is quickly coming to an end. My physical body is becoming progressively weaker with each moment that passes by. My mouth is very dry. The saliva that is in it is of a thick consistency, making it difficult to swallow. My heartbeat is becoming weaker. My breathing pattern is changing. Each inhalation of my breath is becoming shorter and shallower. It will only be a matter of an hour or so before it is all officially over. I am taking myself to experience the reality of physical death. I have been a warrior in all that I have done along my life journey. This is to be my final test. It is a test to see if all that I have been learning within the natural elements is real.

If all of what I have been opening myself up to within me is real, I will be able to physically die and then be reborn once again into my present physical embodiment – only this time I will be totally new in my earthly expression. If, on the other hand, all of what I have been learning is an illusion, I won't have to worry about anything any longer, especially matters pertaining to the earthly plane.

It has now been seven and a half days since I have taken any food or liquid into my body. I have not touched a drop of water either. I am choosing to do this at this time, for it appears that this is all there is left for me to do. I have done and seen everything there is to do and see on this earthly plane within my inner channels. This last experience will either connect me completely to all that is on the physical plane – the reality of the one – or it will connect me with all that is beyond the physical plane. Either way I will find out for sure what is real.

My journey to find my truth has been an enlightening one so far. I need to know the extent of all the realities that are possible on this plane of existence – the outer physical plane. I want the purity, and that is what I am going for. I have never been one for philosophical concepts of reality. I have been a realist in all that I have ever done, and this journey is to be no exception. I am consciously aware that I am now going to have to physically die in order to find the purest expression of my truth. I have known for a long time now that it all might come down to this, and I am prepared as I have never been prepared before.

I have been stalking death for close to five years now, and I have never been affected by what it supposedly stands for. To me, it is an illusion. The more I have gone after it, the further away it appeared to move from me. I see death as a coward. It is fearful of me. I am not fearful of it. I never have been, and I never will be. This time I am stalking death with focused intensity within all of my inner and outer world movements.

I am observing closely everything that is coming to my inner visual screen of mental thought. I am consciously retreating into the central core of my being, pulling back from everything. I am as ready as I will ever be. I welcome the illusion of death to come to me. I am moving toward it and showing it that I am not afraid of what it seemingly stands for. I have experienced expressions of death many times before. This is to be no different. I know that I shall once again show death that it has no reality within my living expression. I am a warrior who thrives on the very essence of death. I purposely feed off all that it stands for. I am consciously going after what almost all people here on this plane fear. I fear nothing, for I am nothing. Through this unfolding movement that I am creating, I will become everything either within this physical embodiment or outside this physical embodiment. A warrior always chooses his time to die. I am choosing now....

I have been steadily working on my book for the past three months – June, July, and August, 1986. The days have been long, twelve to fourteen hours in front of a typewriter. That has been quite an experience in itself. I have been teaching myself how to type as I have been moving along. I am feeling excited about writing my personal account of my own living expression over the past four and a half years. I am not writing this for anyone else but me. I am finding it an extremely valuable tool. It has enabled me to go back into those living experiences I have already had and see them from slightly different angles. I am using this entire unfolding experience to open me up to more of that which I already know.

I have been totally supported by my outside world within my current movement. My housemate has been very supportive and nurturing all through my inner journey. She has been a great gift that I have given myself in this lifetime in order to become all that I am – the functional creative essence of white light. Without her unconditional love, I would never have gotten as far as I am right now.

I can't help but think that I am still missing a few pieces to my own wholeness puzzle. I am not at all clear, at this time, as to what these pieces might be. I am finding, though, that each time I go back into the content of my past experiences, I become more aware that I am slowly getting closer to solving the whole mystery that exists within my self. I know that through doing this experience of writing the book, I will uncover all that I need in order that I can fully realize my ultimate truth.

I know that I will eventually succeed in my endeavor, for I have yet to come up short on any of my journeys. I need only be patient, and all that I need shall arrive when I am most able to utilize it. Patience is one thing I have learned well over the past four and a half years, and it is one tool that continually comes in handy. Whenever I am in doubt, I wait to see what will unfold within any given unfolding experience. I have found that if I wait long enough, it all generally takes care of itself. If I don't try to force things, things always work out. Regardless of how it turns out in the end, it always works out in my favor, for there is always something I can use from all the experiences I create, as long as I do not judge them or compare them to each other.

This book represents only a small portion of my living experiences. I have been spending countless hours looking at my life. As a result of my intensity in looking, I am uncovering all sorts of knowing gifts that are hidden within everyday experiences. By doing nothing, I have been successfully opening myself up to the mechanics of everything that exists on the earthly plane. It has all been so simple! In the inner world, one does not have to 'do' in order to receive. In the outer world of man one has to 'do' in order to receive. What one receives from doing in the outer world is the illusion of what this earthly plane is all about – the illusionary accumulation of power and control. What one receives from doing nothing within the inner world is the simplicity of how all living expressions express themselves on this plane, and how to get the most out of your life from creatively living here on this plane.

Life here is truly never the way that it seems. It is always the way that is. It is only the way that it is if I say that it is that way. If I am not absolutely sure, then it will always be the way that it seems. The way that it seems will always be determined by who I end up listening to. If I am always listening to the voices I hear outside my person, I will always live my life in the way that it seems. As long as I listen to the voices that exist and dialogue within my own personal living expression, I will always live my life in the way that it is.

How do I know this to be so? That is an easy question to answer. I am the one who determines how I will live from moment to moment. I know that my all-knowing sense of reality exists entirely within my inner world, and that it creatively and functionally expresses itself within my outer world. I also know that my all-thinking sense of illusion exists entirely within my outer world, and that it expresses itself abstractly within the competitive world of man. From within my inner world, I am able to move through my outer world, and the fragmented world of man, totally centred within the functional reality of all that I am. If I am always to live within the realities of my outer world illusions, I will never be able to enter into my own inner kingdom of free-flowing creativeness. I will always be limited in the way that I express myself outside myself. I am absolutely free within my inner movement. I will always be limited and restricted by my outer world expressions.

Sometimes, I feel that I want to be in the outer world doing something creative for myself and other people. I want to share what I have been learning with whoever would like to listen and search within himself to open more to the purity of who they are. I am always open to learning. There is always so much more to see and do here. I am finding that I am becoming restless in my inner and outer world movements. I wonder sometimes if maybe I haven't gone just a little too far in my inner search for truth. I wonder if, maybe, all those people who have been critical of my inner drive to find the purity, haven't been right all along. I question myself like this only when I want to dig even deeper into the simple mysteries that make up this plane of existence.

I know where I am going. I know what I am doing. I always have, and I always will. I am getting closer and closer to having it all. Soon everything will work itself out. Harmony shall prevail in my life, for that is how I am creating it. Everything in my life is moving to a constant state of flowing, ever-changing, ever-unfolding harmony. I am waiting patiently for the right moment to arrive, and when it finally does, I will be open and receptive to flowing with it and receiving all that there is. I know that I will soon arrive within the central core of who I am within my total functional living expression.

I know that my experience with my inner teacher (when I was in my room for fifty-two hours) is all there is on this plane. I still feel that it will not be totally complete until such time I am able to fully experience all of it within my outer world movements. I want and need that emotional bonding in order that I might receive the full impact of what it was all about. I have been opening myself up more with the information I have received from that experience. I know that there is still much more within that experience that I will be able to open myself to, once I journey to that place within myself, through myself, and in a conscious state of being.

When I sit quietly and ask my inner teachers for guidance, all I have been getting is this: "All that needs to be done at this point in your living expression is being done. Realize that all will come to you. Nurture yourself with that which is at hand. Look no further than the moment that is unfolding. Your gift of life will come through your ability to see all that is before you. All that is before you is not as you perceive it to be. Like your writings that keep changing in the inner expressions each time you read them, so too does everything you centre yourself with these days (in your outer world) change within its expression. But only if you allow yourself to fully experience the seemingly unimportant things. The greatest treasures for you at this time are the ones that are too simple. Turn your entire focus onto the simple expressions of life. Know that it is set up by you so that you might fully experience all of your inner teachings. You cannot speed the internal process up, for you are the internal process. All that you need at this time is before you. Quiet your thoughts about outside things, and open your inner eyes and you will be able to see it all so clearly."

I know that these words are all I need to hear. My internal questioning is always so that I won't become stagnant or lazy in my movements, and also so that I don't take what I am doing in my life for granted. A warrior never takes anything for granted. A warrior is sure of only one thing – that he is not afraid to die in order to fully realize his ultimate truth. I will continue to move along with my book, as I know that everything I will need in order to complete this next phase of my journey is within its contents. I know that I am divinely guided from within my being, and that my divine guidance will continually provide me with all that I need. I trust the all-knowing feelings that continually manifest within the depths of my being. I will continue to observe and to listen as I progressively move along.

## *December 30, 1986*

*This story begins one week earlier, and outlines the days prior to, during, and after the seven and a half day fast of food and liquids, that was my death and my rebirth.*

My lady friend has returned to Victoria and we meet at the airport. As we leave the airport on our way into Victoria, we decide that we are going to spend some quiet time together, looking at all the different things that have come up for each of us since we last spoke.

While we are in a restaurant talking, I mention that I am feeling as though I am going to go deeper into myself, deeper than I have ever been before; that I am consciously going after death. I mention that I do not know when my death-seeking journey will begin, but I do know that, at any given time now, I will stop talking, eating, and drinking fluids. I ask her if she will support me in my journey. I mention that I do not know how long it will take to complete the process. I only know that I will have to physically die in order to find out all that I need to know. She agrees to support me in whatever I choose to do, saying that she knew before she came back that I was going to be doing something like this, and that I was not going to be speaking to anyone.

We enter the house and are greeted by my housemate. The three of us sit on the cushions and talk about different things, and then I mention to my house-mate what I am choosing to do. I ask her if she will also support me in my jour-ney. She says that she will do whatever is necessary in order for me to complete my journey in the way that I want to create it.

Later in the evening, I mention that I would like to share my last meal with them. I know that my last inner journey will be starting soon. We proceed to go downtown to a restaurant. While we are there, I begin to feel that this will definitely be my last night out in the world of man. My journey will start some-time tomorrow. I proceed to explain everything I will need from each of them in order to complete my journey in the manner I want. I mention that it would be important for me to have a totally loving and supportive environment in order to move through all that will present itself. I mention that I will need silence, as much as possible, to minimize the distractions that could possibly interfere with my desire of focus and intention. I also mention that I do not want to talk to them about what is going on in their lives at this time. I tell them that I need each of them in order to complete this leg of my life journey. Without their support, it would not be possible. When everything is clear, we all leave the restaurant and go home.

My lady friend and I talk more after we arrive home. I tell her that I need her to love me, touch me, hold me and stay close to me. I know it will be through her that everything will be shown to me. I mention that I have gone as far as I can go on my own. I know that I cannot go any further in my life without a woman by my side. I mention that she is the woman I have chosen to complete this leg of my earthly journey with. I know that a man cannot make it here on this plane without a woman, and that a woman cannot make it here on this plane without a man. I know this, for it took the union between a man and woman in order for me to get here to this plane. Only through surrendering unto each other can they show each other how to live in the way of the creative Child.

I need her to guide me (by nurturing me) back into the expressional state of the Child. I am consciously reversing the flow of my living expression. I am going back into the womb. I am going back into the depths of her womb. She will be my mother and the provider of my life. I also say that I will not be talking to her except through sign language.

I tell her that I will not be able to reach out to her or touch her, for I am choosing to completely release myself from all wants and desires on this plane. If I am to reach out and touch her, it would show me that I am still attached to either her or to my life. I cannot afford to be attached to either. I will only succeed in my quest if I can completely detach myself from all of my illusionary hooks in the world of man. I tell her that I am going to find the purest state of self-less love I can, and that the only way to fully express the love is to totally leave this plane of reality and then come back again.

I also tell her that I am not at all sure of what I am doing. I am more or less feeling my way through it all. I only know that all the signs I have been receiving are showing me that this is the appropriate direction for me to be heading at this time. I know that it is so, because there is no resistance from anyone in my living space, as to what I am going to do. There is no resistance to anything, from anyone, anywhere. I am being guided entirely from a greater, inner source of knowing.

## December 31, 1986

I have been lying here for the past few hours, looking over all that has been happening within my living expression over the past week. I feel as though my last inner journey is close at hand. I am not at all sure when this process will officially begin. All I know is that I am feeling different within the wholeness of my being. I can feel things shifting within me on many different levels of awareness. I am waiting patiently for the right impulse to come – an impulse that will come from deep within my being. I know that I cannot push my way into this experience. If I do, then I will surely die and not come back.

I feel like I need to dialogue with the Plants in the living room. I get up, put on some warm clothes and walk out into the dimly lit room. I sit down in the centre of the three cushions, close my eyes, take two long, deep breaths and begin to align myself with the shifting frequencies the various Plants have. I am opening myself to dialoguing with whichever one or ones would like to. I ask a question and a dialogue unfolds, "Is it necessary for me to eat any food?"

"No."

"Is it necessary for me to drink any fluids?"

"No."

"Will anything happen to me if I don't eat or drink?"

"No"

"Is it appropriate for me to go after death at this time?"

"Yes."

"Will I be able to experience physical death?"

"Yes."

"Will I be able to come back to this plane again once I leave?"

"Yes."

"Is it really necessary that I die?"

"No."

"Will I be able to receive all that I seek without dying?"

"No."

"Do I need to go about all this in any special way?"

"No. There is no way to go about doing any of it."

"I know what I will do. I will go on a 'liver flush' for a couple of days to clean out my system and rid myself of all waste material."

"That will not be necessary."

"You mean I could start right now?"

"Yes. Now is the appropriate time to begin."

"It is not necessary that I wait?"

"No. There is no need for you to wait any longer. It is time for you to begin right now."

"If this is so, then my body will release itself from holding on to any unnecessary waste material. If this is to happen, then I will know for sure that all of what I have been hearing is so."

"Your physical body will indeed release itself shortly, and then you will know."

A couple of hours have now passed since my dialogue with the Plants, the release of waste material from my body, and the official beginning of my new journey toward death. The other two people in the house are beginning to move around, and I explain to them that I am on my way.

My journey toward death has given me a new outlook on life. I am seeing that there is no such thing as life. There is only death. Through my continual journey toward death, I am creating a new living expression each and every moment I am here.

## January 5, 1987

I am well into my fifth day without eating or drinking. My body is feeling weak and tired on the outside, but inside I am getting stronger. There has been a constant shifting of energies within my body, all of them supportive. There has been much happening within my world, as well as within the worlds of the other two people in this living space. It is a death journey for each of us in our own unique ways.

My friend and I have been getting closer as each day has come and gone. There is no illusion between us. We both know that I am going to die. We know that this is the only course of movement for me to take. As a result of our awareness, we are continuing to live totally within the unfolding moment. The past is of no concern to either of us. We are both very much aware that our time together is limited. She is very clear that I have to do what I am doing. She has not questioned it at all. She has to continually release herself from any possible attachment she might have to me. If she doesn't, then it might very well kill me and possibly her, as well.

We keep nurturing each other, and each of us unconditionally supports the other. I am seeing the importance of having another human being in my life to share all of my experiences with. It is not through the sharing of the experience that I will see what I see, but rather, it is what I will become aware of once the experience is over.

Both my friend and I have acknowledged that what we have is not a relationship. What we have is nothing. It is only what it is when it is in the process of unfolding – and that's it. We have not been trying to 'build' a relationship. If we say that we have a relationship, then we are saying we have a picture of what a relationship is. In our past relationships, we carried pictures around of what a relationship was, and they didn't work out. We both realize that there is no such thing as a relationship. We see that all there actually is, is creative movement between people. We can create anything we want between the two of us. We both see that we never have to get tired of each other, or of what we are doing, as long as we are willing to surrender all of our pictures of ourselves, of each other, and of the world. We are realizing that if we get rid of all of our stagnant beliefs, then we will always be free within an unfolding moment to be creative and spontaneous within our movements, individually or together.

Knowing that we do not have a relationship, we are both free to create a relationship with each other that is based on our experiences together. We both realize that it doesn't take a lot of work in order to have a loving and supportive relationship with another human being. (We had both heard that relationships have to be worked at. Because we believed that approach for a while, that was the way it was.) We both now see that it is really easy to have a supportive, creatively unfolding relationship with each other. We are finding that the key to having it all is in not wanting to have anything. Neither of us wants to put our personal security into something as nebulous as an illusionary relationship. On the contrary, we are focusing on ridding ourselves of all the insecurities that have been responsible for communication breakdowns in our past relationships with each other and with other men and women.

I know that what I am choosing to do in my life (at this time) has nothing to do with another human being. I am not doing what I am doing for my friend or because of her. I am doing what I am doing because I want to know more about myself. She is not allowing me to die because it is important to her. She is allowing me to die because it is important to me. She knows that I am doing it because I love myself enough, and because I need to know how much more I can love myself. If I love myself more, then I will love all those in my life more. She knows that she will only gain more of herself by allowing me to become more of myself. There is no guarantee that I am even going to come back to this plane once I leave. She knows the risk that I am taking, but she loves herself enough to allow me to do what I need to without feeling threatened.

It is strange how it all seems to work out sometimes. Here we are, each of us now having what we have always been looking for within ourselves and within a communicating relationship with another person, and we are willing to give it all up with no picture of what will come out of it. I know that we will have more because of what I am doing, although that is not the purpose behind doing it. It is just one of the fringe benefits that one gets when one goes after something else like death.

I never get tired of having my friend around. I am truly amazed at how many hours in a day we spend together, and we have not had a disagreement or confrontation of any kind. There has only been creativeness flowing between us. We know that there is no point in bitching or complaining at each other. We have both seen that those things are only indicative of power struggles – wanting control of the relationship or the movements of the other person – and they are usually centred on attaching security to something or someone outside of ourselves. It didn't work in our past relationships, so we are not even trying to make it work in our ever-unfolding, non-relationship.

My whole movement has been focused on me. I am the only person I look out for. I know that if I look out for me, then I will be able to be with every other human being equally. If I see through the illusions of security and insecurity, then I will be free to be totally secure within my insecurities. This way I will never have to depend on another person to make my world worth living in. I will continually create the world that I choose to live in and creatively express myself in. To give myself this freedom will assure that I will, in all ways, remain a Child in my approach to life on this plane of reality.

My friend has been taking care of me all along, not because she feels she has to for me, but because she wants to for her. She came to stay with me because she wanted to learn about unconditional love, and that is exactly what she has been learning. She has been seeing that the more she loves me, the more she opens up to within herself – to who she is and what she wants to do in her life. She has to love me unconditionally, for if she is to put a condition on what we have or don't have, it will create an emotional imbalance within her that will have a disastrous effect on the outcome of my journey. She knows that I need her in order to do what I am doing, and that she has the power within her movements to create pain and suffering within me and within herself. She knows that the only way that will happen is if she gets caught thinking about past relationships within herself and with other people that exist outside herself. As long as she stays right with me in the unfolding moment, she knows that all will work out for the best for each of us. We are both creating and learning, and learning about creating, as we journey along together, equally.

I see her as a part of me, not separate from me. She is me. I also see that I am her. As I hold this reality within my creatively unfolding living expression, there never seems to be anything worth worrying about, mainly because I know that I am creating a life of harmony for myself and all those I surround myself with. I see her as the outer, physically manifested side of me that is loving and nurturing. The more I get to identify with this side, the more I can readily love all the other sides of me in the same way. She has been a tremendous gift that I have created for myself. I know that what we share together can only grow into many other multi-dimensional aspects of creative expression, for both her and me. The more I surrender to this simple truth, the more I see within the limitless boundary of this truth.

Throughout this fasting period of time, my physical body has been going through some major changes. The outward appearance of my physical form has changed drastically from having no food or water. It is changing itself according to what I will need within my movements on the earthly plane when I come back after I die. The texture of my skin is smoother and softer. My outer eyes are clear and have been turning different colors: sometimes green, then gray-blue, then deep, deep, blue, like those of a newborn child. The size of my muscles is slowly shrinking, and my muscle strength is decreasing. I am not concerned, though, as I am no longer attached to what my physical body looks like. I know that my body knows all that is taking place, and that it also knows exactly which form will be most efficient for its next movement on the earthly plane. I am not wanting to control any of what is taking place. I am strictly an observer, patiently waiting to see and feel all of what will unfold within me.

My heart remains strong. My kidneys are still functioning efficiently. I have been releasing substantial amounts of urine up to four times a day, which is interesting, considering I haven't had any fluids for almost six days. I have tasted my urine each time to make sure I am not losing valuable electrolytes. I want to make sure that I am not just blindly following my inner communications.

I know that each moment is a new moment, and that a truth-seeking warrior takes nothing for granted. I know that I will only receive all there is within this experience if I continually stay awake and see each moment as an opportunity to discover more about myself. I am very much aware that the reality of death is actually nothing. The way that I get my nurturing food is by what I see while I am making my journey toward death.

My endocrine system is fully functional once again. My pineal and pituitary glands, within the deeper layers of my physical brain, are flowering. My pituitary has activated my thyroid gland, and it in turn is activating and stimulating my other glands to full capacity. Now that my organs are only functioning at a minimal capacity, my glandular system is able to initiate new growth and movement within the deeper levels of the cellular structure within my body. My brain has been going through drastic changes. The three separate entities of brain matter that make up the totality of my physical brain are now aligning and combining to form a new, totally integrated brain.

The energies that are constantly racing throughout my body are of a much higher frequency than I have ever felt previously. I am now able to feel the textural differences between the energies within my central core, and they will slowly begin to move outward as my body continues to move through its evolutionary growth processes. I am not sure what is going to happen from this movement. I do know that it will be something I have not fully experienced before within my conscious earthly movements.

My friend and I have been working together on my book since her return to Victoria. I have been doing the writing and editing, and she has been typing the manuscript. It has been a tremendous gift having her do this with me. She has been learning quite a lot about herself through this process. I have been keeping myself focused on one thing while I make this journey to my death – my life.

As I am reading the book and doing the necessary corrections, I am being provided with insight into what is happening within my unfolding process. It appears that I have already written about all that is happening right now. I am reading a dialogue that I have had with Raven, and also other aspects of my Higher Self, which has already explained fully the entire process. As I read them, I can feel the integration of all the information throughout my entire being. This has been a constant confirmation that it is indeed the right time for me to be making this journey.

My whole book is focused on death. My whole life now is focused on death. I am living entirely so that I can die. I am going after death within my living expression so I can spend the rest of my life creating things, without fear of losing anything. I will become death in all that I choose to do. When I die this time and come back, I will not be able to die again. I know this to be a truth, but I am not sure, at this point in my journey, how it all works. I know that before this is all over I will know how everything works.

My body is producing lots of rich and sweet saliva within my mouth. My body appears to be creating its own source of water at this time. I am also aware that my body is re-absorbing the waste material that lies within my intestinal tract. There isn't much, but what is there is reentering into my system and being turned into useful food materials. I know that my body is also taking my seminal fluid and using it as a food source as well. My body knows exactly what it is doing. I am learning a tremendous amount about my body by carefully observing the whole process. I am not concerned where it is taking me or what the outcome will be. I am content with just moving along within it.

I have surrendered completely. I have no want for my life. There is no questioning within my thought processes. I have relinquished all of my attachments to this plane of existence. I have been clear in my intention right from the beginning. I am not attached to anyone because I am not attached to myself. If I am not attached to my self, then it is impossible for me to be attached to anyone else. I am the creator of all those who are in my world.

*January 6, 1987*

*The Seventh Day*

It is now ten o'clock in the evening. I am aware that my movement toward death is quickly becoming a reality. Since yesterday, I have been slipping fast within my physical embodiment. Without having a will to live, and only seeking death, everything within the process has sped up. I now know that tomorrow is the day. I will be leaving this plane in the early hours of the morning. I am neither excited nor am I afraid. I am remaining centred in my focus, and that is all. To me, there is nothing else.

I have been snuggled up into the arms of my friend for about an hour. We have been talking mostly about past experiences within our relationship. I have mentioned that I do not know whether I will be coming back, or if I can come back. I am continually opening more within myself. I am feeling waves of movement within the central cortex of my physical brain. I am getting clear, inner knowing pictures of all mankind's journeys ever since time began and well beyond when time will end. They are not being presented in the form of words. They are in the form of expressive light textures that make up all the all-knowing thought patterns in the universal language. I am entering into that place where all the great Masters, who have walked the surface of Mother Earth, reside.

As I am observing all that is being presented, I am overwhelmed by the stupidity of man. I see all that he has done on this plane to himself and to all other forms of life, and none of it makes any sense. Life is so simple. So simple, in fact, that man cannot see it. Tears spill onto my cheeks. They are not tears for me, but rather, they are tears for the foolishness of man's behavior on this plane.

Man is too stuck on the illusionary reality of power and control. He is blind to the fact that there is more to living on this plane than what he knows. He believes that he is the most important aspect of reality on this plane of existence. He continually worships this god and that god. Yet, the pure and simple truth is – he has made power and control into gods within his movements. He worships power and control in every facet of his living expression. Yet he continually says that he is a god-fearing man. He creates gods whenever and wherever he chooses, as long as he gets what he wants. He will call anything a god, and then outwardly say that it is not a god. He is sure that there is only one god – many variations of the one – and that he doesn't live here. No one seems to know, with absolute sureness, where he lives, yet everyone says that he does live. Man creates foolishness outside himself so he never has to look at his own internal foolishness. Man is the fool!

I outwardly express more of what I am seeing to my two friends. I tell them one last time that I love them, that I always have, and that I always will. I know that this will be the last time I will ever see them. When I die and then come back, I know that I will not be the same person. They might think they see the same person, but I know that I will not be the same. I will be a totally new person – a new Child of the universe; a free Child of the universe. I turn to my friend, look deeply into her eyes and say, "I love you, my friend. I have always loved you, ever since the first day we met."

"I know you have. I have always loved you, as well."

"You know, I am not really sure that I'll be coming back."

"I know. I also know that you will be coming back."

"Yeah, I'll be back, because I want to taste the fresh mountain water from the waterfall out at Sombrio Beach. That's pretty funny, don't you think? I'm dying for a glass of water. Seems kind of silly, doesn't it?"

"There are worse things you could be dying for, you know."

We both laugh at the absurdity of what we are talking about. It doesn't really matter what happens, for nothing will ever look the same in my outer world again once this is over. We are both still very much centred within ourselves, giving total freedom for the creative movement to unfold. My friend has been trusting that I know what I am doing. I have been trusting that the voice inside me knows what I need to be doing.

I tell my friend, "Tomorrow is the day. I know that I will have a choice as to whether I will come back to this plane."

"Why wouldn't you want to come back?"

"I don't know. I will have to leave first. Once I do, then I will be able to tell you. Can you wait for an answer?"

"I think so. Are you going to come back and tell me?"

"Of course. I'm coming back because I'm going to change the world. You haven't forgotten, have you?"

We both laugh and embrace each other in a nurturing hug. We both know that the time is quickly approaching, and that the truth is close at hand. We are both going to learn from this experience more than we could have learned living a whole lifetime together.

*January 7, 1987*

*Wednesday, early morning*

… I am patiently waiting for my moment of truth to arrive. I have been lying on my back on the cushions in the middle of our living room for well over an hour. I have been internally dialoguing with the Plants about things that have been unfolding within the deeper levels of my being. I have been opening myself to the all-knowing aspects of myself, and seeing more of what this earthly plane is all about. It is truly a simple plane of reality to move through. I clearly see that all of it is only a three-dimensional holographic illusion.

Nothing here is ever worth getting upset over unless I choose to put some importance onto any one expression of reality. As long as I remain unattached to everything, I will be able to utilize everything that is here. When I solely identify with something that is supposedly here, I become trapped by that thought, and it ends up controlling and shaping my internal and external worlds. I have a sense that death is much like this observation. I see that death is, in reality, an illusion that my beliefs have created to be real. I am going to find out for sure very shortly.

It is now nine o'clock in the morning. My friend and housemate have come into the living room. It is important that they witness what is about to take place – if indeed anything does. My housemate is sitting on the cushions against the wall. My friend kneels by my side. I motion to her to come to the end of the cushions where my head is. I want her to put her hands on my head so she can feel all that will be taking place within me.

I am growing weaker by the minute. My arms and legs are so weak that I am not able to move them. My mouth has dried up almost completely. I am having great difficulty swallowing. My heartbeat and blood pressure are steadily growing weaker. My breath is getting much shorter and shallower. I can feel myself beginning to slip from this plane of existence. I am beginning to lose touch with my physical body. I am floating in and out of physical consciousness. The time periods in between these two states of being seem to go on forever, each one being a lifetime in itself.

I am now free-flowing deep within my own inner channels. I am moving within the inner dimensions of my being. I am doing this in a totally conscious manner. It is very different from anything I have ever witnessed before through my inner channels. I see the illusions of all that is supposed to exist here on this plane. I also see the realities of all that exists here on this plane. I am moving deeper and deeper within the central core of my being, moving inwardly to the most central point. There is nothing but darkness. Yet within this darkness, there is light.

I arrive at the innermost threshold that separates my total reality here on this plane and all the other realities that simultaneously exist on this plane. I am standing on one side of the forever opening and closing portal. During one element of time, I am on one side. During another element of time, I am on the other. I am not at all sure what is happening. When I go to move through the portal, it closes. When I remain still, the portal opens again. Whenever I make a move, so does the portal. When the portal is open, I see everything. When it is closed, I see nothing.

When the portal is open, the movement of creative energies goes on and on. There is no end. There is no beginning. They are both the same. It is continually expressing itself in an infinite number of ways. There is no form or structure to its movement. It is all *what* it is, and only *when* it is. When the portal is closed, there is no expression. There is only solidification of form and structure. There are no creative energies moving and interacting. It all doesn't make very much sense to me. I need to explore it from a different angle.

I ascend through the greater depths of my being, back to the state of consciousness that is typical of this earthly plane. I open myself to entering into a dialogue with my friend. I make the statement, "The portal keeps opening and closing. Every time I make a move to go through it, it disappears. Why?"

"There is still a piece of the puzzle you are not getting."

"What is that?"

"I can't say."

I know that what I am asking her is of no importance. What I hear behind the words from our dialogue is the necessary key to this unfolding experience. I know that it is a simple solution I am looking for. All the information that I have been receiving since I first began this death-seeking journey, has been very simple. I must release myself from wanting to know. The more I want to know, the further away it seems to be – the key, that is.

I am looking at my friend's reply 'I can't say'. What does that mean to me? What I put out isn't important. What I hear back is important. What does it all mean? 'I can't say. I can't say.' Say what? Words. Words. That's it. That's it! It's all got to do with words. There are no words to describe what I see. I cannot describe what I see with words. Words limit all things, yet words create all things. There are no words that will fully describe the process that is currently unfolding within me. To put words to it means that I am separating myself from the unfolding process. Whenever I search for words to describe the process, it changes within its expressional manner. Whenever I seek to have a thought regarding the movement of the portal, the creative portal closes and I cannot get through. When there are no words, the creative portal is free to move within its own creative formless form.

I am always on the very edge of the forever-shifting threshold of the portal of life and death. It is a highly sensitive, delicate fabric that can never be moved through. It can only be moved within. I am that transparent sensitive fabric. I am the forever-shifting portal. I am the ever-unfolding doorway. I've got it. I am it – I am it! I know that this is so. Now I must go and see for myself, through my living conscious experience – but without thought. How do I get there without thought? I am already there. I do not need thought if I am already there. I must totally surrender my illusional reality that I am not there.

I am once again moving within the central core of my being – the place of all-knowing. Once again I am on the threshold of the forever opening and closing portal. I surrender myself within myself. I am now within the ever-unfolding delicate fabric. I am totally free within myself, so free that I am no longer in my physical embodiment. I am my physical embodiment, but I am not in my physical embodiment. I am now floating freely within every form and formless expression of life on the earthly plane, and within all the other planes that have ever existed, that exist now, and that will exist in the days ahead.

This place is nothing the way man has described it to be through his religious dogmas. There are no angels. There is no God *per se*. There is a God Consciousness, but there is definitely no God entity. The pure and simple truth is: We are all gods, for we are all of this God Consciousness. There is no devil. There are no spirit forms. There are no forms here, yet there are all forms here, but they are totally without form. There are the knowing formless that create the forms for those in form to see. It is all so simple.

There are so many other planes of reality that I am now free to go to. There is no point to going there, though, not as long as I know that man is living totally in the dark on the earthly plane. I know that I must go back to open man's eyes to what is really on the physical plane called Earth, and to show man how to ascend to the higher places within the God Consciousness that he is.

In no time, I am back within the greater depths of my earthly physical embodiment, heading toward the outer expression of my being. As I am fully reinstating myself, I feel the vibrations of a higher frequency energy being generated throughout my entire being. I have brought back with me, into this old earthly form, a new and vibrant life. I am the light of the Creative Principle – I am God. I have successfully created a new expression of life.

I now know what the sentence, 'in order to enter the kingdom of heaven, one must die and be reborn and live through the eyes of a Child,' possibly means. The kingdom of heaven is within. It has nothing to do with somewhere outside the physical embodiment.

I open my outer eyes, look directly into my friend's eyes and ask, "Why can't I go through the portal?"

"There is no portal?"

"That's right! I am the portal. I was there. I saw it all."

Not really understanding my words, she just nods her head and smiles.

An incredible surge of energy is pulsating throughout my entire beingness. I am becoming alive within my new awarenesses. There is no such thing as death. All things are forever in a constant state of movement and transformation. Life and death are only illusionary concepts of reality that my belief system has made into a functional reality.

There is no such thing as death. It is all just an illusion. There is only death if I choose there to be death. There is no life, either, unless I create it to be here. There is only the creatively unfolding moment, and that is all, for it is only within that moment that one can truly see everything that is. That is the only true reality that exists. Everything else is an illusion. I feel so alive, and that is only because I am dead. I can never die again, for I have never really lived.

My friend tells me that she is glad that I came back, and that she loves me. I tell her that I love her. I also tell her that I have a date with Mother out at Sombrio Beach – a two-hour drive from Victoria. I need a drink of water, and the only water I will touch is from that waterfall. I ask my housemate if I can borrow her car to make the journey. I bound up off of the cushions and put my clothes on. I hug each person and tell them how much I love them. I know that I wouldn't be where I am right now if it wasn't for each of them.

My friend and I have been driving for nearly ninety minutes. There hasn't been much talking along the way. There hasn't been a need for any. We have been feeling each other constantly – feeling the subtle changes that have been occurring in each of us as a result of my death experience. My physical body continues to get stronger. I can still feel the energies pulsating throughout my entire being. I am creating new patterns within my physical embodiment. The currents of energy are of a much higher frequency. My heartbeat has slowed down and is much stronger. I can feel the resonations coming from the contractions within each chamber bouncing off my internal chest wall.

As I am driving, everything looks so very different out there in the natural elements. It all looks so new. Although I have driven this road before, I am not recognizing it. I am not holding on to any picture of what it is once I move through it. I am seeing all of it through the fresh new eyes of a Child. I am excited about seeing this new world I have entered into. I know that this is only the beginning. I can take it anywhere I want it to go.

I recall that when my hiking buddy and I were at Sombrio Beach a while back, I couldn't get up to the waterfall because there was a ten-foot ledge. I know that it will still be that way. I also know that I will need help if I am going to climb up to where the waterfall is. I am going to need the assistance if I am going to complete my journey as I have planned. I retreat inwardly and ask for guidance from my all-knowing self. I ask myself, "What shall I do about creating something to aid me in getting up to the waterfall?"

As my words are finishing, I receive my own answer from myself, "It is not necessary to concern myself about this. All will be provided for me, for I am creating it to be this way. I am giving myself all that I will need in order to complete this journey."

We pull off the main road onto a rarely used sideroad that will dead end at the top of a bluff at the east end of Sombrio Beach. I get out of the car, carrying my kit bag that contains two one-gallon-sized and five quart-sized glass jars. I am going to bring some pure water home with me to drink. If I am going to consume water, I want to make sure it flows directly from Mother Earth. My friend says that she will carry the kit bag for a while, to allow me to see what kind of physical condition I am in.

The trail that leads to the beach is a good mile long, and the switchback terrain is fairly steep in places. It will be a test for me just to get down to the bottom. I have only one objective – to get to the waterfall to have a shower and a drink. There is nothing that is going to stop me from completing this journey. Death hasn't stopped me, so I know nothing will unless, of course, I create it to be otherwise.

As we start our descent down the steepest parts of the trail, I spot a small man-made ladder-like structure leaning up against the bank on my left. I know that this is for me. I know that this is the means that will allow me to make it up to the waterfall. As I walk closer to where it is, I mention to my friend that life has provided this for me so that I can make it up to the waterfall. We both look at each other and smile.

I sling the ladder over my shoulder and we move along on our way. My upper thigh muscles are still a little weak. They haven't been exercised in any way for nearly eight days. With each step down this steep trail, it feels as though my legs are going to give out. I know that is not real. I know that I have plenty of strength in them, and that they will service me in the way that I am choosing to create. I am right on the edge of being totally out of control and totally in control. Just when I think I am losing it all, I regain it all. I am the ever-shifting portal that separates all the infinite realities that can be manifested here on this plane of existence.

I am totally living within the unfolding moment. I am not even sensitive to the fact that I haven't eaten any food or taken in any fluids for seven and a half days. I feel that there is no need to remember any of what I have done in the moments gone by. I know that all that there is, is within the unfolding moment I am continually creating.

At one point, I bring back (by way of my memory banks) the possibility that I might die on the way down. My greatest fear is that I will not make it to the waterfall – that I will die just before I get there. When I look at it all, though, I begin to laugh at the silliness of having such an illusionary thought. I begin to laugh inside myself, knowing full well that it is impossible for me to die. I am death in all that I choose to do. And because I am, I will be able to do whatever I desire without fear. Realizing this once again gives me a burst of electrical stimulation within my physical embodiment. I can feel this energizing current moving steadily throughout all the dimensional levels within my beingness. I am consciously connecting with the current of life that is forever free-flowing within the movement of Mother Nature. I am very much alive and creating.

We emerge from the dense bush and trees onto the beach, and are officially greeted by the all-giving, unconditionally, ever-loving Sun. It is a sign to me that my own internal sun is now one with the Sun that creates and sustains all life on this Planet. I am now the living essence of my central core of creativity. I am now able to create new life for myself and for everyone I come into contact with. I will do this by unconditionally loving everyone on this Planet. I know that we are all brothers and sisters looking for the same things in life. We are all like lost children trying desperately to find our way back home again, to the place inside ourselves that gives us a knowing feeling as to what living here on this plane is all about.

We walk a short distance along the beach before we come to signs of the creek that will lead us to the waterfall. As we proceed to make our way up the creek bed, with its twenty-foot-high sloping to forty-foot-high walls on either side, I clearly see that I am (symbolically) returning this earthly body of mine – that I have been using for the first thirty-six years of my life – back into the depths of the uterus of Mother Nature.

I am moving toward surrendering all that I am not, to become all that I am – which lies behind all the illusions of what I have thought this plane to be about. My excitement is mounting. I know that my death-seeking journey is officially coming to a close, and that I will soon begin a new journey, in a whole new way.

I will be the way in all that I choose to do. I will be the life in all that I choose to create. I will be the truth in all that I am, regardless of what it might be.

The temperature of the outside air is a cool 36°F. There is a breeze running through the narrow channel we are moving through. There is a vibrant electrical current stirring in the surrounding air. The closer I get to the waterfall, the stronger it becomes. My body is beginning to be affected by the electrical stimulation coming from the light spray of water. I walk up to the furthest point – approximately two hundred yards from the beach – and lay the ladder against the uneven surface of the wall that leads to the upper ledge. This is the place where I will take my first drink and be cleansed by the soothing waters of Mother. I take my kit bag and lay it beside the ladder, and then we begin removing our clothes.

I lay the last of my things down on my wet windbreaker and begin to walk toward the ladder. My body is warm and alive. I am aware that the electrical stimulation I am feeling is not the same kind of electricity I have experienced previously. This is much different. I have no awareness of hot or cold, for I am both of these things. I am the ever-shifting portal once again. I am the creator of hot and of cold. If I do not think with patterns of words, then I will not be separate from any of that which is unfolding before me.

I slowly make my way up the ladder. I am now aware that the ladder is not quite long enough to allow me to get to the top of the ledge. I am going to have to balance myself on a water-sculptured section of rock in order to hoist myself to the higher level. I am not concerned about it, though. My focus is still on one objective – to take a drink and have a shower from the waterfall. I know that nothing will stop me, for I am the creator of this entire experience.

I gingerly reposition my body so my centre of balance is well ahead of my present position. I take a short breath, and at the same time, push off with my supporting foot and lean my whole body weight forward. I have made it. I have successfully arrived inside the womb of Mother. I look down the full length of the narrow channel with its forty-foot-high walls that create this place of being. I turn and look straight up forty feet along the continuously wavering sheet of water as it falls freely from the upper levels of its creative path.

I acknowledge to myself and to Mother that I have returned home, and express verbally, "Mother, I have made this journey so that I might once again be born within my own being. I have come here to the depths within you to ask that I be granted the opportunity of being reborn through the purest channel I know. I am but a humble servant of that which is much greater than I. I only wish to become a pure vessel through which the Creative Principle may flow through freely and creatively. I ask that I be granted a new physical life so that I might be of pure self-less service to all mankind."

Upon finishing these words, I lean over and scoop up a palmfull of water. I bring it into my mouth and swallow. Instantly, I can feel the electrifying effect it is having on me. I know that I have been accepted within the life-giving creativeness of Mother.

I walk under the falling water and stand motionless. I am feeling only the oneness with all that is taking place within and around me. I am once again at the *centre* of it all. It has a much different texture this time, but it has the same sense of knowing. I begin to laugh outwardly. I see the depth of humour that there is in everything. I am everything. I am the humour. Without me, there is nothing. With me, there is nothing. It is all so simple. I am now seeing more of all that I had seen when I left this plane of reality through the process of physical death.

I turn around, look at my friend, and exclaim, "I've made it! I've made it! I am being reborn again. Come up here and be with me. Let us be (symbolically) reborn together. Come and be with yourself, with me. This is a time for life and a time for death. Come and die with me again so we can be reborn together, separately."

She makes it to the top of the ladder and can come no further on her own. She is not tall enough to use the same handholds as I did. I walk over to where I can reach out and give her my hand. As I reach out to her, I say, "Let me help you. Take my hand and let me guide you."

She looks at my hand and reaches out. She firmly takes it and allows me to pull her up to the higher place. We stand together before the rushing water, looking deeply into each other's eyes. We have both made our own individual journeys, but we have made them together. I look deep within her and say, "I love you, my friend. I need you to be my friend."

She replies, "I love you. I need you to be my friend."

I take her by the hand and walk under the falling water. We stand here and embrace in a warm and supportively loving hug. Nothing else seems to matter. The two of us have become one in essence and in form. We shall always be together, regardless of what might happen in our individual life journeys. We step out of the rushing water and cry out with excitement. We are like two little children playing under a water sprinkler in the middle of summer. We both feel the electrical creativeness that is ever-present through spontaneous movement. I step back under the water for one last supportive embrace by Mother. I am soaking up all the unconditional love that Mother is showering me with. Mother and I are one in the same. I love Mother. Mother loves me.

As my friend goes to make her way down, I have to guide her from where I am. She is not able to see anything below her. She has to rely on my guidance if she wants to make it down safely. She listens to my directions and finds the appropriate places to secure her footing. I have hold of her wrist to secure her while she is in transition onto the ladder. She has made it to the bottom and looks back up. She asks me how I am going to get down. I tell her that I will need her help. She will have to help guide my foot onto the top of the ladder.

As she begins to climb the ladder again, I slowly position myself in such a way that I am now ready to extend my left foot down toward her. She reaches out, takes the sole of my foot and applies sufficient resistance against it so I can slowly lower myself.

Within seconds, I am once again on stable and secure ground. All is well. We embrace each other and kiss. One journey has ended, and another one begins. Where it is going, we have no idea. We know that it will go wherever we want it to. We both know that we can create anything we want within our non-relationship.

As we are getting dressed and filling the water jugs, we begin to look at this experience in a whole new, life-supporting way. I tell my friend that I would never have been able to make it here today if it wasn't for her. I could never have done it alone. She replies that she wouldn't have been able to see all that she has seen along my death-seeking journey, if it wasn't for me. I then say, "I made it up to the waterfall and then turned and helped you when you most needed it. I can keep taking you to the higher places inside yourself. All you have to do is support me in going to those higher places within myself."

She replies, "You helped me to get up there and then to get down. Without your guidance, I would never have made it. I am also seeing that without my guidance, you would not have been able to get down off that ledge."

I tell her that I know I need her as much as she needs me. I explain that I don't mean I need her to make me who I am, but I need her to show me how I can become more of who I am. I will, in all ways, be open to having her guide me within an unfolding experience. She says that she needs me too, in the same way. We both begin to laugh, for we both know that it really doesn't matter. We both know that nothing matters any more. We both know that everything matters now.

When the water jugs are filled, we make our way along the creek, stopping once and a while to look back at the disappearing waterfall. As we come out of the creek bed and onto the open beach once again, I put my kit bag down on the sand, stand up straight and look open-eyed into the life-giving Sun. I am aligning with the nuclear power that generates from its very essence. I am feeling all that it is within me. I am it. It is me. My eyes are seeing and feeling the purity of its simple truth: give unconditionally, and you will, in all ways, create new life. I close my outer eyes so I can feel all that I have been taking in within my being. I am a self-generating powerhouse.

As I pick up my kit bag in my right hand, and put my left arm around my friend's shoulder, my outer eyes are drawn to a partially obscured image I see off to my right. As I turn my head, I see a very familiar occurrence within the interacting movements of the natural elements. I see a partially buried log in the sand near the shoreline. I cannot help but think of the day, several years ago on Mystic Beach, when I was forced to look at the log in the sand, and what happened to it when the water came in and moved it to another place. I also remember asking myself this simple question: "What will it take to develop that kind of peace and harmony within my worlds?"

As I continue to look, I see that I have indeed obtained that kind of harmonious relationship within my inner and outer worlds. I have once again returned to the place where it all began and where it all ends. I am also at the same place where it all ends and where it all begins. It has taken me five short years to return here. But what is time, anyway? There is no place to go.

As we climb back up the endless steep path toward the car, I feel my body responding to the new surge of life-giving nurturing I have created for myself. I am getting stronger with each step I take. My body is becoming more alive within its unfolding movements. I am gliding over the surface of the ground with my bare feet. It is stimulating and energizing.

I am now recalling the same feeling I used to have in my physical training days, back in the early seventies. I am seeing and feeling the same flow of energy within me that I had opened myself up to back then. It has been fourteen years, and I see that I really haven't gone anywhere either inside myself or outside. I can try and tell myself that I have, but I know that I haven't.

I am not holding on to any of the steps I have taken along this steep trail. I am seeing everything as being new. I am seeing everything through the innocent eyes of the Child. I am seeing that without memory, I am always free to be spontaneously creative in all that I do. As long as my intention is pure and focused on creating new life, I will always be supported by mankind. The key is to put mankind first, before everything.

Since I have died, I no longer live. I never have to be concerned about me, for I am not. I am now totally free to be self-less in all that I do from now until the day I consciously choose to leave this plane for good. When I leave, I will return to the same state of beingness I was in when I first arrived – and that I am in now: the purest essence of white light. Only this time I will be taking my whole conscious beingness and returning it into the all-encompassing essence and reality of the white creative energy – that which generates life within the central core of all things.

We arrive back at the car. I open the trunk and put the full water jugs in a secure position so they won't fall over and leak. I pull the car back onto the main road, heading toward Victoria.

As the car rounds a bend in the road, I hear the familiar voice of Raven calling on my inner channels. As I look upward and ahead of me, I see him clearly. He is waiting for me, and begins to fly on the same route we are taking. He is criss-crossing the road and as he continues to glide effortlessly, he presents his new-life supporting message:

"Welcome, my brother. You have indeed learned well all that you have been shown. It is because of your purity of intention that you have made it into the innermost creative reality within your living expression. You have seen the illusions within all the things that have form and structure, and you have also created the necessary realities so you could clearly see those illusions. You are now the master of illusion and master of reality. Use what you have attained within yourself wisely for the purest self-less expression within all of your movements on this earthly plane. All that you will create will aid man in ascending to those higher creative places inside his consciousness: The God Consciousness that he truly is, but does not realize he is.

"Realize, my brother, that the road you are commencing to create and travel on has never before been created on this plane. Although you may be clear within yourself as to what is, there are others who will strongly object to all that you choose to create. Know that this is one means that will enable you to open up more within yourself to all that you know. You will never come to a place where you will be at peace with what you see, for this plane is forever shifting and changing within the textures of reality. You can continually create new expressions of being, and as you do, there will be more expressions that are created off those that you create. It is a truly endless circle – one that is ever-unfolding and life-supporting. Only you can determine what you will ultimately create.

"Always stay attuned to the purity, and the world will be yours to create whatever you choose and desire. Remain focused on having no purpose for being here, and you will always create things that will have a humanitarian purpose. There is always more and more, my brother. There is never less. You are free within yourself to move in any direction you so choose. It truly doesn't matter what you do. Your movement will affect the entire world.

"It is now appropriate that you rest for a while before your outer world journey begins. There are still some matters that need attending to within your personal living expression from your last life. They need to be cleared away before you can fully attain that level of knowingness within your physical embodiment. The knowingness is yours within its entirety, consciously. Now the vehicle must be fully attuned to that all-encompassing frequency, to secure the ever-changing harmonious relationship that is needed in order for you to do what you will.

"There is still more for you to see along this road. It is now time for me to leave."

At this point, he takes a wide arc to the right and begins to fly back toward us. As he passes by, he turns and looks straight into my eyes. For the very first time since our initial introduction some years ago, I feel his loving, supportive beingness. As he is about to disappear out of sight, I hear him say, "Take care, my brother. Remember that I have always loved you, and that you are always loved by everyone, in all that you do. Love is the basis of all Life."

I am feeling my Brother as I have never felt him before. I know that his words have come from his heart. I know now who he truly is. I am feeling the very core essence of his living expression. I know all that he *is* within himself, and all that he *is not* outside himself. He has shown me his greatest gift throughout all the experiences I have had with him in the natural elements – pure unconditional love. I am now seeing that I am unconditional love. His gift is simple, as it always is. I am seeing more and more of nothing the further I journey along this road – my new earthly road.

As we continue to drive along the gravel road, I begin to feel the presence of another ally. It is the vibrational essence of Bald Eagle. I am feeling that he is near, and that he has come to offer his new-life supporting love. As we continue along the road, I catch a glimpse of him as he is flying over the tree tops just off to my left. I see him land on the very top of a tree.

I ask my friend if she saw him, and she says she did not. I want to look at him and see if I can talk with him for a few moments. I turn the car around and go back a couple hundred yards, then turn again to retrace my route, hoping to catch a glimpse of him once more. I pull over to the side of the road where I can get a good look. He is still sitting there, looking out over everything that lies within his domain.

As I stop the car and turn the motor off, I can hear him beginning to speak,

"Greetings, my brother. Today is truly your day, as is every day. I wish to acknowledge that you have attained the highest and purest level of expression that is attainable here on this plane of existence.

"You have consistently proven that you are worthy of such a place within your total beingness. Now that you have left all that there is on this plane, and have successfully returned to all that is not on this plane, this plane is now yours to do with whatever you so choose. I know that you are going to create only things that will uplift all mankind and show him a true and pure reflection of all that he is within himself.

"What you have done, my brother, no one else has done before on this plane. You are pure within your earthly movements, and that purity will enable you to create wondrous things for the entire world you are creating. It is now time for you to rest and allow yourself to become fully aware of all that you have done. It will take an element of time before your new earthly movement begins. Be patient, and know that that time will soon arrive.

"Sit high above the Earth so you can get a much closer look at all that is going on within its continually unfolding realities. The best way for you to attain this knowing is to be still and quiet and let all that you need come to you.

"Although we have only met a few times along your journey, my brother, I have been feeling you within the flowing current of all creative life expressions. You and I are, and always have been, one in the same ribbon of light."

I pause for a moment, honored by his words, and then reply, "Yes, my Brother. I have always felt your presence within my being. The few occasions we have met previously, I have always known that one day we would meet like this. I am one within you. You are one within me. We are both of the one. There is truly nothing else."

That is all that needs to be said, for it says it all. I know that his presence within my new life will always be inside me to continually use as a creative gift. It will give me the strength and the insight to always do nothing. It will be through the doing of nothing that I shall do everything in my new living expression here on this plane of existence called Earth.

*January 19, 1987*

## THE FINAL INTEGRATION CREATES ENLIGHTENMENT

I am lying in bed, letting my thoughts come and go without wanting to organize them into any particular order. I receive a strong inner feeling with regard to a newspaper clipping I saw early this morning. It concerned a young woman who was suspected of being abducted and assaulted while she was out jogging near her home. The area she went missing is near Mt. Doug Park in Saanich, a municipality of greater Victoria. I am feeling as though this young woman is not dead. I have a sense that she is still alive, and that she is lying in the bushes near the park. I am also sensing that she is just barely alive, continually moving in and out of consciousness.

My body is beginning to react to my inner feelings. My heartbeat is increasing and my breathing is beginning to speed up. My body's surface skin is beginning to sweat. I have an overpowering urge to go to this place and check it out to confirm my inner feelings one way or another. I ask my lady friend if she wants to go for a drive. She agrees. We get dressed and leave.

We are sitting in the car along the side of the road about two hundred yards from where I feel this young person might be. I ask my friend for the candle she has brought so I can make my way through the darkness of the surrounding bush. We get out of the car and proceed to move up the closed fire road that leads to the foot of the main mountain.

It is 12:30 a.m., Tuesday morning. I take a lighter out of my pocket and flick it three times before it finally creates a flame with which I can light the candle. I hold the candle in my right hand, and use my left hand as a shield in front of the flame to make sure the candle doesn't go out as I walk. Without the aid of the burning candle, I am not able to see a whole lot of anything, as the bush is fairly dense.

As I am moving, I am aware that the different areas I am travelling through have all been well travelled over by others, perhaps others who have come out here in search of the young woman earlier on. The candle has gone out twice since I arrived. I am clearly aware that without it, I am lost. My eyes are not able to discern anything in the darkness other than outlines of shapes and forms, but not distinct shapes or forms.

I am walking on paths that have been made by man, and through untravelled sections of bramble bush and Scottish broom, making my own trails as I move along. Part of me knows that there is nothing out here. I feel as though I am walking around looking for something that doesn't exist, except if I choose to believe what I have read in the local paper concerning this whole matter. I am out here looking at death and looking at life. In my earlier inner feeling, I saw this person moving in and out of consciousness between life and death, and that there was a very thin thread separating her two worlds. I now see that there might possibly be another purpose to my being out here at this time.

I am now aware that I am not out here to discover whether this woman is dead or alive. I am here to look deeper into the realities of whether I am half alive or half dead; whether I am moving in and out of the total consciousness I have been awakened to. This is just another journey into the depths of my being, looking for the answers to my two most frequently asked questions, "What is it all about here on this earthly plane? What is the purest truth I can find within this plane of reality?"

As I continue to walk, I begin to have a dialogue within the darkened depths of my inner sanctuary. There are two distinct voices conversing. One belongs to my earthly self, and the other to an aspect of my Higher, Spiritual Self.

My earthly self begins a dialogue, "Shall I go home?"

"No. Keep going, you are getting closer."

"Closer to what?"

"Keep moving, you will see."

"Is there someone out here to find?"

"There is no one else out here outside of yourself. Your friend who has come here with you remains isolated from you to allow you to move freely within your inner depths so that you might discover the gifts that this experience holds for you."

"I had better go and make sure that she is all right."

"That will not be necessary. She is very sensitive to all that is unfolding within you. She might not know it on a conscious level, but she knows."

"Is there any point to doing any more of this?"

"There is never any point to doing anything unless you decide there is."

"Yes, of course, I know that. But what I am referring to is this walking around out here in the darkness, looking for something that doesn't even exist in my world, except that I invited it into my reality by attaching myself to the emotional impact it had on me through reading about it in the illusionary newspaper. I don't have to do this any more. There is no point."

"That is so. There is no point. Now you are free to look at this whole experience through new eyes and discover the valuable gifts that lie at the very heart of it."

"And what might that be?"

"It is not for me to say. It is for you to open yourself to. If you do not look so fixedly at it, it will show itself in simple terms. Be open and receptive to all that will present itself to you. Through careful and diligent observation, you will see all that you need to see."

"Of course. That's it. To continue walking but observe how I am walking, and what is allowing me to walk through this ever-changing environment I am finding myself moving through."

"Be quiet and still within your movement, and you will clearly see. If you continue dialoguing, you will miss the sensitive gifts that are arriving shortly."

I am seeing that if I didn't have the flame from the candle, I wouldn't be able to move as freely or as surely along these paths or the makeshift paths I am creating. I see that my vision is limited by the amount of light coming from the flame. I am aware that I have to use my left hand as a shield, or reflecting mirror, so that I can throw more light on to the path ahead of me as I walk. When I take my left hand away from behind the flame, the light that is cast from the flame becomes more diffuse. As a result, I am unable to see very much ahead of me. It also affects my eyes, for the intensity of that diffused light dilates the pupils and partially blinds me for a few seconds. When I return my hand behind it as a shield between the flame and my eyes, I am able to see further and also more detail.

As I am moving, I am aware that I am the bearer of the light. I am the one who is controlling what I see as I journey along. I am the one who chooses to see the quality of what I am seeing. I am the one who creates a visual picture of all that I am seeing. I can either make my intensity of intention within seeing like that of a laser or a diffused light bulb. I have seen this in the way that I have been shielding myself from the brightness of the candle flame. If my intention is pure, I will always see what I need to at that particular point in my evolutionary growth. If my intention is not so pure, then I will get all caught up within an outside, third-party dialogue.

My earthly self continues, "This can't be all of it. There has to be more. What am I missing?"

"You are missing nothing, my friend. You are getting it all. Allow yourself to remain free from consciously activated thought, and all will come to you. Be patient."

"Is there any point to being out here any more?"

"No. It is now time to leave this area. All that you need, you have received. Allow time now for it to be clearly presented to you. Remain quiet and still within yourself. Keep your intention focused like that of a laser, but only on this experience at this time. Do not engage in idle conversation on your way home. If you do, then all will disappear into the depths of darkness from where it is now in the process of coming.

"Your friend will not interfere with the unfolding of this process," my inner voice continued, "for she knows all that is moving and the degree at which it is moving. Be sensitive to yourself and your quest to find your purest expression of truth. Know that the hour is finally at hand. All that you have been looking for (along your life journey) shall be presented to you shortly. Remain focused within the purity of that which you have asked for. Trust me not. Believe not that which you have experienced here this evening. Release yourself from all things within the processes of your thought, and everything shall be shown to you. Be absolutely quiet and still within all of your movements, or else you will lose all that you have spent so long looking for."

"Yes, I know," I reply. "It is my internal feeling that shall guide me to the place inside myself that will provide me with all the answers to the unlimited universes that exist within my own internal universe. I am that which I feel. At this moment, I am nothing. Nothing is real within my own internal dimensions of reality. I am the ultimate creator of all that is within my inner and outer dimensions. You are another part of me, a deeper aspect of me, but no different than this aspect of me. I am the creator that has brought you here. We are both one in the same. We are the same. There is no difference between you and I, is there?"

"There is no difference between you and I unless you or I determine there is. We are indeed one in the same; you and I, I and you."

"How is it that we can split like this and have a dialogue?"

"We are not split. That is the illusion. The reality is that you and I are one. Within the wholeness of the one, there are many separate divisions, each of which is still very much the whole. If you stand back far enough and take a good close look at it all, you will see that everything is part of the whole, yet it is also part of the separateness. We are all like that. All things are like that on this earthly plane. Look deeper into your experience this past hour, and you will see the plain and simple truth. Allow it all to come back into your visual screen now, but this time use your new awareness and all shall be felt within you. As you are able to feel, you will unlock the combination inside your internal essence and your all-knowingness shall stream forth within your entire beingness."

I am now recalling the whole experience over again. As it is returning, I am seeing it with different eyes. I am seeing the subtle, delicate gifts that are hidden within the textures that make up the structural fabric of the experience. I am seeing that the light provided by the candle may be symbolic of the light of creation. It allows me to create those things in my outer world that have been created from within my inner world. Many people on this plane might call this light the 'Christ vibration'.

I see that the darkness that surrounded the area I had been walking in is representative of the darkness within the void from which all expressions of life are brought forth. It holds within its delicate fabric the purest essence of the light. "If the light of the candle represents the light of the Christ vibration," asks my earthly self, "and the darkness represents the 'Creative Principle' that allows the light to be cast, who am I who is holding the light and walking forth within the covering of the darkness?"

"That is the question that will open up all the doorways leading into the all-encompassing chamber of your all-knowing self," replied my inner voice. "Keep looking. Look deeper at it and you will see."

"I am the bearer of the light and the keeper of the darkness. I am both, yet I am neither."

"Do not take it so lightly. If you do, you will lose it all forever. Go slowly, and with focused intension, and your way shall open within you."

"How far do I take it back?"

"How far can you take it back?"

"How far back? Back to right here. Back to you and I. Who are you?"

"Who are you?"

"I am nothing. Or I mean, I am no particular thing."

"Yes, but where did you come from?"

"I have always been. Who are you? And where did you come from?"

"I am nothing. Or I mean, I am no particular thing. I have always been."

"How is that so? How can we both be nothing? And how is it that both of us have always been. How is that possible? Unless—."

"That's right," said my inner voice. "Unless we are all that is, all that ever has been, and all that ever will be. We are, my friend, we are. We are pure reflections of the one. And the one is a pure reflection of each of us. We are divided, yet we are whole."

Every thing is just one. There is nothing except the aspect of the one. In totality, that is who I am. I am the oneness of all things. I see it. I mean, I really see it, like I have never seen it before. The key is to fully remove myself from the earthly plane of reality, to go beyond the stars that I know exist and move within the far-reaching galaxies of other dimensional pathways. That is where it all lies. The key to this earthly existence cannot be found on the surface of the Earth. I had to leave everything behind in order to fully and freely have everything that is here. It is all so simple. As long as I look at all things strictly from an earthly point of view, I will never be able to see the simplicity that exists within the divisional aspects of the whole of what this plane truly stands for.

Once a being comes to this plane of existence called Earth, they are subject to following the Laws that govern its form and structure. One must leave this plane entirely and re-enter back into it through the process called death, and when one does so freely within one's own movements, then one will see the gifts that are here. One will also see the simplicity of all that this plane stands for.

That is (possibly) what Jesus meant when he (supposedly) said that in order to enter into the kingdom of heaven, one must die and be born again. Only by being born again can one clearly see everything, without attachment to any of it; for that person would have to clearly release himself from all earthly attachments in order to die and then return within the same physical embodiment.

The Child's view of this world, and all the different galaxies that exist and that are created, is the only way one can truly see the simplicity of all that exists within and around the textured surfaces of the earthly plane.

"Yes, my friend," said my inner voice. "You are indeed looking in the clearest light. Can you still go deeper into it? Is this as far back as you can take it?"

"How much further can I possibly take it back?"

"How far would you like to take it back?"

"What does that mean?"

"Look at it seriously, and you will see."

"How far would I like to take it back? I am the Creative Principle. I can take it back and back and back. There is no end in sight. How can there be if I am the Creative Principle?"

"How do you know that you are the Creative Principle?"

"I know that I am."

"Who is the I who says that it knows?"

"The I is the Creative Principle."

"Who said that the I is the Creative Principle?"

"I did."

"Yes, but who is the I who is saying that the I is?"

"I am the Creative Principle."

"Yes, I hear you saying that. But who says that you are the Creative Principle?"

"I have already told you, I did."

"Yes, I know that, you have already told me. But who said that you are the Creative Principle?"

"If we are one, why are you arguing with me?"

"I am not arguing with you. I am only asking questions because I want to know the answer. It is only you who is choosing to see it as arguing."

"Well, if I am not the Creative Principle, who is?"

"Are you now saying that you are not the Creative Principle?"

"No, I am not. I am only repeating what you said. I know that I am the Creative Principle."

"If you know like you say you know, why are you doubting what you know?"

"I am not doubting what I know. I know what I know."

"What is it that you know? What is it that you are so sure of? Is it that you know, or is it that you are the Creative Principle?"

"It is both of those. Why are you trying to make this more difficult than it actually is?"

"It is not me, my friend, who wants to make it all more difficult. It is you who is causing the separation here."

"I do not see it as separation. I see that what I am saying is that I know that I am the Creative Principle, and you keep saying that I am not."

"No, that is not so. I have not said that you are not the Creative Principle. You did. I merely questioned the statement you made saying that you are the Creative Principle. Are you attached to being the Creative Principle?"

"No! I am not attached to anything. I am everything."

"If you are everything, then you are attached to that which you think everything represents. If this is so, then you cannot be the Creative Principle, for the Creative Principle is not attached to that which it creates."

"Look, I've told you, I am not attached to anything. And I am the Creative Principle."

"If you are not attached to anything, like you say you're not, then why are you becoming frustrated and upset within your movements?"

"I am not frustrated, and I am not upset. Look, why don't we just end this whole thing right here and pretend that it didn't even happen."

"No. This has to be fully addressed, and it has to be addressed right now while it is here. Now is the time for the final integration to take place. We are one, my friend. But within that one, we are separated. The unification process of connecting us to the essence of one vibration must be complete before you can enter into the deepest chamber within your beingness – the one that holds all the information to this universe and all the other universes within this universe. You cannot make it there without me. I am already there, and so are you. The difference, my friend, is that I know that I am, and you just think you are. You must surrender unconditionally unto yourself and unto me before your greatest hour shall arrive. Without me, you are truly nothing. And you will stay that way. But with me, you will be everything, just as you have said."

"How do I know that I can trust what you say is true?"

"I thought you told me that you knew everything? If you truly do know what you say you know, then you would not question any of it – and you surely wouldn't be wasting your time talking to me, now would you?"

"Well, no, I guess I wouldn't. What are you telling me I have to do?"

"I am not telling you to do anything. If you truly want what you say you want, then you must surrender all that you think you are unto the thought that makes you that which you think you are."

"I want to know how you want me to go about doing that."

"You know full well that which I have spoken of. I cannot interfere with any of that which you will do. I have never interfered in any of the things that you have chosen to do along your life journey. I am here to aid you in your quest to become whole within your earthly expression this time around. I am only a reflection of that which you represent on the earthly plane of reality. I am not the Creative Principle any more than you are. But we are both the Creative Principle. We will only be able to fully see that and realize that when our alignment is completed. And that, my friend, is entirely up to you. You will have to surrender, for it is you who has established an attachment to the earthly plane of illusionary realities."

"I want it all. I want all of me. I have come too far within myself. I will not give it all up, not now; not when I am right on the threshold of obtaining it all."

"That's just it, my friend. You will have to give it all up. You will have to leave it all behind. If you choose not to, then you cannot complete your alignment. Without alignment, you cannot be fully self-realized here on this plane of existence. It is entirely your choice. This is it. Take it or leave it. There is no other way around it."

"Okay, okay. I need time to think about it. Can you give me a minute?"

"This is not about time, my friend. This is about eternal life. How can you be focusing on time when we are talking about all time? You have a clear choice. It is all so simple. Why are you trying to think your way back into the world of complexity? You can either choose to let go within yourself and surrender all that you think, or you can hold on tight to all that you think you know and move along your earthly journey like everyone else, knowing that some day you are going to physically die.

"If you choose to surrender, then you will choose eternal life. In case you do not realize what that means, allow me to tell you. It means that you will not be able to physically die on this plane of existence. When your total movement is complete on this plane, you will ascend – within your full physical embodiment – into the heavens within, into the limitless inner depths of darkness, back to the beginning of all things. You will join the other great Masters who have walked on the earthly plane, and who now take residence in other loftier dimensions of self-less expression. Upon leaving in this way, you will never return to this form of expression again.

"Can you see that time is not an issue here? You decide what you truly want. Is it really your ultimate truth that you want? Or is it that you want the fragmented thought about what the ultimate truth is?"

"I want my ultimate truth, and I am willing to pay any price in order to have it. I am a fearless warrior. I am seeking the purity of myself and everything that exists on this plane of reality."

"If that is your truth, then release yourself so you may become your entire and complete self. Make the necessary move. It is the only way that you will become all of that which 'is' within your purest form of movement."

"I am surrendering my entire essence to the formless Creative Principle that has created me. I am choosing to become nothing in order that I may see the totality of that which is within the all-loving Creative Principle. To myself, I do hereby surrender. I surrender myself unto the all-encompassing 'i', and I relinquish all that I perceive to be me to the all-encompassing i. I surrender my essence to become all essences. I surrender, I surrender."

"That which has been ordained, has now officially been completed. I am one within all that is. And within all that is, i am one," replies my Higher Self.

Within this unification process, I have fully returned to the essence of all that is. i am floating within all the textured matrixes that make all the different realities within this plane and beyond. I am everything at the same time as i am nothing. I have no knowledge, yet i am all-knowing.

i am not my physical body. I have created my physical body the way that it is now, but i am not the body that I have created. i am not the food that I choose to put into my physical body. i am the creator of the food that I choose to put into my body, but i am not the food that I create. i am not the thoughts that I am in the process of putting to this paper. i am the creator of the thoughts that I am choosing to put to this paper, but i am not the words that I choose to create. i am not the light that shines within my outer world. i am the creator of the light that shines within my outer world, but i am not the light that I have created through the ever-loving Sun. i am not the darkness that holds the creative light. i am the creator of the darkness, but i am not the darkness that I have created.

i am not any of those things. All of those things have come to be through I, yet i am none of those things. All of those things, as well as everything else that exists here on this plane of existence, are the illusions that keep me and everyone else forever spinning, desperately searching for answers that don't even exist.

i am not death. I have created my own physical death, but i am not the death that I have created. i am not life. I have created my own new life, but i am not the new life that I have created. i am not the thoughts that have created either one of these two illusionary realities. i am that which creates the equal realities of the light and the dark, yet i am neither of these that I have created. I am that which creates all the infinitely different divisions and fragmentations within all the textures that this plane of existence has to offer. I am the nebulous creative element of life, but i am not life. I am that which brings into being all things, but i am not any of those things that I bring into being. I am that which creates all forms, but i am not any of the forms that I choose to create.

i am all that I am not. i am all that does not exist as yet. i am none of that which is. I am the Christ in knowing that i am that which is not yet in form. I am the anti-christ when I identify with any of that which has form. I am the Creative Principle of Life. i am not the creations of that which has created them, nor am i the creator, for they both have form. I am that which has created the world, but i am not the world. I am that which creates the universes, but i am not the universes that I have created. I am the GOD principle, but i am not GOD. i am the Creative Principle – I am GOD. I am the I am, but the I am is not the i. i... But i am not the I, i am. And what is, is not the am. What am i? Who is the 'I' who does all the speaking in the dialogues I have with people? Who is it? What is it?

I see it all so clearly now. It is all simple in its expression. I use it all the time. The i is nothing more and nothing less that an instantaneous expressive reality of thought. The i is thought. That's it! That's the ultimate truth that exists here on this plane, or any other plane. Thought determines what I will see within my entire journey on this plane of reality. All there is, is thought. The Creative Principle is thought. Thought brings into manifestation all things. Without thought, there is nothing. With thought, there is everything. Without thought, there is everything within the formless Creative Principle. With thought, there is nothing, for it solidifies the existence of form and structure. Thought is everything. Thought is nothing.

Life is a paradox of ever-changing dimensional pathways that simultaneously lead to nowhere and to everywhere. They will continually lead a person to those places that exist nowhere in particular, and to those places that lead to everywhere there is. One thing is for certain though: they will always return to the place from where they were created – from thought. The i is thought.

Thought is the I. Thoughts create, thoughts destroy. Paradoxically, thoughts that destroy in the same breath create something new. Thoughts that create something new in the same breath destroy something old. This is all done through the conceptual reality of thought. Thought is the Creative Principle. My whole existence on this plane is evaluated through the structure of my own thoughts. It is all so simple. My life is a continuous alignment of various thought patterns, based entirely on what I believe there is to do on this plane.

To live freely without premeditated thought patterns is to live within the totality of the Creative Principle. Thoughtlessness is the key to having nothing on this plane and to having everything on this plane.

I need to look at all this a little closer. Could this really be all there is to functionally living here on this plane? I know that this is a simple truth that I have uncovered, and one that we all know all too well here on this plane. I also know that there are many hidden depths within a simple truth. The more I look at this one, the more I will see what lies behind its seemingly innocent simplicity. I have continually observed, through many of my journeys, that the seemingly simple creative expressions (within the natural elements) are usually the most complicated within their structure and their form (electricity, wind). Those that appear to be really complicated are generally the most simple within their structure and their form (tree, Sun).

Behind all these things that exist, there is one common ingredient: they can only exist here if I say they exist here. In order for me to say that they exist here, I must use thought. In order for me to use thought, I must know what thought is. In order for me to know what thought is, I must be thought. I am thought. But thought is not me. Thought is the Creative i Principle. Thought is not the i. The i is not thought. Thought and i are one in the same, but they are not each other. The thought is given life through the i. And the i is given creative expression through thought. The i is given creative expression through the thought, but the thought is not the i.

The 'I' that is writing this to paper, is not the same 'I' who answers the telephone when it rings. The 'I' that answers the telephone each time is not always the same 'I'. It is a continually changing 'I' that moves freely within the earthly plane of illusionary reality. I believe that the I that I am by my birth name – Blaise – is always the same I. This is the grandest illusion that this plane has to offer, and one that keeps man chasing himself around in circles, trying to find answers to questions that have been posed by the many different 'I's'. The number of individual 'I's' that each person has is infinite. Once I consciously see this, I am free from ever judging myself again.

If the reality is that the universe is always unfolding (that it has been going on for millennia, and that it will go on for millennia), then it must also be a reality that the I will go on for millennia within my own evolutionary process.

The universe and I are one, for it is through the organization of the universal matter that I have come into being. Without that alignment outside my physical embodiment, I could not possibly be within my physical embodiment, writing these words to paper. I am a creation of the universal energies. I continually utilize the free-flowing creative universal energies while I am on this plane of existence, or any of the other planes of reality.

I am a continuum of movement while I am here. My physical body shows me this within each infinitesimal time sequence. My body is always in a constant state of movement. It cannot stop any of the processes that move within it. It can easily control the duration of each sequence of movement, but it cannot stop them. My body did not create itself from nothing. There is another force outside of and within the element of my physical body that is responsible for bringing it here and sustaining it.

Within my physical embodiment, I have all the universal information – as does every human being. How do I know that this is a fact? It is very simple, as all truth is.

> In the beginning, there is nothing. From nothing comes the movement of something. Something is a thought impulse created through the simplicity of movement. Movement circulates within and around thought. Thought is an amassment of collective energies that are forever unfolding and changing within their own arrangements and alignments. The swirling energies of creative thought created the structure and the form of the ever-unfolding, ever-changing universes that exist within all the inter-galactic movements.
>
> The ever-unfolding, ever-changing universe continually creates new and ever-changing-in-expression thought vibrations. These thought vibrations create all form and all structure within all life forms. All forms of living expressions (on this earthly plane of reality) are created through thought. All forms of living expression are actually just forms and structures of thought held in time sequences and space allotments, both proportional to the vibration of the thought that created them and that sustains them. When the thought pattern is acted upon or interacted

with by another thought vibration, the form or structure of that original thought pattern is altered and a new thought form or structure is created.

Every thought that exists within my being is continually being affected by all the other vibrational thought forms within this earthly dimension of reality. The thought forms that constitute my physical beingness are never constant in their creative process of unfolding. They are only constant if I choose to create a thought form vibration that holds them that way. This feat, in reality, is impossible. But because I create a thought form that supports it being possible, it is. The thought forms that make up all things on this earthly plane of reality, and all the other planes of reality, can create anything they want. The key is to keep the thought forms free within their own movement so that they are able to show, in entirety, the complete ever-unfolding universe. The ever-unfolding universe is only a continuum of thought moving through and within its own ever-creatively infolding matrix of colour vibrations.

There is nothing else for me to look for. I have arrived within the swirling central matrix of my ever-unfolding darkened void. I have arrived at the eternal resting place of the all-knowing thought of creation. I am that which I perceive. All that I perceive, I am. The I, the thought, the universe are all one. Everything is of the one. I am the central core of all life. It is through me that all things have been given life on this plane. It is through me that all things are what they are and are what they are not. I am within the totality of all things. All things are within the totality of who I am. I am the universe. I am the infinite number of 'I's' that make up my physical embodiment, that are ever-changing and ever-creating within their own creative vibrations.

I cannot control all that I am, for I am all that is. In order for me to control anything, I must be separate from that which I want to control. I cannot control the unfolding of the universe, and I cannot control the unfolding of my own being, for the universe and I are one. I am the thoughts that make all forms within this dimension of reality. I cannot control the unfolding of the universe, so I cannot control the ever-unfolding 'I' that makes up my person, or the ever-creating thought forms that make up my living expressions. I am forever changing within my own form, just as the universe is forever within a progressional movement of unfolding.

The I cannot control anything. The I is always trying to control everything. It does not realize that it is everything. It is constantly trying to gain control of everything – everything that it already controls – by using illusionary, static thought forms that are not static at all, but are always in a constant form of movement and unfolding.

The Creative Principle is thought. Thought has created the Creative Principle. In the beginning, there is quiet. From within the depths of the quiet comes movement. From movement comes thought, and thought is the movement. The movement unfolds from within its central core. Thought is the movement of quiet which creates the voice of all language. The language is the means by which the thought expresses itself. The language and the thought are one in the same. The thought and the movement are one in the same. The movement is one within itself and within the quiet. The quiet and the thought are one in the same. The 'I' and the thought are one in the same. The 'I' and the quiet are one in the same. The 'I', the Thought, the quiet, the movement, the universe, are all one. The 'I' that I am is all that is, within its simplistic movement.

What this means is that the 'I' that I think I am at any given time is, in reality, all the combined 'I's' that I will ever be, or that anyone else will be, within the textures of the ever-unfolding and ever-creating universe. If I release myself from identifying with any one 'I' within a particular time sequence, I will allow myself to enter into the free-flowing stream of all-knowing wisdom. To release myself completely from the earthly plane will ensure that I have full utilization of all the things that exist on this earthly plane.

The key is not for me to want to control the 'I' that is moving in the creative way at any given time. If I do, then I am saying that the 'I' that is moving is the Creative Principle. It is the Creative Principle, but only for that specific unfolding moment. And that's it! To be totally unattached to anything gives me full access to everything.

It is all so simple. I have arrived at the end and the beginning once more. Only this time I know that I am all that I am, without question and without conflicting thought.

> 'I' am the thought that I create within any given time sequence.
> 'I' am thought. Thought is whatever 'I' want it to be. Thought
> is totally formless yet encompasses all forms. 'I' am thought in
> all that I do. 'I' am the Creative Principle in all that I am to do
> within my earthly expression.

My ultimate truth is always shown in the simple movements I choose to create during any sequence of time, regardless of how long or how short. Movement is all there is. All there is, is movement.

'I' am that which I am. I am whatever 'I' choose to be: "I am the physical embodiment of Life Consciousness, inclusive of all life, and I am here to bring myself into form and to creatively express my all-knowing consciousness through my self-created experiences. I am the Body: Human."

---

## BOOK 2

*Beyond the Inner Circle, and Back Again:*
*The CHILD's Perspective*
**C**reative **H**uman **I**nfinitely **L**iving **D**ivinely
from within

Question: *Who am I?* Answer: I am the Body: Human.

*Where did I come from?*

*What am I doing here?*

A guide book for living on the Earth as the Body: Human.

# Blaise Eagleheart

DanBatchelor.com

Blaise Eagleheart lives in Victoria, B.C., where he is the owner and operator of Natural Movement Centre. He is an Integrated Movement Specialist, Medical Exercise Specialist and Personal Trainer.

As someone who has always 'walked his own creative path,' Blaise became passionately aware of how the mind, body and emotions are functionally integrated and how they operate individually and collectively. He has openly shared his awareness with others to make the world a better place.

Blaise has always been a warrior, consciously confronting illusionary beliefs to find his own experiential truths. He physically trained as a fanatic throughout his twenties, challenging his self-imposed beliefs in order to find the endless possibilities of his creative movements through unorthodox training methods. He played and coached rugby at club, Island and Provincial levels, before immersing himself in the martial art of Chien Lung. He also studied Eastern healing arts and other energy-based disciplines. He then opened a dojo with his Teacher, where he taught biomechanics of movement and life skills, as well as martial art classes for children and adults. Blaise continues to incorporate this martial art philosophy in his work at Natural Movement Centre.

Contact Blaise Eagleheart through www.NaturalMovementCentre.com.

Printed in the United States
140294LV00006B/2/P